IFIP Advances in Information and Communication Technology 720

IFIP Advances in Information and Communication Technology

The IFIP AICT series publishes state-of-the-art results in the sciences and technologies of information and communication. The scope of the series includes: foundations of computer science; software theory and practice; education; computer applications in technology; communication systems; systems modeling and optimization; information systems; ICT and society; computer systems technology; security and protection in information processing systems; artificial intelligence; and human-computer interaction.

Edited volumes and proceedings of refereed international conferences in computer science and interdisciplinary fields are featured. These results often precede journal publication and represent the most current research.

The principal aim of the IFIP AICT series is to encourage education and the dissemination and exchange of information about all aspects of computing.

More information about this series at https://link.springer.com/bookseries/6102

Zhongzhi Shi · Michael Witbrock · Qi Tian
Editors

Intelligence Science V

6th IFIP TC 12 International Conference, ICIS 2024
Nanjing, China, October 25–28, 2024
Proceedings

Springer

Editors
Zhongzhi Shi
Chinese Academy of Sciences
Beijing, China

Michael Witbrock
University of Auckland
Auckland, New Zealand

Qi Tian
Huawei Technologies
Huawei, China

ISSN 1868-4238 ISSN 1868-422X (electronic)
IFIP Advances in Information and Communication Technology
ISBN 978-3-031-71255-5 ISBN 978-3-031-71253-1 (eBook)
https://doi.org/10.1007/978-3-031-71253-1

This Springer imprint is published by the registered company Springer Nature Switzerland AG
The registered company address is: Gewerbestrasse 11, 6330 Cham, Switzerland

Preface

This volume comprises the proceedings of the Sixth International Conference on Intelligence Science (ICIS). Artificial Intelligence research has made certain substantial progress in some special areas so far. However, the deeper understanding of the essence of intelligence is far from sufficient and, therefore, many state-of-the-art intelligent systems are still not able to compete with human intelligence. To advance research in artificial intelligence, it is necessary to investigate intelligence, both artificial and natural, in an interdisciplinary context. The objective of this conference is to bring together researchers from brain science, cognitive science, and artificial intelligence to explore the essence of intelligence and the related technologies. The conference provides a platform for discussing some of the key issues that are related to intelligence science.

For ICIS 2024, we received 32 papers, of which 23 papers were included in the program as regular papers, and 2 papers as short papers. We are grateful for the dedicated work of both the authors and the referees, and we hope these proceedings will continue to bear fruit over the years to come. All papers submitted were reviewed by three referees.

A conference such as this cannot succeed without help from many individuals who contributed their valuable time and expertise. We want to express our sincere gratitude to the Program Committee members and referees, who invested many hours for reviews and deliberations. They provided detailed and constructive review reports that significantly improved the papers included in the program.

We are very grateful for the sponsorship of the following organizations: Chinese Association for Artificial Intelligence (CAAI), IFIP TC12, China Chapter of the International Society for Information Studies; to the organizers, Nanjing University of Science and Technology, China, and CAAI Mind Computation Technical Committee, China; and for the support of IFIP Technical Committee 12 and the Institute of Computing Technology, Chinese Academy of Sciences. Thanks to Jinhui Tang as Chair of the Local Organizing Committee and Haofeng Zhang as Secretary General. We specially thank Zechao Li, Liang Xiao, Chunyan Xu, and Xiangbo Shu for carefully preparing the proceedings.

Finally, we hope you find this volume inspiring and informative.

July 2024

Zhongzhi Shi
Michael Witbrock
Qi Tian

Organization

Sponsors

Chinese Association for Artificial Intelligence (CAAI)
China Chapter under International Society for Information Studies

Organizers

Nanjing University of Science and Technology, China
Technical Committee of Mind Computation, CAAI

Support

IFIP Technical Committee 12
Institute of Computing Technology, Chinese Academy of Sciences

General Chairs

Yixin Zhong	Beijing University of Posts and Telecommunications, China
Ben Goertzel	AGI Society, USA
Mengyin Fu	Nanjing University of Science and Technology, China

Program Chairs

Zhongzhi Shi	Institute of Computing Technology, CAS, China
Michael Witbrock	University of Auckland, New Zealand
Qi Tian	Huawei, China

Program Committee

Mihir Chakraborty	Jadavpur University, India
Zhen Cui	Nanjing University of Science and Technology, China
Zhihua Cui	Taiyuan University of Science and Technology, China
Andre de Carvalho	University of São Paulo, Brazil
Shifei Ding	China University of Mining and Technology, China
Zhisheng Huang	Vrije Universiteit Amsterdam, The Netherlands
Xiangkui Jiang	Xi'an University of Posts and Telecommunications, China
Yixuan Ku	Sun Yat-sen University, China
Yu Li	Université de Picardie Jules Verne, France

Zechao Li	Nanjing University of Science and Technology, China
Kai Liu	Bohai University, China
Chenguang Lu	Liaoning Technical University, China
Dingsheng Luo	Peking University, China
Wenjian Luo	Harbin Institute of Technology, China
Baoliang Lv	Shanghai Jiao Tong University, China
Tamás Mihálydeák	University of Debrecen, Hungary
Wenjia Niu	Beijing Jiaotong University, China
Yuhua Qian	Shanxi University, China
Chuan Shi	Beijing University of Posts and Telecommunications, China
Zhiping Shi	Capital Normal University, China
Zhongzhi Shi	Institute of Computing Technology, CAS, China
Huajing Tang	Zhejiang University, China
Jinhui Tang	Nanjing University of Science and Technology, China
Guoyin Wang	Chongqing University of Posts and Telecommunications, China
Pei Wang	Temple University, USA
Xiaofeng Wang	Shanghai Maritime University, China
Michael Witbrock	University of Auckland, New Zealand
Liang Xiao	Nanjing University of Science and Technology, China
Chunyan Xu	Nanjing University of Science and Technology, China
Pen Yang	Southern University of Science and Technology, China
Wanqi Yang	Nanjing Normal University, China
Yiyu Yao	University of Regina, Canada
Hong Yu	Chongqing University of Posts and Telecommunications, China
Haofeng Zhang	Nanjing University of Science and Technology, China
Junping Zhang	Fudan University, China
Fuzhen Zhuang	Beihang University, China

Local Organization Committee

Chair

Jinhui Tang — Nanjing University of Science and Technology, China

Vice Chair

Zechao Li — Nanjing University of Science and Technology, China

Secretary General

Haofeng Zhang — Nanjing University of Science and Technology, China

International Liaison

Guangyu Li — Nanjing University of Science and Technology, China

Abstracts of Keynotes and Invited Talks

The Law of Paradigm Revolution for an Emerging Discipline

Yixin Zhong

AI School, BUPT, Beijing, China
zyx@bupt.edu.cn

Abstract. The paradigm for a discipline is defined as the scientific worldview and its methodology observed by that discipline and is thus the supreme force regulating the research of the discipline. It can only be summarized from the practice of that discipline and its establishment will lag far behind the occurrence of that discipline. As a result, an emerging discipline will have no paradigm of its own available in the initial stage of its development and should borrow a paradigm from other disciplines existing already. Consequently, the borrowed paradigm for an emerging discipline will not match its research needs, leading to the emerging discipline being in an abnormal state of development. To escape this abnormal development, the paradigm for the emerging discipline should be summarized, and then the replacement of the borrowed paradigm by its own paradigm should be carried out. This is the so-called paradigm revolution in the emerging discipline. Artificial intelligence (AI in brief) is an emerging discipline at the present time. Therefore, a paradigm revolution in AI is absolutely necessary.

Complex Systems Approaches to Diseases, Climate Change, and the Future: Why Now? Why AI?

Jiming Liu

Department of Computer Science, Hong Kong Baptist University
jiming@comp.hkbu.edu.hk

Abstract. The future sustainability challenges that the world will face will be unprecedented, ranging from (re-)emerging infectious diseases to climate change and beyond, which could potentially pose serious threats to humanity. To be best prepared for, and to effectively respond to, future global challenges, in view of their intrinsic complexity resulting from dynamically interweaving (in)tangible factors, it is of critical importance that we embrace and leverage complex systems approaches to addressing such challenges now. In this talk, I will present the key rationales for why complex systems approaches would be essential, why now, and moreover, in doing so, why and how artificial intelligence (AI) and especially machine learning (ML) could aspire to open up new horizons, and towards this end, what would be the fundamental scientific research questions to ponder.

Exploring Statistical Learning in Multi-View Deep Joint Subspace Analysis

Pradipta Maji

Machine Intelligence Unit, Indian Statistical Institute, Kolkata, India
pmaji@isical.ac.in

Abstract. Multi-view data analysis is an important machine learning paradigm which explores the consistency and complementary properties of multiple views to discover patterns hidden in data. One of the important issues associated with real-life high-dimensional multi-view data is how to integrate relevant and complementary information from multiple views, while generating discriminative joint subspaces for analysis. Although the integration of multi-view data is expected to provide an intrinsically more powerful model than its single-view counterpart, it poses its own set of challenges. The most important problems associated with multi-view data analysis are handling the heterogeneous nature of different views and high-dimension low-sample size nature of individual views, selection of relevant and complementary views while generating discriminative joint subspaces for analysis, and capturing the lower dimensional non-linear geometry of each view. In a multi-view scenario, it is expected that the joint subspace should be learned in such a way that the similarity in the latent space implies the similarity in the corresponding concepts. The joint subspace should also reflect the intrinsic properties of each of the individual views and should efficiently capture the non-linear correlated structures across different views. In this regard, some novel deep learning algorithms will be discussed which are developed based on the theory of statistical learning. The theory of canonical correlation analysis is judiciously integrated with the learning objective of the multimodal discriminative deep Boltzmann machine to learn a joint subspace from the maximally correlated subspaces, while the concept of Hilbert-Schmidt independence criterion helps to encapsulate the cross-view dependency in terms of consensus and/or complementary knowledge from the input pairs of views. Based on the Bayes error analysis, an upper bound on the error probability of the novel deep models is estimated, which facilitates determining the optimal architectures of the models.

Application Cases of Intelligent Techniques for Sustainable Cities

Tianrui Li

School of Computing and Artificial Intelligence, Southwest Jiaotong University
trli@swjtu.edu.cn

Abstract. With the rapid development of urbanization, massive data has been accumulated around urban management-related fields. Sustainable urban management has entered the era of big data intelligence. How to effectively obtain useful knowledge from these big data by deep mining and intelligent learning techniques has become the key problem to be solved in current sustainable urban development. This report focuses on application cases of intelligent techniques for sustainable cities, e.g., urban taxi route recommendations, rental suggestions, ambulance deployment strategies, food delivery optimization, and subway stop scheduling. It concludes by discussing the challenges of sustainable urban big data analysis.

Towards brain-like machine intelligence with large-scale spiking neural networks

Yonghong Tian

Department of Computer Science, School of Electronic and Computer Engineering, Peking University
Network Intelligence Research, Pengcheng Laboratory
yhtian@pku.edu.cn

Abstract. The brain's structure and functions have long served as a wellspring for advancements in intelligent technologies throughout human history. Brain-inspired spiking neural networks (SNNs) emulate neural dynamics through event-based computations, effectively capturing temporal information for brain-like, energy-efficient processing. Currently, SNNs have found successful applications in diverse fields such as image recognition and object detection which are poised to potentially revolutionize artificial intelligence. However, the scalability of SNNs has remained limited, impeding further performance enhancements and their practical deployment. Therefore, developing methods and theories for constructing large-scale SNNs is crucial to unlocking their full potential. In this presentation, I will discuss recent breakthroughs in the development of large-scale SNNs, covering advancements in spiking neuron technologies, network architectures, algorithms, programming frameworks, and applications in neuromorphic computing.

Contents

AI for Science

Medical Artificial Intelligence

Author Index

Machine Learning

Difference-Enhanced Learning of the Deep Semantic Segmentation Networks for First Break Picking

Zhongyang Wen and Jinwen Ma(✉)

Department of Information and Computational Sciences, School of Mathematical Sciences and LMAM, Peking University, Beijing 1000871, China
{zywen,jwma}@pku.edu.cn

Abstract. The precise estimation of seismic arrival times, commonly referred to as first-break picking, is a critical problem in seismic research due to its important role in various seismological applications such as statics correction processing. In recent years, there have been several deep learning algorithms designed specifically for 2D seismic arrival time picking. A widely used approach is to treat the 2D arrival picking problem as a 2D image segmentation problem and employ a deep semantic segmentation model for end-to-end first break picking. However, the first break mask generated from this method often fails to meet the uniqueness of first arrival time according to certain noises. In order to alleviate this problem, we propose a difference-enhanced learning method of the deep semantic segmentation network for the first break picking problem by designing a new kind of loss function, which actually improves the quality of mask generation and arrival time accuracy. It is demonstrated by extensive experiments on a real seismic dataset that our proposed difference-enhanced learning method is effective and outperforms the conventional learning methods for deep semantic segmentation models on the estimation of seismic arrival times.

Keywords: First-break picking · Seismic data · Semantic segmentation · Loss function

1 Introduction

In seismic prospecting, first break picking identifies the earliest signal arrivals of the primary wave within a specified set of seismic traces following a seismic shot. Its importance is widely acknowledged in seismic prospecting. Actually, it is a critical initial phase in seismic data processing and has been applied to Q-estimation, travel time tomography, statics correction processing and so on. This task can be manually accomplished by experts in the specialized field. However, manual detection of these arrivals is a laborious and time-consuming work. Moreover, it becomes a rather challenging task when the seismic data are obtained in intricate near-surface conditions or when the signal-to-noise ratio is

Published by Springer Nature Switzerland AG 2025
Z. Shi et al. (Eds.): ICIS 2024, IFIP AICT 720, pp. 3–15, 2025.
https://doi.org/10.1007/978-3-031-71253-1_1

low. Over the past few decades, there has been an exponential growth in seismic data volume with the development of seismic exploration industry. Therefore, it is very necessary to develop automatic picking methods that offer high efficiency and accuracy.

Before the emergence of deep learning methods, automatic picking methods had been investigated over four decades, as reviewed in [1]. One typical representative of these traditional methods is the STA/LTA method which calculates the ratio of the average energy between the short-term window and the long-term window [2]. These methods often exhibit unsatisfactory performance when confronted with irregular surfaces, intense noise, or energy loss. Additionally, there are also some early methods using artificial neural networks (NN) [10,11]. However, the simplicity of the network architecture, typically comprising three fully connected layers, and limited computational resources generally constrain the accuracy of these methods. In recent 10 years, deep learning methods have achieved great success in fields such as computer vision and pattern recognition. In response, researchers have turned to deep neural networks to address the challenges in seismology, leveraging the abundance and accessibility of seismic datasets [12]. In fact, an increasing number deep learning models have been applied to the first break picking task. For instance, CNNs have been utilized to identify the first arrivals on multi-trace seismic data [5,19]. Additionally, some methods treat first break picking as a classification problem, where each pixel in a moving window is classified [4,19]. Hu et al. [6] considered first break picking as a binary segmentation problem and trained a UNet [14] to identify first arrivals on seismic data. Yuan et al. [17] proposed an end-to-end approach incorporating a U-net for segmentation and a recurrent neural network for picking. Mousavi et al. [13] proposed a global deep learning model for earthquake signal detection including arrival picking using a hierarchical attention mechanism. Tsai et al. [16] trained a deep learning model with expert-selected data, significantly reducing training time and the need for human-labeled data. Yuan et al. [18] trained a fully-convolutional Seg Net to pick densely-sampled first breaks directly from common-shot gathers with sparsely distributed traces. Jiang et al. [7] utilized the Swin-Transformer as the backbone network for picking. Research [12] compares deep learning models with classical characteristic function-based models and concludes that deep learning models outperform traditional models significantly in terms of performance, speed, generalization capability, and noise resistance.

Despite the widespread use of deep semantic segmentation models in 2D first break picking problems, they still have certain limitations. Semantic segmentation models conduct pixel-level classification to produce the masks. However, these masks may not always meet the requirement for first arrival times, which necessitates a precise boundary point along the time-sample direction for each trace. Specifically, all points before this boundary point are classified as background, while points after it are classified as foreground. In this paper, we propose a difference-enhanced learning method for the deep semantic segmentation neural network for First Break Picking, which is implemented by designing a compounded loss function to enhance the difference of the previous signals to the first arrival. In this way, this difference-enhanced learning method effectively alleviates the issue that the arrival time from generated masks may deviate the real arrivals according to certain possible noise. Therefore, it can improve the accuracy of 2D arrival picking significantly. We have conducted the experiments using various semantic segmentation methods with different loss functions on diverse training datasets and the experimental results demonstrate that our proposed difference-enhanced learning method can significantly enhance the quality of first arrival mask generation and improve the first break picking performance under almost any condition.

2 First Break Picking Through Image Segmentation

2.1 Deep Segmentation Methods

Image semantic segmentation aims to classify pixels within an image. For this purpose, researchers have proposed the encoder-decoder structure, which represents one of the most popular end-to-end architectures, including fully convolutional networks (FCNs) [9], U-Net [14], DeeplabV3+ [3], etc. These structures typically employ an encoder to extract image features and a decoder to restore these features to the original image size, ultimately producing the final segmentation results. While the end-to-end structure proves practical for image segmentation tasks, it diminishes the interpretability of the models. The UNet, initially proposed by Ronneberger et al., stands as the pioneering encoder-decoder structure and has found extensive application in medical, remote sensing, industrial applications, etc. UNet addresses issues encountered with typical CNN architectures utilized in image segmentation by adopting a symmetric structure and skip connection. UNet adeptly integrates low-level and high-level image features by merging low-resolution and high-resolution feature maps through skip connections, presenting an optimal solution for many actual image segmentation tasks. The first break picking problem can be defined as an image segmentation task, where the objective is to divide the seismic image into two distinct regions. The process of utilizing deep semantic segmentation models for 2D first break picking is roughly illustrated in Fig. 1.

2.2 Limitations of Picking by Deep Segmentation Models

If we consider 2-dimensional seismic data images as 2D images, the first break picking problem is essentially seeking a two-part segmentation along the time-sample direction of the image. It's a problem about finding a 1D curve in the 2D seismic data, in other word, finding a segmentation point along the time-sample direction for each trace. However, if we only consider the positions of the arrival times as the learning target for the deep learning model, this approach is highly data imbalanced. Therefore, the common practice is to treat the portion before the arrival time as background and the portion after the arrival

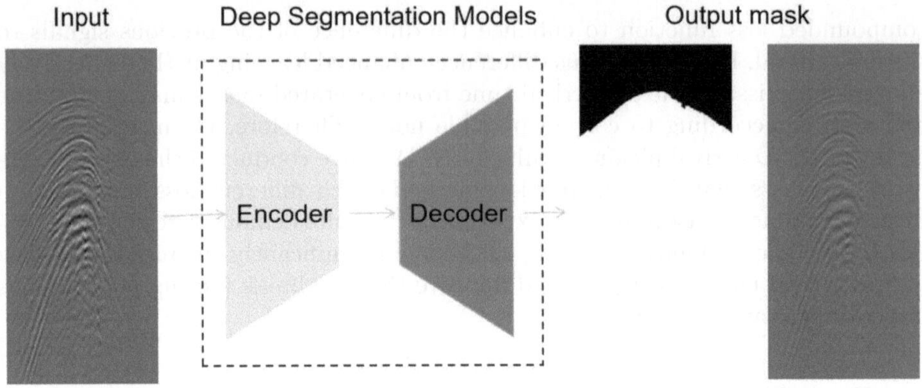

Fig. 1. A Brief diagram showing the process of 2D first break picking.

time as foreground, using a deep learning model for binary semantic segmentation. Since semantic segmentation models inherently perform pixel-level binary classification to generate masks, these masks may not necessarily satisfy the condition of the first arrival times, i.e., having a strict boundary point along the time-sample direction for each trace, where all points before this point are classified as background and points after this point are classified as foreground. Figure 2 illustrate situations that may arise when deep semantic segmentation models extract masks from input data. Figure 2(a) shows a mask generated by the model that is divided into two disconnected parts, while Fig. 2(b) demonstrates a mask from the model that notably fails to delineate the exact arrival boundaries in the left and middle traces. These masks evidently fail to meet the conditions required for arrival picking tasks.

To measure the proportion of poorly performing traces on arrival picking traces by a trained deep model, we define the **Deformation Rate (DR)** by the proportion of the number of deformed picking traces to all the picking traces:

$$DR = \frac{N_{Deformed}}{N_{All}}$$

If the mask on a 1D trace does not strictly adhere to the conditions required for arrival picking, meaning there is no clear boundary strictly separating foreground from background, then that picking on the trace is considered deformed. The deformation rate represents the proportion of traces on the seismic dataset where the generated masks fail to meet the arrival conditions. Experimental results on a test set consisting of 40 shots, with a UNet model trained via transfer learning on a 10-shots training set, yield a deformation rate of **14.44%**. Further details regarding experimental setup will be discussed in Sect. 3. Deformed picking of segmentation models significantly affects the performance of arrival picking.

Typically, post-processing is often required for the masks obtained from the semantic segmentation models to obtain arrival times. Post-processing is not

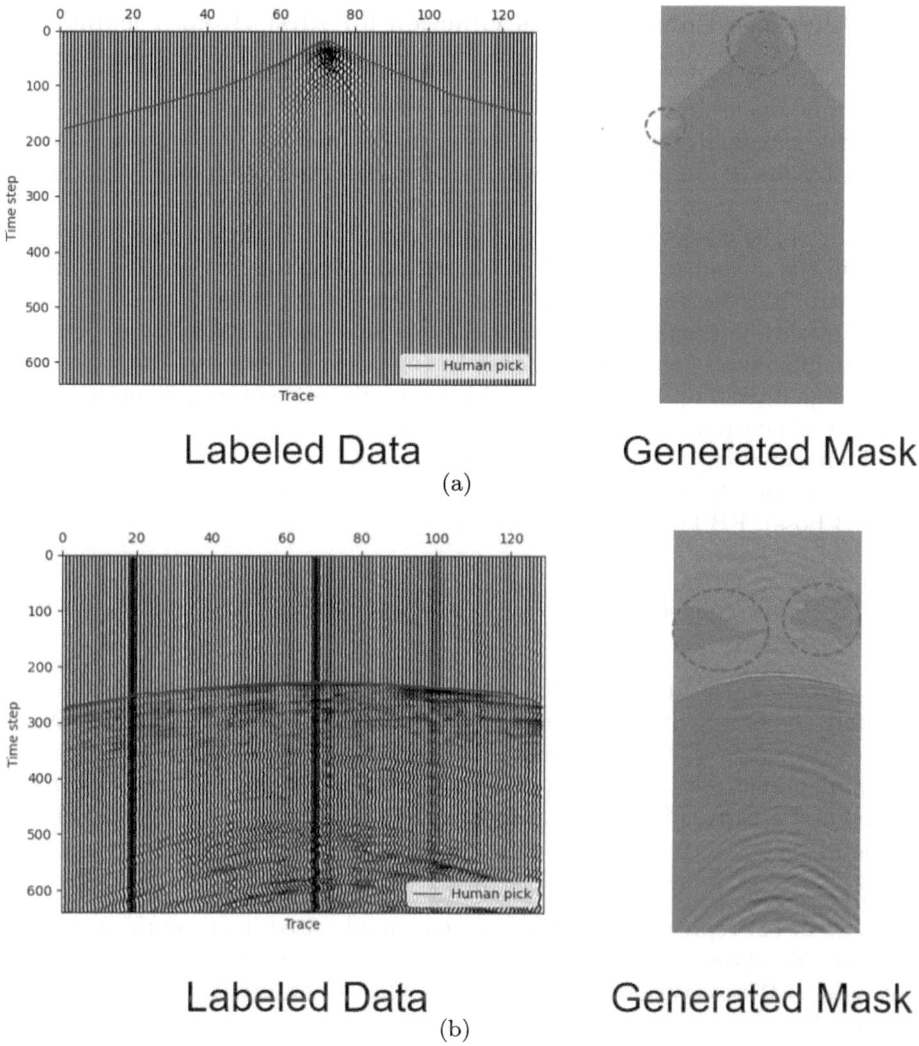

Fig. 2. These images display the 2D seismic data and the corresponding masks obtained from a trained deep learning model.

a fundamental modification of the model itself and often does not consistently yield good picking results. Another approach is to train the deep learning model with a larger dataset, allowing the model to better learn the conditions satisfied by first arrival masks when increasing the observed data. However, in practice, obtaining a sufficient amount of manually annotated seismic data for a new seismic exploration area can be really difficult and time-consuming.

2.3 Difference-Enhanced Loss Function for First Break Picking

Unlike other methods that rely on post-processing or enlarging the dataset, we aim to fundamentally ensure that the model learns to meet the conditions of first break picking during training process. To address this issue, we aim to add soft constraints on the semantic segmentation masks by appropriately modifying the loss function used for semantic segmentation. This is to enhance the picking capability of the masks for arrival picking tasks. To achieve this goal, we need to constrain the output probabilities of the segmentation model. We hope to make the probabilities for the first half along the time-sample direction as close to 0 as possible, while those for the second half as close to 1 as possible. It is noted that the difference of the output along the time direction are very important for seismic signal picking. We consider taking the difference of output probabilities along the time-sample direction, and calculating the mean squared error with the difference along the time-sample direction of ground truth (gt). We apply this loss function to the 2D first break picking task, referring to it as First-Break Loss(FB Loss). FB Loss can be expressed by:

$$FBLoss = \frac{1}{N}\sum_{i=1}^{N}|\Delta_{ts}p_i - \Delta_{ts}gt_i|^2 \tag{1}$$

The difference of the ground truth along the time direction is essentially a matrix with only the first arrival time point being 1, while other points are all 0. When this loss decreases, the output probabilities will be closer before the first arrival time point and after it, while the probability difference on both sides of the arrival time point increases. Finally, we derived the following semantic segmentation loss function (2):

$$Loss = Loss_{Base} + \alpha FBLoss \tag{2}$$

$Loss_{Base}$ in (2) represents the base loss commonly used in semantic segmentation, like Dice Loss [15], CE Loss, Focal Loss [8], etc. represents the coefficient controlling FB Loss, usually 10 in practice. Our loss function effectively biases the model towards learning a probability output that satisfies the constraint of the arrival mask. Figure 3 shows the computation of our proposed loss function.

3 Experimental Results

3.1 Implementation Detail

Data Preparing. Unlike synthetic datasets commonly used in other studies, we exclusively utilize real seismic exploration datasets for training and testing. This approach allows for a better validation of practicality and real-world applicability. The real land shot gathers are provided by BGP Inc., China National Petroleum Corporation. It has over 200 shots and each shot is consisted of over 8000 space traces and about over time samples. To better utilize the features of the seismic data in deep neural network learning, we have segmented the

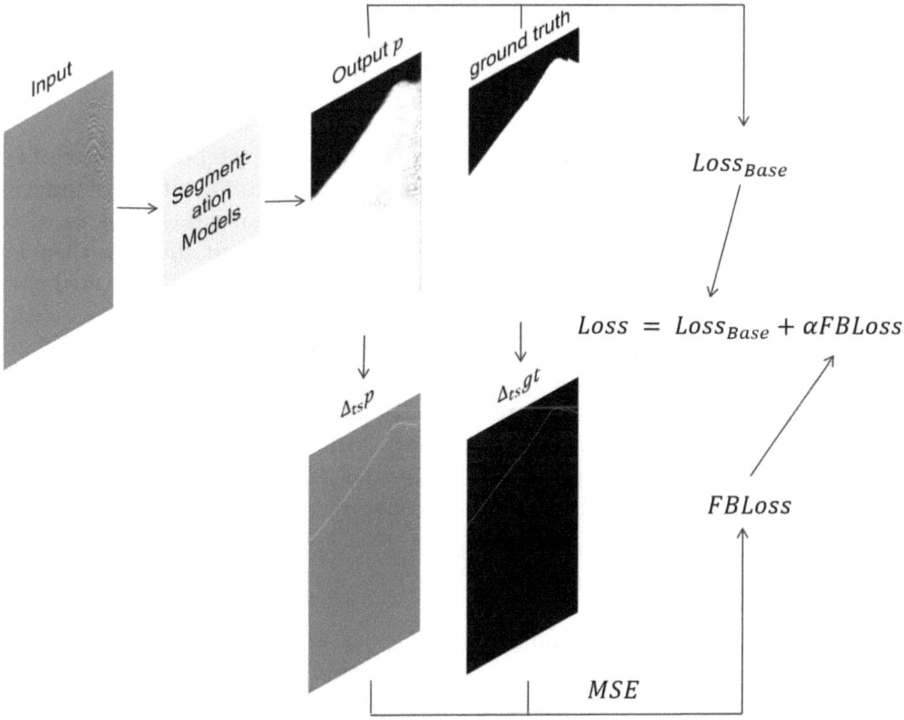

Fig. 3. A conceptual diagram illustrating the computation of our proposed loss function.

data into slices of size 128 space traces × 640 time-samples. Each slice extracted has manually annotated first arrival time for each trace. We randomly select 921 images slices from 40 shot gathers in sequential order as the test set for all model algorithms, which are never involved in training. For the training set selection, we employed 3 groups of datasets ranging from small to large, each containing approximately 100, 200 and 3200 labeled images cut from 5, 10 and over 160 shot gathers, respectively. We will discuss these datasets in detail again in Sect. 3.3. It is worth mentioning that evaluating deep learning models trained with fewer training datasets better reflects the model's generalization performance on first break picking in other working area. That's why we select different sizes of training dataset. If not specifically mentioned, the training dataset used in the subsequent experiments is the "10shots" dataset.

Segmentation Method and Training. To verify the ability of our proposed loss function for first break picking, we mainly employ UNet, which has demonstrated excellent performance for segmentation of medical images. We replace the original encoder in UNet by a ResNext50 with pretrained weights on ImageNet dataset, which often gives a better performance in picking first break. To train the segmentation model, we utilize the Adam optimizer with a learning rate set to 0.0001 and a batch size of 16. If the validation performance does not improve over 25 epochs, the learning rate is reduced to 0.00001.

Parameter Choosing. The selection of α is crucial for the performance of the loss function proposed in our study. Similar to other composite loss function approaches, we experimented with three α selection schemes including constant α, increased α and rebalanced α. The increased α scheme starts with a low value of α, and increases it gradually at the end of each epoch. The rebalanced α scheme rewrite the combined loss as $(1-\alpha)L_{Base} + \alpha L_{FB}$ and starts with a low value of α then increase it over time. Through experimentation, we found that selecting a constant α value between 5 and 10 yields better performance. This may be attributed to the inherent correlation between the base loss and the diff loss itself. As the baseline loss decreases during training, the diff loss also decreases, and vice versa. If not otherwise stated, the loss functions used in the experiments below are all selected with a constant α value of 10.

3.2 Performance

We first select the most commonly used Dice Loss [15], Cross Entropy (CE) Loss, and Focal Loss [8] in semantic segmentation as the base loss functions, which, together with our proposed FB Loss, constitute the first break picking semantic segmentation loss function for training. We use default parameters for Focal Loss:$\alpha = 0$ and $gamma = 2$(α, γ here are the parameters in Focal Loss, representing the prior probability of having positive value in target and the power factor for dampening weight). Figure 4 illustrates the learning curve of our combined loss function during the training process. This demonstrates the effectiveness of our proposed loss function in achieving good learning performance with different base losses.

Table 1 illustrates the arrival picking performance of models trained with different loss functions on the same training dataset and under identical training conditions, evaluated on the test dataset. Unlike the commonly used evaluation methods in semantic segmentation, we adopt the proportion of traces within 1, 2, 5, and 10 time-sample ranges of the true picking time as the evaluation criterion for picking. This evaluation method is more meaningful for arrival picking issues than semantic segmentation evaluation criteria. From the table, it can be observed that the models trained with the addition of our FB Loss to base loss functions such as Dice Loss and Focal Loss exhibit a significant reduction in deformation rate and notable improvements in accuracy at 1, 2, 5 and 10 time-sample. Additionally, models trained with CE Loss show a slight decrease in deformation rate and a minor improvement in picking accuracy. From the experimental results, it can be observed that integrating the composite difference-enhanced loss function significantly enhances the model's ability to pick arrivals and reduces the picking deformation rate. It shows the significant effectiveness of our proposed method for the first break picking problem.

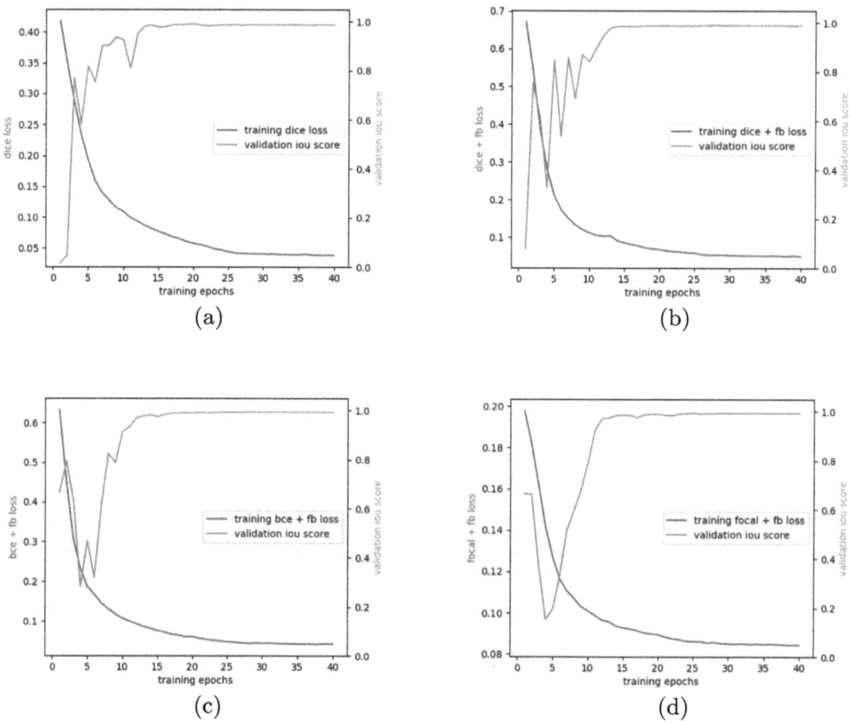

Fig. 4. Learning curves of training loss and validation score for seismic data training. (a), (b), (c), (d) demonstrates the training process using Dice Loss, Dice Loss with FB Loss, BCE Loss with FB Loss and Focal Loss with FB Loss respectively.

Figure 5 illustrates the comparison between masks generated by models trained with and without our proposed loss function on sample seismic data, under otherwise identical conditions. From Fig. 5(a), it is evident that the distortion in the middle part of the generated mask is significantly reduced after training with our loss function. Furthermore, Fig. 5(b) shows that the hollow part in the middle of the mask disappears after training with our loss function. From these results, it can be observed that, under similar conditions, the UNet model trained with our proposed loss function effectively mitigates the deformation issues of the generated masks and improve the picking accuracy.

3.3 Different Models and Datasets

To demonstrate that our loss function is not only applicable to the UNet method, we selecte two classic semantic segmentation methods, PSPNet and Deeplabv3 for training on seismic data. The basic settings for these two methods are consistent with those mentioned in Sect. 3.1 for UNet. Table 1 presents our experimental results. From Table 2, it is evident that our loss function exhibits the

Table 1. Experimental results for the UNet trained with and without FB Loss testing on test seismic data. $[-N, N]$ accuracy stands for the proportion of traces picking error less than N time samples in all test traces.

	Deformation rate	[–1, 1]	[–2, 2]	[–5, 5]	[–10, 10]
Dice Loss	14.44%	45.64%	58.48%	72.47%	80.38%
+ FB Loss	**8.03%**	**61.74%**	**73.19%**	**84.63%**	**91.39%**
CE Loss	17.01%	48.43%	61.11%	73.48%	79.75%
+ FB Loss	**14.86%**	**51.14%**	**62.89%**	**74.81%**	**82.17%**
Focal Loss	14.26%	38.57%	56.56%	76.39%	84.48%
+ FB Loss	**7.70%**	**54.65%**	**67.88%**	**81.26%**	**88.66%**

most significant improvement in picking accuracy for the UNet model. For PSPNet and Deeplabv3, models trained with our loss function also show notable improvements in accuracy at 1 and 2 points, with negligible differences in accuracy at 10 points, possibly due to differences in model architecture. Regardless of the method, introducing our FB Loss to the base loss function results in a certain degree of improvement in arrival picking performance, especially at 1 and 2 points. This indicates that our loss function better distinguishes arrival boundaries compared to conventional semantic segmentation losses.

Table 2. Experimental results for different segmentation models trained with and without FB Loss testing on test seismic data. $[-N, N]$ accuracy stands for the proportion of traces picking error less than N time samples in all test traces.

	[–1, 1]	[–2, 2]	[–5, 5]	[–10, 10]
UNet	45.64%	58.48%	72.47%	80.38%
+ FB Loss	**61.74%**	**73.19%**	**84.63%**	**91.39%**
PSPNet	31.69%	48.18%	71.04%	80.03%
+ FB Loss	**34.16%**	**50.48%**	**72.16%**	79.79%
DeepLabV3Plus	26.24%	41.14%	69.04%	86.91%
+ FB Loss	**31.71%**	**47.71%**	**72.37%**	86.61%

To prove the broad applicability and generalization performance of our loss function, we conduct model training on seismic datasets of different sizes. For the selection of training datasets, we create three datasets. The first dataset consists of a small number of slices extracted from 5 shot gathers, comprising fewer than 100 annotated image slices, referred to as "5-shots". The second dataset comprises over 200 image slices extracted from 10 shot gathers (including those from the first dataset), referred to as "10-shots". The third dataset, referred to as "All-shots", comprises images extracted from over 160 shot gathers excluding the test shot gathers. The 5-shots and 10-shots datasets represent smaller

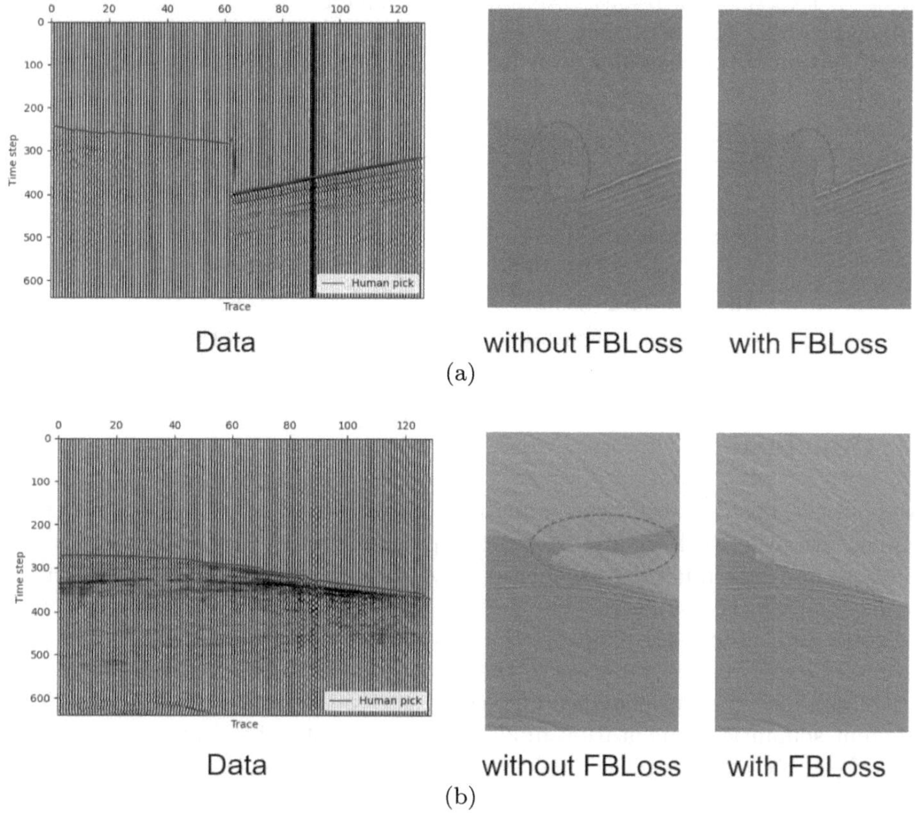

Fig. 5. These images display the 2D seismic data alongside the masks obtained from a trained deep learning model.

training datasets, while the 160 shots dataset represents a relatively large training dataset. Table 3 presents the experimental results. From the table, it can be observed that models trained with our loss function on smaller training datasets exhibit significant improvements in picking performance, even comparable to models trained on larger datasets. Moreover, on larger training datasets where model accuracy is already high, our loss function still leads to further improvements in accuracy. This highlights the versatility of our approach for the arrival picking problem.

Table 3. Experimental results UNet trained on different scales of training datasets with and without FB Loss testing on test seismic data. $[--N, N]$ accuracy stands for the proportion of traces picking error less than N time samples in all test traces.

	[−1, 1]	[−2, 2]	[−5, 5]	[- -10, 10]
5-shots data	30.13%	44.13%	63.37%	72.21%
+ FB Loss	**43.87%**	**56.24%**	**69.73%**	**76.91%**
10-shots data	45.64%	58.48%	72.47%	80.38%
+ FB Loss	**61.74%**	**73.19%**	**84.63%**	**91.39**
All-shots data	86.37%	90.26%	93.92%	97.93%
+ FB Loss	**89.90%**	**91.13%**	93.78%	**98.11%**

4 Conclusion

We have established a difference-enhanced learning method of the deep semantic segmentation network for the first break picking problem by designing a novel compounded loss function. In such a way, the trained semantic segmentation models can effectively address the issue of deformed picking in first break picking tasks and significantly improve the accuracy of arrival time picking. Through extensive experiments, we observe that the difference-enhanced models consistently enhance the performance of picking across different base loss functions, different semantic segmentation models, and different sizes of training datasets. Therefore, the experimental results validate the effectiveness of our difference-enhanced approach.

Acknowledgments. This work was supported by the Natural Science Foundation of China under grant 62071171. Thanks for the private labeled seismic data provided by BGP Inc., China National Petroleum Corporation.

References

1. Akram, J., Eaton, D.W.: A review and appraisal of arrival-time picking methods for downhole microseismic data. Geophysics **81**(2), KS71–KS91 (2016). https://doi.org/10.1190/geo2014-0500.1
2. Allen, R.V.: Automatic earthquake recognition and timing from single traces. Bull. Seismol. Soc. Am. **68**(5), 1521–1532 (1978)
3. Chen, L.C., Zhu, Y., Papandreou, G., Schroff, F., Adam, H.: Encoder-decoder with atrous separable convolution for semantic image segmentation. In: Proceedings of the European Conference on Computer Vision (ECCV), pp. 801–818 (2018)
4. Duan, X., Zhang, J., Liu, Z., Liu, S., Chen, Z., Li, W.: Integrating seismic first-break picking methods with a machine learning approach, pp. 2186–2190 (2018). https://doi.org/10.1190/segam2018-2998293.1. https://library.seg.org/doi/abs/10.1190/segam2018-2998293.1

5. Hollander, Y., Merouane, A., Yilmaz, O.: Using a deep convolutional neural network to enhance the accuracy of first-break picking, pp. 4628–4632 (2018). https://doi.org/10.1190/segam2018-2982650.1. https://library.seg.org/doi/abs/10.1190/segam2018-2982650.1
6. Hu, L., Zheng, X., Duan, Y., Yan, X., Hu, Y., Zhang, X.: First-arrival picking with a U-net convolutional network. Geophysics **84**(6), U45–U57 (2019). https://doi.org/10.1190/geo2018-0688.1
7. Jiang, P., Deng, F., Wang, X., Shuai, P., Luo, W., Tang, Y.: Seismic first break picking through swin transformer feature extraction. IEEE Geosci. Remote Sens. Lett. **20**, 1–5 (2023). https://doi.org/10.1109/LGRS.2023.3248233
8. Lin, T.Y., Goyal, P., Girshick, R., He, K., Dollár, P.: Focal loss for dense object detection. In: Proceedings of the IEEE International Conference on Computer Vision, pp. 2980–2988 (2017)
9. Long, J., Shelhamer, E., Darrell, T.: Fully convolutional networks for semantic segmentation. In: Proceedings of the IEEE Conference on Computer Vision and Pattern Recognition, pp. 3431–3440 (2015)
10. Maity, D., Aminzadeh, F., Karrenbach, M.: Novel hybrid artificial neural network based autopicking workflow for passive seismic data. Geophys. Prospect. **62**(4), 834–847 (2014)
11. McCormack, M.D., Zaucha, D.E., Dushek, D.W.: First-break refraction event picking and seismic data trace editing using neural networks. Geophysics **58**(1), 67–78 (1993)
12. Mousavi, S.M., Beroza, G.C.: Deep-learning seismology. Science **377**(6607), eabm4470 (2022). https://doi.org/10.1126/science.abm4470. https://www.science.org/doi/abs/10.1126/science.abm4470
13. Mousavi, S.M., Ellsworth, W.L., Zhu, W., Chuang, L.Y., Beroza, G.C.: Earthquake transformer-an attentive deep-learning model for simultaneous earthquake detection and phase picking. Nat. Commun. **11**(1), 3952 (2020)
14. Ronneberger, O., Fischer, P., Brox, T.: U-Net: convolutional networks for biomedical image segmentation. In: Navab, N., Hornegger, J., Wells, W.M., Frangi, A.F. (eds.) MICCAI 2015. LNCS, vol. 9351, pp. 234–241. Springer, Cham (2015). https://doi.org/10.1007/978-3-319-24574-4_28
15. Sudre, C.H., Li, W., Vercauteren, T., Ourselin, S., Jorge Cardoso, M.: Generalised dice overlap as a deep learning loss function for highly unbalanced segmentations. In: Cardoso, M.J., et al. (eds.) DLMIA/ML-CDS -2017. LNCS, vol. 10553, pp. 240–248. Springer, Cham (2017). https://doi.org/10.1007/978-3-319-67558-9_28
16. Tsai, K.C., Hu, W., Wu, X., Chen, J., Han, Z.: Automatic first arrival picking via deep learning with human interactive learning. IEEE Trans. Geosci. Remote Sens. **58**(2), 1380–1391 (2020). https://doi.org/10.1109/TGRS.2019.2946118
17. Yuan, P., Wang, S., Hu, W., Wu, X., Chen, J., Nguyen, H.V.: A robust first-arrival picking workflow using convolutional and recurrent neural networks. Geophysics **85**(5), U109–U119 (2020)
18. Yuan, S.Y., Zhao, Y., Xie, T., Qi, J., Wang, S.X.: Segnet-based first-break picking via seismic waveform classification directly from shot gathers with sparsely distributed traces. Pet. Sci. **19**(1), 162–179 (2022)
19. Yuan, S., Liu, J., Wang, S., Wang, T., Shi, P.: Seismic waveform classification and first-break picking using convolution neural networks. IEEE Geosci. Remote Sens. Lett. **15**(2), 272–276 (2018). https://doi.org/10.1109/LGRS.2017.2785834

A Framework of Reinforcement Learning for Truncated Lévy Flight Exploratory

Quan Liu[1,2], Shile Feng[1(✉)], and Zixian Gu[2]

[1] Kashi University, Kashi 844006, Xinjiang, China
1373118521@qq.com
[2] Soochow University, Suzhou 215006, Jiangsu, China

Abstract. Deep reinforcement learning (DRL) still explores insufficiently when dealing complex tasks with high-dimensional and large state spaces. Therefore, developing better exploration strategies is still one of the important tasks in reinforcement learning. The paper introduces a new exploration strategy ATLF (Adjustment of Truncated Lévy Flight exploration framework, ATLF) which augments the existing exploration mode with Lévy flight, making action selection more stochastic to boost exploration. The ALTF framework is combined with discrete-space algorithm DQN and continuous space-algorithm SAC to handle reinforcement learning tasks. Compared with a variety of reinforcement learning algorithms on OpenAI gym environments such as MountainCar-v0 and Walker2d-v2, the result shows that our algorithm has better exploration ability than vanilla DQN or SAC, obtaining higher overall rewards, and is less likely to fall into local optimization, and is more stable. Additionally, the result shows that the ALTF is highly compatible with existing deep reinforcement learning algorithms.

Keywords: sequential decision · deep reinforcement learning · Lévy flight · exploration framework · random walk

1 Introduction

In recent years, Deep Reinforcement Learning (DRL), as an important research hotspot in the field of machine learning, which is typically characterised by its data-driven nature [1], has been widely used in the fields of game playing [2], robot control [3], etc. DLR has emerged as a highly effective technique for addressing various scientific and applied problems [4], but its practicality is restricted in real-time environments due to its short response time, high computational complexity, and instability in learning [5].

The problem of balancing exploration and utilization is an important challenge in DRL. For this task, many researches have proposed novel exploration strategies, such as the exploration strategy of adding maximum entropy to the value function [6], the curiosity-driven exploration strategy [7], etc. The algorithm of adding maximum entropy to the state value function, take SAC [6]

Published by Springer Nature Switzerland AG 2025
Z. Shi et al. (Eds.): ICIS 2024, IFIP AICT 720, pp. 16–29, 2025.
https://doi.org/10.1007/978-3-031-71253-1_2

(Soft Actor Critic) as an example, the state value function of SAC is denoted as $V(s_t) = \mathrm{E}_{a \sim x}\left[Q(s_t, a_t) - \log \pi(a_t \mid s_t)\right]$, and its basic idea is to add the maximum entropy of the strategy as the action uncertainty measure into the value function to improve the value of the state-action pairs that have a low number of visits, and the SAC algorithm is effective in most of the continuous control tasks. For example, the count based exploration strategy, UCB (Upper Confidence Bound) [8], UCB modifies the Q-value of the algorithm to the actual distribution of the current action gain and the sum of the action uncertainty metrics, denoted as $Q_t(a) + U_t(a)$, where $U_t(a) = c\sqrt{\frac{\ln t}{N_t(a)}}$, $N_t(a)$ denote the number of times action a has been selected, and $\ln t$ denotes the logarithm of the total number of times the action has been selected.

The basic idea of the UCB method is to use the uncertainty of the action as a reward addition value function, so that the intelligent body is biased to choose the uncertainty of the large the UCB method is effective in discrete control tasks, but its use in continuous action space is limited by the need to count the number of times each state action is used. There are still two problems in solving large-scale tasks:

1. All three exploration strategies are 1-step random walk, 1-step random walk is unable to explore a large unknown region in a short time, which severely limits the exploration ability of the intelligent body.
2. The implementation of all three exploration strategies requires modification of the value function, and the algorithms suffer from slower convergence and unstable results when the state uncertainty changes too quickly and the value function changes at any time.

To solve these two problems, this paper proposes a adjustment of truncated Lévy flight exploartion framework (ATLF), where Lévy flight is a multi-step random walk algorithm with a step size sampled from a truncated Lévy distribution [9], i.e. the walking process has a relatively high probability of a large spanning step.

Through experiments, this paper demonstrates that ATLF plays a good role in exploring unknown environments, and the AC algorithm incorporating the ATLF exploration framework improves the cumulative total rewards by 47.88%, 12.21%, and 40.73%, respectively, compared to the classical SAC algorithm in the Mujoco environments Ant-v2, Walker2d-v2, and Hopper-v2. The ATLF exploration framework is a modification of the step size of the random walk, so the framework is not exclusive with other exploration strategies. In this paper, we combine the ATLF exploration framework with other exploration strategies, and experiments prove that such a combination can produce better results in most tasks. In the OpenAI Gym LunarLander-v2 experiments, compared to the classical algorithms ICM-DQN [7] and Noisy-DQN [10], the algorithms combined with the ATLF framework increase the cumulative total rewards by 223.01% and 155.31%, respectively.

2 Background Knowledge

2.1 Reinforcement Learning

The goal of reinforcement learning is to train an intelligent body to learn strategies that maximise cumulative rewards through its interaction with the environment. Where interaction is the process of an intelligent body walking in an unknown environment, at each time step t, the environment provides the intelligent body with a state S_t, based on which the intelligent body chooses an action a_t to perform according to the strategy, and at the next time step $t+1$, the intelligent body receives a reward r_t from the feedback from the environment and the next momentary state S_{t+1}. The interaction model can be modelled by the Markov Decision Process (MDP) [11], and the MDP model can be represented by a quaternion (S, A, R, P), where S is the set of states, A is the set of actions, R is the reward function, and P is the state transfer function.

2.2 Intrinsic Curiosity-Based Reinforcement Learning Algorithms

ICM (intrinsic curiosity module, ICM) [6] proposed in 2017, increases the curiosity of intelligences towards unknown states from the perspective of prediction modelling. ICM divides the prediction model into three modules: feature extraction, forward model, and backward model. Among them, the feature extraction module converts the state S_t into feature vectors:

$$\phi\left(s_t\right)=\phi\left(s_t;\theta_e\right) \tag{1}$$

where θ_e is the parameter of the feature extraction model. For the forward model, the ICM takes the extracted feature $\phi\left(s_t\right)$ with the intelligent body action a_t as input and outputs the predicted features of the next state:

$$\hat{\phi}\left(s_{t+1}\right)=f\left(\phi\left(s_t\right), a_t;\theta_f\right) \tag{2}$$

where θ_f is a forward prediction model parameter and ICM defines curiosity reward as the distance between the predicted feature and the true feature:

$$r_t^c=\frac{\eta}{2}\left\|\hat{\phi}\left(s_{t+1}\right)-\phi\left(s_{t+1}\right)\right\|_2^2 \tag{3}$$

2.3 Random Walks and Lévy Flights

Lévy Flight, as a classical random walk strategy, has played an crucial role in the development of intelligent optimization algorithms since its discovery [12]. Lévy flight belongs to a class of random walks in which there is a relatively high probability of large steps. Lévy flights, compared to random walks in which the distribution of step lengths is not heavy-tailed, have trajectories as if they could fly from time to time. In essence, Lévy flight is a class of non-Gaussian random processes and it is characterized by selecting a series of instantaneous jumps from the probability density function which has a heavy tail [13].

In a previous study [14], a simple version of the Lévy distribution was defined as follows:

$$L(s, \gamma, \mu) = \begin{cases} \sqrt{\frac{\gamma}{2\pi}} \exp\left[-\frac{\gamma}{2(s-\mu)}\right] \frac{1}{(s-\mu)^{3/2}}, \\ \qquad 0 < \mu < s < \infty \\ 0 \qquad \quad othewise \end{cases} \tag{4}$$

where $\mu > 0$ denotes the minimum step size and γ is the scaling parameter when $s \to \infty$ the equation can be deformed as:

$$L(s, \gamma, \mu) \approx \sqrt{\frac{\gamma}{2\pi}} \frac{1}{s^{3/2}} \tag{5}$$

Lévy flights are superior to random walks when exploring large unknown environments, many theories can prove this fact, one of them is the variance theory of flight distance [9], the variance of the distance of Lévy flights from the starting position grows faster than that of normal random walks, and the expression of the variance of Lévy flights [9] is shown below:

$$\sigma^2(t) \sim t^{3-\beta}, \quad 1 \leq \beta \leq 2 \tag{6}$$

where β is the symmetric Lévy stable distribution coefficient, compared to the variance $\sigma^2(t) \sim t$ of the random walk [15], the variance of the Lévy flight distance from the starting position grows faster with time and can explore a larger unknown area. The experiments in this paper also prove that Lévy flights can explore a larger area than the 1-step random walk and the Brownian motion.

3 Path Adjustment Truncated Lévy flight exploration framework

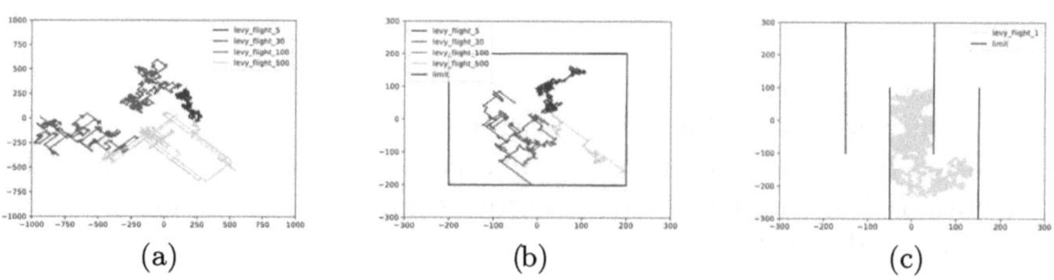

Fig. 1. Comparison of flight paths with different truncation steps in different environments

Unlike the traditional 1-step random walk algorithm, the path adjustment based truncated Lévy flight exploartion framework (ATLF) proposed in this section belongs to Lévy flight, whose step size is sampled from the truncated Lévy distribution. In this section, it is experimentally demonstrated that Truncated

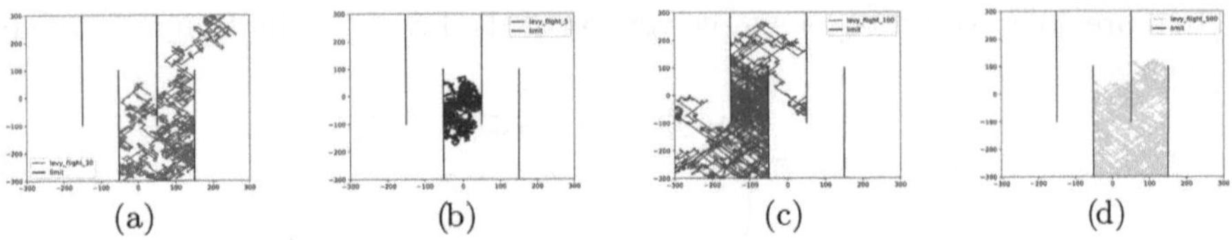

Fig. 2. Comparison of flight paths with different truncation steps in different environments

Lévy Flight Exploartion Strategy (TLF) can effectively improve the exploration ability of intelligences. The ATLF exploration framework is based on the TLF with the addition of a path adjustment mode, which tries to avoid repeated flights of the intelligent body to a poor state while maintaining the exploration ability. The experiment proves that the path adjustment mode effectively improves the performance of the algorithm and increases the stability of the algorithm.

3.1 Truncated Lévy flight exploration strategies

DRL is weakly exploratory in complex environments. In order to effectively solve this problem, this section proposes a truncated Lévy flight exploartion strategy (TLF) based on truncated Lévy flight. This section describes the implementation process of the TLF strategy and conducts comparative experiments in different environments with different truncation step parameters to prove the importance of the number of truncation steps to the Lévy flight algorithm of Lévy's flight algorithm. Section 3.2 combines this exploration strategy with the DQN algorithm, and experiments prove that the algorithm combining this exploration strategy can achieve better results compared with the classical algorithm.

TLF is a variant of Lévy flight that truncates the maximum step size, and the truncation is done to avoid too many time steps in a single flight. The implementation of the TLF exploration strategy is divided into the following two steps:

1. Flight manoeuvre selection. This selection process can be any strategy from the current work on reinforcement learning;
2. Generation of a randomised step size based on the selected truncated Lévy distribution. The intelligent body interacts with the environment based on the actions and the step size;

There are other methods for selecting flight actions in 1, such as -greedy in DQN, soft strategy in SAC [6], etc. While the step size generation in 2 is more complex, previous work usually uses Mantegna's algorithm [8], McCulloch's algorithm and Rejection's algorithm to model the Lévy distribution. The most efficient method [16] for realising the symmetric Lévy distribution in most cases is the Mantegna algorithm, which is used in this paper to generate the symmetric Lévy stable distribution.

In the Mantegna algorithm, the step size of the smart body can be calculated by the following formula:

$$s = \frac{u}{|v|^{1/\beta}} \tag{7}$$

β is the symmetric Lévy stable distribution coefficient. In reinforcement learning, action selection replaces flight direction selection, so there is no case where the step size S is negative. In this section, the maximum step size of the Lévy flight is truncated so that the final S is calculated as follows:

$$s = max\left(\left|\frac{u}{v^{1/\beta}}\right|, S_{max}\right) \tag{8}$$

where S_{max} is the maximum step of the flight, and both u and v are sampled on a normal distribution and are sampled from the normal distribution:

$$u \sim N\left(0, \sigma_u^2\right), v \sim N\left(0, \sigma_v^2\right) \tag{9}$$

Among them:

$$\sigma_u = \left\{\frac{\Gamma(1+\beta)\sin(\pi\beta/2)}{\Gamma\left[(1+\beta)/2\right]\beta 2^{(\beta-1)/2}}\right\}^{1/\beta}, \sigma_v = 1 \tag{10}$$

where $\Gamma(1+\beta)$ is the Gamma function, the distribution of this step follows $|s| \geq |s_0|$ in the expectation Lévy, where S_0 is the minimum step, set in the TLF exploration strategy $s_0 = 1$.

In the unconstrained environment, this subsection compares the trajectories for four cases with truncation steps of 5, 30, 100 and 500. As shown in Fig. 1(a), it is easy to see that the larger the truncation step, the larger the area that can be explored. However, the experiment is not applicable to reinforcement learning tasks, most reinforcement learning tasks have constraints, and too many repetitive steps are dangerous or wasteful, and there are two possibilities for the constraints to appear in the task as follows:

1. Performing wrong actions in certain dangerous states will lead to direct task failure for the intelligent body, for example, in the Walker2d-v2 task, performing wrong actions will cause the intelligent body to fall, which will lead to direct task failure.
2. Performing certain actions in certain states will cause the intelligent body to stay in place, e.g. in the Grid World mission the intelligent body will stay in place after hitting an obstacle.

For the case described in 1, experiments were conducted in the restricted environment in this section, as shown in Fig. 1(b), the intelligences with truncation step sizes of 5 and 30 did not experience task failure in the restricted environment, while the intelligences with truncation step sizes of 100 and 500 reached the hazardous boundary at the beginning of the flight, leading to task failure. Therefore, for tasks with low exploration requirements and dangerous boundaries, it is more appropriate to use a small number of truncation steps, and the

Table 1. Comparison of data after the average of 100 experiments in barrier environment

	1-step	5-step	30-step	100-step	500-step
Percentage of valid data%	97.63	96.12	89.46	79.73	66.37
Distance starting point(1cm)	130	185	200	205	192
standard deviation of distance(cm)	72.25	86.71	78.13	94.18	96.38
Average flight step(cm)	1	1.4	1.93	2.32	2.81

experiments in the Mujoco environment in Sect. 3.2 all use a truncation step of $S_{max} = 5$.

For the case described in 2, the experiments in this section are conducted in an environment with obstacle barriers, where the intelligent body remains in place when passing through the obstacle barriers until the next action no longer passes through the obstacle barriers. As shown in Fig. 1(c) and Fig. 2(a) to 2(d), these experiments represent the walking paths of a 1-step random walk and a truncated Lévy flight with step lengths of 5, 30, 100 and 500, respectively. The experiments show that the 1-step random walk in Fig. 2(c) and the 5-step truncated Lévy flight in Fig. 2(a) are too inefficient to explore, and the exploration ability of the 500-step truncated Lévy flight in Fig. 2(d) is lower than that of the 1-step random walk in Fig. 2(c). The exploration ability of the 500-step truncated Lévy flight in Fig. 2(d) is less than that of the 30-step truncated Lévy flight in Fig. 2(b) and the 100-step truncated Lévy flight in Fig. 2(c).

Table 1 shows the average data obtained by each truncation step in the restricted environment for 100 times, comparing from the perspective of distance from the starting point, the intelligent body with a truncation step of 500 is less effective than that of 100 and 30 steps, which can be concluded that in the space with obstacles, not the larger the truncation step the better the exploration ability, and too high truncation step will also have a lack of exploration problems.

The large truncation step length will have the problem of data invalidity, as shown in the effective data percentage in Table 1, this paper compares the effective data percentage produced by Lévy flights with truncation step lengths of 1, 5, 30, 100 and 500 in 100 experiments, and the results show that the amount of effective data decreases with the increase of the number of truncation steps, and the effective data in the 500-step truncation is only 66. 4%, so the effective data in the 500-step truncation is only 66.4%, and the effective data in the 500-step truncation is only 66.4%. Therefore, when choosing the truncation step length, it is necessary to consider both exploratory and data validity at the same time. In the experiments in Sect. 3.2, the TLF framework in the OpenAI Gym environment adopts a truncation step size of $S_{max} = 50$, which retains more explorability under the premise of data validity as high as possible.

3.2 Path Adjustment Based Flight Frames

Section 3.1 describes three problems that can occur when intelligences explore: lack of exploration, crossing dangerous boundaries, and data invalidity. Although the TLF framework mitigates the above problems, due to the uncertainty of flight, the TLF will still fly into known worse states or even dangerous boundaries with sufficient training. To avoid the above situation, this paper proposes the Path Adjustment Based Truncated Lévy Flight (ATLF) framework to add a path adjustment strategy to the TLF framework, i.e. to adjust the path when the flight is about to reach a known worse state.

Path adjustment is a basic strategy for natural organisms, e.g. a fly will not keep hitting an obstacle when it encounters one during its flight, but will change the direction of its flight; a sheep searching for food will change its path when it encounters wolves in front of it, and so on, and path adjustment can effectively improve the ability of intelligences to use their own experience. In the ATLF framework, the conditions for path adaptation are as follows:

$$\begin{aligned} & Q\left(s_t, a_{fly}\right) \geq Q_{\max a'}\left(s_t, a'\right) \\ \text{or } & \left|1-\frac{Q\left(s_t, a_{fly}\right)}{Q_{\max} a'\left(s_t, a'\right)}\right| \leq \rho \end{aligned} \tag{11}$$

where $Q\left(s_t, a_{fly}\right)$ is the value function for maintaining the flight manoeuvre, while $Q_{\max a'}\left(s_t, a'\right)$ is the optimal value function in the current state, and ρ is the threshold for maintaining the flight, the larger ρ indicates that the current intelligence has less tolerance for the flight manoeuvre, and it is harder for bad flight manoeuvres to occur: the smaller ρ indicates that the tolerance is greater, and it is easier for bad flight manoeuvres to occur. Lemma 1 proves that path-adapted truncated Lévy flight is superior to Brownian motion in exploring unknown domains using mathematical statistics. Lemma 1. Introducing the quantized equation for the distance of a random variable $\Delta \equiv log_{10}\frac{T(0)}{N_s(0)}$ [17], $T(0)$ has the following equivalence if Δ is the probability distribution of a TLF random variable returning to the starting point and $N_s(0)$ is the probability distribution of a Gaussian random variable returning to the starting point:

$$\begin{aligned} \Delta \simeq & \log_{10}\frac{2\Gamma(1/\beta)}{\pi\beta}+\frac{2-\beta}{2}\log_{10} l \\ & +\frac{1}{2}\log_{10}\left(\frac{\Gamma(1+\beta)\sin(\pi\beta/2)}{2-\beta}\right) \end{aligned} \tag{12}$$

where l is the truncation step and β is the symmetric Lévy stabilisation distribution coefficient.

Theorem 1. The ATLF random variable and the Brownian motion random variable satisfy the conditions in Lemma 1, and the probability distribution distance between the two to return to the starting point is Δ. When the coefficient of the symmetric Lévy stabilizing distribution is $1 \leq \beta < 2$, $\Delta > 0$ is constant, the expected displacement distance of the path-adjusted truncated Lévy flight distribution is superior to Brownian motion.

The specific process of the ATLF framework is shown in Algorithm 1:

Algorithm 1: DQN algorithm

Initialisation state action value network Q parameter θ
Initialise target state action value network Q parameter $\theta^- = \theta$
Initialise size n, experience buffer d
for episode=1,2,..., H: **do**
  Initialise the environment space
  for t = 1,2,...,T: **do**
    if The flight step parameter is **then**
      Choose not to fly down with probability ε
      The other cases are sampled from the distribution to obtain step S
      Selection of actions $a_t = argmax_a Q\left(\phi\left(s_t\right), a; \theta\right)$
    else
      Path adjustment is required:
      select $a_t = argmax_a Q\left(\phi\left(s_t\right), a; \theta\right)$
      No adjustments are made:
      Adoption of the previous moment's action $a_t = a_{t-1}$
      Flight steps minus 1
      Perform action a_t, get reward r and next state S_{t+1}
      Deposit experience $(s_t, a_t, r_{t+1}, s_{t+1}, d)$ into D
      Randomly sample n samples from the empirical buffer pool D
      Calculate $y_i = r_j + d\gamma {max}_{a'} \hat{Q}\left(\phi_{j+1}, a_j; \theta^-\right)$
      Update state action value network Q
      Minimising the loss function $L(\theta)$
      Update target network parameters: $\theta^- \leftarrow \tau\theta + (1-\tau)\theta^-$
    end if
  end for
end for

Path tuning can largely prevent intelligences from flying into bad states or dangerous boundaries with sufficient training, and the presence of the ρ parameter can adjust the relationship between exploration and exploitation in the algorithm. A lower ρ implies a lower flight state lower bound but with high exploration, while a higher ρ improves the flight state upper bound but indirectly hinders the intelligence's ability to explore new domains. In this paper we use a fixed parameter $\rho = 0.1$ in the ATLF framework. For most of the tasks tested in this paper, the use of a fixed parameter significantly improved the training effect of the intelligences.

3.3 ATLF Algorithm Incorporating Exploratory Action Selection

The section takes the SAC algorithm as an example to introduce how to combine the ATLF exploration framework with traditional algorithms. A major feature of SAC is the entropy regularisation, where the policy is trained to maximise the trade-off between expected return and entropy, with higher entropy representing a more stochastic policy, and the method increases the explorability of the policy. In entropy-regularised reinforcement learning algorithms, the intelligence receives a reward at each step proportional to the entropy corresponding to the current time step. The reward in reinforcement learning becomes of the following form:

$$\pi^* = \underset{\pi}{argmax}\mathbb{E}\left[\sum_{\tau\sim\pi}^{\infty} \gamma^t \left(R\left(s_t, a_t\right) + \alpha H\left(\pi\left(\cdot \mid s_t\right)\right)\right)\right] \tag{13}$$

where α is the entropy regularisation parameter, also called the temperature parameter, whose value function is set as follows:

$$V\left(\, s_t\right) = \mathbb{E}_{a_t\sim\pi}\left[Q\left(s_t, a_t\right) - \log\pi\left(a_t \mid s_t\right)\right] \tag{14}$$

SAC intelligences output action at according to the current state st each time they interact with the environment, while the ATLF exploration framework samples the step size from the truncated Lévy distribution before the intelligences interact with the environment, and obtains the step size through Eq. 8, and then standardises the action value a_t, a_{t+1}, a_{t+2}, $\ldots$, a_{t+s-1} in the time step t, $t+1$, $t+2,\ldots$, $t+s-1$ to a_t for the environment interaction, and at each flight step, the algorithm adjusts the decision based on the adjustment Eq. 11, and if adjustment is needed, the flight action is $a_{t'} = argmaxQ\left(s_{t'}, a_{t'}\right)$. When the time step is exceeded $t+s-1$, the new step size is resampled, and the previous process is repeated.

4 Experiments and Analysis of Results

In order to verify the effectiveness and compatibility of the ATLF exploration framework, this section conducts comparison experiments by combining the ATLF exploration framework with classical algorithms under the Open-AI Gym platform [18]. Gym is an environment platform under the OpenAI company that includes a rich experimental environment. In the discrete environments MountainCar-v0, CartPole-v0, LunarLander-v2, and Acrobot-v1 tasks, this section conducts comparison experiments between the ATLF-DQN algorithm, which combines the ATLF exploration framework with the Noisy-DQN algorithm, and the Noisy-DQN [10] and ICM-DQN [7] algorithms to verify the performance of the ATLF exploratory framework in discrete space tasks, and the comparison experiments between the ATLF-DQN and TLF-DQN algorithms show that the path adjustment method effectively improves the performance of the algorithms.

In the Swimmer-v2, Humanoid-v2, Walker2d-v2 and Hopper-v2 tasks in the continuous environment Mujoco, this section compares the ATLF-AC and ATLF-Noisy-SAC algorithms, which incorporate the ATLF exploration framework, with the classical SAC [6] and Noisy-AC [10] algorithms, which validate the effectiveness of the ATLF framework for continuous-space tasks.

Table 2. The data of the last 10000 steps of the five experiments of each model in the openai gym game are averaged

	MountainCar-v0	Acrobot-v1	CartPole-v0	LunarLander-v2
TLF-DQN	–163.97	-85.1	**200**	142.37
ATLF-DQN	**–132.79**	**–84.17**	**200**	**252.35**
ICM-DQN	–199.23	-97.18	164.79	65.75
TLF-ICM	–165.91	-96.58	84.31	**176.62**
ATLF-ICM	**–146.62**	**–93.4**	**174.2**	167.87
Noisy-DQN	–199.36	-211.5	183.38	71.31
TLF- Noisy	–129.67	-84.25	**200**	212.58
ATLF- Noisy	**–111.22**	**–81.62**	**200**	**230.32**

4.1 Experimental Parameter Setting

To ensure the fairness of the experiment, the parameters used in this paper are consistent with those of the base algorithm. In the DQN algorithm, the empirical buffer pool capacity is set to $m = 20000$, the number of batch-selected samples $n = 64$, the maximum number of time steps per episode $S_{max} = 1000$, and the target network update method is set to soft update, with the soft update parameter $\tau = 0.005$, the discount coefficient $\gamma = 0.99$, and the update rate $\alpha = 0.0003$. In the AC algorithm, the empirical buffer pool capacity is set to $m =$ 1,000,000, the number of samples selected in the batch $n =$ 256, the maximum number of time steps per episode S_{max} $= 1000$, the discount factor $\gamma = 0.99$, the update rate $\alpha = =0.0003$, and the temperature parameter is in the form of a gradual decrease. For Noisy-AC, this paper adopts the noise network approach, which adds noise to the state and action networks with parameter space. For the probability σ(uncertainty about characters) of selecting the Lévy flight strategy, this paper sets the parameter to vary from 1, decreasing with time. The adaptation factor is set to $\rho = 0.1$ in all tasks.

4.2 Comparison of Experimental Effects of TLF Strategies

This section verifies the effectiveness of the TLF strategy applied to the DQN algorithm and proves that the algorithm combined with the Truncated Lévy Flight strategy can achieve a good improvement in effectiveness even without path adjustment. As shown in Fig. 3, this section compares TLF-DQN with Noisy-DQN and ICM-DQN in the experiments, and the results prove that the DQN algorithm combined with TLF achieves higher cumulative rewards compared to Noisy-DQN and ICM-DQN algorithms in all tasks. As shown in Table 2, the TLF-DQN algorithm achieves 17.75%, 59.76%, 9.06%, and 50.09% higher cumulative rewards compared to the Noisy-DQN algorithm in four tasks, namely MountainCar-v0, Acrobot-v1, Cartpole-v0, and LunarLander-v2, respectively, and compared to the ICM-DQN algorithm in terms of cumulative reward

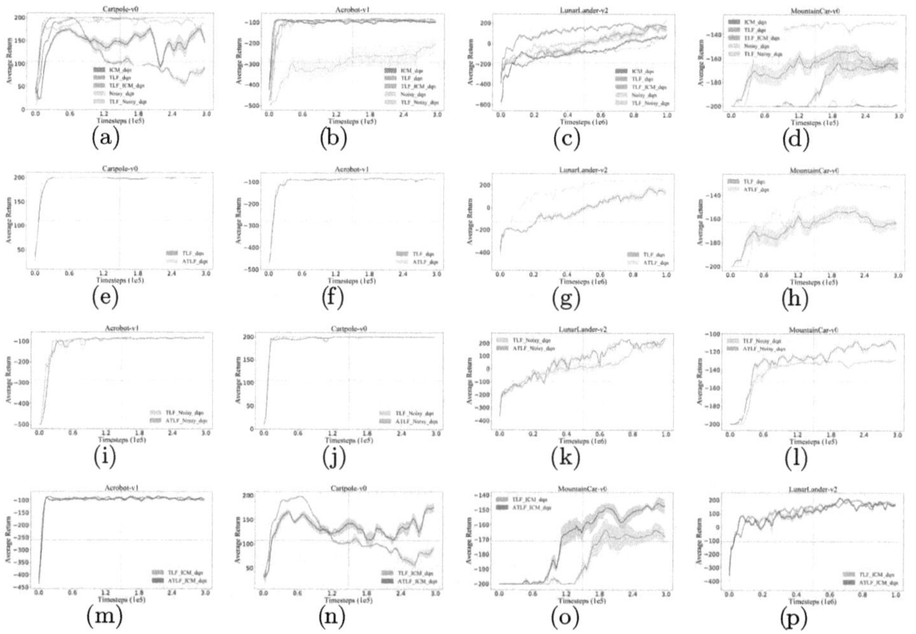

Fig. 3. Comparative experiment of TLF and ATLF framework combined with DNQ, ICM-DQN and Noisy DQN in OpenAI Gym environment

improved by 17.70%, 12.43%, 21.37%, and 118.53%, respectively. This section also validates the compatibility of TLF strategies by combining TLF strategies with Noisy-DQN and ICM-DQN algorithms, and the results show that the corresponding algorithms combining TLF exploration frameworks achieve higher rewards in most tasks compared to Noisy-DQN and ICM-DQN algorithms.

As shown in Figs. 3(a), 3(c) and 3(d), the algorithms incorporating the TLF framework outperform the corresponding classical algorithms both in terms of final training results and stability in the three environments Acrobot-v1, LunarLander-v2 and MountainCar-v0. As shown in Table 2, in the simple task Acrobot-v1, the TLF-Noisy-DQN and TLF-ICM-DQN algorithms improve the results by 60.17% and 0.61%, respectively, compared to the corresponding classical algorithms. In the complex LunarLander-v2 task, the TLF-ICM-DQN and TLF-Noisy-DQN algorithms are 168.62% and 198.11% more effective than their classical counterparts, respectively. In the difficult Mountaincar-v2 task, the TLF-Noisy-DQN and TLF-ICM-DQN algorithms are 34.96% and 26.5% more effective than the corresponding classical algorithms.

The feedback reward for the difficult task MountainCar-v0 is sparse and only reaches the end position to get a positive reward value, while the rest gets a -1 reward. Figure 3(a) shows that Noisy-DQN and ICM-DQN do not reach the endpoint at the end of training, i.e. they cannot solve the task well. After combining the TLF exploration strategy with Noisy-DQN and ICM-DQN, both algorithms achieved better results and successfully completed the task early in training.

The above experiments proved that the TLF framework has a strong exploration capability and is also compatible with the three algorithms, DQN, Noisy-DQN and ICM-DQN, which have good compatibility. On the simple Cartpole-v0 task, the TLF-ICM-DQN algorithm showed unstable results in the late stage of training, as shown in Fig. 3(b).

5 Conclusion

The paper proposes a truncated Lévy flight reinforcement learning exploration framework based on path adjustment, which starts from the perspective of the walking step size and uses the truncated Lévy flight to jump out of the one-step random walk framework, solving many exploration problems that Lévy flight may have in complex environments, such as flying to a known poor or dangerous state during the flight process, and the data validity reduction that occurs when the truncation step size is too large, the data validity reduction that can occur with large truncation steps, etc. The exploration framework is able to explore a larger region, avoiding the repetitive region walking of traditional exploration algorithms and improving the explorability of the algorithm while ensuring data validity.

The ATLF exploration framework is not exclusive to other exploration strategies, and the ATLF framework can be combined with different exploration algorithms. Through experiments, this paper shows that the algorithms combined with the ATLF exploration framework can train better strategies than the classical algorithms. The ATLF framework only uses simple decreasing random probabilities to choose the flight time, but intuitivelyunsrt [19], the ATLF framework should adopt a flight strategy for states with a high degree of unknowns and reduce the flight probabilities for states that are well known.

Acknowledgments. This paper is sponsored by Natural Science Foundation of Xinjiang Uygur Autonomous Region (2022D01A238); National Natural Science Foundation of China (62376179);

References

1. Osinenko, P., Dobriborsci, D., Aumer, W.: Reinforcement learning with guarantees: a review. IFAC-PapersOnLine **55**(15), 123–128 (2022)
2. Wang, X., et al.: SCC: an efficient deep reinforcement learning agent mastering the game of starcraft ii. In: International Conference on Machine Learning, pp. 10905–10915. PMLR (2021)
3. Apolinarska, A.A., Pacher, M., Li, H., Cote, N., Pastrana, R., Gramazio, F., Kohler, M.: Robotic assembly of timber joints using reinforcement learning. Autom. Constr. **125**, 103569 (2021)
4. Song, Y., Suganthan, P.N., Pedrycz, W., Ou, J., He, Y., Chen, Y., Wu, Y.: Ensemble reinforcement learning: a survey. Appl. Soft Comput. **149**, 110975 (2023)
5. Kim, M.J., Kim, J.S., Ahn, C.W.: Evolving population method for real-time reinforcement learning. Expert Syst. Appl. **229**, 120493 (2023)

6. Haarnoja, T., Zhou, A., Abbeel, P., Levine, S.: Soft actor-critic: Off-policy maximum entropy deep reinforcement learning with a stochastic actor. In: International Conference on Machine Learning, pp. 1861–1870. PMLR (2018)
7. Burda, Y., Edwards, H., Pathak, D., Storkey, A., Darrell, T., Efros, A.A.: Large-scale study of curiosity-driven learning. arXiv preprint arXiv:1808.04355 (2018)
8. Contal, E., Buffoni, D., Robicquet, A., Vayatis, N.: Parallel gaussian process optimization with upper confidence bound and pure exploration. In: Blockeel, H., Kersting, K., Nijssen, S., Železný, F. (eds.) ECML PKDD 2013. LNCS (LNAI), vol. 8188, pp. 225–240. Springer, Heidelberg (2013). https://doi.org/10.1007/978-3-642-40988-2_15
9. Yang, X.S.: Metaheuristic optimization: nature-inspired algorithms and applications. In: Artificial Intelligence, Evolutionary Computing and Metaheuristics: In the Footsteps of Alan Turing, pp. 405–420. Springer, Heidelberg (2013). https://doi.org/10.1007/978-3-642-29694-9_16
10. Tasfi, N., Capretz, M.: Noisy importance sampling actor-critic: an off-policy actor-critic with experience replay. In: 2020 International Joint Conference on Neural Networks (IJCNN), pp. 1–8. IEEE (2020)
11. Baum, L.E., Petrie, T.: Statistical inference for probabilistic functions of finite state Markov chains. Ann. Math. Stat. **37**(6), 1554–1563 (1966)
12. He, Q., Liu, H., Ding, G., Liangping, T.: A modified lévy flight distribution for solving high-dimensional numerical optimization problems. Math. Comput. Simul. **204**, 376–400 (2023)
13. Wang, Z., Chen, Y., Ding, S., Liang, D., He, H.: A novel particle swarm optimization algorithm with lévy flight and orthogonal learning. Swarm Evol. Comput. **75**, 101207 (2022)
14. Crovella, M.E.: Performance evaluation with heavy tailed distributions. In: Haverkort, B.R., Bohnenkamp, H.C., Smith, C.U. (eds.) TOOLS 2000. LNCS, vol. 1786, pp. 1–9. Springer, Heidelberg (2000). https://doi.org/10.1007/3-540-46429-8_1
15. Einstan, A.A.: On the movement of small particles suspended in stationary liquids required by the molecular-kinetic theory of heat. Phys. (Leipzig) **17**, 549 (1905)
16. Syberfeldt, A., Lidberg, S.: Real-world simulation-based manufacturing optimization using cuckoo search. In: Proceedings of the 2012 Winter Simulation Conference (WSC), pp. 1–12. IEEE (2012)
17. Mantegna, R.N., Stanley, H.E.: Stochastic process with ultraslow convergence to a Gaussian: the truncated lévy flight. Phys. Rev. Lett. **73**(22), 2946 (1994)
18. Van Hasselt, H., Guez, A., Silver, D.: Deep reinforcement learning with double q-learning. In: Proceedings of the AAAI Conference on Artificial Intelligence, vol. 30 (2016)
19. Sharma, S., Srinivas, A., Ravindran, B.: Learning to repeat: fine grained action repetition for deep reinforcement learning. arXiv preprint arXiv:1702.06054 (2017)

Detection of Depression in EEG Signals Based on Convolutional Transformer and Adaptive Transfer Learning

Qianqian Tan(✉) and Minmin Miao

School of Information Engineering, Huzhou University, Huzhou 313000, China
1002537620@qq.com, 02746@zjhu.edu.cn

Abstract. Electroencephalography (**EEG**) signals provide an objective reflection of the inner workings of the brain, making them a promising tool for the diagnosis of depression. However, the classification of EEG signals for depression is severely affected by individual differences among subjects, complex intrinsic properties, and low Signal-to-Noise Ratio (**SNR**), which limits the classification accuracy. Additionally, traditional convolutional neural networks extract local features but fail to capture long-term dependencies in EEG decoding. To address the aforementioned issues, we introduce an adaptive transfer learning method based on a convolutional transformer model for depression detection. The experimental results demonstrate the effectiveness of the proposed model on the public MODMA dataset and EDRA dataset. The results indicate that the MODMA and EDRA datasets exhibit optimal accuracies of 100% and 98.61%, respectively, outperforming some state-of-the-art depression identification methods. Our findings provide new perspectives on the recognition of depression, which could be used as an assisted diagnostic tool in the future.

Keywords: Transfer learning · EEG · Depression detection · Convolutional transformer

1 Introduction

[1] Depression is a common mental disorder that causes persistent sadness, feelings of hopelessness, and low self-esteem [4]. Unfortunately, clinical diagnostic methods for depression have some limitations, which can delay effective treatment for patients. That is why we need to develop an objective assessment method to detect depression accurately and quickly. EEG is widely used in the medical field as a rapid, noninvasive tool for monitoring brain activity and is effective in diagnosing a variety of disorders, including depression [19], epilepsy [6],

[1] This work was supported in part by the National Natural Science Foundation of China under Grants 62101189 and U20A20228, and in part by the Zhejiang Provincial Natural Science Foundation of China under Grant LTGC23F010001.

Z. Shi et al. (Eds.): ICIS 2024, IFIP AICT 720, pp. 30–39, 2025.
https://doi.org/10.1007/978-3-031-71253-1_3

and psychiatric disorders [3]. In recent years, there has been a growing interest among researchers in utilizing deep learning models to analyze depression EEG signals. Due to the limitation of the kernel size of Convolutional Neural Networks (**CNNs**), they can only capture features in the local receptive field, thus making it difficult to capture long-term dependencies in a time series. For this reason, researchers have further introduced Recurrent Neural Networks (**RNN**) and Long Short-Term Memory Networks (**LSTM**) to capture temporal features in EEG classification tasks [12,17]. However, such models are not suitable for training in parallel and are prone to lose their hidden states rapidly as the time step increases. Given the significance of global dependency, transformer models based on the attention mechanism have emerged in the field of EEG decoding and have demonstrated promising performance by capitalizing on long-term temporal relationships [10,14]. Moreover, the effect of individual variability on EEG signal data, including differences in individual brain structure and neural response levels, results in significant differences in the distribution of EEG signal data among subjects. Consequently, cross-subject classification tasks frequently exhibit lower accuracy.

In order to address the aforementioned challenges and shortcomings, we introduce an adaptive transfer learning method based on a convolutional transformer model for depression detection. The paper's main contributions include:

- An end-to-end adaptive transfer learning method based on convolutional transformer model for decoding EEG signals with depression. In addition, the necessity of adaptive transfer learning is demonstrated, and the generalization ability of the model is enhanced by a fine-tuning approach.
- An extensive number of experiments using the publicly available datasets MODMA and EDRA are conducted to validate the performance of our model. The results of these experiments provide strong evidence that the proposed model achieves state-of-the-art performance. This suggests that the transfer learning approach is an effective method for addressing the challenges of data distribution differences and limited samples.

2 Related Work

In recent years, the application of deep learning models to analyze depression EEG signals has attracted the attention of many researchers. Qayyum et al. [9] integrated a shallow network of convolutional neural networks and gated recurrent units (**GRUs**) for depression diagnosis. Zhang et al. [21] proposed a 2DCNN-LSTM classification model that fully utilizes spatial and temporal information, achieving an accuracy of 95.1% in depression diagnosis. Zhang et al. [20] introduced LSTM to extract temporal-domain features and a two-dimensional convolutional neural network to extract spatial-domain features. The detection of major depressive disorder (**MDD**) through the temporal and spatial feature fusion approach achieved an accuracy of 96.33%. Wan et al. [16] proposed a transformer-based EEG analysis model, EEGformer, which employs a one-dimensional convolutional neural network to automatically extract EEG channel features and combines multiple transformer modules in order to uniquely capture multiple EEG features.

3 Methodology

This study introduces an adaptive transfer learning method based on a convolutional transformer model for EEG signal decoding in depression. The model employs convolution to learn local features, and then employs self-attention to encapsulate global features, enhancing the model's generalization ability through different methods of fine-tuning the scheme. The architecture of this network is shown in Fig. 1.

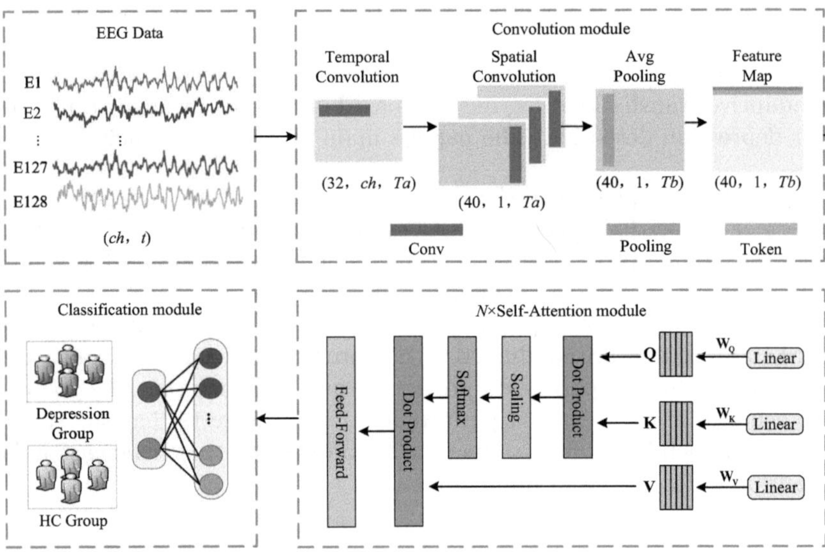

Fig. 1. The convolutional transformer model consists of four modules: data input, convolution, self-attention, and classification, where t, Ta, and Tb represent the sampling points, ch represents the number of channels, and **Q**, **K**, and **V** represent matrices.

3.1 Convolution Module

First, two 1D convolutional layers are employed to design the convolutional module for temporal and spatial dimensions, respectively, with the objective of extracting local features effectively. Subsequently, the batch normalization technique is introduced to simplify the training process and alleviate the overfitting problem. Meanwhile, the exponential linear unit (**ELU**) nonlinear activation function is chosen. In the subsequent stage of feature extraction, we employ the average pooling operation along the time dimension. Finally, the feature maps of the convolution module are rearranged, and each sample point is input as a token to the self-attention module.

3.2 Self-attention Module

In this module, we use self-attention mechanisms to capture the global time dependence of EEG features in depression. The process starts by creating query vectors ($\mathbf{Q}$), key vectors ($\mathbf{K}$), and value vectors ($\mathbf{V}$) using three linear layers. The dot product of the $\mathbf{Q}$ and $\mathbf{K}$ vectors is used to compute the pairwise similarities between each query and all the keys. To prevent the gradient from vanishing, we normalize these similarities by dividing by the scaling factor. Next, we apply the softmax function to obtain the weight matrix. Finally, the weight matrix is multiplied with the values ($\mathbf{V}$) by a dot product operation [15]. This entire attention computation is repeated N times in the self-attention module. The process can be expressed as follows:

$$\text{Attention}(\mathbf{Q}, \mathbf{K}, \mathbf{V}) = \text{softmax}\left(\frac{\mathbf{Q}\mathbf{K}^{\mathrm{T}}}{\sqrt{d}}\right)\mathbf{V} \tag{1}$$

In order to enable the model to perceive the global dependence of depressed EEG signals from different locations, we used a multi-head strategy. This requires dividing the feature map token of the previous module into H segments and then merging the output of each head to form the final output of the module. This process can be described as follows:

$$\begin{aligned} \text{MultiHead}(\mathbf{Q}, \mathbf{K}, \mathbf{V}) &= \text{Concat}(head_0; \cdots; head_{H-1}) \in \mathbf{R}^{N\times d} \\ head_h &= \text{Attention}(\mathbf{Q}_h, \mathbf{K}_h, \mathbf{V}_h) \in \mathbf{R}^{N\times \frac{d}{H}} \end{aligned} \tag{2}$$

where the dimension of the input feature map is $N \times d$, $head_h$ denotes the output of the hth head after the attention mechanism, Concat denotes the operation used to splice all $head_h$.

3.3 Classification Module

In this module, the output of the self-attention module is employed as the input of the fully connected layer. Subsequently, the category with the greatest probability value is regarded as the final classification result through the softmax function. The loss function of the entire framework is based on cross entropy, which is calculated as follows:

$$Loss = -\frac{1}{N_c}\sum_{i=1}^{N_c}\sum_{j=1}^{n} y_{ij}\log\left(\hat{y}_{ij}\right) \tag{3}$$

where N_c denotes the number of samples in the current batch and n denotes the number of categories. In addition, y_{ij} and $\hat{y}_{ij}$ are the true and predicted labels, respectively.

3.4 Transfer Learning Strategy

CNN-based classification algorithms generally require a significant amount of training data, which can lead to longer computation times. To address this issue, transfer learning is commonly used to obtain pre-trained models. Due to the differences in data distribution between the source and target domains, the application of transfer learning to the EEG classification task for depression faces certain challenges. In this study, the source domain consists of data from non target subject, while the target domain consists of data from target subject. To achieve domain adaptation, this study employs a fine-tuning strategy so that the model trained using the source domain can be better adapted to the properties of the target domain. Hence, the adaptation scheme focuses on fine-tuning the model parameters using a part of target subject data to optimize the model's performance in the EEG depression classification task in the target subject. This study considered two different classification strategies: subject-independent and subject-adaptive. In the subject-independent classification, all data except for the target subject were used for training. For each target subject, we performed a 2-fold cross validation on the data from remaining subjects for model selection. Since the model never observes any data from the target subjects during training, this is prone to inter-subject variation. Therefore, in the subject-adaptive classification method, different proportions of target subject data (see Sect. 4.2 for dataset partitioning) are used to fine-tune the pre-trained model in order to investigate the effect of different degrees of adaptive α on classifier accuracy. In this study, three different adaptation schemes AS-1 , AS-2 and AS-3 were employed. Each scheme fine-tunes different parts of the pre-trained model to improve the classification performance on the target subject. In the first adaptation scheme AS-1, the fully connected (**FC**) layer has been optimized while the rest of the network parameters remain unchanged. In the second adaptation scheme AS-2, the transformer module and the fully connected layer have been retrained using adaptation data, while the rest of the network parameters remain unchanged. In the third adaptation scheme AS-3, the entire network model has been retrained using adaptation data. The framework of the scheme is illustrated in Fig. 2.

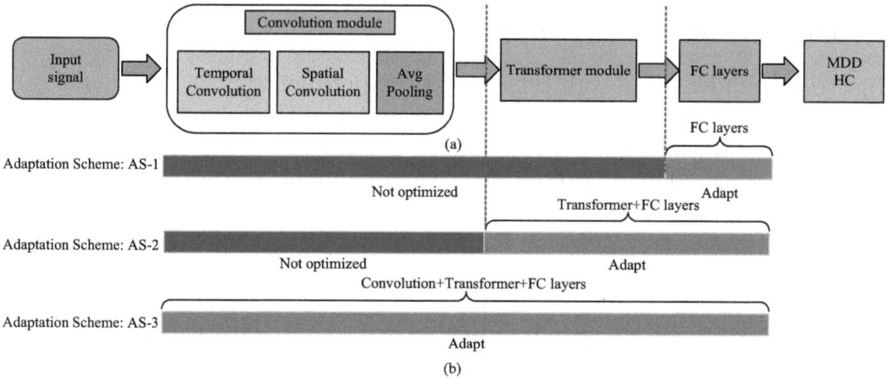

Fig. 2. Illustrations of (a) Network architecture and (b) three different adaptation schemes AS-1, AS-2 and AS-3.

4 Experiments and Results

This section presents the dataset preprocessing, experimental setup, and results for various schemes, which are then compared with state-of-the-art algorithms to validate the superiority of our approach.

4.1 Dataset Preprocessing

In this paper, we use the MODMA dataset [1] and the EDRA dataset [18]. For the MODMA dataset, the dataset consists of 53 subjects, of which 24 are diagnosed depression patients and 29 are healthy individuals. The device sampling frequency was 250 Hz and the reference electrode was a Cz electrode. The data recording time for each subject was approximately 5 min. The raw EEG data signals from all 128 channels were filtered using a band-pass filter from 0.5 Hz to 50 Hz, and then re-referenced using the common average reference (**CAR**) method. To reduce computational resources, we chose to study 64 of the 128 electrodes in this paper [20]. For uniform processing, we divided each participant's data into 150 segments of 2 s each, for a total of 7950 segments. For the EDRA dataset, which consisted of 50 subjects, 26 were categorized as being at high risk for depression, while 24 were considered to be at low risk. The EEG signal acquisition device was an EEG cap with 64 electrodes, in accordance with international standards. Following the final screening, 62 valid electrodes were selected for further experimental studies. The reference electrode for the online recordings was the FCz electrode, while the offline recordings used a global average reference. The EEG signals were filtered using a 0.05–100 Hz online band-pass filter. The sampling frequency was 500 Hz. Independent component analysis (**ICA**) was used to correct for ocular artifacts. Each subject intercepted a 1-minute continuous EEG recording and divided it into 60 equal-length segments of one second in length. Finally, a total of 3000 samples were obtained.

4.2 The Setting of Experiment

Subject-independent and subject-adaptive experiments were conducted separately in the current study. (1) In subject-independent classification, all data except for the target subjects were used for training. For each target subject, we performed a two-fold cross-validation of the remaining subjects' data for model selection. (2) In subject-adaptive classification, the model with minimum validation loss across cross-validation folds in the subject-independent classification is used as the base model. We used only the first 60% of the target subjects' data to fine-tune the network, ranging from 10% to 100% in steps of 30%. The model was implemented in the PyTorch framework and deployed on a GeForce RTX 3090. The Adam optimizer [5] is employed to minimize the loss function, with a learning rate of 0.00008, and the batch size to 50. We set the number of filters in the convolution module to 32, the number of self-attention executions N to 6, and the number of heads h to 10.

4.3 Experimental Results and Analysis

This section presents a discussion of the accuracy of subject-independent and subject-adaptive classification models. In subject-independent experiments, the average accuracy among all subjects on the MODMA dataset was 51.36%. The experimental results reflect that the generalization ability of the model varies due to differences in the distribution of the collected EEG signal data among subjects. In order to reduce the individual differences among subjects and enhance the model's generalization performance, the method of fine-tuning was employed. Table 1 provides the average results for all subjects in the subject adaptive experiment for the MODMA dataset. For the MODMA dataset, the accuracy of scheme AS-1 can exceed 97% at an adaptation rate of 10%, and can reach 100% at an adaptation rate of 40%. The remaining schemes achieve 100% accuracy. To further validate the effectiveness of the model, we conducted further experiments on the EDRA dataset according to scheme AS-3, which showed an average accuracy of 98.61% among all subjects, which is better than some of the state-of-the-art depression recognition methods. Experimental results show that the model has a certain generalization ability. A comparison was made between our method and other state-of-the-art depression identification methods to demonstrate the superiority of our work. Table 2 and Table 3 list the state-of-the-art studies and their corresponding performances in recent years for the MODMA dataset and EDRA dataset, respectively. The following methods have achieved impressive results on the MODMA dataset or EDRA dataset. For example, the study [2] fully considered all channel information in EEG-based major depressive disorder recognition and designed a random search algorithm to select the best discriminative features describing each channel. The study [8] transformed EEG signals into brain maps containing temporal, frequency and spatial information, and utilized CNNs and GRUs to achieve classification of depressed and healthy individuals. The study [21] presents a hybrid neural network based on CNN and LSTM for the automatic detection of depression. In study [13], a novel Twin Pascal's Triangles Lattice Pattern (**TPTLP**) was employed to extract local texture features from raw depression EEG signals and subbands. The study [22] proposed a new model for learning depression detection from EEG signals by adaptive channel optimization (**MGCL-ACO**) multi-view contrast. Research [18] proposed a graph-based adaptive least absolute shrinkage and selection operator model (**GA-LASSO**) to learn the discriminant features of FC matrices.

Table 1. The average accuracy (%) of the fine-tuned pre-trained model among all subjects on the MODMA dataset, where AS denotes the adaptation scheme and α denotes the proportion of adapted data.

Scheme	Adaptation Rate			
	$\alpha = 10\%$	$\alpha = 40\%$	$\alpha = 70\%$	$\alpha = 100\%$
AS-1	97.70	100	100	100
AS-2	100	100	100	100
AS-3	100	100	100	100

Table 2. Results of our model compared to state-of-the-art models of depression diagnosis using the MODMA dataset.

Method	Accuracy (%)
BrainMap + CNN + GRU [8]	89.63
CNN-LSTM [21]	95.10
GA-LASSO [18]	97.43
MGCL-ACO [22]	99.19
BLDA-RSSA [2]	99.32
TPTLP+Greedy algorithm [13]	**100**
Proposed model	**100**

* GRU: Gate Recurrent Unit; LSTM: Long Short-Term Memory; GA-LASSO: Graph-based Adaptive Least Absolute Shrinkage and Selection Operator; MGCL-ACO: Multi-view Graph Contrastive Learning via Adaptive Channel Optimization; TPTLP: Twin Pascals Triangles Lattice Pattern.

Section 4 validates its effectiveness and robustness through numerical experiments on artificial and UCI datasets, with comparative analyses demonstrating its performance advantages. Finally, Sect. 5 summarizes the findings and suggests future research directions.

2 Related Work

2.1 LSSVR

LSSVR is an improved version of SVR, mainly proposed by Suykens, etc. LSSVR improves computational efficiency in solving regression problems by simplifying the optimization process, making it an effective tool for handling large-scale data and regression problems. It aims to find a linear regression function:

$$f(x) = \omega^T x + b, \tag{1}$$

Among them, $\omega \in R^n, b \in R$.

In LSSVR, the optimization problem is defined as [4]:

$$\begin{aligned} &\min_{\omega,b,\xi} \tfrac{1}{2}\|\omega\|^2 + \tfrac{C}{2}\sum_{i=1}^{l}\xi_i^2, \\ &s.t.\ y_i - (\omega \cdot x_i + b) = \xi_i, i = 1, 2, \cdots l. \end{aligned} \tag{2}$$

In the formula, $C > 0$ is the adjustment factor, which plays a role in adjusting weights, ξ_i represents the error of each sample point from the hyperplane.

The meanings of the objective functions of the model are to maximize the margin and minimize the error, respectively. LSSVR fits the training points by finding a pair of fitting functions. Since its constraint condition only contains the equality constraint, the solution of the optimization problem is more straightforward, significantly improving the solution efficiency, which is more evident when solving larger-scale problems. However, all training points in LSSVR contribute to the regression function, making it lack sparsity.

Clearly, not all regression problems can be fitted with a linear function. In the nonlinear case, a transformation Φ is introduced to map the training points into a high-dimensional Hilbert space. Linear regression is then performed on the training set in that space, and a kernel function $K(x, x')$ is used to obtain the regression function under the nonlinear condition [10, 11].

2.2 $\varepsilon-$ TSVR

The process of solving regression problems requires the choice of an appropriate loss function. The ε- insensitive loss function is defined as follows [8]:

$$e(y, f(x)) = |y - f(x)|_\varepsilon = \begin{cases} 0, |y - f(x)| \le \varepsilon \\ |y - f(x)| - \varepsilon, \text{others} \end{cases} \tag{3}$$

The meaning of the ε-insensitive loss function is that when the difference between the observed value y of point x and the predicted value $f(x)$ does not exceed a certain value ε, it is considered that the predicted value $f(x)$ of this point is lossless, i.e., the loss is zero; when $|y - f(x)| > \varepsilon$, the loss is recorded as $|y - f(x)| - \varepsilon$. The geometric representation of the loss function is shown in the Fig. 1, it can be seen from the figure that the ε- insensitive loss function can ignore errors within a certain range in $[-\varepsilon, \varepsilon]$, ensuring the existence of a global optimum solution while also guaranteeing the sparsity of the solution.

The core idea of ε-SVR (Standard Support Vector Regression) is to construct an ε-insensitive loss band for training points, allowing as many training points as possible to fall within the band region, that is, using an ε-insensitive loss function to measure empirical risk [12].

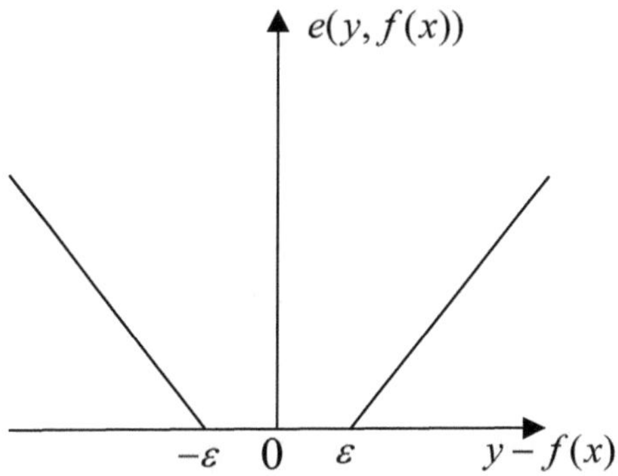

Fig. 1. $\varepsilon-$ insensitive loss function

Both ε-SVR and LSSVR fit the training set through a pair of parallel functions, whereas TSVR removes the parallel restriction and constructs two non-parallel functions:

$$f_1(x) = \boldsymbol{\omega}_1^T \boldsymbol{x} + b_1, f_2(x) = \boldsymbol{\omega}_2^T \boldsymbol{x} + b_2, \tag{4}$$

where $\boldsymbol{\omega}_1 \in R^n, \boldsymbol{\omega}_2 \in R^n, b_1 \in R, b_2 \in R$, then take the mean of the two functions $f(x) = \frac{1}{2}(f_1(x) + f_2(x))$ as the final regression function.

ε-TSVR is proposed in combination with ε-SVR and TWSVM, that is, a regularization term is added to the original TSVR, and the loss function used is the ε-insensitive loss function. The optimization problem is defined as:

$$\begin{aligned} &\min_{\boldsymbol{\omega}_1, b_1, \boldsymbol{\xi}} \frac{C_3}{2}\left(\|\boldsymbol{\omega}_1\|^2 + b_1^2\right) + \frac{1}{2}\|\boldsymbol{Y} - (\boldsymbol{A}\boldsymbol{\omega}_1 + \boldsymbol{e}b_1)\|^2 + C_1\boldsymbol{e}^T\boldsymbol{\xi}, \\ &s.t.\ \boldsymbol{Y} - (\boldsymbol{A}\boldsymbol{\omega}_1 + \boldsymbol{e}b_1) \geq -\varepsilon_1\boldsymbol{e} - \boldsymbol{\xi}, \\ &\qquad \boldsymbol{\xi} \geq 0, \end{aligned} \tag{5}$$

$$\begin{aligned} &\min_{\boldsymbol{\omega}_2, b_2, \boldsymbol{\eta}} \frac{C_4}{2}\left(\|\boldsymbol{\omega}_2\|^2 + b_2^2\right) + \frac{1}{2}\|(\boldsymbol{A}\boldsymbol{\omega}_2 + \boldsymbol{e}b_2) - \boldsymbol{Y}\|^2 + C_2\boldsymbol{e}^T\boldsymbol{\eta}, \\ &s.t.\ (\boldsymbol{A}\boldsymbol{\omega}_2 + \boldsymbol{e}b_2) - \boldsymbol{Y} \geq -\varepsilon_2\boldsymbol{e} - \boldsymbol{\eta}, \\ &\qquad \boldsymbol{\eta} \geq 0, \end{aligned} \tag{6}$$

where $\boldsymbol{A}$ represents the inputs of the training set composed of all training points, and $\boldsymbol{Y}$ represents the outputs of the training set composed of all training points; C_1, C_2, C_3, C_4

is a penalty factor greater than zero, playing a balancing role in the objective function; ε_1 and ε_2 is a bandwidth greater than zero, which is a pre-given parameter; $\boldsymbol{\xi}$ and $\boldsymbol{\eta}$ are slack variables.

The objective function of Eq. (5) consists of three main components: the first term is the regularization term and maximizing the margin, i.e., the width of the band; the second term minimizes the distance between $f_1(x)$ and the training points, ensuring it fits the training points as closely as possible; the third term minimizes the error, and combined with the subsequent constraints, it requires the training points to be as large as possible or equal to the lower bound $f_1(x) - \varepsilon_1$, as shown in Fig. 2. Similarly, Eq. (6) has constraints that require the training points to be as small as possible or equal to the upper bound. The regularization term ensures the model achieves structural risk minimization. In practical situations, different sizes for the lower and upper bands can be set, making TSVR more flexible [6].

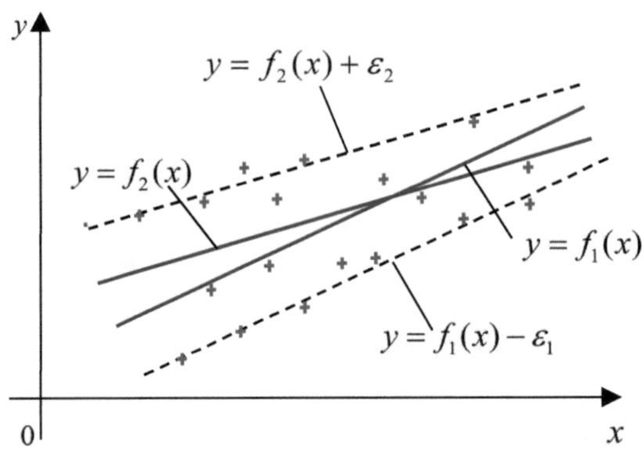

Fig. 2. $\varepsilon-$ TSVR

3 Twin Bounded Least Squares Support Vector Regression (TBLSSVR)

In this chapter, we introduce the Twin Bounded Least Squares Support Vector Regression (TBLSSVR) by incorporating regularization terms into the combined LSSVR and TSVR models to minimize structural risk. TBLSSVR determines the final decision function by fitting training points using two non-parallel hyperplanes. The model includes only equality constraints, making it computationally efficient and fast. We subsequently present TBLSSVR and its solution algorithms for linear and nonlinear cases.

3.1 Linear Model

Like TSVR, TBLSSVR also fits training points by constructing two non-parallel hyperplanes:

$$f_1(x) = \boldsymbol{\omega}_1^T \boldsymbol{x} + b_1,\ f_2(x) = \boldsymbol{\omega}_2^T \boldsymbol{x} + b_2, \tag{7}$$

where $\omega_1 \in R^n, \omega_2 \in R^n, b_1 \in R, b_2 \in R$, then take the average as the regression function:

$$f(x) = \frac{1}{2}(f_1(x) + f_2(x)) \tag{8}$$

The TBLSSVR model is:

$$\begin{aligned} &\min_{\omega_1, b_1, \xi} \frac{C_3}{2}\left(\|\omega_1\|^2 + b_1^2\right) + \frac{1}{2}\|Y - (A\omega_1 + eb_1)\|^2 + \frac{1}{2}C_1\xi^T\xi, \\ &s.t.\ Y - (A\omega_1 + eb_1) = -\varepsilon_1 e - \xi, \end{aligned} \tag{9}$$

$$\begin{aligned} &\min_{\omega_2, b_2, \eta} \frac{C_4}{2}\left(\|\omega_2\|^2 + b_2^2\right) + \frac{1}{2}\|(A\omega_2 + eb_2) - Y\|^2 + \frac{1}{2}C_2\eta^T\eta, \\ &s.t.\ (A\omega_2 + eb_2) - Y = -\varepsilon_2 e - \eta, \end{aligned} \tag{10}$$

where A represents the inputs of the training set composed of all training points, and Y represents the outputs of the training set composed of all training points; C_1 , C_2, C_3, C_4 is a penalty factor greater than zero, playing a balancing role in the objective function; ε_1 and ε_2 is a bandwidth greater than zero, which is a pre-given parameter; ξ and η are slack variables.

The first term of the objective function in Eq. (9) is a regularization term and maximizes the margin, ensuring the minimization of structural risk; the meaning of the second term is to minimize the distance between $f_1(x)$ and the training points, making it fit as closely as possible to the training points, with the minimum sum of square losses; the third term is to minimize the sum of square errors; the constraint is an equality constraint, making the distance ε_1 from the training points to $f_1(x)$ be plus a slack variable ξ. The same principle applies for Eq. (10).

The TBLSSVR has added a regularization term $\frac{C_3}{2}(\|\omega_1\|^2 + b_1^2)$ and $\frac{C_4}{2}(\|\omega_2\|^2 + b_2^2)$. The meaning of the regularization term is the same as in ε-SVR, that is, to maximize the bandwidth of ε_1 and ε_2. We introduce a transformation from R^n to R^{n+1}: $\mathbf{X}=[x, 1]$, $W_1 = [\omega_1, b_1]$. Then the functions $f_1(x) = \omega_1^T x + b_1$ and $y = f_1(x) - \varepsilon_1 = \omega_1^T x + b_1 - \varepsilon_1$ transform respectively $f_1(x) = W_1^T\mathbf{X} = [\omega_1, b_1]^T[x, 1]$ and $y = f_1(x) - \varepsilon_1 = W_1^T\mathbf{X} - \varepsilon_1 = [\omega_1, b_1]^T[x, 1] - \varepsilon_1$. Therefore, the bandwidth between the above two functions can be obtained:

$$\frac{\varepsilon_1}{\|W_1\|} = \frac{\varepsilon_1}{\sqrt{\omega_1^T\omega_1 + b_1^2}} \tag{11}$$

Similarly, another bandwidth is:

$$\frac{\varepsilon_2}{\|W_2\|} = \frac{\varepsilon_2}{\sqrt{\omega_2^T\omega_2 + b_2^2}} \tag{12}$$

In TBLSSVR, the constraint condition is an equality constraint, which turns the optimization problem from solving quadratic programming problems into solving systems of linear equations. This reduces the complexity of the solution and improves its speed. The advantage is more apparent when solving problems with larger samples.

Taking Eq. (9) as an example for solving, for simplicity, from the constraint conditions:

$$\boldsymbol{\xi} = (A\boldsymbol{\omega_1} + \boldsymbol{e}b_1) - \varepsilon_1\boldsymbol{e} - \boldsymbol{Y} \tag{13}$$

Substituting it into the objective function, solve the unconstrained extremum problem:

$$L(\omega_1, b_1) = \frac{C_3}{2}\left(\|\omega_1\|^2 + b_1^2\right) + \frac{1}{2}\|Y - (A\omega_1 + eb_1)\|^2 + \frac{C_1}{2}\|(A\omega_1 + eb_1) - e\varepsilon_1 - Y\|^2 \tag{14}$$

By taking partial derivatives with respect to $\boldsymbol{\omega_1}$ and b_1, we get:

$$\frac{\partial L}{\partial \boldsymbol{\omega_1}} = C_3\boldsymbol{\omega_1} - \boldsymbol{A}^T(\boldsymbol{Y} - \boldsymbol{A}\boldsymbol{\omega_1} - \boldsymbol{e}b_1) + C_1\boldsymbol{A}^T(\boldsymbol{A}\boldsymbol{\omega_1} + \boldsymbol{e}b_1 - \boldsymbol{e}\varepsilon_1 - \boldsymbol{Y}) = 0 \tag{15}$$

$$\frac{\partial L}{\partial b_1} = C_3 b_1 - \boldsymbol{e}^T(\boldsymbol{Y} - \boldsymbol{A}\boldsymbol{\omega_1} - \boldsymbol{e}b_1) + C_1\boldsymbol{e}^T(\boldsymbol{A}\boldsymbol{\omega_1} + \boldsymbol{e}b_1 - \boldsymbol{e}\varepsilon_1 - \boldsymbol{Y}) = 0 \tag{16}$$

By arranging, we get:

$$\begin{bmatrix}\boldsymbol{\omega_1} \\ b_1\end{bmatrix} = \frac{1}{C_3}\left(\frac{1}{1+C_1}\left(\boldsymbol{G}^T\boldsymbol{G}\right)^{-1} + \frac{\boldsymbol{I}}{C_3}\right)^{-1}\frac{1}{1+C_1}\left(\boldsymbol{G}^T\boldsymbol{G}\right)^{-1}\boldsymbol{G}^T[(1+C_1)\boldsymbol{Y} + C_1\boldsymbol{e}\varepsilon_1] \tag{17}$$

where $\boldsymbol{G} = [A, e]$. Similarly, from Eq. (10) we get:

$$\begin{bmatrix}\boldsymbol{\omega_2} \\ b_2\end{bmatrix} = \frac{1}{C_4}\left(\frac{1}{1+C_2}\left(\boldsymbol{G}^T\boldsymbol{G}\right)^{-1} + \frac{\boldsymbol{I}}{C_4}\right)^{-1}\frac{1}{1+C_2}\left(\boldsymbol{G}^T\boldsymbol{G}\right)^{-1}\boldsymbol{G}^T[(1+C_2)\boldsymbol{Y} - C_2\boldsymbol{e}\varepsilon_2] \tag{18}$$

The final decision function is then:

$$y = f(x) = \frac{1}{2}(f_1(x) + f_2(x)) = \frac{1}{2}(\boldsymbol{\omega_1} + \boldsymbol{\omega_2})^T\boldsymbol{x} + \frac{1}{2}(b_1 + b_2) \tag{19}$$

3.2 Non-linear Model

To extend the model to non-linear situations, we introduce transformations Φ and a kernel function $K(\boldsymbol{x}, \boldsymbol{x}') = (\Phi(\boldsymbol{x}), \Phi(\boldsymbol{x}'))$ to find two non-parallel hyperplanes.

$$f_1(x) = K\left(\boldsymbol{x}, \boldsymbol{A}^T\right)\boldsymbol{\omega_1} + b_1, \; f_2(x) = K\left(\boldsymbol{x}, \boldsymbol{A}^T\right)\boldsymbol{\omega_2} + b_2, \tag{20}$$

Then the TBLSSVR model with a kernel function is:

$$\min_{\omega_1, b_1, \xi} \quad \frac{C_3}{2}\left(\|\boldsymbol{\omega_1}\|^2 + b_1^2\right) + \frac{1}{2}\left\|\boldsymbol{Y} - \left(K(\boldsymbol{A}, \boldsymbol{A}^T)\boldsymbol{\omega_1} + \boldsymbol{e}b_1\right)\right\|^2 + \frac{1}{2}C_1\boldsymbol{\xi}^T\boldsymbol{\xi},$$
$$s.t. \; \boldsymbol{Y} - \left(K(\boldsymbol{A}, \boldsymbol{A}^T)\boldsymbol{\omega_1} + \boldsymbol{e}b_1\right) = -\varepsilon_1\boldsymbol{e} - \boldsymbol{\xi}, \text{ and} \tag{21}$$

$$\begin{aligned} \min_{\omega_2, b_2, \eta} \quad & \frac{C_4}{2}\left(\|\omega_2\|^2 + b_2^2\right) + \frac{1}{2}\left\|\left(K(A, A^T)\omega_2 + eb_2\right) - Y\right\|^2 + \frac{1}{2}C_2\eta^T\eta, \\ s.t. \quad & \left(K(A, A^T)\omega_2 + eb_2\right) - Y = -\varepsilon_2 e - \eta, \end{aligned} \tag{22}$$

where A represents the inputs of the training set composed of all training points, and Y represents the outputs of the training set composed of all training points; C_1 , C_2, C_3, C_4 is a penalty factor greater than zero, playing a balancing role in the objective function; ε_1 and ε_2 is a bandwidth greater than zero, which is a pre-given parameter; ξ and η are slack variables.

Referring to the solution process in the linear situation, substitute the constraint conditions into the objective function, construct the Lagrange function, derive it, and arrange to get:

$$\begin{bmatrix} \omega_1 \\ b_1 \end{bmatrix} = \frac{1}{C_3}\left(\frac{1}{1+C_1}\left(H^T H\right)^{-1} + \frac{I}{C_3}\right)^{-1} \frac{1}{1+C_1}\left(H^T H\right)^{-1} H^T[(1+C_1)Y + C_1 e\varepsilon_1] \tag{23}$$

$$\begin{bmatrix} \omega_2 \\ b_2 \end{bmatrix} = \frac{1}{C_4}\left(\frac{1}{1+C_2}\left(H^T H\right)^{-1} + \frac{I}{C_4}\right)^{-1} \frac{1}{1+C_2}\left(H^T H\right)^{-1} H^T[(1+C_2)Y - C_2 e\varepsilon_2] \tag{24}$$

where $H = \left[K(A, A^T)\ e\right]$. Then, the final decision function is:

$$y = f(x) = \frac{1}{2}(f_1(x) + f_2(x)) = \frac{1}{2}(\omega_1 + \omega_2)^T K(A, x) + \frac{1}{2}(b_1 + b_2) \tag{25}$$

4 Experiments

To validate the feasibility and effectiveness of the model TBLSSVR, we conduct numerical experiments on 4 artificial datasets and 9 UCI datasets and compare them with LSSVR, $\varepsilon-$ TSVR, and TLSSVR to analyze their strengths and weaknesses. All numerical experiments are conducted on a system with an Intel Core i7 processor (2.30 GHz), 6GB memory, running Windows 11 operating system, using MATLAB R2017a software.

Since all the algorithms depend on the selection of parameters, we use the Gauss kernel function $K(x_i, x_j) = \exp(-\left\|x_i - x_j\right\|^2/\sigma^2)$ for calculation during the experiment. In ε-TSVR and TBLSSVR, in order to reduce the computational complexity, we set $C_1 = C_2$ $C_3 = C_4$ and $\varepsilon_1 = \varepsilon_2$. The grid search method is used to select the optimal parameters. The parameter σ of the Gauss kernel function is chosen from among $\left\{2^i | i = -2, -1, \cdots, 6\right\}$, the parameter C_1 is chosen from among $\left\{2^i | i = -2, -1, \cdots, 8\right\}$, the parameter C_3 is selected from $\left\{2^i | i = -3, -2, \cdots, 7\right\}$, and the parameter ε_1 is chosen from $\{0.1, 0.2, \cdots, 0.9\}$ [11, 13].

In order to better evaluate the feasibility and effectiveness of the algorithm, we use the ten-fold cross-validation method in the numerical experiment. In the experimental results we obtain, the time is the average of ten cross-validations, and the accuracy is the average of ten prediction accuracies plus its standard deviation.

4.1 Metrics

In this section, we use the following statistical standards to evaluate regression methods: MAE (Mean Absolute Error), RMSE (Root Mean Square Error), NMSE (Normalized Mean Square Error), R^2 (R-squared) [14].

4.2 Artificial Datasets

We use 2D Sinc function to test TBLSSVR, the definition of the Sinc function is:

$$y = \sin c(x) = \frac{\sin(x)}{x}, \quad x \in [-4\pi, 4\pi] \tag{26}$$

Four data sets are generated by adding four different noises to the base of the Sinc function, respectively:

$$y_i = \frac{\sin(x_i)}{x_i} + \xi_i, \ x \sim U[-4\pi, 4\pi], \ \xi_i \sim N\left(0, 0.1^2\right) \tag{27}$$

$$y_i = \frac{\sin(x_i)}{x_i} + \xi_i, \quad x \sim U[-4\pi, 4\pi], \ \xi_i \sim N\left(0, 0.2^2\right) \tag{28}$$

$$y_i = \frac{\sin(x_i)}{x_i} + \xi_i, \quad x \sim U[-4\pi, 4\pi], \ \xi_i \sim U(0, 0.1) \tag{29}$$

$$y_i = \frac{\sin(x_i)}{x_i} + \xi_i, \ x \sim U[-4\pi, 4\pi], \ \xi_i \sim U(0, 0.2) \tag{30}$$

For each dataset, 267 sample points are generated respectively. To eliminate bias, generate five sample sets each time and take their average as the final training set.

The test results are shown in Fig. 3. It can be seen that TBLSSVR has a good fitting effect. At the same time, we also give the regression function $f_1(x) - \varepsilon_1$, which is the Down-TBLSSVR in the figure, and the regression function $f_2(x) + \varepsilon_2$ is represented as Up-TBLSSVR in the figure. It can be seen from the figure that Up-TBLSSVR and Down-TBLSSVR have the same band as TSVR, which has the ability to resist noise disturbance.

Table 1 lists the results in the non-linear case. On the first dataset, the MAE of ε-TSVR and TBLSSVR are the same, but the RMSE and NMSE of TBLSSVR are the smallest, and is the largest, so the regression effect of TBLSSVR is the best. In the second artificial dataset, the MAE, RMSE, and NMSE of TBLSSVR are all the smallest, and is the largest, the accuracy is higher; ε-TSVR is the best in the last two artificial datasets, and TBLSSVR is the second, but the speed is nearly 20 times faster than the former.

As shown in Fig. 4 and Table 2, the analysis of the experimental results under linear conditions is basically consistent with that under non-linear conditions.

4.3 UCI Datasets

To verify the effectiveness of TBLSSVR, we conduct experiments on 9 UCI datasets. The results are presented in Table 3 and Table 4, where the numbers in parentheses of the dataset represent the sample size and dimensions of each dataset. The accuracy is reported as the average prediction accuracy over ten trials plus the standard deviation.

From Table 3 and Table 4, it is evident that TBLSSVR achieves the highest regression accuracy in six of the nine UCI datasets (Stock, Concrete Slump Test, Computer Hardware, Servo, Automobile, Yacht Hydrodynamics), indicating its effectiveness. Specifically, in the Stock, Concrete Slump Test, and Yacht Hydrodynamics datasets, TBLSSVR achieves optimal values in MAE, RMSE, and NMSE, showing the best regression performance. In the remaining three datasets, TBLSSVR ranks second in computing precision. Overall, TBLSSVR outperforms TLSSVR without the regularization term across all datasets and is approximately ten times faster than TSVR, which also has good regression accuracy. Similar results are observed under linear conditions.

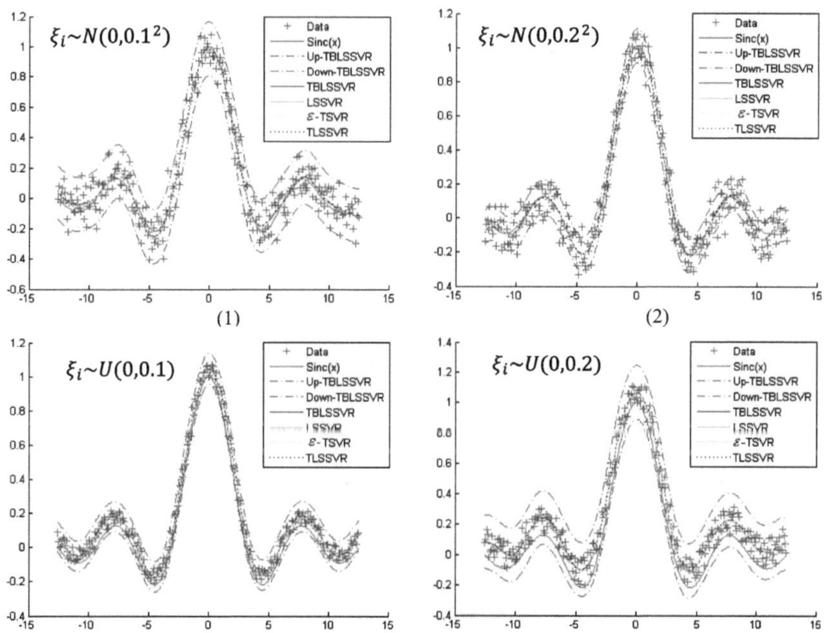

Fig. 3. Prediction result diagram on the artificial dataset (non-linear)

Table 1. Experimental results on the artificial datasets (non-linear)

dataset	model	MAE	RMSE	NMSE	R^2	time(s)
Type1	LSSVR	0.0752 ± 0.0133	0.0933 ± 0.0157	0.0934 ± 0.0735	0.9188 ± 0.0772	0.0084
	ε-TSVR	0.0751 ± 0.0128	0.0932 ± 0.0151	0.0939 ± 0.0709	0.9190 ± 0.0761	0.2826
	TLSSVR	0.0754 ± 0.0134	0.0935 ± 0.0160	0.0933 ± 0.0713	0.9276 ± 0.0759	0.0125
	TBLSSVR	**0.0751 ± 0.0132**	**0.0931 ± 0.0155**	**0.0934 ± 0.0743**	**0.9230 ± 0.0806**	**0.0156**
Type2	LSSVR	0.1644 ± 0.0232	0.2001 ± 0.0295	0.2813 ± 0.0904	0.7568 ± 0.1732	0.0088
	ε-TSVR	0.1641 ± 0.0235	0.1998 ± 0.0300	0.2804 ± 0.0905	0.7667 ± 0.1744	0.3262
	TLSSVR	0.1647 ± 0.0236	0.2005 ± 0.0300	0.2822 ± 0.0902	0.7692 ± 0.1757	0.0134
	TBLSSVR	**0.1618 ± 0.0280**	**0.1991 ± 0.0343**	**0.2787 ± 0.0920**	**0.7556 ± 0.1779**	**0.0139**
Type3	LSSVR	0.0509 ± 0.0049	0.0590 ± 0.0046	0.0359 ± 0.0119	0.9531 ± 0.0633	0.0093
	ε-TSVR	**0.0504 ± 0.0062**	**0.0588 ± 0.0054**	**0.0356 ± 0.0109**	**0.9618 ± 0.0691**	**0.2831**
	TLSSVR	0.0512 ± 0.0051	0.0591 ± 0.0047	0.0360 ± 0.0116	0.9630 ± 0.0626	0.0130
	TBLSSVR	0.0508 ± 0.0047	0.0591 ± 0.0044	0.0360 ± 0.0121	0.9579 ± 0.0646	0.0164
Type4	LSSVR	0.1028 ± 0.0104	0.1194 ± 0.0094	0.1253 ± 0.0330	0.8715 ± 0.1125	0.0091
	ε-TSVR	**0.1023 ± 0.0110**	**0.1185 ± 0.0110**	**0.1224 ± 0.0369**	**0.8984 ± 0.1098**	**0.2632**
	TLSSVR	0.1032 ± 0.0096	0.1200 ± 0.0087	0.1268 ± 0.0331	0.8866 ± 0.1141	0.0165
	TBLSSVR	0.1025 ± 0.0100	0.1190 ± 0.0092	0.1247 ± 0.0333	0.8835 ± 0.1145	0.0168

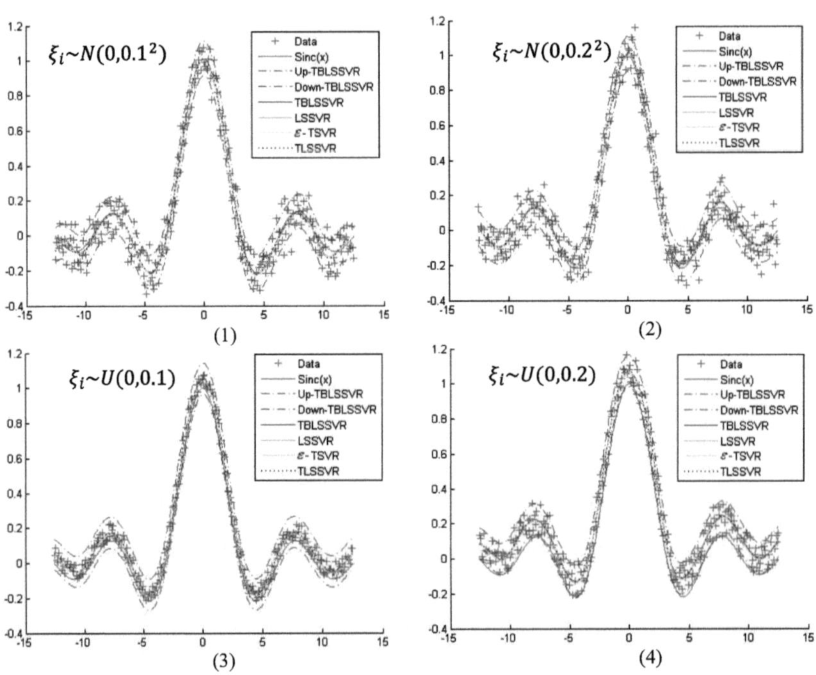

Fig. 4. Prediction result diagram on the artificial dataset (linear)

Table 2. Experimental results on the artificial datasets (linear)

dataset	model	MAE	RMSE	NMSE	R^2	time(s)
Type1	LSSVR	0.2553 ± 0.0371	0.3396 ± 0.0456	0.0579 ± 0.1334	1.0407 ± 0.1356	0.0073
	ε-TSVR	0.2437 ± 0.0384	0.3406 ± 0.0515	0.0546 ± 0.0726	1.0572 ± 0.0756	0.2329
	TLSSVR	0.2434 ± 0.0364	0.3356 ± 0.0472	0.0533 ± 0.0723	1.0594 ± 0.0779	0.0081
	TBLSSVR	**0.2407 ± 0.0332**	**0.3319 ± 0.0465**	**0.0507 ± 0.0713**	**1.0607 ± 0.0746**	**0.0109**
Type2	LSSVR	0.3027 ± 0.0562	0.3985 ± 0.0695	0.0546 ± 0.0526	1.0475 ± 0.1732	0.0057
	ε-TSVR	0.2965 ± 0.0542	0.3977 ± 0.0669	0.0435 ± 0.0503	1.0482 ± 0.1779	0.2423
	TLSSVR	0.2961 ± 0.0539	0.3974 ± 0.0640	0.0429 ± 0.0394	1.0503 ± 0.1757	0.0096
	TBLSSVR	**0.2956 ± 0.0535**	**0.3971 ± 0.0627**	**0.0423 ± 0.0379**	**1.0524 ± 0.1744**	**0.0113**
Type3	LSSVR	0.2463 ± 0.0351	0.3371 ± 0.0493	0.0871 ± 0.0619	1.0571 ± 0.1258	0.0073
	ε-TSVR	**0.2238 ± 0.0342**	**0.3342 ± 0.0454**	**0.0735 ± 0.0526**	**1.0877 ± 0.0591**	**0.2531**
	TLSSVR	0.2266 ± 0.0451	0.3338 ± 0.0497	0.0751 ± 0.0596	1.0537 ± 0.0726	0.0096
	TBLSSVR	0.2257 ± 0.0430	0.3321 ± 0.0488	0.0746 ± 0.0581	1.0754 ± 0.0646	0.0119
Type4	LSSVR	0.2620 ± 0.0572	0.3842 ± 0.0494	0.0984 ± 0.0745	1.0715 ± 0.0735	0.0057
	ε-TSVR	**0.2473 ± 0.0361**	**0.3573 ± 0.0410**	**0.0799 ± 0.0669**	**1.0831 ± 0.0638**	**0.2686**
	TLSSVR	0.2504 ± 0.0396	0.3682 ± 0.0477	0.0868 ± 0.0731	1.0826 ± 0.0641	0.0085
	TBLSSVR	0.2474 ± 0.0373	0.3606 ± 0.0458	0.0852 ± 0.0713	1.0851 ± 0.0673	0.0123

Table 3. Experimental results on UCI dataset (non-linear)

dataset	model	MAE	RMSE	NMSE	R^2	time(s)
Stock	LSSVR	0.0305 ± 0.0098	0.0402 ± 0.0130	0.1875 ± 0.0274	0.9587 ± 0.2578	0.0021
(63*7)	ε-TSVR	0.0308 ± 0.0102	0.0412 ± 0.0134	0.1956 ± 0.2940	0.9160 ± 0.2570	0.1277
	TLSSVR	0.0301 ± 0.0093	0.0393 ± 0.0129	0.1827 ± 0.2607	0.9773 ± 0.2586	0.0027
	TBLSSVR	**0.0295 ± 0.0083**	**0.0383 ± 0.0126**	**0.1661 ± 0.1948**	**1.0211 ± 0.3278**	**0.0041**
Concrete	LSSVR	0.8551 ± 0.2225	1.0171 ± 0.2426	0.0248 ± 0.0197	0.9013 ± 0.1096	0.0027
Slump	ε-TSVR	0.6941 ± 0.1012	0.8704 ± 0.1537	0.0179 ± 0.0105	0.9482 ± 0.0797	0.0599
Test	TLSSVR	0.7191 ± 0.1119	0.9300 ± 0.1601	0.0194 ± 0.0117	0.9451 ± 0.0777	0.0044
(103*8)	**TBLSSVR**	**0.6814 ± 0.0851**	**0.8669 ± 0.1353**	**0.0165 ± 0.0092**	**0.9512 ± 0.0830**	**0.0058**
Forecasting	**LSSVR**	**0.0701 ± 0.0756**	**0.1001 ± 0.1125**	**0.0178 ± 0.0192**	**0.9688 ± 0.0994**	**0.0029**
Orders	ε-TSVR	0.1138 ± 0.1086	0.1531 ± 0.1898	0.0526 ± 0.0534	0.9887 ± 0.1803	0.0357
(60*13)	TLSSVR	0.0948 ± 0.0861	0.1331 ± 0.1360	0.0320 ± 0.0303	0.9986 ± 0.1273	0.0032
	TBLSSVR	0.0896 ± 0.0808	0.1234 ± 0.1243	0.0268 ± 0.0251	1.0060 ± 0.1279	0.0038
Computer	LSSVR	0.0765 ± 0.0991	0.1918 ± 0.3327	0.0694 ± 0.1070	0.9003 ± 0.2114	0.0058
hardware	ε-TSVR	0.0677 ± 0.0869	0.1743 ± 0.3134	0.0602 ± 0.0978	0.9131 ± 0.2815	0.1786
(209*9)	TLSSVR	0.0616 ± 0.0841	0.1649 ± 0.3071	0.0525 ± 0.0915	0.9249 ± 0.2594	0.0083
	TBLSSVR	**0.0588 ± 0.0826**	**0.1599 ± 0.3012**	**0.0481 ± 0.0870**	**0.9211 ± 0.2463**	**0.0108**
Servo	LSSVR	0.4139 ± 0.1478	0.6561 ± 0.2712	0.2659 ± 0.2142	0.7818 ± 0.3507	0.0044
(167*5)	ε-TSVR	0.3693 ± 0.1466	0.5885 ± 0.2839	0.2097 ± 0.1613	0.9303 ± 0.3996	0.1050

(*continued*)

Table 3. (*continued*)

dataset	model	MAE	RMSE	NMSE	R^2	time(s)
	TLSSVR	0.3646 ± 0.1401	0.5949 ± 0.2682	0.2195 ± 0.1767	1.0002 ± 0.4466	0.0063
	TBLSSVR	**0.3589 ± 0.1366**	**0.5933 ± 0.2572**	**0.2146 ± 0.1645**	**0.9936 ± 0.4277**	**0.0116**
Automobile	LSSVR	0.3296 ± 0.1358	0.4949 ± 0.2126	0.3056 ± 0.2204	0.7546 ± 0.1704	0.0054
(159*25)	ε-TSVR	0.3240 ± 0.1333	0.4904 ± 0.2119	0.2991 ± 0.2165	0.7355 ± 0.1551	0.0914
	TLSSVR	0.3201 ± 0.1357	0.4971 ± 0.2133	0.3094 ± 0.2251	0.7916 ± 0.1797	0.0067
	TBLSSVR	**0.3165 ± 0.1357**	**0.5010 ± 0.2147**	**0.3145 ± 0.2291**	**0.8100 ± 0.1853**	**0.0097**
CSM	LSSVR	0.6119 ± 0.1306	0.8767 ± 0.2989	0.9192 ± 0.2166	0.2109 ± 0.2203	0.0051
(187*12)	**ε-TSVR**	**0.5963 ± 0.1390**	**0.9189 ± 0.3164**	**0.9738 ± 0.0847**	**0.1637 ± 0.2004**	**0.1261**
	TLSSVR	0.6246 ± 0.1290	0.9216 ± 0.2841	1.0177 ± 0.1890	0.2919 ± 0.4031	0.0074
	TBLSSVR	0.6048 ± 0.1420	0.8992 ± 0.3264	0.9863 ± 0.3337	0.4834 ± 0.3501	0.0146
Yacht	LSSVR	0.0919 ± 0.0209	0.1537 ± 0.0532	0.0249 ± 0.0099	0.9197 ± 0.1588	0.0128
Hydrody	ε-TSVR	0.1060 ± 0.0244	0.1536 ± 0.0417	0.0263 ± 0.0120	0.9441 ± 0.1272	0.2988
namics	TLSSVR	0.0865 ± 0.0207	0.1219 ± 0.0344	0.0169 ± 0.0085	0.9559 ± 0.1010	0.0181
(308*7)	**TBLSSVR**	**0.0804 ± 0.0168**	**0.1096 ± 0.0294**	**0.0137 ± 0.0068**	**0.9615 ± 0.0901**	**0.0237**
Auto MPG	**LSSVR**	**0.2345 ± 0.0307**	**0.3268 ± 0.0661**	**0.1191 ± 0.0597**	**0.9264 ± 0.1181**	**0.0171**
(392*8)	ε-TSVR	0.2405 ± 0.0315	0.3278 ± 0.0656	0.1196 ± 0.0577	0.9042 ± 0.1150	0.6823
	TLSSVR	0.2366 ± 0.0344	0.3290 ± 0.0686	0.1208 ± 0.0599	0.9335 ± 0.1176	0.0271
	TBLSSVR	0.2364 ± 0.0343	0.3280 ± 0.0667	0.1193 ± 0.0552	0.9268 ± 0.1174	0.0338

Table 4. Experimental results on UCI dataset (linear)

dataset	model	MAE	RMSE	NMSE	R^2	time(s)
Stock	LSSVR	0.0734 ± 0.0163	0.0933 ± 0.0276	0.8228 ± 0.5276	0.9964 ± 0.7561	0.0009
(63*7)	ε-TSVR	0.0773 ± 0.0219	0.0999 ± 0.0273	0.8125 ± 0.2677	0.3779 ± 0.2400	0.0983
	TLSSVR	0.0734 ± 0.0164	0.0933 ± 0.0277	0.8238 ± 0.5289	0.9981 ± 0.7579	0.0015
	TBLSSVR	**0.0733 ± 0.0163**	**0.0932 ± 0.0274**	**0.8184 ± 0.5185**	**0.9968 ± 0.7565**	**0.0026**
Concrete	LSSVR	2.0395 ± 0.5662	2.6557 ± 0.6522	0.1693 ± 0.1426	0.9151 ± 0.2058	0.0025
Slump	**ε-TSVR**	**2.0136 ± 0.5484**	**2.6592 ± 0.68013**	**0.1685 ± 0.1346**	**0.9226 ± 0.2015**	**0.0513**
Test	TLSSVR	2.0530 ± 0.5580	2.6760 ± 0.6429	0.1713 ± 0.1430	0.9264 ± 0.2098	0.0025
(103*8)	TBLSSVR	2.0189 ± 0.5428	2.6655 ± 0.6764	0.1690 ± 0.1341	0.9233 ± 0.2014	0.0048
Forecasting	LSSVR	0.0015 ± 0.0020	0.0023 ± 0.0039	0.0000 ± 0.0000	0.9996 ± 0.0017	0.0036
Orders	ε-TSVR	0.0049 ± 0.0037	0.0059 ± 0.0041	0.0003 ± 0.0004	0.9991 ± 0.0037	0.0345
(60*13)	TLSSVR	0.0026 ± 0.0022	0.0042 ± 0.0024	0.0001 ± 0.0003	0.9993 ± 0.0024	0.0016
	TBLSSVR	**0.0007 ± 0.0012**	**0.0011 ± 0.0023**	**0.0000 ± 0.0000**	**0.9999 ± 0.0008**	**0.0027**
Computer	LSSVR	0.1469 ± 0.0573	0.2175 ± 0.1166	0.3492 ± 0.7889	1.5925 ± 1.2184	0.0045
hardware	ε-TSVR	0.1422 ± 0.0594	0.2168 ± 0.1305	0.3036 ± 0.6606	1.4521 ± 1.0385	0.1594
(209*9)	TLSSVR	0.1428 ± 0.0553	0.2165 ± 0.1376	0.3239 ± 0.6830	1.4339 ± 1.1419	0.0073
	TBLSSVR	**0.1418 ± 0.0515**	**0.2143 ± 0.1321**	**0.2985 ± 0.6510**	**1.4039 ± 1.0337**	**0.0127**

(*continued*)

Table 4. *(continued)*

dataset	model	MAE	RMSE	NMSE	R^2	time(s)
Servo	LSSVR	0.9219 ± 0.1969	1.1189 ± 0.2476	0.9850 ± 0.6983	1.0255 ± 0.8802	0.0031
(167*5)	ε-TSVR	0.8831 ± 0.2206	1.1756 ± 0.2961	1.0086 ± 0.7048	1.1058 ± 0.8424	0.1143
	TLSSVR	0.9257 ± 0.2179	1.1138 ± 0.2714	0.9558 ± 0.7108	1.0716 ± 0.8447	0.0055
	TBLSSVR	**0.8796 ± 0.2217**	**1.1677 ± 0.2976**	**0.9782 ± 0.7267**	**1.0751 ± 0.8549**	**0.0091**
Automobile	LSSVR	0.4650 ± 0.0815	0.5933 ± 0.1050	0.3991 ± 0.1687	0.7811 ± 0.2243	0.0051
(159*25)	**ε-TSVR**	**0.4628 ± 0.0783**	**0.5923 ± 0.1021**	**0.3987 ± 0.1614**	**0.8561 ± 0.2240**	**0.1015**
	TLSSVR	0.4716 ± 0.0921	0.6031 ± 0.1108	0.4092 ± 0.1693	0.7845 ± 0.2894	0.0047
	TBLSSVR	0.4695 ± 0.0824	0.5956 ± 0.1026	0.4012 ± 0.1630	0.8088 ± 0.2411	0.0072
CSM	LSSVR	0.6466 ± 0.1318	0.9406 ± 0.2655	1.0872 ± 0.3304	0.4686 ± 0.5348	0.0029
(187*12)	**ε-TSVR**	**0.6335 ± 0.1355**	**0.9580 ± 0.2593**	**1.1636 ± 0.4593**	**0.5899 ± 0.6884**	**0.1430**
	TLSSVR	0.6518 ± 0.1340	0.9547 ± 0.2598	1.1322 ± 0.3590	0.5528 ± 0.6103	0.0059
	TBLSSVR	0.6425 ± 0.1325	0.9416 ± 0.2648	1.0991 ± 0.3546	0.5037 ± 0.5926	0.0106
Yacht	LSSVR	0.4828 ± 0.0505	0.5940 ± 0.0874	0.3784 ± 0.0735	0.7631 ± 0.3417	0.0066
Hydrody	ε-TSVR	0.4921 ± 0.0496	0.5959 ± 0.0804	0.3851 ± 0.0918	0.8233 ± 0.3723	0.3275
namics	TLSSVR	0.4846 ± 0.0498	0.5957 ± 0.0878	0.3809 ± 0.0761	0.7665 ± 0.3469	0.0146
(308*7)	**TBLSSVR**	**0.4826 ± 0.0501**	**0.5942 ± 0.0885**	**0.3794 ± 0.0784**	**0.7498 ± 0.3425**	**0.0297**
Auto MPG	LSSVR	0.3252 ± 0.0569	0.4265 ± 0.0793	0.1935 ± 0.0522	0.8178 ± 0.1488	0.0099
(392*8)	ε-TSVR	0.3227 ± 0.0497	0.4266 ± 0.0835	0.1937 ± 0.0642	0.7998 ± 0.1527	0.8850
	TLSSVR	0.3372 ± 0.0631	0.4373 ± 0.0875	0.1928 ± 0.0619	0.8042 ± 0.1508	0.0246
	TBLSSVR	**0.3242 ± 0.0516**	**0.4247 ± 0.0710**	**0.1921 ± 0.0522**	**0.8183 ± 0.1403**	**0.0288**

5 Conclusion

This paper proposes the TBLSSVR, which introduces a regularization term into a model that combines LSSVR and TSVR. The model retains both advantages while achieving structural risk minimization and enhancing regression accuracy and solution speed. Numerical experiments on different datasets validate the effectiveness and feasibility of the model, showing potential in practical applications such as financial forecasting, engineering optimization, high-dimensional data analysis, and complex system modeling. However, similar to TLSSVR, TSVR, and LSSVR, the proposed TBLSSVR model lacks sparsity. Designing a sparse TBLSSVR model is one of the future research directions.

Acknowledgements. This work was supported by the Natural Science Foundation of China under grant 62071171.

Supported by High-performance Computing Platform of Peking University.

References

1. Vapnik, V.: The Nature of Statistical Learning Theory. Springer, Heidelberg (2013). https://doi.org/10.1080/00401706.1996.10484565

2. Bishop, C.M.: Pattern Recognition and Machine Learning, vol. 2, pp. 1122–1128. Springer,Heidelberg (2006)
3. Smola, A.J., Schölkopf, B.: A tutorial on support vector regression. Stat. Comput. **14**, 199–222 (2004)
4. Suykens, J.A., Vandewalle, J.: Least squares support vector machine classifiers. Neural. Process. Lett. **9**, 293–300 (1999)
5. Khemchandani, R., Chandra, S., et al.: Twin support vector machines for pattern classification. IEEE Trans. Pattern Anal. Mach. Intell. **29**(5), 905–910 (2007)
6. Shao, Y.H., Zhang, C.H., Wang, X.B., Deng, N.Y.: Improvements on twin support vector machines. IEEE Trans. Neural Netw. **22**(6), 962–968 (2011)
7. Peng, X.: Tsvr: an efficient twin support vector machine for regression. Neural Netw. **23**(3), 365–372 (2010)
8. Shao, Y.H., Zhang, C.H., Yang, Z.M., Jing, L., Deng, N.Y.: An ε-twin support vector machine for regression. Neural Comput. Appl. **23**, 175–185 (2013)
9. Zhao, Y.P., Zhao, J., Zhao, M.: Twin least squares support vector regression. Nerocomputing **118**, 225–236 (2013)
10. Schölkopf, B., Smola, A.J.: A short introduction to learning with kernels. In: Advanced Lectures on Machine Learning: Machine Learning Summer School 2002 Canberra, Australia, 11–22 February 2002 Revised Lectures, pp. 41–64. Springer, Heidelberg (2003). https://doi.org/10.1007/3-540-36434-x_2
11. Khemchandani, R., Jayadeva, Chandra, S.: Optimal kernel selection in twin support vector machines. Optim. Lett. **3**, 77–88 (2009)
12. Burges, C.J.: A tutorial on support vector machines for pattern recognition. Data Min. Knowl. Disc. **2**(2), 121–167 (1998)
13. Hao, P.Y.: New support vector algorithms with parametric insensitive/margin model. Neural Netw. **23**(1), 60–73 (2010)
14. Demšar, J.: Statistical comparisons of classifiers over multiple data sets. J. Mach. Learn. Res. **7**, 1–30 (2006)

MLEE: Event Extraction as Multi-label Classification Task at Token Level

Jinshun Yang, Shuangxi Huang(✉), and Mingfeng Huang

Tsinghua University, Beijing, China
{yjs22,huangmf21}@mails.tsinghua.edu.cn, huangsx@tsinghua.edu.cn

Abstract. Event Extraction is an important task in natural language understanding, which aims to identify event trigger of pre-defined event types and their arguments of specific roles, has attracted a lot of attention from industry and academia. The previous works failed to address some issues, including error propagation problem, overlap and nest problem, and high complexity of model. This work proposes a novel model MLEE, which models Event Extraction task as Multi-Label classification task at token level, and processes the extraction task in a joint paradigm, can help solving issues mentioned above. The experiment verifies our model's effectiveness. Empirical results on DuEE and FewFC shows that MLEE outperforms previous best model, pushing trigger extraction F1 to 85.03% (+4.45%), argument extraction F1 to 78.85% (+2.72%) on DuEE, pushing trigger extraction F1 to 76.69% (+1.63%), argument extraction F1 to 76.53% (+5.27%) on FewFC.

Keywords: Event extraction · pre-trained language model

1 Introduction

Event extraction entails the extraction of structured event information from unstructured text, aiming to discern various predefined elements of different event types within the text. These elements are instrumental in answering the "who, when, where, what, why," and "how" related to events depicted in texts. Figure 1 exemplifies this process, depicting a sentence that contains the event information: an Event Type "movement transport" triggered by the Trigger "left", and two Arguments, "Saddam's family" and "three days ago", playing the Roles "Artifact" and "Time-within" respectively.

Event extraction constitutes a crucial aspect of information extraction research, enabling the efficient retrieval of event information from vast corpora of text. Its applications are broad and significant, enhancing capabilities in information retrieval, recommendation systems, intelligent question answering, knowledge graph construction, and other event-related applications, as cited in the literature [1]. Despite its establishment as a focal point of scholarly attention, event extraction continues to face a myriad of challenges that demand concerted

Published by Springer Nature Switzerland AG 2025
Z. Shi et al. (Eds.): ICIS 2024, IFIP AICT 720, pp. 55–65, 2025.
https://doi.org/10.1007/978-3-031-71253-1_5

scholarly effort. These issues not only underscore the complexity of accurately modeling and interpreting real-world data but also highlight the ongoing need for advanced methodologies in the field.

Event Type: movement transport

Sentence: Saddam's family[artifact] left[trigger] that city three days ago[time-within].

Fig. 1. An illustration of Event Extraction

The first challenge pertains to the issue of error propagation. Event extraction can be partitioned into several sub-tasks: Trigger Identification, Event Classification, Argument Identification, and Argument Role Classification. Table 1 delineates these sub-tasks along with other terminologies pertinent to event extraction. Error propagation issues frequently arise in pipeline-based event extraction frameworks, where the event extraction process is segmented into multiple sub-tasks, each addressed by a series of pipeline models. Subsequent models in this setup typically depend on the outputs of preceding models, although the earlier models do not rely on their downstream counterparts. Consequently, errors produced by upstream models cannot be rectified or mitigated by downstream models, leading to significant issues with error propagation.

The second issue involves the overlap and nesting of event elements. A single sentence may contain different elements of events, with some elements potentially overlapping or even sharing the same textual span. A 'flat event' describes scenarios where the elements (trigger words, arguments) of multiple events do not overlap and can be effectively processed by many existing models. In contrast, overlapping and nested events, where multiple events share the same trigger or the same argument, respectively, pose significant challenges for certain models, particularly those based on multi-classification.

The third challenge is the complexity of extraction models. With the rapid advancement of deep learning, numerous deep learning-based models have been proposed, characterized by numerous parameters and intricate network structures. This complexity results in significant spatial and temporal demands, which in turn create several difficulties in model training and application: 1) A high demand for data and expertise to train these models; 2) Increased costs in computing power and memory, necessitating greater investment during the application phase; 3) Elevated computational complexity, leading to time-consuming inference processes that are unsuitable for effective real-time event information extraction from large-scale texts.

In response to these challenges, this paper introduces a new event extraction model designed to address the issues of overlap and nesting in event extraction, circumvent the problem of error propagation, and reduce the number of model parameters wherever feasible.

Table 1. Terminology related to event extraction

Terminology	Meaning
Event Mention	Sentences describing events which contain event triggers and arguments
Event Type	The category of events that occurred
Trigger	Event trigger is a word or a phrase that most clearly expresses the occurrence of the event
Argument	Event arguments are entities that are part of the event Including participants and attributes
Role	Role is the relationship between an event and its arguments
Trigger Identification	To identify if a text contain event trigger
Event classification	To decide the event type described by a text
Argument Identification	To identify all arguments contained in a certain event type from a text
Role Classification	To decide roles of arguments play in a event

2 Related Work

2.1 Event Extraction

Numerous approaches for event extraction have been proposed to date. Based on the manner of extraction, these methods can be categorized into classification-based, sequence annotation-based, multi-round question answering-based, and generative-based approaches.

Multi-classification-based methods [2] simplify the event extraction process by treating it as multiple classification tasks. These methods typically begin by extracting a candidate set of event arguments through named entity recognition, followed by determining the appropriate argument role and event type for each candidate. The reliance on a predefined set of candidate arguments inherently leads to the problem of error propagation. Furthermore, due to their design, these methods are unable to process overlapping and nested events since they assign each candidate argument a singular role within a specific event type.

Sequence labeling-based methods [3–5] operate independently of named entity recognition efforts, opting instead to directly label each token according to the "BIO" tagging scheme associated with elements of events. Here, 'B' stands for "Beginning," 'I' for "Inside," and 'O' for "Outside." These methods, which essentially engage in a token-level multi-classification task, generally also struggle to adequately handle overlapping and nested events. Some approaches within this category [5] adopt a pipeline strategy for event extraction, which subsequently leads to the propagation of errors throughout the process.

Multi-round question answering-based methods [6,7] approach event extraction through iterative rounds of question answering, targeting the extraction of triggers, event types, arguments, and roles. This methodology entails a sequential process wherein the model first identifies the event type within the text, followed by the extraction of each argument role associated with the event type through a series of question-and-answer interactions. At each round of questioning, the relevant queries and extracted text are concatenated into a cohesive sequence and fed into the model, with the model output providing the corresponding answers. This approach exhibits the capability to extract flat, nested, and overlapping events, showcasing robust generalization capabilities. However, it is accompanied by high computational complexity and diminished inference efficiency.

Generative-based methods [8,9] frame the event extraction task as an encoding-decoding problem, enabling the direct generation of structured event information. These techniques typically leverage encoding-decoding architectures such as T5 and BART, facilitating the extraction of flat, overlapping, and nested events from textual data. Theoretically, these models are devoid of error propagation issues. Nevertheless, they pose challenges in training due to their propensity to generate chaotic and non-standard tokens. Moreover, these methods exhibit a heightened demand for data and entail higher computational complexity compared to conventional models. Despite these challenges, they represent a promising avenue for advancing event extraction capabilities, particularly in capturing nuanced event structures within text.

All categories of methods, despite their advancements and unique approaches, continue to face significant challenges in accurately and efficiently extracting complex event structures from text, highlighting the need for ongoing innovation and development in the field of event extraction.

2.2 Pre-trained Language Model

A pre-trained language model refers to a language model that learns a universal language representation from large-scale corpus in advance, without the need to retrain a new model when performing downstream natural language processing tasks. GPT (Generative Pre-training) [10] is a Transformer based one-way autoregressive language model, improves the state of the art in 9 of 12 tasks. In order to encode context bidirectionally, BERT [11] adopts the self-encoding approach, but causes two problems: 1) The mismatch problem. "[MASK]" tokens exists in the pre-training stage, but don't exist in the fine-tuning stage; 2) Probability calculation of masked tokens depends on the assumption that masked tokens are independent of each other, which is not consistent with the real scenario. XLNet [12] is a Transformer-XL based model, introduces two methods, the permutation language model and dual stream self-attention mechanism, to encode bidirectional information with no information leakage and the mismatch problem.

3 Method

Event extraction involves identifying event trigger words and arguments within text and classifying them according to predefined event types and argument roles. In this study, we model the task of event extraction as a multi-label classification at the token level. Here, each token may be annotated with multiple labels, denoting its association with various arguments or triggers across different event types. This approach effectively addresses the challenges associated with overlapping and nested event structures.

3.1 Event Extraction Model

Our proposed model, designated as MLEE, is predicated on a multi-label classification framework underpinned by the feature representation capabilities of Pre-trained Language Model. The architecture of MLEE is outlined in Fig. 2 and comprises an input layer, a feature representation layer, a probability calculation layer, and an output layer.

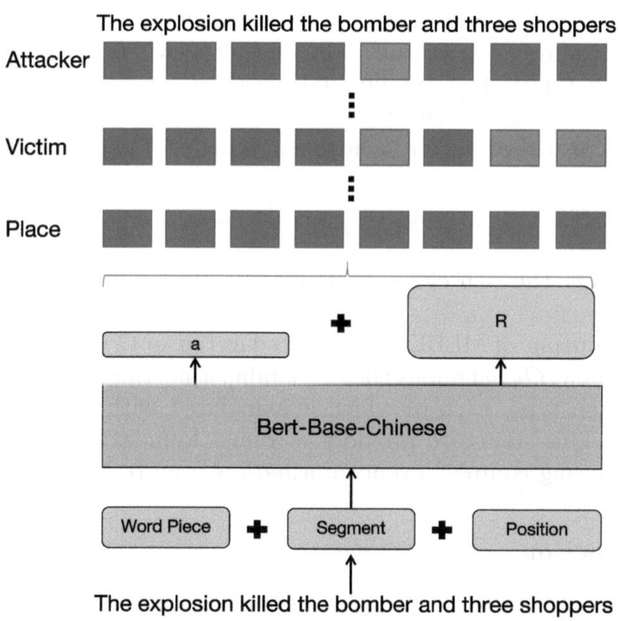

Fig. 2. The architecture of MLEE

In the input layer, text is decomposed into a series of token embeddings through a tokenization process. These embeddings are aggregates of WordPiece embeddings, position embeddings, and segment embeddings. "[CLS]" and "[SEP]", which are special tokens of Pre-trained Language Models like BERT and XLNet, are positioned at the beginning and end of the token sequence, respectively. This token sequence is represented as:

$$T = (t_1, t_2, ..., t_n) \tag{1}$$

in which $t_i(i = 1, 2, ..., n)$ denotes the embedding of the i-th token, and n is the total number of tokens in the sequence.

Subsequently, this token sequence T is input into BERT, where it is transformed into a rich semantic vector representation H:

$$H = (h_1, h_2, ..., h_n) \tag{2}$$

with h_i representing the vector corresponding to t_i.

In the probability calculation layer, two Feed-Forward Networks are utilized to compute the vector a and the tensor R:

$$a = (a_1, a_2, ..., a_n) = W^{(a)}H + b^{(a)} \tag{3}$$

$$R = (r_1, r_2, ..., r_n) = W^{(R)}H + b^{(R)} \tag{4}$$

Here,a_i indicates the likelihood of the i-th token being a trigger or an argument within an event, and r_i is a vector of dimension m, where m corresponds to the number of token types. The weights and biases of the networks are denoted as $W^{(a)}, b^{(a)}, W^{(R)}, b^{(R)}$, respectively.

The output probabilities for each token being of a particular type are computed using:

$$O_{i,k} = \frac{1}{1 + e^{-(a_i + r_{i,k})}} \tag{5}$$

where a_i represent the i-th element of vector a. and $r_{i,k}$ is the k-th element of vector r_i

Finally, the output of MLEE is formulated as tensor O with dimensions $n \times m$, where each element $O_{i,k}$ signifies the probability that the i-th token corresponds to the k-th token type, each of which is associated with a specific role within an event type. This structure provides a robust foundation for accurately and efficiently extracting complex event information from text.

3.2 Loss Function

In our work, we use two kinds of loss function to train our model: Binary Cross Entropy Loss and Circle Loss [13].

As widely Acknowledged, binary classification task aims to classfy inputs into two categories: the positive and negtive classes. Multi-label classification task seeks to identify a subset of relevant categories from a broader set of candidate categories. In this case, we can define the tokens which play an element role belong to positive class, while those that don't play any element role are designated as negtive class. For each specified element role, our model is tasked with selecting tokens that represent the positive class from the sequence of tokens. Thereby, it is possible to change a multi-label classification into several binary classification tasks, utilizing the summation of Binary Cross Entropy from these binary tasks as the overarching loss function.

However, this approach encounters signigicant challenges due to category imbalance. For each element role, the quantity of tokens corresponding to the positive class (K) is markedly smaller compared to the length of the token sequence (n), i.e. $n >> K$. Thus, the task of event extraction becomes a profoundly imbalanced multi-label classification scenario, necessitating strategies to mitigate this imbalance. To this end, we have developed a modified version of the Binary Cross Entropy Loss, which incorporates weights to amplify the influence of the positive class and diminish that of the negative class. The Binary Cross Entropy Loss with Weights is as follow:

$$\ell = \sum_{i=1}^{n} \sum_{k=1}^{m} \beta_{i,k} Y_{i,k} O_{i,k} + \gamma_{i,k} \times (1 - Y_{i,j}) \times (1 - O_{i,k}) \tag{6}$$

where $Y_{i,k}$ is the label, which value is 0 or 1, $\beta_{i,k}$ and $\gamma_{i,k}$ are weights, can be obtained through:

$$\beta_{i,k} = \frac{n+2}{2 \times \sum_{i=1}^{n} I(Y_{i,k} = 1) + 1} \tag{7}$$

$$\gamma_{i,k} = \frac{n+2}{2 \times \sum_{i=1}^{n} I(Y_{i,k} = 0) + 1} \tag{8}$$

in which $I(\cdot)$ is indicator function.

From another perspective, multi-label classification can be regarded as a generalization of multi classification task. In multi classification task, the objective is to identify a single target class from n candidate classes, while multi-label classification aims to ascertain K tokens corresponding to the positive class from n tokens. In multi classification task, Entropy Cross Loss is employed to maximizing socre of target class while minimizing score of non-target class, i.e.:

$$-log \frac{e^{s_t}}{\sum_{i=1}^{n} e^{s_i}} = log \sum_{i=1}^{n} e^{s_i - s_t} = log(1 + \sum_{i=1, i \neq t}^{n} e^{s_i - s_t}) \tag{9}$$

$$\approx max(s_1 - s_t, ..., s_{t-1} - s_t, 0, s_{t+1} - s_t, ..., s_n - s_t) \tag{10}$$

in which s_t is the score of target class and $s_i, i \in \{1, .., t-1, t+1, ..., n\}$ is score of non-target classes. For multi-label classification, The approach naturally extends to maximizing the scores of target classes while minimizing those of non-target classes, which can be achieved by minimizing circle loss, in our specific scenario, are as follow:

$$\ell = log[1 + \sum_{O_{i,k} \in O_k^{pos}} exp(a_{i,k}^{pos} O_{i,k}) \sum_{O_{j,k} \in O_k^{neg}} exp(a_{j,k}^{neg} O_{j,k})] \tag{11}$$

in which $a^{pos}_{i,k}$ and $a^{neg}_{j,k}$ are non-negtive weighting factors, O^{pos}_{k} is the output set of positive class, O^{neg}_{k} is the output set of negtive class. $a^{pos}_{i,k}$ and $a^{neg}_{j,k}$ are defined as:

$$a^{pos}_{i,k} = [Y_{i,k} - O_{i,k}]+ \tag{12}$$

$$a^{neg}_{j,k} = [O_{j,k} - Y_{j,k}]+ \tag{13}$$

where $[\cdot]+$ is the "cut-off at zero" operation.

4 Experiment

4.1 Experiment Setting

Datasets. We conduct our event extraction experiment on two widely used datasets which are DuEE [14] and FewFC [15]. For a fair comparison, we split the same training, validation and test sets as in previous works.

DuEE dataset has 17,000 sentences and 65 event types, includes 20,000 events. The input of the dataset is one or several continuous and complete sentences which contains event information, the output is event element word belonging to predefined event types and roles.

FewFC dataset is from real financial news and has been annotated by professionals. The dataset has 10 types of financial event and 8982 samples, contains 12890 events.

Evaluation Metric. We use Precision(P), Recall(R) and F-measure(F1) as the evaluation metrics. P,R,F1 are defined as:

$$P = \frac{TP}{T+} \tag{14}$$

$$R = \frac{TP}{D+} \tag{15}$$

$$F1 = \frac{2 \times PR}{P + R} \tag{16}$$

In Trigger Extraction task, TP is the number of tokens shared by predicted triggers and annotated triggers, $T+$ is the tokens count of predicted triggers, $D+$ is the tokens count of annotated triggers.

In Argument Extraction task, TP is the number of tokens shared by predicted arguments and annotated arguments, $T+$ is the tokens count of predicted arguments, $D+$ is the tokens count of annotated arguments.

Comparison Methods. We use PLMEE, MQAEE, CasEE as Comparison methods in event extraction experiment. PLMEE [5] proposed an model to overcome the roles overlap problem by separating the argument prediction in terms of roles, and divided event extraction into two subtasks: trigger extraction, argument extraction. MQAEE [6] formulated event extraction as multi-turn question answering, and proposed a history answer embedding strategy for the model to make full use of history answers. CasEE [16] proposed a joint learning framework with cascade decoding for overlapping event extraction.

Implementations. We optimize our models by using BCE loss function and AdamW optimizer with learning rate 2e-5 in first 50 epochs, using circle loss function and AdamW optimizer with learning rate 2e-6 in the next 30 epochs. our model is implemented in pytorch with AdamW optimizer. our experiment goals are: 1) Verifying the improvement of our model over the baselines approaches. 2) Providing quantitative evidence of the model's complexity is lower than the baseline models. The batch size in the training is 10. we leverage the BERT-Base-Chinese model in the feature representation layer, which has 12 layers, 768 hidden units and 12 attention heads. The max sequence length is set to 400.

4.2 Results in Event Extraction Experiment

We evaluate our event extraction model on DuEE and FewFC dataset. Table 2 presents the Comparisons between our model and other baselines. As shown in the table, on DuEE dataset, our model outperforms the previous best model CasEE by 4.45% in trigger extraction F1 score, and 2.72% in argument extraction F1 score. On FewFC dataset, out model outperforms CasEE by 1.63% in trigger extraction F1 score, and 5.27% in argument extraction F1 score.

Table 2. Results of event extraction on DuEE

Dataset	Model	Trigger Extraction			Argument Extraction		
		P	R	F1	P	R	F1
DuEE	PLMEE	78.89	76.95	77.91	74.78	73.41	74.09
	MQAEE	79.27	73.42	76.23	76.78	72.22	74.43
	CasEE	81.74	79.45	80.58	77.32	74.98	76.13
	Ours	93.45	78.00	**85.03**	82.75	75.30	**78.85**
FewFC	PLMEE	76.82	75.16	76.16	73.59	65.51	69.32
	MQAEE	81.87	70.42	75.71	74.25	63.46	68.43
	CasEE	77.87	78.25	78.06	71.19	71.33	71.26
	Ours	77.66	81.82	**79.69**	73.70	79.60	**76.53**

The possible reasons of why our model has better performance are as follow: 1) The previous works divided event extraction into subtasks, result in error propagation problem. Such as PLMEE first identified event type, then performed argument extraction according to event types, and CasEE also divide event extraction into two stage works. We use a joint extraction paradigm for event extraction, which complete all subtasks of event extraction in a unified model, avoiding error propagation problem. 2) We uses multiple sets of vectors to represents output, each set of vectors serve for a role to determin the spans of all elements (including trigger and argument) that play it. Since we extract elements that play different roles in different types of events separately, our model can extract trigger-sharing and argument-sharing events, thus achieving high performance on nested and overlapping event.

4.3 Complexity Analysis

Furthermore, we conducted a comparative analysis between our model and the previously leading model, CasEE, focusing on computational costs during both training and inference phases, as well as GPU memory consumption. Given that our model incorporates fewer parameters and layers, it inherently exhibits a reduced complexity compared to baseline models.

Table 3. Comparative evaluation in terms of computational cost between the propsed MLEE and CasEE

Dataset	Training Speed		Inference Speed		GPU Memory Usage	
	CasEE	MLEE	CasEE	MLEE	CasEE	MLEE
DuEE	1×	8.40×	1×	10.62×	10222 MiB	4162 MiB
FewFC	1×	6.21×	1×	5.31×	9830 MiB	7160 MiB

The comparative results are presented in Table 3. As illustrated in Table 3, our model, MLEE, demonstrates a superior speed relative to CasEE. Additionally, MLEE requires less GPU memory than CasEE.

5 Conclusion

This work introduces an innovative event extraction model that employs a joint paradigm to address the task, thereby avoiding the issue of error propagation. By modeling the extraction task as a multi-label classification problem at the token level, the model is effective for nested and overlapping events extraction. Notably, the model's complexity is significantly reduced, featuring fewer parameters than its predecessors. Empirical comparisons and analytical experiment results varify its effectiveness, demonstrating its superiority over previous approaches.

Acknowledgment. This work was supported by the National Key R & D Program of China under grant 2022YFF0903300.

References

1. Li, Q., et al.: A survey on deep learning event extraction: approaches and applications. IEEE Trans. Neural Netw. Learn. Syst. **35**, 6301–6321 (2022)
2. Mekala, D., Shang, J.: Contextualized weak supervision for text classification. In: Proceedings of the 58th Annual Meeting of the Association for Computational Linguistics, pp. 323–333 (2020)
3. Chen, L., Ruan, W., Liu, X., Lu, J.: Seqvat: virtual adversarial training for semi-supervised sequence labeling. In: Proceedings of the 58th Annual Meeting of the Association for Computational Linguistics, pp. 8801–8811 (2020)

4. Ramponi, A., van der Goot, R., Lombardo, R., Plank, B.: Biomedical event extraction as sequence labeling. In: Proceedings of the 2020 Conference on Empirical Methods in Natural Language Processing (EMNLP), pp. 5357–5367 (2020)
5. Yang, S., Feng, D., Qiao, L., Kan, Z., Li, D.: Exploring pre-trained language models for event extraction and generation. In: Proceedings of the 57th Annual Meeting of the Association for Computational Linguistics, pp. 5284–5294 (2019)
6. Li, F., Peng, W., Chen, Y., Quan Wang, L., Pan, Y.L., Zhu, Y.: Event extraction as multi-turn question answering. In: Findings of the Association for Computational Linguistics: EMNLP 2020, pp. 829–838 (2020)
7. Guo, S., et al.: A frame-based sentence representation for machine reading comprehension. In: Proceedings of the 58th Annual Meeting of the Association for Computational Linguistics, pp. 891–896 (2020)
8. Lu, Y., et al.: Text2event: controllable sequence-to-structure generation for end-to-end event extraction. arXiv preprint arXiv:2106.09232 (2021)
9. Hsu, I., et al.: Degree: a data-efficient generation-based event extraction model. arXiv preprint arXiv:2108.12724 (2021)
10. Radford, A., Narasimhan, K., Salimans, T., Sutskever, I., et al.: Improving language understanding by generative pre-training (2018)
11. Devlin, J., Chang, M.-W., Lee, K., Toutanova, K.: Bert: pre-training of deep bidirectional transformers for language understanding (2019)
12. Yang, Z., Dai, Z., Yang, Y., Carbonell, J., Salakhutdinov, R.R., Le, Q.V.: Xlnet: generalized autoregressive pretraining for language understanding. In: Wallach, H., Larochelle, H., Beygelzimer, A., d' Alché-Buc, F., Fox, E., Garnett, R. (eds.) Advances in Neural Information Processing Systems, vol. 32. Curran Associates, Inc. (2019)
13. Sun, Y., et al.: Circle loss: a unified perspective of pair similarity optimization. In: Proceedings of the IEEE/CVF Conference on Computer Vision and Pattern Recognition (CVPR) (2020)
14. Li, X., et al.: DuEE: a large-scale dataset for Chinese event extraction in real-world scenarios. In: Zhu, X., Zhang, M., Hong, Yu., He, R. (eds.) NLPCC 2020. LNCS (LNAI), vol. 12431, pp. 534–545. Springer, Cham (2020). https://doi.org/10.1007/978-3-030-60457-8_44
15. Zhou, Y., Chen, Y., Zhao, J., Wu, Y., Xu, J., Li, J.: What the role is vs. what plays the role: semi-supervised event argument extraction via dual question answering. In: Proceedings of AAAI-2021. AAAI Press (2021)
16. Sheng, J., et al.: Casee: a joint learning framework with cascade decoding for overlapping event extraction. arXiv preprint arXiv:2107.01583 (2021)

Research on Improvement of Sweeping Learning Chain Algorithm Based on Factor Space Theory

Yaru Liu(✉), Fanhui Zeng, and Sihang Ren

College of Science, Liaoning Technical University, Fuxin 123000, China
820516560@qq.com

Abstract. In order to improve the classification accuracy of sweeping learning chain (SLC) algorithm in factor space and solve the problem that SLC is error-prone to classify samples in mixed domain, this paper proposes sweeping learning chain-K-Nearest Neighbor (SLC-KNN) algorithm. When SLC encounters the problem of undivisible data, KNN is used to classify the samples to be tested that fall into the mixed domain. It not only solves the problem of undivisible data encountered by the SLC, but also reduces the amount of computation and storage of KNN algorithm. And extended to multi-classification problem, proposed BT-SLC-KNN multi-classification algorithm. According to the maximum class center distance, firstly the algorithm makes the two most easy to separate classes separate. And defines the Class center distance on sweeping vector, a normal binary tree is generated step by step by comparing the distance of the remaining categories on the sweeping vector of the two classes with the furthest distance. It reduces the time complexity of merge sweeping learning chain (MSLC) algorithm and improves the multi-classification accuracy. Finally, the experiments are carried out on UCI data sets, and the results show that the two algorithms are feasible and effective.

Keywords: factor space · sweeping learning chain algorithm · K-Nearest Neighbor · binary tree

1 Introduction

With the advent of the information revolution, intelligent science and data science emerge as the times require. Intelligent network makes human beings face great opportunities and challenges. Under this background, new mathematics has begun to sprouts, promoting the development of intelligent science and data science. In 1982, the Chinese scholar Wang P Z firstly put forward the new concept of factor space, and used factor space to describe big data and intelligent science, which has its advantages in theory, method and goal. In theory, it can describe and deal with problems more clearly and more rigorously, and in method, it can make the algorithm simple and fast.

At present, the main difficulty in the field of artificial intelligence is to find the key factors in practical problems. How to reveal the key factors has become an important

Published by Springer Nature Switzerland AG 2025
Z. Shi et al. (Eds.): ICIS 2024, IFIP AICT 720, pp. 66–80, 2025.
https://doi.org/10.1007/978-3-031-71253-1_6

research topic. When the key factors are found, we can use key factors to classification, prediction, inference, making decision, etc. The theory of explicit and implicit factors in factor space is to find hidden key factors by some method, so as to distinguish objects and divide concepts, and break through the bottleneck problem in the field of artificial intelligence. Based on this idea, we propose the sweeping learning chain algorithm (SLC) for the classification problem of machine learning. Experimental result show SLC algorithm is feasible and effective for small data samples binary classification.

However, the SLC algorithm may fail in big data application scenarios, and it is easy to misclassify the points in the projection mixed domain, which makes the accuracy of classification not ideal. Therefore, based on the combination theory, this paper fully combines the advantages of SLC algorithm which has high recognition rate for samples far away from the boundary of the projection mixed domain with the advantages of KNN algorithm which has high recognition rate for samples closer to the boundary of the projection mixed domain, and proposes a SLC-KNN algorithm. And it is extended to multi-classification problem, which is transformed into multiple binary classification problems, and BT-SLC-KNN multi-classification algorithm is proposed. Experimental results show that the algorithm is feasible and effective.

2 Factor Space Theory

2.1 Sweeping Learning Chain Algorithm

When human eyes classify two classes of things, it can be summed up as sweeping from the center of one class to the center of the other class, and the overall vision notices is the sweeping direction. Although the sweeping direction conforms to the overall judgment of the human eye, it is not necessarily a visible and hidden factor. But each sweep vector can make a contribution to the classification, so SLC algorithm is proposed.

Definition 1: Let $S = \{x_i = (x_{i1}, x_{i2}, \cdots, x_{in})\}$ is a separable set binary classification training set, $Y = \{+, -\}$ is a label set, $S \times Y = \{x_i = (x_{i1}, x_{i2}, \cdots, x_{in}; Y)\}$ is called a binary classification training set. Let $S^- = \{x_i^- | i = 1, \cdots, k\}$, $S^+ = \{x_j^+ \big| j = 1, \cdots, l\}$, where $x_i^-, x_j^+ \in R^n$. The centers of two classes of data sets are $o^- = (x_i^+ + \cdots + x_k^+)/k$, $o^+ = \left(x_j^+ + \cdots + x_l^+\right)/l$, denoted $w = o^+ - o^-$, w is called sweeping vector(sweeping direction).

Definition 2: Denote.

$$a^+ = \arg\min_j\left\{\left(x_j^+, w\right)|j = 1, \cdots, l\right\}, a^- = \arg\min_i\{(x_i^-, w)|i = 1, \cdots, k\},$$

a^+ and a^- are called the positive class lower bound and the negative class upper bound.

Denote

$$J^* = \left(a_t^+ - a_t^-\right)/2.$$

J^* is called partition wall.

If $a^+ > a^-$, then the two categories can be completely separated by w and J^*. If $a^+ \le a^-$, the two categories cannot be completely separated by w, which $\left[a^+, a^-\right]$ is called the projection mixing domain. The sample points in the projected mixing domain are called mixing point.

Sweeping Learning Chain Algorithm Steps

Input: two training set $S^- = \{x_i^- | i = 1, \cdots, k\}$, $S^+ = \left\{x_j^+ | j = 1, \cdots, l\right\}$, where $x_i^-, x_j^+ \in R^n$.

Output: a sequence of criteria $\pi = \{\{w_t, H_t = [a^+, a^-]\}(t = 1, 2, \cdots, T-1); w_T; J^*\}$.

Step1: $t := 1$, calculate the centers of the two classes o_t^+,o_t^- and $w_t := o_t^+ - o_t^-$.

Step2: calculate (x_i^+, w_t) and $\left(x_j^-, w_t\right)$, obtained

$$a_t^+ = \min\{(x_i^+, w_t)|x_i^+ \in S_t^+\},$$

$$a_t^- = \max\left\{\left(x_j^-, w_t\right)|x_j^- \in S_t^-\right\}.$$

If $a_t^+ \le a_t^-$, then there exists projection mixing domain $\left[a_t^+, a_t^-\right]$,record w_t, $H_t = \left[a^+, a^-\right]$; In this case, the two classes cannot be completely separated, and deleted the non-mixing points of the two classes, and the sample data sets are updated

$$\begin{aligned} S_{t+1}^- &:= S_t^- - \{x_i^- \in S_t^- | (x_i^-, w_t) < a_t^+\} \\ S_{t+1}^+ &:= S_t^+ - \left\{x_i^+ \in S_t^+ | \left(x_j^+, w_t\right) > a_t^-\right\}, \end{aligned}$$

let $t = t + 1$, go back to step 1.

If $a_t^+ > a_t^-$, then there is no projection mixing domain, and there is a partition wall J^* to separate the two classes. Record $w_T := w_t$, J^* and turn to Step 3.

Step 3: Outputs the sequence of criteria

$$\pi = \{\{w_t, H_t = [a^+, a^-]\}(t = 1, 2, \cdots, T-1); w_T; J^*\}.$$

Sweeping Learning Chain Algorithm Test Steps.

Input: Testing set $Z \times Y = \{z_i = (z_{i1}, z_{i2}, \cdots, z_{in}; Y)\}$,$z_i \in R^n$.

Output: Classification result.

Step1: $t :=$ 1,calculate (z_i, w_t).

Step2: determine the relationship between (z_i, w_t) and $H_t = \left[a^+, a^-\right]$,if (z_i, w_t) is not in $H_t = \left[a^+, a^-\right]$, turn to Step 3; otherwise, turn to Step 4.

Step3: if $(z_i, w_t) < a^+$, z_i is negative class; If $(z_i, w_t) > a^-$,z_i is positive class, the operation is stopped and output result.

Step4: Let $t := t + 1$,if $t \ne T$ go back to Step 1. If $t = T$, there is a partition wall J^*,if $(z_i, w_T) < J^*$, z_i is judged as negative class; if $(z_i, w_T) > J^*$,z_i is judged as positive class. Stop the operation and output result.

2.2 Merge Sweeping Learning Chain Algorithm

SLC algorithm is used to solve binary classification problems, and can't be directly applied to multi-classification problems. How to effectively extend binary classification problem to multi-classification problems is still worth to be studied. At present, there is also a corresponding multi-class classification algorithm in the factor space: merge sweeping learning chain algorithm.

For the n classification problem, let the category index set $J := \{1, \cdots, n\}$,the data set $X_1 = \{x_1^1, x_1^2, \cdots, x_1^{n_1}\}, X_2 = \{x_2^1, x_2^2, \cdots, x_2^{n_2}\}, \cdots, X_n = \{x_n^1, x_n^2, \cdots, x_n^{n_n}\}$.

Definition 3: (Merge classes) Selected $X_j (j = 1, 2, \cdots, n)$ form dataset X, and the remaining classes are merged.

$$H_j := \underset{i \neq j}{\wedge} X_i i, j = 1, 2, \cdots, n.$$

Call H_j is the merge class of the $X_j X_j$

$$H_j = \{X_1, \cdots, X_{j-1}, X_{j+1}, \cdots, X_n\}.$$

Definition 4: (Absolute difference) Give J^* and w_T, the test point z,the absolute difference is

$$D = |(w, z) - J^*|.$$

The principle of MSLC: multiple SLC are combined to solve multi-class classification problems. According to the one-against-rest rule, SLC are trained n times, and selected one class as the positive class, and the other classes are merged together as the negative class to train. Finally, n criterion sequences are obtained. Given a test sample point z, it is substituted into the results of the trained n criterion sequences to obtain n classification results. The mode discrimination is used to select the most frequent class as result.

Merge Sweeping Learning Chain Algorithm Steps

Step1: Selected X_j denoted as the positive class, the merged class H_j denoted as the negative class. There are n pairs.

Step2: Calculate the center of the positive class X_j and negative class H_j,and sweeping vector $w = o^+ - o^-$.Calculate the minimum inner a^+ of the positive class and the maximum inner b^- of the negative class.

Step3: Calculate J, if J is positive, get w_T,$J^* = (b^- - a^+)/2$,if J is negative,the mixing domain is $[a^+, b^-]$.

Using MSLC algorithm, n pairs of criteria sequence $\{\pi_1, \pi_2, \cdots, \pi_n\}$ are obtained.

Merge Sweeping Learning Chain Algorithm Test Steps

Step1: Checks whether X_j and H_j is separate. If so, then calculates J^*, obtained $\pi_j = \{\{w_t, H_t = [a^+, b^-]\}(t = 1, 2, \cdots, T-1); w_T; J^*\}$.

Step2: For test point z,calculate (w, z) and determine whether it is in $[a^+, b^-]$.

①If (w, z) is on the left of $[a^+, b^-]$, z is judged as negative, otherwise z is judged as positive. Stop the operation and output result.

②If (w, z) is in the mixed domain, can't judge, turn to Step3.

Step3: Calculate (w_T, z),if $(w_T, z) > J^*$,z is judged as positive class, otherwise z is judged as negative class.

Step4: Make the attribution discrimination of the test point z:

① Use mode discrimination method, the class with the most occurrence is result. Output result and the algorithm ended, otherwise②.
② Use absolute difference discrimination method, and the class correspond to the smallest absolute value of the difference is taken as classification result.

2.3 K-Nearest Neighbor Algorithm

KNN algorithm was proposed by Cover and Hart in 1967. The basic idea of the algorithm is: according to the distance between samples to classify, select the nearest K samples as neighbors, and vote to decide the classification of samples. KNN models usually use Euclidean distance to find the nearest "neighbor". Euclidean distance is defined as follows:

$$d(x, y) = \sqrt{\sum_{k=1}^{n} (x_k - y_k)^2}$$

Figure 1 shows the state of the classification when K = 5.

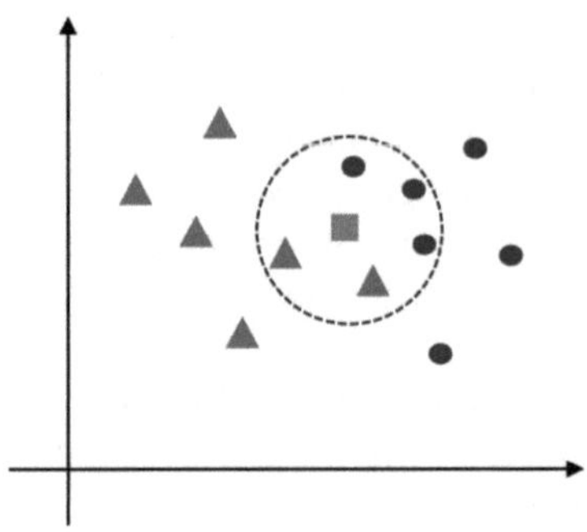

Fig. 1. The state of the classification when K = 5

The KNN algorithm is simple and easy to understand. It doesn't require complex preprocessing and model. It doesn't need estimate parameters and training time. KNN algorithm is suitable for multi-classification problems and rare event classification. It has the advantage of high accuracy, not sensitive to outliers, and does not need to make any assumptions of data.

The disadvantage is KNN algorithm needs to store all the samples in the computer, and the distance between the sample must be calculated and compared, which leads to a large amount of storage and calculation.

3 SLC-KNN Algorithm

In order to improve the accuracy of the SLC algorithm when the number of mixed points decreases very slowly or even not decreases or the datasets cannot be divided. We proposes sweeping learning chain-K-Nearest Neighbor (SLC-KNN) algorithm.

3.1 SLC-KNN Algorithm Principle

With the number of mixed points decreases rapidly, the distance between the projection of the lower bound of the positive class and the projection of upper bound of the positive class decreases rapidly. The projection of the of the negative class and the projection of the lower bound of the negative class also decreases rapidly, so that the negative interval quickly becomes positive interval and explicit implicit factors are obtained. However, the number of mixed points may decrease very slowly or even not decrease or data cannot be divided, explicit implicit factors can't be found, thus affecting accuracy.

Example1: Given two datasets.

$$S^+ = \{x_1^+ = (0, -1), x_2^+ = (1, 0), x_3^+ = (0, 3), x_4^+ = (-5, 2), x_5^+ = (-10, -10)\}$$

$$S^- = \{x_1^- = (2, -4), x_2^- = (4, -2), x_3^- = (0, -4), x_4^- = (2, -2), x_5^- = (10, 10)\}$$

The processing of classification by SLC is as follows:

Step1: Let $t := 1$,$S_1^+ := S^+$,$S_1^- := S^-$,calculate the center of positive and negative sample points $o_1^+ = (-2.8, -1.2)$, $o_1^- = (3.6, -0.4)$,the sweep class vector is

$$w_1 = o_1^+ - o_1^- = (-6.4, -0.8)$$

for simplicity of the example, taken $w_1 = (-15, -2)$.

Step2: Calculates $(x_i^+, w_1)(x_i^+ \in S_1^+)$ and $\left(x_j^-, w_1\right)\left(x_j^- \in S_1^-\right)$, get

$$\begin{aligned} a_1^+ &= \min\{(x_1^+, w_1) = 2, (x_2^+, w_1) = -15, (x_3^+, w_1) \\ &= -6, (x_4^+, w_1) = 71, (x_5^+, w_1) = 170\} = -15 \end{aligned}$$

$$\begin{aligned} a_1^- &= \max\{(x_1^-, w_1) = -22, (x_2^-, w_1) = -56, (x_3^-, w_1) \\ &= 8, (x_4^-, w_1) = -26, (x_5^-, w_1) = -170\} = 8 \end{aligned}$$

There is a projection mixing region $H_1 = [-15, 8]$, see Fig. 2(a). Store into $\pi = \{w_1 = (-15, -2); H_1 = [-15, 8]\}$, delete non-mixing points and update the data set:

$$S_2^- := S_1^- - \{x_i^- \in S_1^- | (x_i^-, w_1) < -15\} = \{x_3^-\}$$

$$S_2^+ := S_1^+ - \left\{x_i^+ \in S_1^+ | \left(x_j^+, w_1\right) > 8\right\} = \{x_1^+, x_2^+, x_3^+\}$$

Let $t := t + 1$,go back to Step1.

Step1: recalculate $o_2^+ = (1/3, 2/3)$; $o_2^- = (0, -4)$, get sweeping vector

$$w_2 = o_2^+ - o_2^- = (1/3, -10/3)$$

for simplicity of the example, taken $w_2 = (1, -10)$

Step2: computes $(x_i^+, w_2)(x_i^+ \in S_2^+)$ and $\left(x_j^-, w_2\right)\left(x_j^- \in S_2^-\right)$,get

$$a_2^+ = \min\{(x_1^+, w_2) = 10, (x_2^+, w_2) = 1, (x_3^+, w_2) = -30\} = -30$$

$$a_1^- = \max\{(x_3^-, w_1) = 40\} = 40$$

There is a projection mixing domain, see Fig. 2(b).

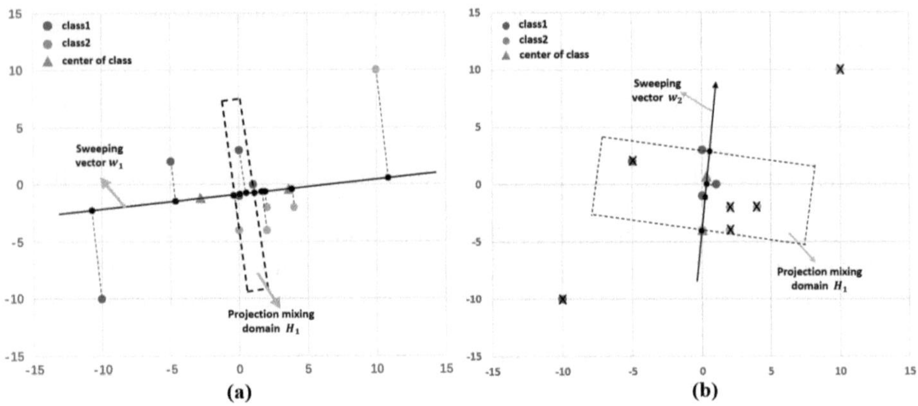

Fig. 2. (a) w_1 and H_1 **(b)** w_2 and H_2

Update
$\pi = \{\{w_1 = (-15, -2); H_1 = [-15, 8]\}, \{w_2 = (1/3, -10/3), H_2 = [-30, 40]\}\}$
and update data set

$$S_3^- := S_2^- - \{x_i^- \in S_2^- | (x_i^-, w_2) < -30\} = \{x_3^-\}$$

$$S_3^+ := S_2^+ - \left\{x_i^+ \in S_2^+ | \left(x_j^+, w_2\right) > 40\right\} = \{x_1^+, x_2^+, x_3^+\}$$

Data set has not changed, so stop the operation and go to step 3.

Step3: Output
$\pi = \{\{w_1 = (-15, -2); H_1 = [-15, 8]\}; T = 2; w_T = (1, -10); J^* = 5\}$.

However, result still exist a projection mixed region, and there are a number of sample points in projection mixed region. At this time, the partition wall couldn't classify successfully, so misjudgment may occur which will reduce the accuracy rate.

Example1 shows that SLC algorithm isn't omnipotent, it will fail. In order to improve the classification performance, we need to pay attention to mixing points. KNN algorithm is only related to the classes of K nearest neighbors, and it has a good classification effect for the datasets containing overlapping samples. However, it is a lazy learning algorithm, and when the training set is large, its huge computing space will lead to high time complexity. Combining the advantages of two algorithms, we can use the SLC-KNN algorithm to improve the accuracy of classification. The SLC-KNN model can be described as follows: when classify the sample, firstly use SLC algorithm for classification, then if the sample finally falls into the projection mixed domain use KNN algorithm. It solves the problem that SLC algorithm easy to misclassification for the sample in projection mixed domain, and also solves the problem that the KNN algorithm has too much calculation (Fig. 3).

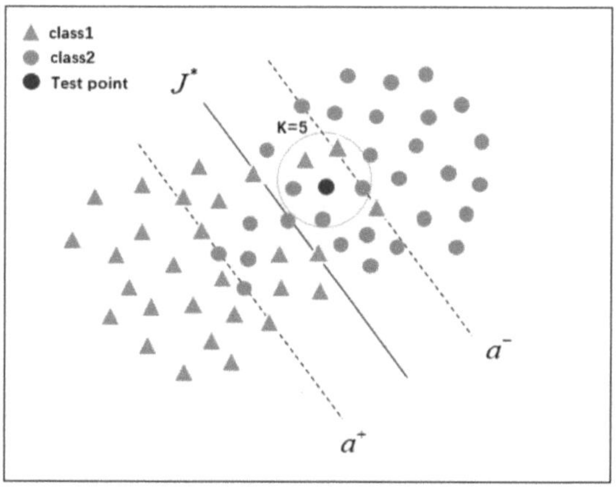

Fig. 3. When K = 5 SLC-KNN algorithm

3.2 SLC-KNN Algorithm Steps

When training the SLC-KNN algorithm combined classifier, the steps are as follows:

Input: Training set and testing set.

Output: Classification result.

Step1: Training set are trained by SLC algorithm to obtain the criterion sequence π.

Step2: Selected a test sample x from the testing set. If testing set is empty, the algorithm ends.

Step3: Firstly, classify the samples by π. If it can be judged, the recognition results are directly output. If the testing samples fall into mixed domain, go to Step4.

Step4: Use KNN algorithm, train KNN model and output optimum K. Sort the obtained distances according to the order from small to large, select the top K small distances, and according to the majority voting rule output result.

Step5: Update the testing set and return to Step2.

Time complexity is an important index to measure the efficiency of an algorithm. The time complexity of SLC-KNN algorithm mainly includes two parts: training phase and testing phase. Let d is the number of conditioning factors, t is iterations and n is the number of training set, where l is the number of positive class and k is the number of negative class. The complexity of the SLC algorithm in the training phase and testing phase are $O(n * d)$ and $O(t * d)$. The complexity of the KNN algorithm in the training phase and testing phase are $O(1)$ and $O(n * d)$.

The time complexity of the SLC-KNN algorithm is calculated as follows (Fig. 4):

1) Training phase: $O(n * d)$.
2) Testing phase: $O((l_1 + k_1) * d)$.

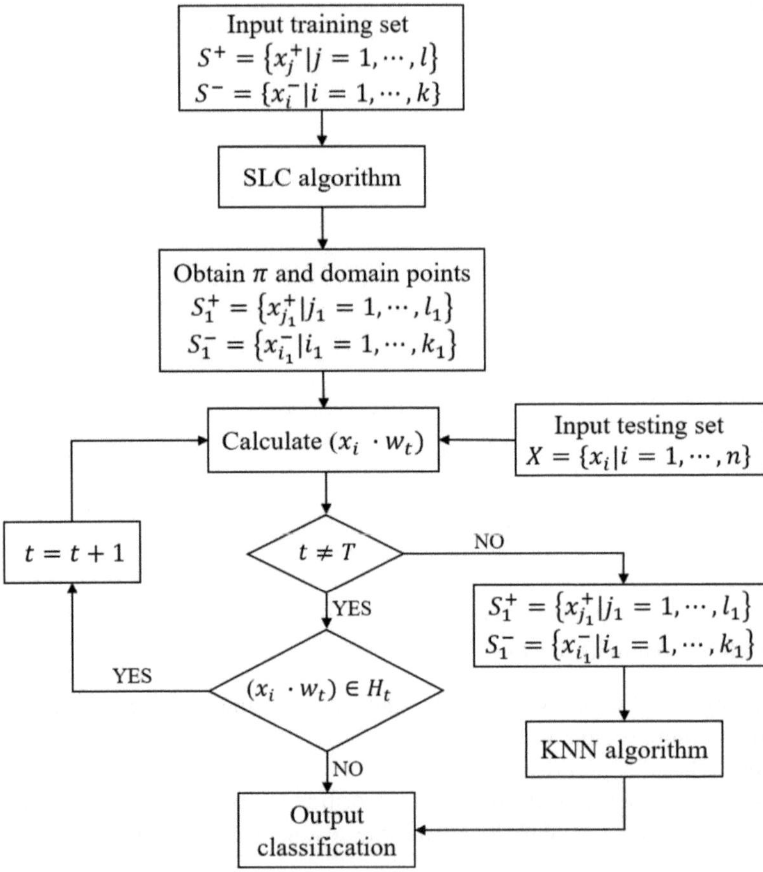

Fig. 4. Flow chart of SLC-KNN algorithm

3.3 Instance Analysis

In order to test the effectiveness of SLC-KNN algorithm, experiments are carried out on three different UCI datasets. Use SVM algorithm and KNN algorithm as comparison algorithms, and the specific test process is obtained.

The datasets used in the empirical analysis of the algorithm comes from the UCI database, and the specific information of the dataset is as follows:

Cryotherapy Dataset is used to diagnose wart treatment result of using cryotherapy according to Sex, Age, Time, Number of warts, Type, Area, the results are cured and not cured.

Immunotherapy Dataset is used to diagnose wart treatment result of using immunotherapy according to Sex, Age, Time, Number of warts, Type, Area, Induration diameter, the results are cured and not cured.

Rice(Cammeo and Osmancik) Dataset is used to judge the category of rice according to Area, Age, Perimeter, Major_Axis_length, Minor_Axis_Length, Eccentricity, Convex_Area, Extent.

The specific structure of each dataset in Table 1.

Table 1. The structure of experimental dataset.

Name	Number	Positive class	Negative class	Training set	Testing set	Dim
Cryotherapy	90	42	48	62	18	7
Immunotherapy	90	19	71	53	16	8
Rice	3810	1630	2180	2400	800	8

The training set were respectively input into SVM, KNN and SLC-KNN classifiers for comparative experiments to establish corresponding classification models, and then tested on the test samples. The indicators of algorithms are shown in Table 2.

Table 2. Comparison of indicators of four algorithms.

Name	Indicator	SLC	KNN	SVM	SLC-KNN
Cryotherapy	Accuracy	0.7222	0.9444	0.6111	**1.0000**
	Precision	1.0000	0.8889	1.0000	1.0000
	Recall	0.3750	1.0000	0.1250	1.0000
	F1	0.5455	0.9412	0.2222	1.0000
Immunotherapy	Accuracy	**0.8125**	0.75	**0.8125**	**0.8125**
	Precision	0.7857	0.7333	0.7857	0.7857
	Recall	1.0000	1.0000	1.0000	1.0000
	F1	0.8800	0.8461	0.8800	0.8800
Rice	Accuracy	0.4575	**0.9087**	0.9025	**0.9087**
	Precision	0.1476	0.7899	0.7723	0.7899
	Recall	0.245	0.865	0.865	0.865
	F1	0.1842	0.8257	0.816	0.8257

The results of experiments show that SLC-KNN algorithm has higher accuracy than the single SLC and SVM algorithm. The SLC-KNN algorithm solves the problem of poor classification effect of SLC algorithm when it is not separable, overcomes the defects of SLC's error-prone classification of samples in mixed domain and the high time complexity of KNN. It combines the advantages of SLC and KNN classification, and can classify more accurately.

4 BT-SLC-KNN Multi-classification Algorithm

At present, the merge sweeping learning chain (MSLC) algorithm need to construct n 1-against-rest classifiers. However, MSLC will produce unclassifiable regions, and the training and testing time is long. In order to improve the multi-classification performance and reduce the time complexity, this paper proposes a SLC-KNN multi-classification algorithm based on normal binary tree structure.

4.1 BT-SLC-KNN Multi-classification Algorithm Principle

The binary tree structure can naturally decompose a complex multi-class classification problem into multiple binary classification problems, and only n-1 classifiers need to be constructed. Each child node in the binary tree represents a classifier, so the classes that have already been classified will not be used for classification, reducing the training time and testing time. There are two kinds of binary tree structure. One is skewed binary tree, which is divided by one class and the rest of the classes at each internal node. The other is at the inner node, which is a split of multiple classes and multiple classes, which is a normal binary tree. In the classification of each level of the decision tree, if a classification error occurs at a node in the upper level, the error will be carried over to the next level of the node. Particularly, the errors occur closer to the root node, and the final classification error accumulates more. This error accumulation is fatal if the classes are large. Normal binary tree can effectively reduce the number of levels of the decision tree, so when building a decision tree model, normal binary tree structure is a priority method.

BT-SLC-KNN multi-classification algorithm firstly divides all classes into two sub-classes, and then divides the sub-classes into two sub-classes, and so on until all nodes only contain a single class. The method decomposes a multi-class classification problem into a series of binary classification problems, and the SLC-KNN algorithm is used to classify the two sub-classes. Compared with the one-to-rest method of MLSC, the binary tree method can solve the inseparable problems, and it does not necessarily need to calculate all the classifiers, which can save testing time.

The design of binary tree hierarchy is one of the key factors affecting the performance of multiple classifiers. For different binary tree structures, the segmentation region of each class is different, the performance of the resulting classification model will be different. The classification performance of the upper node sub-classifier has a greater impact on the performance of the whole classification model. Therefore, in the process of generating a normal binary tree, the class that is furthest apart from the other classes should be split firstly. Based on this idea, construct a normal binary tree.

Definition 5: (Class center distance)Let the Euclidean distance between the center o_i of Class i and the center o_j of Class j be the class center distance d_{ij},then.

$$d_{ij} = \left\| o_i - o_j \right\|$$

Definition 6: (Class center distance on sweeping vector) Let the sweeping vectors of Class i and Class j be w_{ij},and let the projector distance between class k and class i in w_{ij} is.

$$d_{ik} = \left| \left(o_k, w_{ij} \right) - \left(o_i, w_{ij} \right) \right|$$

and the projector distance between class k and class j in w_{ij} is

$$d_{jk} = \left| \left(o_k, w_{ij} \right) - \left(o_j, w_{ij} \right) \right|$$

In order to describe the process clearly and intuitively, a two-dimensional space is taken as an example to illustrate the generation process of the algorithm, see Fig. 5.

4.2 BT-SLC-KNN Multi-classification Algorithm Steps

The steps of BT-SLC-KNN multi-classification algorithm are given below:

Step1: For the $N(N > 2)$ classification problem, the category index set $J := \{1, \cdots, n\}$, the category data set $S = \{X_1, X_2, \cdots, X_n\}$,calculate the center $O = \{o_1, o_2, \cdots, o_n\}$ of N class data, select the two categories with the largest distance between the center of the class X_i and X_j,respectively put them into S_1 and S_2, calculate the sweeping vector w_{ij}.

Step2: $\forall X_n (n \neq i, j)$, calculate the projector distance d_{in} and d_{jn} on w_{ij} of center o_n,if $d_{in} > d_{jn}$,then add the class n to S_2,if $d_{in} < d_{jn}$, then add to S_1.

Step3: Take the sets and as the left and right subtrees of the binary tree respectively, and use SLC-KNN algorithm once.

Step4: Update $S = S_1$,until each subtree contains only one category that cannot be further divided. At this time, this category is taken as a leaf of the binary tree as a leaf node of the binary tree, and the algorithm ends. Otherwise, turn to step 1 and split the left subtree into 2 secondary subtrees.

Step5: Update $S = S_2$, and the following is same as Step 4.

4.3 Instance Analysis

In the experiment, three UCI datasets were used to evaluate the performance of BT-SLC-KNN, and the data information is shown in the Table 3.

In order to test the performance of BT-SLC-KNN multi-class classification algorithm, used MSLC and multi-class SVM as comparison experiments.

Table 4 shows that the BT-SLC-KNN multi-classification algorithm is significantly better than MSCL, which indicates that the algorithm is feasible and effective. And we need to compare and optimize algorithm time in the future.

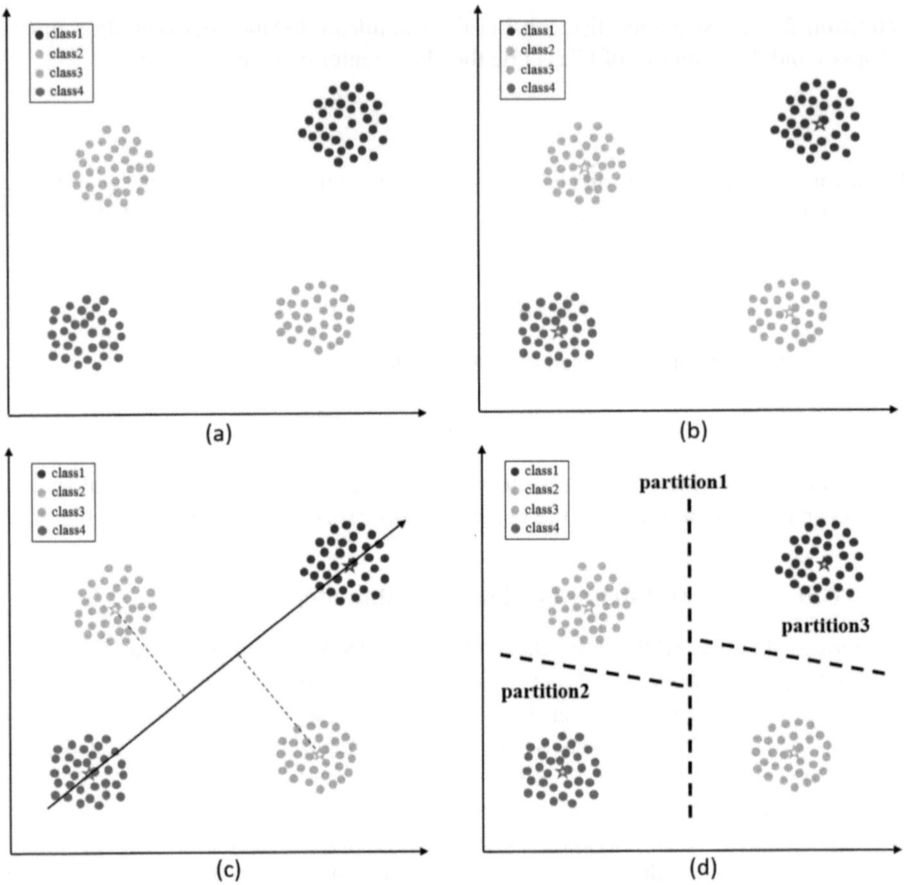

Fig. 5. Example of generation process of binary tree ($N = 4$).**(a)** Visualization of 4 classes of sample points. **(b)** Calculate the centers of four classes of sample points.**(c)** Class1 and Class4 have the largest center distance, calculate w_{14} and compared $d_{12}, d_{13}, d_{42}, d_{43}$ **(d)** $d_{12} > d_{42}$,Class2 is added to Class4;$d_{13} < d_{43}$, Class3 is added to Class1.

Table 3. Experimental Dataset Information.

Name	Class	Number	Training	Testing	Dim
Iris	3	150	105	29	4
User Knowledge Modeling Data Set	4	358	258	77	6
Zoo	7	100	59	34	17

Table 4. Comparison of accuracy of the three algorithms.

Name	MSLC	SVM	BT-SLC-KNN
Iris	0.9031	0.9031	**0.9655**
User Knowledge Modeling Data Set	0.8571	0.8718	**0.8831**
Zoo	0.8823	0.7941	**0.9411**

5 Conclusion

Based on the SLC algorithm in factor space, this paper proposes SLC-KNN algorithm and BT-SLC-KNN algorithm. The specific research process and conclusion are as follows:

1. Taking the explicit and implicit factor space as the background, this paper mainly studies the situation that the number of mixed points in SLC algorithm decreases very slowly or even doesn't decrease or the situation that the data cannot be divided. Then this paper proposes the SLC- KNN algorithm and analysis the time complexity. It solves the problem of poor accuracy of SLC algorithm in the case of inseparable, overcomes the defects of SLC's error-prone classification of samples in mixed domain and the high computational time complexity of KNN. The feasibility and effectiveness of the SLC-KNN algorithm are proved by the comparative analysis of examples.
2. On the basis of SLC-KNN algorithm combined with binary tree structure, constructed a multi- class classification algorithm, which effectively reduces the amount of calculation of training and learning and significantly speed up the training time. The feasibility and effectiveness of the BT-SLC-KNN multi-classification algorithm can be illustrated by the comparative analysis of examples.

Acknowledgments. Supported by Liaoning Revitalization Talents Program (XLYC2211085), Liaoning Province Education Department project (JYTQN2023210; LJKZZ20220047), Fuxin City social science Project (2023Fsllx154;2023Fsllx017;2023Fsllx144).

Disclosure of Interests. It is now necessary to declare any competing interests or to specifically state that the authors have no competing interests.

References

1. Wang, P.: Factor spaces and factor data-bases. J. Liaoning Tech. Univ. (Nat, Sci.) **32**(10), 1297–1304 (2013)
2. Zeng, F., Wang, Y., Wang, P., et al.: Algorithm of sweeping multiplex classification based on factor space theory. J. Liaoning Tech. Univ. (Nat. Sci.) **43**(1), 111–118 (2024)
3. Fu, Z., Xu, Y., Wu, Z., et al.: SVM-KNN network intrusion detection method based on incremental learning. Comput. Eng. **46**(4), 115–122 (2020)
4. Pu, L., Zeng, F., Wang, P.: Base point classification algorithm based on factor space theory. CAAI Trans. Intell. Syst. **15**(3), 528–536 (2020)

5. Wang, Y., Zeng, F., Sun, H., et al.: Factor implicit model of machine classification learning based on factor space theory. Comput. Sci. Math. Forum **2023** (2023)
6. Teng, K.-D., Zhao, Q., Tan, H.-R., et al.: Emotion classification using EEG signals based on SVM-KNN algorithm. Comput. Syst. Appl. **31**(2), 298–304 (2022)
7. Li, Y.L.: Application of BT-SVM Multi classification Algorithm in the Evaluation of Teaching Quality. Guangxi University, Nanning (2014)
8. Wang, H.Q., Wang, B.: Application of optimized proximal support rector machine in image retrieval. J. Chongqing Univ. Technol. Nat. Sci. **9**, 66–71 (2014)
9. Song, Z.Q., Chen, Y.: The review of the multi class classification algorithm based on SVM. J. Naval Aeron. Eng. Inst. **30**(5), 442–446 (2015)
10. Zhao, L.: An improved multi class classification method based on support vector machine. Comput. Appl. Softw. **31**(12), 233–236 (2014)
11. Tang, F.M., Wang, Z.D., Chen, M.Y.: A new cross tree support vector machine algorithm. Comput. Eng. Appl. **41**(7), 24–26 (2005)
12. Fan, B.C., Wang, J.Y., Bao, Y.M.: Combined with feature selection of binary tree SVM multi classification algorithm. Comput. Eng. Des. **31**(12), 2823–2825 (2010)
13. Zheng, W., Ma, N.: An improved decision tree after pruning algorithm. Comput. Dig. Eng. **6**, 960–966+971 (2015)
14. Xia, S.Y., Pan, H., Jin, L.Z.: Non balanced binary tree multi class support vector machine classification method. Comput. Eng. Appl. **45**(17), 167–169 (2009)
15. Xie, J.Y., Zhang, B.Q., Wang, W.Z.: Multi class classification algorithm based on double support vector machine. J. Nanjing Univ. Nat. Sci. Ed. **47**(4), 354–363 (2011)

End-To-End Control of a Quadrotor Using Gaussian Ensemble Model-Based Reinforcement Learning

Qiwen Zheng[1(✉)], Qingyuan Xia[1], Haonan Luo[2], Bohai Deng[3], and Shengwei Li[3]

[1] Nanjing University of Science and Technology, Nanjing, China
{mr_zhqw,xqy}@njust.edu.cn
[2] Southwest Jiaotong University, Chengdu, China
lhn@swjtu.edu.cn
[3] National Key Laboratory of Rotorcraft Aeromechanics, Nanjing University of Aeronautics and Astronautics, Nanjing 210016, China
dengbohai@nuaa.edu.cn

Abstract. In recent years, the rapid development of deep reinforcement learning has provided a new way to solve the robot control problems. However, the low sample efficiency and slow convergence speed of deep reinforcement learning have become one of the obstacles when transitioning from simulation to the real world. In this paper, we propose a quadrotor control policy using Gaussian ensemble model-based reinforcement learning. Unlike traditional control methods, this method uses an actor-critic deep neural network which is updated with a reward function to achieve end-to-end control of the quadrotor by establishing a mapping between the quadrotor's states and motor control signals. Additionally, we improve sample efficiency by constructing an ensemble model following a Gaussian normal distribution, which differs from conventional model-free RL methods. The environment model is trained using data from the agent's interaction with the real environment and reduces the number of interactions with the real environment by generating simulated data. The approach is evaluated in the AirSim which is a high-fidelity visual and physical simulator. The results show that the proposed approach improves the sample efficiency, eliminates oscillations and steady error, and demonstrates robustness to external disturbances.

Keywords: Quadrotor · Soft Actor-Critic · Ensemble Model · AirSim

1 Introduction

Efficient and stable motion control of quadrotor drones is crucial for successful flight missions. Researchers have proposed various control theories. In addition to traditional linear control methods like PID and LQR control, advanced nonlinear control methods such as model predictive control (MPC), sliding mode control (SMC) [1], robust control, and adaptive control have been utilized. However, these methods often require precise quadrotor dynamics models, which can be challenging to establish.

Published by Springer Nature Switzerland AG 2025
Z. Shi et al. (Eds.): ICIS 2024, IFIP AICT 720, pp. 81–92, 2025.
https://doi.org/10.1007/978-3-031-71253-1_7

In the past decade, machine learning has made significant contributions to the field of control, particularly with the application of deep reinforcement learning. Nathan et al. [2] used model-based reinforcement learning algorithms to control quadrotor hovering. Wang et al. [3] proposed a deterministic policy gradient algorithm with an integral compensator to address steady-state errors. Liu et al. [4] addressed oscillation and instability in quadrotor control by proposing a deep reinforcement learning strategy based on a reference model.

In the existing research on deep reinforcement learning for quadrotor control, most researchers have focused primarily on issues related to control precision and stability. However, there has been relatively less emphasis on studying the training efficiency of reinforcement learning. Minimizing interactions with the environment is crucial for improving sample efficiency, considering quadrotors' static instability. This paper aims to address these issues and the main contributions can be summarized as follows:

1. A quadrotor control algorithm based on Gaussian ensemble model reinforcement learning is proposed. This algorithm utilizes an ensemble model following a Gaussian normal distribution as the environmental model, effectively improving the sample efficiency.
2. Based on this model, the paper optimizes and improves the reward function and termination condition design. The control performance of the algorithm is validated using the AirSim platform, demonstrating its effectiveness in reducing oscillations and steady errors, as well as robustness against external disturbances.

2 Background

The motion of a quadrotor consists of translational motion driven by forces and rotational motion driven by torques [5]. For translational motion, the position dynamics model can be derived from Newton's second law

$$m^e\dot{\boldsymbol{V}} = m\boldsymbol{g} - {}^e\boldsymbol{F} \tag{1}$$

where ${}^e\ \dot{\boldsymbol{V}} = \left[\dot{v}_x, \dot{v}_y, \dot{v}_z\right]^T, \boldsymbol{g} = \left[0, 0, g\right]^T$, ${}^e\boldsymbol{F}$ is the joint force of thrust force ${}^b\boldsymbol{T}$ and aerodynamic drag $\boldsymbol{f}_d$. In the modeling process, the aerodynamic drag $\boldsymbol{f}_d$ is typically negligible and can be ignored. The thrust force ${}^b\boldsymbol{T} = \left[0, 0, f\right]^T$, where $f = \sum_{i=1}^{4} T_i$. To facilitate analysis, the thrust force is transformed from the body coordinate system to the inertial coordinate system using a rotation matrix $\boldsymbol{R}_b^e$, which is

$$\boldsymbol{R}_b^e = \begin{bmatrix} C_\theta C_\psi & C_\psi S_\theta S_\phi - S_\psi C_\phi & C_\psi S_\theta C_\phi + S_\psi S_\phi \\ C_\theta S_\psi & S_\psi S_\theta S_\phi + C_\psi C_\phi & S_\psi S_\theta C_\phi - C_\psi S_\phi \\ -S_\theta & S_\phi C_\theta & C_\phi C_\theta \end{bmatrix}$$

where $S_{\{\cdot\}}$ and $C_{\{\cdot\}}$ represent $\sin(\cdot)$ and $\cos(\cdot)$ respectively. ϕ, θ and ψ represent the roll, pitch, and yaw angles respectively.

For rotational motion, the attitude dynamics model can be derived from Euler's equation:

$$\boldsymbol{I}\dot{\boldsymbol{w}} + \boldsymbol{w} \times \boldsymbol{I}\boldsymbol{w} = \boldsymbol{M}_g + \boldsymbol{M}_\tau + \boldsymbol{M}_d \tag{2}$$

where $\boldsymbol{I} = diag(I_x, I_y, I_z)$ is the diagonal moments of inertia matrix of the quadrotor, $\boldsymbol{w} = [p, q, r]^T$ is the angular velocity with respect to three axes in body coordinate system, $\boldsymbol{M}_g = [-I_r\Omega q, I_r\Omega p, 0]^T$ is the gyroscopic torque, where I_r is the inertia moment of each rotor, $\Omega = \omega_1 + \omega_2 + \omega_3 + \omega_4$ is the total speed of the propeller. $\boldsymbol{M}_\tau = [\tau_x, \tau_y, \tau_z]^T$ is the torque generated by the propellers along the body axis. $\boldsymbol{M}_d$ is the rotational dynamic drag torque which can be ignored.

Combined with (1) and (2), the quadrotor overall dynamics model can be expressed as follows:

$$\begin{aligned}
\dot{v}_x &= -\tfrac{f}{m}(\cos\psi\sin\theta\cos\phi + \sin\psi\sin\phi)\\
\dot{v}_y &= -\tfrac{f}{m}(\sin\psi\sin\theta\cos\phi - \cos\psi\sin\phi)\\
\dot{v}_z &= g - \tfrac{f}{m}\cos\phi\cos\theta\\
\dot{p} &= \tfrac{1}{I_x}\left[\tau_x + qr(I_y - I_z) - I_r\Omega q\right]\\
\dot{q} &= \tfrac{1}{I_y}\left[\tau_y + pr(I_z - I_x) + I_r\Omega p\right]\\
\dot{r} &= \tfrac{1}{I_z}\left[\tau_z + pq(I_x - I_y)\right]
\end{aligned} \tag{3}$$

Reinforcement learning focuses on how an agent can maximize the rewards in a complex and uncertain environment [6]. The state, action, state transition probability function and reward function together form a Markov four-tuple (S, A, P, R).

For the quadrotor control problem, the goal of reinforcement learning is to find an optimal policy, thus achieving stable and fast control of the quadrotor. Define the target policy as π_θ and the objective function of policy learning as $J(\theta)$. According to the policy gradient theorem:

$$\nabla_\theta J(\theta) = \mathbb{E}_{\pi_\theta}\left[Q^{\pi_\theta}(s, a)\nabla_\theta \log \pi_\theta(a|s)\right] \tag{4}$$

where $Q^{\pi_\theta}(s, a)$ is the action-value function. In recent years, researchers have proposed many new algorithms by improving the computation methods of action-value function, which are the basis of this paper.

3 Methods

3.1 GEM-SAC Algorithm

Our GEM-SAC algorithm is developed based on soft actor-critic (SAC) algorithm [7, 8] which is an actor-critic algorithm based on maximum entropy. On the basis of policy learning, the actor-critic algorithm [9] introduces critic to estimate the action-value function $Q^{\pi_\theta}(s, a)$, so as to help the actor learn the policy better.

To incorporate entropy into the objective, the new objective function is defined as:

$$\pi^* = \arg\max_\pi \mathbb{E}_\pi\left[\sum_t r(s_t, a_t) + \mu H(\pi(\cdot|s_t))\right] \tag{5}$$

where $H(\pi(\cdot|s_t))$ represents the level of randomness of the policy π in state s. μ is a regularization coefficient used to control the importance of entropy. To automatically adjust μ, the loss function is constructed as follows:

$$\mathcal{L}(\mu) = \mathop{\mathbb{E}}_{\substack{a_t \sim \pi(\cdot|s_t) \\ s_t \sim \mathcal{D}_{env}}} \left[-\mu \log \pi(a_t|s_t) - \mu \mu_{target} \right] \tag{6}$$

where μ_{target} is the target value of the entropy.

To mitigate the problem of Q-values overestimation, two critic networks Q^{w_1} and Q^{w_2} are utilized. To ensure stable neural network training, two target networks, $Q^{\bar{w_1}}$ and $Q^{\bar{w_2}}$ are employed. The loss function of the critic network is defined as:

$$\mathcal{L}_Q(w) = \mathop{\mathbb{E}}_{(s_t, a_t, r_t, s_{t+1}) \sim \mathcal{D}_{env}} \left[\frac{1}{2} (r_t + \gamma V_{w^-}(s_{t+1}) - Q_w(s_t, a_t))^2 \right] \tag{7}$$

where $\mathcal{D}_{env}$ represents the replay buffer of the real environment, which stores the quadruple data (s_t, a_t, r_t, s_{t+1}) obtained from the real environment. $V_{w^-}(s_{t+1})$ is the state-value function which is calculated by the target network:

$$V_{w^-}(s_{t+1}) = \min_{i=1,2} Q_{w_j^-}(s_{t+1}, a_{t+1}) - \alpha \log \pi(a_{t+1}|s_{t+1}) \tag{8}$$

The actor network is updated by minimizing the KL divergence, and the loss function obtained after employing the reparameterization trick is:

$$\mathcal{L}_\pi(\theta) = \mathop{\mathbb{E}}_{\substack{a_t \sim \mathcal{N} \\ s_t \sim \mathcal{D}_{env}}} \left[\alpha \log(\pi_\theta(\tilde{a}_t|s_t)) - \min_{i=1,2} Q_w(s_t, \tilde{a}_t) \right] \tag{9}$$

where $\mathcal{N}$ represents standard Gaussian distribution. $\tilde{a}$ represents the action after reparameterization.

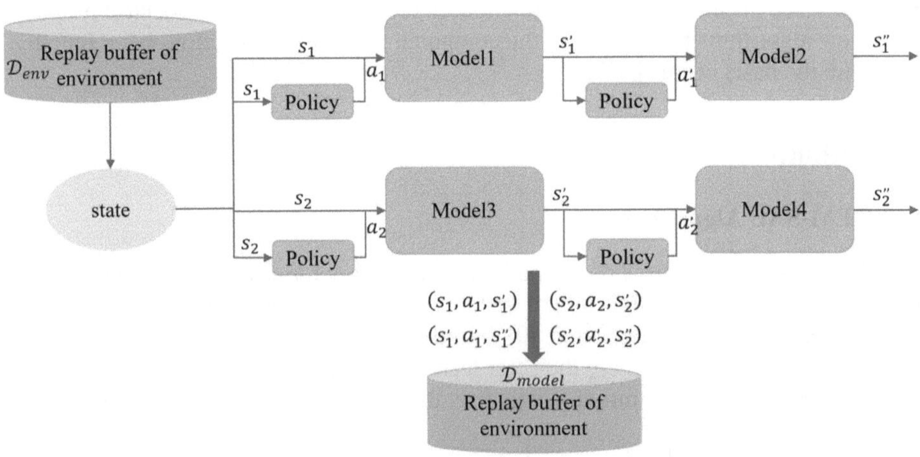

Fig. 1. Gaussian ensemble model

In the formula above, both the actor and critic networks rely on quadruple data from the real environment, collected through continuous interaction and trial-and-error.

However, for quadrotors, minimizing this process is desired. This paper adopts the model-based reinforcement [10, 11, 14] approach, improving the sample efficiency.

On the basis of the above policy optimization algorithm, this paper introduces an ensemble model satisfying Gaussian distribution as an environment model. The environment model generates additional training data that assists in optimizing the quadrotor's policy. As the environment contains inherent noise and random uncertainty [12], the Gaussian distribution is employed to characterize this uncertainty. The environment model is defined as $\hat{P}$, with parameters θ, then based on the current state-action pair (s_t, a_t), the distribution of the next state s_t can be written as:

$$\hat{P}(s_t, a_t) = \mathcal{N}(\mu_\theta(s_t, a_t), \Sigma_\theta(s_t, a_t)) \tag{10}$$

Using neural network to construct μ_θ and Σ_θ, the loss function is defined as

$$\mathcal{L}_G(\theta) = \sum_{n=1}^{N} \left[\mu_\theta(s_n, a_n) - s_{n+1}\right]^T \Sigma_\theta^{-1}(s_n, a_n)\left[\mu_\theta(s_n, a_n) - s_{n+1}\right] + \log\det \Sigma_\theta(s_n, a_n) \tag{11}$$

To enhance the accuracy of the environment model, an ensemble learning approach is employed to construct multiple identical Gaussian distribution neural networks. These networks take state-action pairs as inputs and output mean vectors and covariance matrices of the next state's Gaussian distribution. The data from these networks are stored in the replay buffer of the environment model $\mathcal{D}_{model}$ and used for agent training, as shown in Fig. 1.

3.2 Model-Based Network Structure

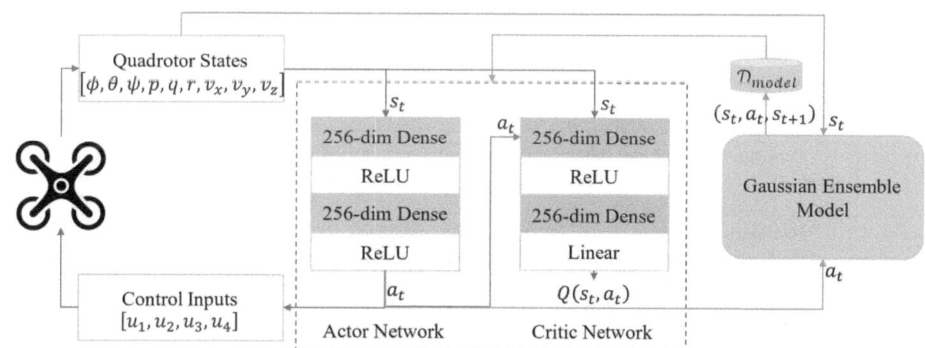

Fig. 2. Model-based network structure

A deep neural network can be used to directly output the PWM values of the four motors $[u_1, u_2, u_3, u_4]$, enabling end-to-end control of the quadrotor. $[u_1, u_2, u_3, u_4]$ is the action space of deep reinforcement learning. To facilitate the calculations of policy entropy and neural network fitting, the action space is normalized within $[-1, 1]$.

To implement the GEM-SAC algorithm for quadrotor control, it is necessary to select appropriate states to describe the motion. The attitude angle $[\phi, \theta, \psi]$ and angular velocity $[p, q, r]$ are selected to describe the rotation motion of the quadrotor. The quadrotor's translational motion is described using the velocity $[v_x, v_y, v_z]$. Finally, the observation space of the quadrotor is defined as $[\phi, \theta, \psi, p, q, r, v_x, v_y, v_z]$.

In this paper, deep reinforcement learning is designed as a velocity controller. The negative sum of squared velocity error, denoted as $-\left(v_{xe}^2 + v_{ye}^2 + v_{ze}^2\right)$, is used as part of the reward function, where $v_e = v - v_d$, v_d are the desired velocities. Additionally, to maintain the quadrotor's heading direction towards true north during flight, the negative of the squared heading angle is also included in the reward function, denoted as $-\psi^2$. To encourage flight, a positive constant c is added to the reward function. In summary, the reward function is defined as:

$$r_t = -\left(v_{xe}^2 + v_{ye}^2 + v_{ze}^2 + \psi^2\right) + c \tag{12}$$

In summary, the model-based network structure of the GEM-SAC algorithm is illustrated in Fig. 2. The actor network takes a 9-dimensional state vector as input and outputs a 4-dimensional action vector. The critic network takes a 13-dimensional vector combining the state and action as input and outputs the Q-value. The Gaussian ensemble model takes a 13-dimensional vector combining the state and action as input and outputs the value of the next state.

The GEM-SAC algorithm is summarized in Algorithm 1.

Algorithm 1: GEM-SAC

Randomly initialize the parameter w_1, w_2 of critic network $Q_{w_1}(s,a)$, $Q_{w_2}(s,a)$
Randomly initialize the parameter θ of actor network $\pi_\theta(s)$
Initialize the target critic network $Q_{w_1^-}$ and $Q_{w_2^-}$ by $w_1^- \leftarrow w_1$, $w_2^- \leftarrow w_2$
Initialize Gaussian ensemble model G_θ, environment replay buffer $\mathcal{D}_{env}$, model replay buffer $\mathcal{D}_{model}$
for *N episodes* **do**
  train model G_θ on $\mathcal{D}_{env}$
  for *T timesteps* **do**
    Take action in environment according to $\pi_\theta(s)$; add (s_t, a_t, r_t, s_{t+1}) to $\mathcal{D}_{env}$
    for *E model rollouts* **do**
      Randomly sample s_t from $\mathcal{D}_{env}$
      Perform i steps model rollout starting from s_t using model G_θ; add to $\mathcal{D}_{model}$
    end
    for *G gradient updates* **do**
      Randomly sample (s_t, a_t, r_t, s_{t+1}) from $\mathcal{D}_{env}$ and $\mathcal{D}_{model}$
      Update critic network following formula (7)(8)
      Update actor network following formula (9)
      Update entropy regularization coefficient μ following formula (6)
      Update target network using soft-update $w^- \leftarrow \tau w + (1-\tau)w^-$
    end
  end
end

---

4 Experiments and Results

In this paper, we utilize AirSim as the simulation platform. AirSim is a high-fidelity visual and physics simulation platform based on the Unreal Engine [13], which can be used as a plugin in any UE project. We add a quadrotor model to AirSim, based on the real quadrotor in our lab for the further work, and the simulation parameters for the quadrotor are shown in Table 1.

Table 1. Parameters of the quadrotor

Parameter	Value	Parameter	Value
Mass m	1 kg	Moments of inertia of body I_y	$0.022\ \mathrm{kg} \cdot \mathrm{m}^2$
Body radius d	0.225 m	Moments of inertia of body I_z	$0.036\ \mathrm{kg} \cdot \mathrm{m}^2$
Moments of inertia of body I_x	$0.021\ \mathrm{kg} \cdot \mathrm{m}^2$	Moments of inertia of motor I_r	$0.00015\ \mathrm{kg} \cdot \mathrm{m}^2$

To use AirSim for reinforcement learning, we build the interface for Gym. The deep reinforcement learning algorithm is developed based on PyTorch and Python, and the communication between Python and AirSim is achieved through RPC. The experiments run on Windows 10 operating system with an Intel Core i9-12900KF @ 3.19 GHz, and neural network computations are accelerated using Nvidia 3080Ti GPU. The training parameters are listed in Table 2. The training framework for quadrotor in AirSim is shown in Fig. 3.

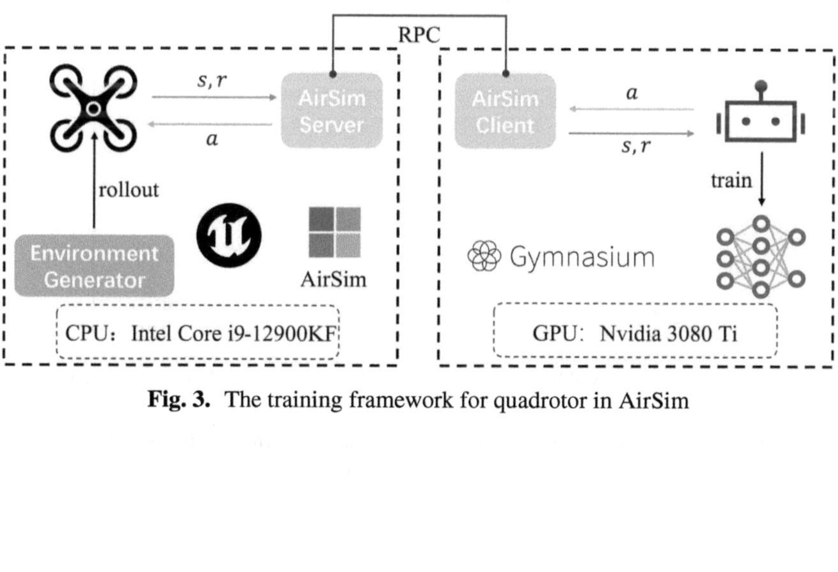

Fig. 3. The training framework for quadrotor in AirSim

Table 2. Parameters of training

Parameter	Value	Parameter	Value
Learning rate of critic network α_w	5e−4	Batch size N	256
Learning rate of actor network α_θ	1e−3	Soft update coefficient τ	5e−3
Learning rate of entropy regularization coefficient α_μ	1e−3	Discount factor γ	0.99
Size of $\mathcal{D}_{env} M_{env}$	1e6	Time between every step t	0.01(s)
Size of $\mathcal{D}_{model} M_{model}$	5e5	Maximum steps T	500

4.1 Comparative Evaluation

To analyze the algorithm performance of GEM-SAC, we use the SAC algorithm as a baseline for comparison. The training curves of the average reward per episode and average number of timesteps per episode for both algorithms are shown in Fig. 4 and Fig. 5, respectively. The results of both figures are calculated based on ten consecutive episodes. The solid line represents the average value of these 10 episodes, while the shaded area represents the corresponding standard deviation.

Based on the reward function (15), the average reward per episode comprehensively reflects the magnitude of state errors. Analyzing the curve in Fig. 4, the GEM-SAC algorithm learns faster and achieves higher rewards compared to the SAC algorithm, validating the higher sample efficiency of GEM-SAC.

Figure 4 also records the training duration, where GEM-SAC almost reaches a stable state after 20,000 timesteps, taking 628.1 s, while SAC is much slower, reaching stability after 40,000 timesteps, taking 1329.8 s. GEM-SAC, with its higher sample efficiency, reduces the numbers of interaction between the quadrotor and the environment, significantly improving training speed.

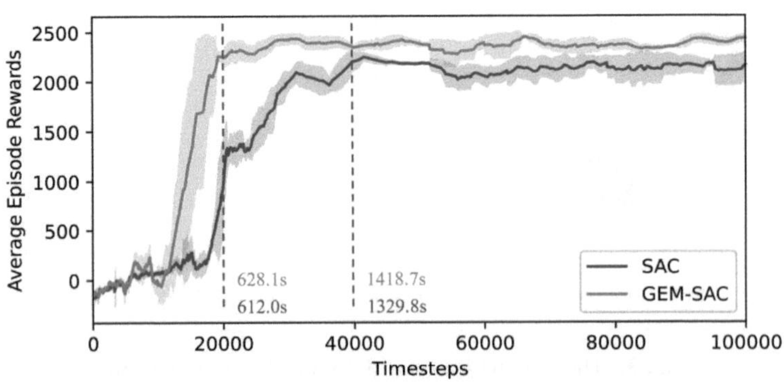

Fig. 4. Average episode reward curve. The solid line represents the average value of 10 episodes, and the shaded area represents the corresponding standard deviation.

For quadrotor control, the average number of timesteps per episode reflects the safety of the quadrotor. Analyzing the curve in Fig. 5, the GEM-SAC algorithm reaches the maximum number of timesteps faster compared to the SAC algorithm. This is advantageous in reducing potential damage to the quadrotor in a real environment.

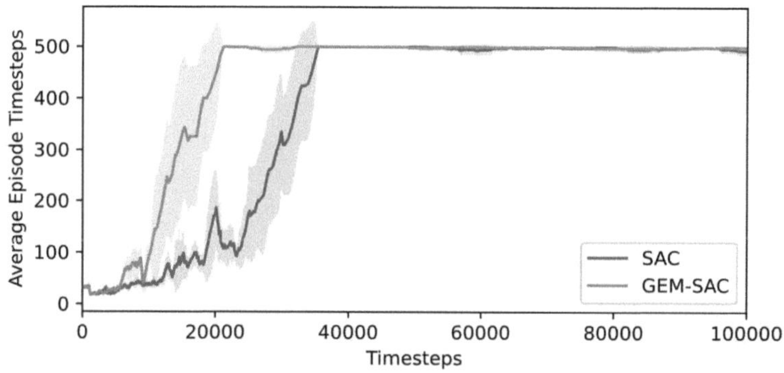

Fig. 5. Average episode timesteps curve. The solid line represents the average value of 10 episodes, and the shaded area represents the corresponding standard deviation.

4.2 Velocity Control Experiment

To further analyze the performance of the GEM-SAC algorithm, we compare its performance with the SAC algorithm on a velocity tracking task. To evaluate both horizontal and vertical control performance simultaneously, a desired velocity is given $[1, 0, -1]$,denoted as $v_x = 1$, $v_y = 0$, $v_z = -1$.

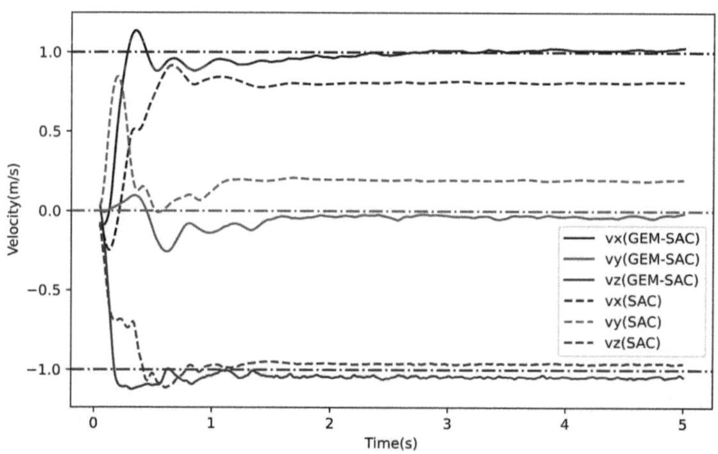

Fig. 6. Velocity response curve. The solid lines and the dashed lines represent the velocity response of GEM-SAC and SAC, respectively.

The velocity response curves of the two control algorithms are shown in Fig. 6. After the desired velocity is given, both GEM-SAC and SAC algorithms can respond quickly. Compared to SAC algorithm after stable control, GEM-SAC algorithm has much smaller steady error and less oscillation. The response curves of the attitude angles are shown in Fig. 7. Compared to the SAC algorithm, the GEM-SAC algorithm demonstrates smaller variations in attitude angles, indicating smoother control.

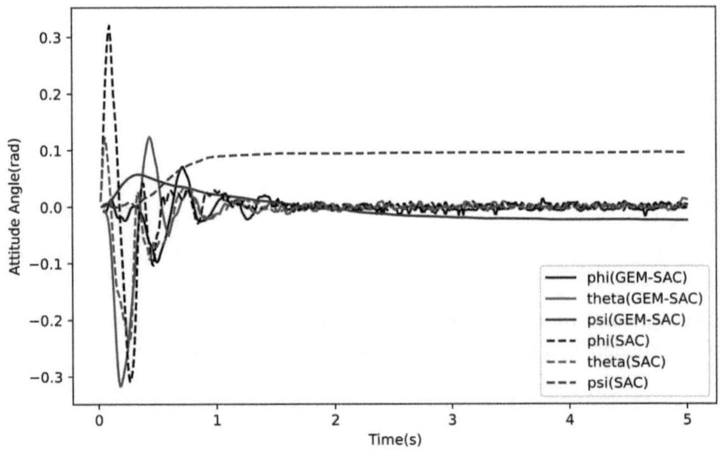

Fig. 7. Attitude angle response curve. The solid lines and the dashed lines represent the attitude angle response of GEM-SAC and SAC, respectively.

4.3 Robustness Experiment

During actual flight, quadrotors are subject to various disturbances from the environment. To verify the robustness of the control strategy, we simulate wind gusts in AirSim and

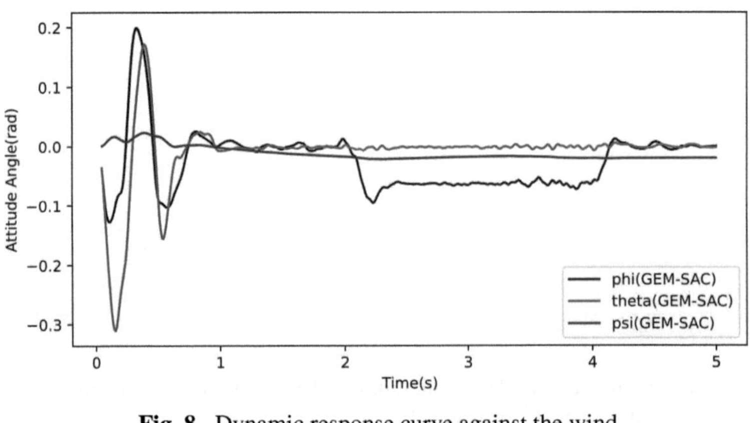

Fig. 8. Dynamic response curve against the wind

observe the effects on the quadrotor during flight. The results are shown in Fig. 8. The quadrotor starts from the initial state and performs a horizontal forward flight task. At $t = 2$ s, a 5 m/s gust is applied along the y-axis, representing a horizontal eastward gust. In order to maintain its position in the y-direction, the control policy quickly adjusts the roll angle to approximately −0.08 radians (5°) and maintains this roll angle to compensate for the gust's influence. The gust is maintained 2 s until $t = 4$ s, and the quadrotor recovers to its normal state in approximately 0.2 s, after the gust is canceled.

5 Conclusions and Future

In this paper, we propose a quadrotor control policy based on Gaussian ensemble model reinforcement learning. First, we construct an actor-critic deep neural network architecture based on the maximum entropy reinforcement learning, which achieves the mapping between the quadrotor's states and motor control signals. Next, we construct an ensemble model following a Gaussian normal distribution as an environment model to improve the sample efficiency. Finally, the proposed GEM-SAC algorithm is evaluated in the AirSim. The results demonstrate that the proposed approach improves the sample efficiency, eliminates oscillations and steady error, and is robust to external disturbances. In the future work, we will continue conducting hardware-in-the-loop (HIL) experiments for quadrotors and extend our experiments for a wider range of drone types, such as tilt-rotor aircraft, with the deep reinforcement learning.

References

1. Xu, B.: Composite learning finite-time control with application to quadrotors. IEEE Trans. Syst. Man Cybern. Syst. **48**(10), 1806–1815 (2017)
2. Lambert, N.O., Drew, D.S., Yaconelli, J., Levine, R.C., et al.: Low-level control of a quadrotor with deep model-based reinforcement learning. IEEE Rob. Autom. Lett. **4**(4), 4224–4230 (2019)
3. Wang, Y., Sun, J., He, H., et al.: Deterministic policy gradient with integral compensator for robust quadrotor control. IEEE Trans. Syst. Man Cybern. Syst. **50**(10), 3713–3725 (2019)
4. Liu, H., Suzuki, S., Wang, W., et al.: Robust control strategy for quadrotor drone using reference model-based deep deterministic policy gradient. Drones **6**(9), 251 (2022)
5. Mahony, R., Kumar, V., Corke, P.: Multirotor aerial vehicles: modeling, estimation, and control of quadrotor. IEEE Robot. Autom. Mag. **19**(3), 20–32 (2012)
6. Sutton, R.S., Barto, A.G.: Reinforcement Learning: An Introduction. MIT press, Cambridge (2018)
7. Haarnoja, T., Zhou, A., Abbeel, P., Levine, S.: Soft actor-critic: off-policy maximum entropy deep reinforcement learning with a stochastic actor. In: International Conference on Machine Learning, pp. 1861–1870. PMLR (2018)
8. Haarnoja, T., Zhou, A., Hartikainen, K., et al.: Soft actor-critic algorithms and applications. arXiv preprint arXiv:1812.05905 (2018)
9. Lillicrap, T. P., Hunt, J. J., Pritzel, A., et al.: Continuous control with deep reinforcement learning. arXiv preprint arXiv:1509.02971 (2015)
10. Luo, F.M., Xu, T., Lai, H., Chen, X.H., Zhang, W., Yu, Y.: A survey on model-based reinforcement learning. Sci. China Inf. Sci. **67**(2), 121101 (2024)

11. Moerland, T.M., Broekens, J., Plaat, A., Jonker, C.M.: Model-based reinforcement learning: A survey. Found. Trends Mach. Learn. **16**(1), 1–118 (2023)
12. Chua, K., Calandra, R., McAllister, R., Levine, S.: Deep reinforcement learning in a handful of trials using probabilistic dynamics models. In: NeurIPS (2018)
13. Shah, S., Dey, D., Lovett, C., Kapoor, A.: Airsim: High-fidelity visual and physical simulation for autonomous vehicles. In: Field and Service Robotics: Results of the 11th International Conference, pp. 621–635. Springer, Heidleberg (2018)
14. Chen, X.H., et al.: Offline model-based adaptable policy learning for decision-making in out-of-support regions. IEEE Trans. Pattern Anal. Mach. Intell. **45**, 15260–15274 (2023)

Causal Reasoning

Research on the Causal Forest Algorithm Based on Factor Space Theory

Fanhui Zeng[1,2], Kaile Lin[1,2](✉), Xiaotong Liu[1,2], Pengxue Zhang[1,2], and Sixing Ren[1,2]

[1] College of Science, Liaoning Technical University, Fuxin 123000, China
464825872@qq.com
[2] Institute of Intelligence Engineering and Mathematics, Liaoning Technical University, Fuxin 123000, China

Abstract. In order to solve the problems in classification, improve the classification accuracy and generalization ability of a single classifier, based on the degree of determination of factor space theory, a causal tree algorithm is proposed; Ensemble multiple causal trees, provide a definition of factor importance, obtain advantage factors, set importance thresholds in numerical experiments to reduce the set of condition factors, randomly select factors and then obtain the causal forest algorithm. Experimental comparison was conducted on the classification datasets of the UCI database to comprehensively evaluate the causal tree algorithm, causal forest algorithm, SVM algorithm and random forest algorithm. The experimental results showed that the causal forest algorithm performed well in terms of accuracy, precision, recall, F1 value, and AUC indexes, especially on the Vote and Cancer datasets, with good predictive and generalization abilities. The research conclusion expands the theoretical and applied research of factor space in data mining.

Keywords: Factor space · Causal tree algorithm · Factor importance · Causal forest algorithm

1 Introduction

In 1982, Wang Peizhuang [1] put forward the theory of factor space from the origin of the understanding of things, providing a theoretical framework for the mathematical description of concepts, judgment and reasoning, and establishing the mathematical theory [2] of knowledge representation. In 2014, Wang Peizhuang defined the degree of determination and domain of condition factors on result factors in discrete cases, and sequentially extracted corresponding reasoning knowledge from the domain, got a new algorithm - factor analysis algorithm [3], the algorithm can quickly extracted in a factor analysis table and inference rules, become one of the core algorithm of factor library theory, provide important tools for artificial intelligence and data mining. Wang Huadong [4] used a column by column advancement method to improve the

Published by Springer Nature Switzerland AG 2025
Z. Shi et al. (Eds.): ICIS 2024, IFIP AICT 720, pp. 95–109, 2025.
https://doi.org/10.1007/978-3-031-71253-1_8

accuracy and running speed of the algorithm when selecting factors for stacking and partitioning. Liu Haitao [5] proposed the inference model of factor analysis algorithm, which effectively solves the problem of non-recognition phenomenon and has a high recognition rate, and improves the accuracy of factor analysis algorithm. Qu Weihua [6] proposed the multi-standard causal analysis algorithm, which expanded the application of causal analysis from single-label classification to multi-label classification. Bao Yanke [7] proposed the differential transfer algorithm to improve the accuracy of the multi-factor classification algorithm. Sun Hui [8] proposed a multi-objective causal analysis dimensionality reduction algorithm to reduce the computational complexity of extracting causal rules using multi-objective causal analysis. Liu Xiaotong [9] proposed the reverse causal analysis algorithm and applied it to predict credit defaults in bank cards, obtaining more accurate default prediction results and more complete causal reasoning rules. The factor analysis algorithm has been widely applied in various fields [10–13].

To further improve the classification accuracy and generalization ability of single classifiers, ensemble learning is currently a widely used learning strategy for handling classification problems and optimizing models. Classic ensemble learning methods include random forest algorithms [14], Adaboost [15], XGBoost [16], etc. The random forest algorithm uses decision trees as the base classifier, enhances the independence between trees in the random forest through random sampling and random subspaces, and reduces generalization errors. The performance of this algorithm mainly depends on two factors [17]: the difference between classifiers and the accuracy of the classifier. When constructing each classifier, the feature attributes of the classifier are randomly selected, which means that the probability of each attribute being selected is equal [18]. However, due to the imbalance of factor importance, the random forest algorithm may randomly select weak factor subsets to generate weak classifiers, leading to a decrease in the convergence speed and performance of the model. Therefore, this paper first proposes a causal tree algorithm using the degree of determination of factor analysis algorithm. Secondly, the causal forest algorithm is proposed to ensemble multiple causal trees, define factor importance, set importance thresholds, and randomly select factors so that the condition factor set of each tree is selected from the condition factors greater than the threshold. Finally, the effectiveness of the causal forest algorithm is verified through experiments on classification datasets in the UCI database. The experimental results show that compared to traditional causal tree algorithms, SVM, and random forest algorithms, causal forest algorithms exhibit better performance in accuracy, precision, recall, F1 value, and AUC indexes.

2 Preliminary Knowledge

The factor space theory emphasizes that the factors are the fundamental root, and each factor can string out a series of attributes or phases of things. For example, gender factor can string out two attributes (phases): male and female. From a mathematical perspective, factors are a type of trait mapping that maps objects to their phases. The basic theories related to factor space are as follows [2]:

Definition 1. Factor f is a map $f : D \to I(f)$, where $D = D(f)$ is a set of a class of things to be discussed, called the theory domain. $I = I(f) = \{a_1, a_2, \cdots, a_k\}$ called the trait space or phase domain of f, a_i is the trait or phase of f.

Definition 2. Note $I_{F^*} = \{I(F)\}_{(F \in P(F^*))}$, refer to $\Phi = (D, I_{F^*})$ as a factor space on D, sometimes also expressed as:

$$\Phi = (D, F^* = \{f_1, \cdots f_n\}) \tag{1}$$

Usually, as long as two things are different, there is at least one factor that makes the factors of these two things completely different.

Determine a division relationship ~ based on factor f: for any $u, v \in D$, $u \sim v$ if and only if $f(u) = f(v)$. An equivalence relationship determines a classification of objects in D, and the class where object d is denoted as

$$[d]_f = \{v \in D|f(v) = f(u)\}$$

Definition 3. Note

$$H(D,f) = \{[a_i]|i = 1, 2, \cdots, n\}$$

Call this classification as the division of f to D. Consider each class $c_i = [a_i]$ as an element to form a set $D/_f = \{c_i|i = 1, 2, \cdots, n\}$, called the quotient space or quotient set of D with respect to f.

Definition 4 (Combination operation of factors). Factor h is called the combination factor of factor f and factor g, denoted as $h = f \vee g$. If h is the largest common sub-factor of f and g, namely $f \geq h$, $g \geq h$, and for any factor e, there must be.

$$(f \geq e, g \geq e) \Rightarrow h \geq e$$

Definition 5 (Disjunctive operation of factors). Factor h is called the disjunctive factor of factor f and factor g, denoted as $h = f \wedge g$. If h takes f and g as subfactors and is the smallest of such factors, namely $h \geq f$, $h \geq g$, and for any factor e, there must be.

$$(e \geq f, e \geq f) \Rightarrow e \geq h$$

Definition 6 (Background relationship). Given the qualitative factor space on D, for any $a = (a_1, a_2, \cdots, a_n) \in I$, the original phase on D is $[a] = F^{-1}(a)= \{d \in D|F(d) = a\}$, $[a]$ may be empty set $\emptyset$, if $[a] = \emptyset$, a is a virtual configuration, otherwise a is a real character particle. The set of all-real traits is denoted as.

$$R = F(D) = \{a = (a_1, a_2, \cdots, a_n) \in X\,|\exists d \in D\}$$

R as the background relationship between factors $f_1, f_2, \cdots, f_n$.

Definition 7. If the background relationship

$$R = [f \vee g](D) = f(D) \times g(D)$$

The factor f is said to be independent of g.

Definition 8 (Background distribution). In a sample with a domain size m, if phase $a_{(1)(2)\cdots(n)}$ appears k times, $p^*_{(1)(2)\cdots(n)} = k/m$ is called the frequency of phase $a_{(1)(2)\cdots(n)}$, and $\{p^*_{(1)(2)\cdots(n)}\}$ is called the background distribution.

3 Causal Tree Algorithm

Factor analysis algorithm in factor space is a algorithm to quickly extract inference rules from data tables (causal analysis tables). This section proposes a causal tree algorithm based on tree structure extraction rules using the degree of determination and factor analysis.

3.1 Basic Concepts

Factors influence, restrict each other and cause and effect each other. In the factor analysis, the concerned factor g is called the outcome factor, and the factor $\{f_1, f_2, \cdots, f_n\}$ that has an influence on the outcome factor is called the condition factor.

In factor analysis, the factor g that is being considered is called the result factor, and the factor $\{f_1, f_2, \cdots, f_n\}$ that affects the result factor is called the condition factor.

The causal analysis table takes objects as rows (the domain), condition factors and result factor as columns, and the specific form shows Table 1. The elements in column j of row i in Table 1 are the i-th object traits under the j-th factor.

Table 1. The causal analysis table

D	$F \to g$			
	f_1	$\cdots$	f_n	g
d_1	$f_j(d_i)$			$g(d_i)$
d_2				
$\vdots$				
d_m				

Each row of the causal analysis table is the coordinate of an object in the factor space. Finite object constitute domain $D = \{d_1, d_2, \cdots, d_m\}$, condition factor is $F = \{f_1, f_2, \cdots, f_n\}$, condition factor trait space is $I(f_j) = \{a_{j1}, a_{j2}, \cdots, a_{jk}\}(j = 1, 2, \cdots, n)$. The result factor is g, and the trait space of the result factor is $I(g) = \{g_1, g_2, \cdots, g_s\}$.

Definition 9 (Degree of determination). Given a condition factor f_j and a trait a_t taken by the factor, denoted as $[a_t] = \{d_i | f_j(d_i) = a_t\}$, if all the objects in $[a_t]$ have the same value (i. e., a trait or grade g_l of the result factor g, so that $[g_l] = \{d_i | g(d_i) = g_l\} \supseteq [a_t]$, $[a_t]$ is a decision class of f_j. The union of all decision classes of f_j is called the domain of determination of that factor on the result factor g. The ratio of the number of rows c occupied by the domain of determination of f_j to the number of rows of the table (the number of total objects) m is called the degree of determination of the result factor g, which is denoted as $d(f_j) = c/m$.

Definition 10. If a class $[a_t]$ of condition factor f_j is a decision class, and all objects in the class have a unique definite result g_l, then "if f_j is in a_t, the result g is g_l" is an inference rule determined by condition factor f_j, denoted as $f_j = a_t \rightarrow g = g_l$.

3.2 Algorithm Principle

The principle of causal tree algorithm is to establish a model by analyzing the degree of determination of condition factors on result factors. The core idea of this algorithm is that in a given causal analysis table, the degree of determination of condition factors on result factors is different. By quantifying this degree of determination, the algorithm can identify the most decisive factor and select the condition factor with the highest degree of determination as the segmentation criterion for the current node. According to this standard, the dataset is divided into subsets, and the values of the data within each subset on that condition factor are the same. In each subset, the causal tree algorithm continues to analyze the degree of determination of the remaining condition factors, repeating the process of selection and partitioning. In this process, each divide corresponds to the generation of an inference rule, which ultimately constitutes a complete causal tree.

3.3 Algorithm Steps

The causal tree algorithm steps are as follows:

Input Causal analysis table $(D, F = \{f_1, f_2, \cdots, f_n\}; g)$, condition factor set $F = \{f_1, f_2, \cdots, f_n\}$, result factor g.

Output A causal tree Tr with node as the root node.

Step 1 Create a new node;

Step 2 Check if the category g_i of the result factor corresponding to the samples in the causal analysis table is the same. If g_i is the same, mark the node as the leaf node of the category;

Step 3 Check the values in the set of condition factors. If the condition factor set is empty or the object in the causal analysis table has the same value on the factor set F, mark node as leaf node and mark its category as the category with the largest number of objects in the causal analysis table;

Step 4 Calculate the degree of determination of each factor in the condition factor set F, and select the condition factor with the highest degree of determination;

Step 5 Traverse each value of the selected condition factor as a branch generated by the node, and each branch contains samples with a value of a_t under that condition factor;

Step 6 Check the result factor of each branch. If the result factor trait is unique, mark the branch node as a leaf node and label its category as the category of objects in that branch. If the result factor trait is not unique, proceed to step 7;

Step 7 Take the sample after removing the condition factor from this branch as input and repeat steps 2–6.

The experimental analysis of the causal tree algorithm is shown in Sect. 5.

Assuming the size of the dataset is *m*, the number of condition factors is *n*, and the average number of condition factor traits is *p*. When using the degree of determination, the results corresponding to each trait value of each factor need to be checked, and the algorithm time complexity is approximately O(*mnp*).

4 Causal Forest Algorithm

In the factor space, the causal tree algorithm performs the classification and induction by using the degree of determination as the division criterion, which is an effective classification and induction method due to its simple and intuitive structure. However, in the process of causal tree formation, when there are too many condition factors or when there are many traits of condition factors, the problem of over-fitting often appears, which will weaken the classification and prediction ability of the model. In order to solve this problem and further improve the classification accuracy of the base classifier as well as the generalization ability, the concept of factor importance is introduced, and the strategy of integrated learning is adopted to propose the causal forest algorithm. The algorithm combines multiple models to enhance prediction performance, effectively reducing the risk of over-fitting by dispersing the decision process among multiple trees, while improving the generalization ability of the model to unseen data.

4.1 Basic Concepts

To measure the impact of condition factors on classification performance, the definition of factor importance is given below.

Definition 11 (Factor importance). Given a causal analysis table $(D, F = \{f_1, f_2, \cdots, f_n\}; g)$, for $\forall f_i \in F$ and factor subset $B = F - \{f_i\}$, the difference between the degree of determination of the composite divide of condition factor set *F* and the degree of determination of the composite divide of factor subset *B* is the importance of factor f_i in the domain *D*, denoted as.

$$M(f_i) = d(F) - d(B) \tag{2}$$

In formula (1), $d(F)$ represents the degree of determination of the composite divide of the set of condition factors $F = \{f_1, f_2, \cdots, f_n\}$, *B* represents the subset of factors after removing factor f_i from the set of condition factors *F*, $d(B)$ represents the degree of determination of the composite divide of the remaining factors after removing factor f_i from the set of condition factors *F*, and $M(f_i)$ represents the importance of factor f_i.

In general, if each object in domain D has different traits under each condition factor, that is, the causal analysis table considers the background distribution of the sample, and the condition factor set F can fully distinguish the objects, then $d(F) = 1$.

Obviously, factor importance can be used to measure its impact on the classification ability of the causal analysis table.

As can be seen from formula (1), the langer the value of the factor importance, the greater the influence of the factor in the classification.

Definition 12. Given a causal analysis table $(D, F = \{f_1, f_2, \cdots, f_n\}; g)$, for $\forall f_i \in F$, *if.*

$$d(F) \neq d(B)$$

f_i is called the advantage factor on domain D, otherwise, f_i is called the disadvantage factor on domain D.

Example 1. Given a causal analysis table for evaluation, as shown in Table 2. The domain $D = \{d_1, d_2, d_3, d_4, d_5, d_6\}$, the condition factor set is $F = \{f_1, f_2, f_3, f_4\}$ and the result factor is g. Calculate the factor importance of each factor.

Table 2. Evaluation and analysis table

D	$F \rightarrow g$				
	f_1	f_2	f_3	f_4	g
d_1	1	1	1	1	0
d_2	1	1	0	0	1
d_3	1	1	0	1	1
d_4	0	1	1	1	0
d_5	0	0	0	1	0
d_6	0	1	0	1	1

Taking the condition factor f_2 as an example, provide the calculation process of factor importance. The composite divide of factors $\{f_1, f_3, f_4\}$ divides the domain D into:

$$\{d_1\{111\}, d_2\{100\}, d_3\{101\}, d_4\{011\}, \{d_5, d_6\}\{001\}\},$$

Because classes $\{111\}$,$\{100\}$,$\{101\}$and$\{011\}$ all contain only one object, they are the decision classes of $\{f_1, f_3, f_4\}$, and the result factor corresponding to class $\{001\}$ are not all the same (there are 0 and 1), and they are not the decision class for $\{\{f_1, f_3, f_4\}$. Therefore

$$d(F - \{f_2\}) = d(f_1, f_3, f_4) = (1 + 1 + 1 + 1)/6 = 4/6$$

And $d(F) = 1$, so, the factor importance of f_2 is

$$M(f_2) = d(F) - d(F - \{f_2\}) = 1 - 4/6 = 2/6$$

Similarly, the factor importance of f_1 is

$$M(f_1) = d(F) - d(F - \{f_1\}) = 1 - 1 = 0$$

the factor importance of f_3 is

$$M(f_3) = d(F) - d(F - \{f_3\}) = 1 - 2/6 = 4/6$$

the factor importance of f_4 is

$$M(f_4) = d(F) - d(F - \{f_4\}) = 1 - 1 = 0$$

According to Example 1, f_2 has the greatest factor importance, indicating that f_2 has the greatest influence on the classification ability of the evaluation analysis table. The factor importance of f_1 and f_4 is 0, indicating that after removing f_1 or f_4, the classification ability of the evaluation analysis table remains unchanged.

4.2 Algorithm Principle

The essence of the algorithm is to construct multiple causal trees through ensemble methods to form a causal forest, improving the stability and accuracy of a single model.The new data classification results are obtained from the voting results of each causal tree in the forest. Before constructing the causal tree for each causal analysis table, filter the condition factors based on their importance.

Specific algorithm principle:

Using a random sampling method with dropout on the original dataset to generate a new training set sample, ensuring that each generated training set is a random subset of the original dataset, increasing the diversity of the model; For each newly generated training set, calculate the importance of each condition factor, set an importance threshold α, and delete condition factors with less importance to reduce factor dimensions and optimize the foundation for constructing a causal tree; Randomly select l factors as candidate factors for nodes during causal tree construction; Select the factor with the highest degree of determination as the dividing node to form a causal tree; Each causal tree predicts the samples on the test set; The predicted results of all causal trees are summarized through a voting mechanism, and the category label with the highest number of votes is the category label of the test sample.

4.3 Threshold α

When using the causal forest algorithm, setting a threshold α is a critical step that affects model performance. This not only affects the simplification and complexity of the model, but also directly affects the generalization ability and accuracy of the model on unknown data.

(1) α too high: almost all condition factors are deleted as unimportant factors, resulting in the oversimplification of the model and the loss of important information, thus reducing the performance of the model.
(2) α too low: some condition factors that actually contribute little to the model's prediction being considered important and retained, resulting in the model being too complex and at risk of over-fitting, thus reducing the model's generalization ability.

The reasonable setting of thresholds requires finding a balance between retaining sufficient information and avoiding the model from being too complex. Through multiple experiments to evaluate the performance of the model, it has been shown that the threshold is usually set between 0 and 0.3. It can be adjusted according to the specific situation.

4.4 Algorithm Steps

Domain $D = \{ d_1, d_2, \cdots, d_m\}$, condition factor is $F = \{ f_1, f_2, \cdots, f_n\}$ and condition factor trait space is $I(f_j) = \{a_{j1}, a_{j2}, \cdots, a_{jk}\}(j = 1, 2, \cdots, n)$; the result factor is g, and the trait space of the result factor is $I(g) = \{g_1, g_2, \cdots, g_s\}$. The causal forest algorithm steps are as follows:

Step 1 Using the self sampling strategy, generate K different causal analysis tables from the original causal analysis table;

Step 2 For each generated causal analysis table, calculate the factor importance of each condition factor, set a factor importance threshold, and delete condition factors with importance lower than the threshold to reduce factor dimensions;

Step 3 When dividing nodes, randomly select a subset from the remaining condition factors, calculate the degree of determination of each factor in these subsets, and select the condition factor with the highest degree of determination as the current node divide criterion;

Step 4 Divide according to the selected condition factors and repeat the above process until the sample data of all nodes belong to the same class or the set of condition factors is empty;

Step 5 Repeat the above steps to construct K causal trees;

Step 6 For the test sample, the results of the K causal trees generated earlier are combined by voting, and the result with the most occurrences is the predicted result of the test sample.

Algorithm 4.1 Causal forest algorithm

Input Causal analysis table $(D, F = \{f_1, f_2, \cdots, f_n\}; g)$, condition factor set $F = \{f_1, f_2, \cdots, f_n\}$, result factor g, and the test sample d.

Output The category label of the test sample d.

Step 1 For any $1 \leq i \leq K$, perform the following cycle:

① Sampling with K times from the causal analysis table of size m, and $T_1, T_2, \cdots, T_K$ represents new training sets after sampling;
② Call algorithm 4.2 to build a causal tree T_i.

Step 2 Use these K causal trees to predict sample d, obtain K prediction results $T_1(d), T_2(d), \cdots, T_K(d)$, and obtain the category labels of test sample d through voting;

Step 3 The algorithm ends and returns the final prediction result of test sample d.

Algorithm 4.2 Single causal tree T_i algorithm

Input Causal analysis table $(D, F = \{f_1, f_2, \cdots, f_n\}; g)$, condition factor set $F = \{f_1, f_2, \cdots, f_n\}$, result factor g, factor importance threshold α.

Output Causal tree T_i.

Step 1 Create a new node includes all objects in the domain;

Step 2 Check if the result factor category C corresponding to the samples in the causal analysis table is the same. If so, mark the node as a leaf node of category C;

Step 3 Check the values in the condition factors set. If the condition factor set is empty or the objects in the causal analysis table have the same values on factor set F, mark the node as a leaf node and mark its category as the category with the highest number of objects in the causal analysis table;

Step 4 Perform factor reduction on the condition factor set:

① Calculate the factor importance of n condition factors;
② Set a threshold α for factor importance, remove condition factors with importance less than the threshold α, and randomly select l factors for the remaining condition factors to obtain the current causal analysis table;
③ Generate the base classifier T_i using the causal tree algorithm on the optimized causal analysis table;

Step 5 The algorithm ends and returns the constructed causal tree.

5 Experimental Analysis

To verify the effectiveness of the causal forest algorithm, three classified datasets from the UCI database were selected for learning, and the results were compared with the cause fruit tree algorithm, SVM and random forest algorithm respectively.

5.1 Data Description

The information of each dataset is as follows:

Vote dataset is a voting record of US House members, with the result factors being Democratic and Republican.

Cancer dataset is used to diagnose breast cancer patients according to the nuclear morphology such as the radius, texture, perimeter shape of the cancer cell nucleus. There are two types of result factors: benign and malignant.

Npha dataset is a national public opinion survey on healthy aging, used to predict the number of doctors that respondents will see within a year. There are two types of result factors: 0–3 doctors as 1and 4 or more doctors as 2.

The specific structure of each dataset is presented in Table 3.

5.2 Experimental Result

Four classification algorithms were used to ten fold cross validation to obtain accuracy, precision, recall, F1 value, and AUC. The F1 value takes into account both the precision and recall of the algorithm. The experimental results are shown in Table 4.

Table 3. Basic information of datasets

Datasets	Number of objects	Number of condition factors	Result category
Vote	435	16	2
Cancer	683	9	2
Npha	714	14	2

In order to visually show the experimental results of the algorithms, the indexes of the four algorithms on different datasets are analyzed by graphical method.

Table 4. Comparison of the experimental results

Datasets	Index	Causal tree algorithm	Causal forest algorithm	SVM algorithm	Random forest algorithm
Vote	Acc	0.8308	**0.9462**	0.9231	0.9308
	Pre	0.9718	**0.9877**	0.9750	0.9873
	Rec	0.8625	**0.9302**	0.9070	0.9070
	F1	0.9139	**0.9581**	0.9398	0.9454
	AUC	0.9117	0.9427	0.9873	**0.9892**
Cancer	Acc	0.9317	**0.9756**	0.9707	0.9519
	Pre	0.9756	**0.9922**	0.9845	0.9769
	Rec	0.9160	**0.9695**	**0.9695**	**0.9695**
	F1	0.9449	**0.9807**	0.9769	0.9732
	AUC	0.9547	**0.9957**	0.9949	0.9645
Npha	Acc	0.5352	**0.7746**	0.7324	0.6761
	Pre	**0.8140**	0.8000	0.7727	0.7581
	Rec	0.7292	**0.9455**	0.9273	0.8545
	F1	0.7693	**0.8667**	0.8430	0.8034
	AUC	0.5920	**0.6643**	0.6330	0.5602

(1) Experiment 1

For the Vote dataset, due to the small number of samples, set the number of base classifiers to 10 and the factor importance threshold α to 0.01. The comparison relationship between the accuracy, precision, recall, F1 value, and AUC indexes of various classification algorithms is shown in Fig. 1.

According to Fig. 1 and Table 4, for the Vote dataset:

① The causal forest algorithm shows the best accuracy, precision, recall and F1 value, and has the best comprehensive performance on this dataset;

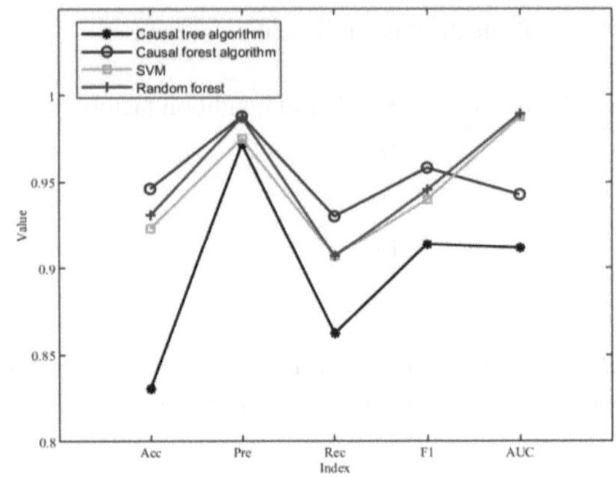

Fig. 1. The indexes of four algorithms on the Vote dataset

② SVM algorithm and random forest algorithm perform well in AUC value, especially the random forest algorithm has a slightly higher AUC value, indicating that their ability to distinguish positive and negative categories is slightly better than other algorithms; ③ The performance of the causal tree algorithm is relatively low, especially in terms of accuracy and AUC value.

(2) Experiment 2

For the Cancer dataset, set the number of base classifiers to 10 and the factor importance threshold α to 0.002. The comparison relationship between the accuracy, precision, recall, F1 value, and AUC indexes of various classification algorithms is shown in Fig. 2.

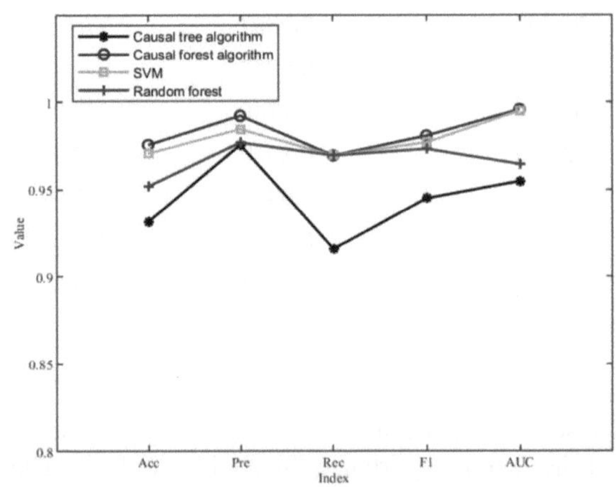

Fig. 2. The indexes of four algorithms on the Cancer dataset

According to Fig. 2 and Table 4, for the Cancer dataset:

① The accuracy, precision, F1 value, and AUC of causal forest algorithm are superior to causal tree algorithm, SVM algorithm, and random forest algorithm, and the AUC value is close to 1, indicating that the algorithm has high classification ability;
② The recall of causal forest algorithm is equal to SVM algorithm and random forest algorithm, and both are better than causal tree algorithm.

(3) Experiment 3

For the Npha dataset, set the number of base classifiers to 10 and the factor importance threshold α to 0.2. The comparison relationship between the accuracy, precision, recall, F1 value, and AUC indexes of various classification algorithms is shown in Fig. 3.

According to Fig. 3 and Table 4, for the Npha dataset:

① The causal forest algorithm outperforms random forest algorithm and SVM;
② In terms of recall, the causal forest algorithm is higher than other algorithms, indicating its effectiveness in identifying positive classes;
③ The causal tree algorithm has a high accuracy, indicating its reliability in identifying positive classes.

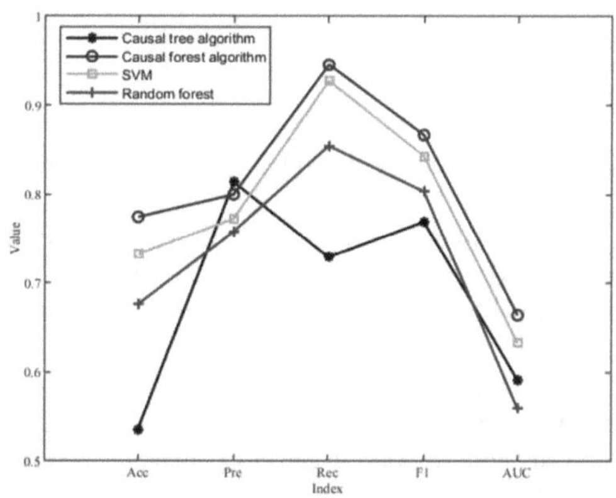

Fig. 3. The indexes of four algorithms on the Npha dataset

Overall, the causal forest algorithm has shown good performance on three datasets, especially in terms of accuracy and recall, effectively handling over-fitting and improving generalization ability. The performance on the Npha dataset also indicates the adaptability and robustness of the algorithm to complex data environments.

6 Conclusion

This paper aims to improve the classification performance and generalization ability of a single classifier by using the degree of determination in factor space theory, defining factor importance, and proposing a causal forest algorithm.

(1) A causal tree algorithm based on tree structure extraction rules was proposed based on the degree of determination.

(2) Define factor importance to evaluate the influence of different condition factors on the classification ability of causal analysis tables.
(3) Propose a causal forest algorithm based on factor importance. This algorithm reduces the set of condition factors by setting an importance threshold, effectively removing redundant factors, and adding randomly selected factors. By combining multiple causal trees, the accuracy of classification is improved.
(4) The performance of the causal forest algorithm was validated through experiments on multiple classification datasets in the UCI database. The experimental results show that compared to causal tree algorithms, SVM algorithms and random forest algorithms, causal forest algorithms shows better performance in accuracy, precision, recall, F1 value, and AUC.

In summary, the causal forest algorithm expands the theoretical basis of factor analysis by defining the factor importance, providing a new solution for practical classification problems. In practical applications, the data that needs to be processed is often very large. Although the causal forest algorithm improve classification accuracy to a certain extent, large datasets inevitably increase computation time. Therefore, how to reduce algorithm complexity is a problem that needs to be solved in the future.

References

1. Wang, P.Z., Sugeno, M.: The factors field and background structure for fuzzy subsets. Fuzzy Math. **2**(2), 45–54 (1982)
2. Wang, P.Z., Li, H.X.: A Mathematical Theory on Knowledge Representation. Tianjin Scientific and Technical Press, Tianjin (1994)
3. Wang, P.Z., Guo, S.C., Bao, Y.K., et al.: Causality analysis in factor spaces. J. Liaoning Tech. Univ. (Nat. Sci.) (7), 865–870 (2014)
4. Wang, H.D., Wang, P.Z., Guo, S.C.: Improved factor analysis on factor spaces. J. Liaoning Tech. Univ. Nat. Sci. **34**(4), 539–544 (2015)
5. Liu, H.T., Guo, S.C.: Reasoning model of causality analysis. J. Liaoning Tech. Univ. (Nat. Sci.) **34**(1), 124–128 (2015)
6. Qu, W.H., Liu, H.T., Guo, S.C.: Multi-target causality analysis in factor space. Fuzzy Syst. Math. **31**(06), 74–81 (2017)
7. Bao, Y.K., Ru, H.Y., Jin, S.J.: A new algorithm of knowledge mining in factor space. J. Liaoning Tech. Univ. (Nat. Sci.) **33**(8), 1141–1144 (2014)
8. Sun, H., Zeng, F.H., Pu, L.J.: Dimension reduction algorithm of multiple targets causal analysis based on factor space theory. J. Liaoning Tech. Univ. (Nat. Sci.) **40**(05), 466–472 (2021)
9. Liu, X.T., Zeng, F.H., Liu, X.J.: Research on bank credit card default prediction based on Factor Space Theory. J. Liaoning Tech. Univ. (Nat. Sci.) **40**(06), 567–574 (2021)
10. Liang, Z.L.: Geological Disaster Rescue Routes Based on Factor Space Optimization Study. Guangzhou University, Guangzhou (2022)
11. Cui, T.J., Wang, P.Z.: Intelligent reliability analysis method based on space fault tree and factor space. CAAI Trans. Intell. Syst. **14**(5), 853–864 (2019)
12. Zhang, Y.N., Zeng, F.H., Bao, Y.K., et al.: Risk factors of hypertension in Fuxin rural areas of Liaoning Province. Chin. J. Hypertens. **25**(10), 937–941 (2017)
13. Liu, X.T.: Research on Default Risk of Personal Credit Based on Factor Space Theory. Liaoning Technical University, Liaoning (2021)

14. Breiman, L.: Random forests. Mach. Learn. **45**(1), 5–32 (2001)
15. Kumari, G., Naveen, M.K., Mary, A.S.: AdaBoost based random forest model for emotion classification of facial images. MethodsX 11102422–102422 (2023)
16. Krishna, K.M., Mohammad, Z.K., Ajay, I.: Credit card fraud prediction using XGBoost: an ensemble learning approach. Int. J. Inf. Retr. Res. (IJIRR) **12**(2), 1–17 (2022)
17. Ding, H.B., Ye, F.Y.: Fuzzy random forest algorithm for uncertain data classification. Comput. Eng. Des. **44**(11), 3373–3379 (2023)
18. Guan, X.Q., Pang, J.F., Liang, J.Y.: Random forest algorithm based on class randomization. Comput. Sci. **46**(02), 196–201 (2019)

Superpositioner – A Non-logical Computation Model

Chuyu Xiong(✉)

New York, USA
chuyux99@gmail.com

Abstract. We have been striving to exceed computational complexity, and in the process, we have come to realize the dilemma of classical computing, and in turn we realize that superpositioner may be a way to solve. A superpositioner is a model formed by several Boolean functions that their variables and function values are feeding back to each other. The component of the superpositioner is the reentry function, which can be fully described by classical logic and can be calculated by classical computation, but the superpositioner as a whole is a non-logical entity, and it is impossible for classical computation to fully compute it. In this article, we present the concept of a superpositioner and discuss its basic properties. We find that the superpositioner + dispositioner will form a new type of computation model whose capabilities can surpass Turing computation. We envision that this new model will help implement these functions in the intelligent agent: a whole new way of programming and a whole new way of learning, endogenous feelings, analogies and associations, forming understanding, dynamic action, participating in the formation of subjectivity, and more. We will also discuss how to implement superpositioner in the most preliminary way.

Keywords: Intelligent Agent · Superpositioner · Dispositioner · Conceiving Space · Exceeding Computational Complexity

1 Introduction

We have been contemplating to establish intelligent agents that can exceed the computational complexity [1]. According to the definition in [5], an intelligent agent is something that perceives its environment through its sensors and acts upon its environment through its actuators. We find that the subjectivity and agency of intelligent agents are key to enhancing their capabilities [2]. If an intelligent agent possesses good subjectivity and positive agency, its capabilities can be greatly improved. If we want to create intelligent agents that exceed computational complexity, it is even more necessary to enable the agents to have good subjectivity and agency.

C. Xiong—Independent researcher.

Published by Springer Nature Switzerland AG 2025
Z. Shi et al. (Eds.): ICIS 2024, IFIP AICT 720, pp. 110–131, 2025.
https://doi.org/10.1007/978-3-031-71253-1_9

However, we also find that if an intelligent agent only adopts classical computation (Turing computation) methods, it is very difficult to achieve true agency [2]. Does this mean that we need to develop a kind of computation different from classical computation in order for intelligent agents to possess true agency? But the Church-Turing thesis states that any computation is equivalent to a Turing machine, so how could we develop a computation different from classical computation? This is a dilemma.

In attempting to overcome this dilemma, we happen to learn a simple model proposed by Findlay, Koch, and Toroni, which we call the PQR circuit [6]. This simple model stimulated us to delve deeper into the question of what computation really is, and to rethink various aspects of computation. After long contemplation in this direction, we conceived the idea of the superpositioner, and thus proposed the superpositioner–a new computation model.

Simply put, the superpositioner is a model formed by supeimpose several Boolean functions together, thus creating a cross-over (reentry is the term) between the variables and values of the functions. The function reentry forms a situation where multiple functions are superimposed. Certainly, this appears to be a rather chaotic situation that cannot be well described by classical logic, one that is non-logical and cannot be fully computed by classical computation–it is an entirely new configuration. Faced with the superpositioner, faced with this chaotic situation, in order to revert to classical logic, we need to impose an external order on the reentry, so that we can locally disentangle this chaotic situation and restore logicality. We call this process "disposition" and what performs the disposition is the "dispositioner". Thus, the superpositioner + dispositioner effectively forms a new computational model. After preliminary exploration of this new computational model, the results left us quite surprised: this model has great potential, and is likely to help us enable agency in intelligent agents, and more. Therefore, in this paper, we write down this computational model.

In this paper, we will discuss the superpositioner + dispositioner computation model and some of its basic properties. We will show that this computation model provides us with a new way of programming and a new way of learning. We will also envision implementing several important functions in intelligent agents using this computation model, such as: innate perception, generating agency, forming understanding, forming analogies and associations, participating in the subjectivity of intelligent agents, and so on. These are extremely difficult to achieve using Turing computation. This is just the initial step in exploring the superpositioner; we will continue to study various aspects of this model, including its applications and implementations.

The arrangement of this paper is as follows: in Sect. 2, we introduce the PQR circuit, a model from researches on consciousness that is also a very simple superpositioner. In Sect. 3, we propose superposition and the superpositioner, as well as disposition and the dispositioner. In Sect. 4, we discuss the conceiving space and intrinsic functions. In Sect. 5, we envision some potential applications of the superpositioner and preliminarily discuss how to implement the superpositioner. In Sect. 6, we provide some discussion.

2 PQR Circuit

The PQR circuit was proposed by Findlay, Koch, Toroni and others [6]. Several years ago, Toroni et al. put forward the famous information integration theory. Information integration refers to: a set of information being causally interdependent, not a one-way influence but rather a mutual influence, thereby closely connected to form a whole. In arguing for this theory, they proposed an extremely simple model to illustrate the concept of information integration. Since this model uses 3 nodes P, Q and R, we call this model the PQR circuit, shown in the following diagram (Fig. 1).

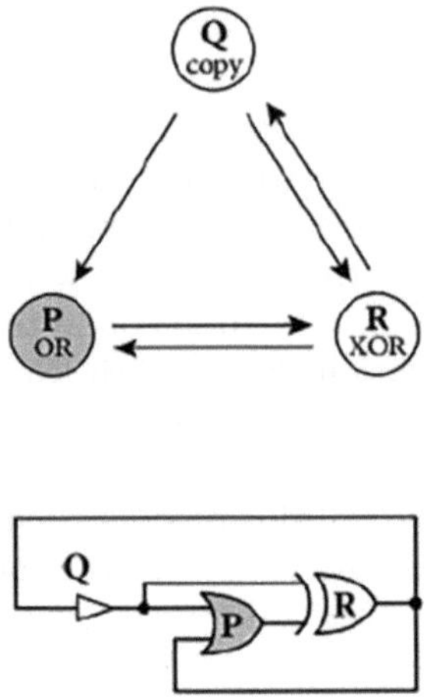

Fig. 1. PQR Circuit, from Koch [7]

It can be clearly seen that this circuit is actually formed by the superposition of several Boolean circuits. The so-called superposition refers to the reuse of a node by two or more Boolean circuits at that node. We can also express this model using Boolean functions. There are 3 Boolean circuits in total, so there are also 3 Boolean functions.

$$P = f_1(P, Q, R) = Q \vee R \tag{1}$$
$$Q = f_2(P, Q, R) = R \tag{2}$$
$$R = f_3(P, Q, R) = P \oplus Q \tag{3}$$

Note that in the expressions (1), (2), (3) above, each function is a simple Boolean function, and there is nothing special about them if considered individually. However, if we put them all together, we can see that a special thing: these variables are both independent variables and function values at the same time. This is what is meant by being causally interdependent. Therefore, they form a superposition. We can view the PQR circuit as a special kind of circuit formed by the superposition of 3 very simple Boolean circuits. In this circuit, there are no traditional input nodes or output nodes, but rather, all nodes are both input and output nodes. It is important to note that such a circuit is very different from so-called feedforward circuits, and also very different from so-called recurrent networks.

Toroni et al. proposed the PQR model, and their main argument was that for such a fully interconnected circuit of nodes, or a model where information is causally interdependent, if one were to simulate it using conventional circuits or functions, it would require far more circuits or functions to express. They used this to argue for and explain what integrated information is and the rationality of integrated information theory. However, they seem to have stopped there. We have not read any literature where they explored the further implications of such circuits, nor have we seen them discuss the potential rules and consequences of such circuits, or envision uses for such circuits.

3 Superpositioner and Dispositioner

After understanding the PQR circuit, we deeply felt that it implied several very important things, and wondered whether these things could help us. Here is how we viewed it: If we decoupled the PQR circuit, it would degenerate into 3 very simple Boolean circuits, with nothing unique, and certainly within the scope of Turing computation. However, if we superimposed these very simple Boolean circuits, the situation would be very different. The superposition causes P, Q, R to be both function values and variable values, i.e.: the cause is also the effect, the effect is also the cause. If viewed as conventional computation, it would inevitably lead to much confusion. As Toroni et al. pointed out, if one insisted on simulating the PQR circuit using classical computation, it would require far more circuits. This means that a PQR circuit using only 3 nodes would require tens of nodes in a feedforward circuit to simulate. Coincidentally, we have been actively thinking about how to exceed computational complexity. Therefore, the PQR circuit, which can do a lot with just 3 nodes, prompted us to consider whether superimposing several Boolean circuits could create an opportunity to make exceeding computational complexity possible. Thus, we engaged in long-term reflection and exploration in this direction.

Based on this reflection, we proposed a model formed by the superposition of Boolean circuits. Boolean circuits are equivalent to Boolean functions, so the superposition of Boolean circuits is equivalent to the superposition of Boolean functions. Since Boolean functions are easier to describe, we adopted Boolean functions for discussion. We first define superposition, superpositioner, and reentry. Note that in this paper, B represents the 1-dimensional Boolean space (binary variable space), and B^N represents the N-dimensional Boolean space.

Definition 1 (Superposition and Superpositioner). *Assuming there are N bits: $T = \{b_1, b_2, \ldots, b_N\}$, and assuming there are N Boolean functions $\{f_1, f_2, \ldots, f_N\}$, $f_i : B^N \to B, i = 1, \ldots, N$, as in the following form:*

$$b_1 = f_1(b_1, b_2, \ldots, b_N)$$
$$b_2 = f_2(b_1, b_2, \ldots, b_N)$$
$$\ldots\ldots$$
$$b_N = f_N(b_1, b_2, \ldots, b_N)$$

Then we call the functions $f_1, \ldots, f_N$ superimposed at nodes $b_1, \ldots, b_N$, and we call $f_1, \ldots, f_N$ and $b_1, \ldots, b_N$ form a superpositioner, calling $b_1, \ldots, b_N$ the nodes of the superpositioner, $f_1, \ldots, f_N$ the reentry functions of the superpositioner, f_i reentry to b_i, and N the scale of the superpositioner. ■

Note that in the definition, the individual functions $f_1, \ldots, f_N$ themselves have nothing unique - they are just ordinary Boolean functions. The uniqueness lies in the fact that the function values of these functions are reentried into the variable values. This is superposition, and the entirety of the superpositions forms the superpositioner. Let's now look at some examples of superpositioners.

Example 1 **(Example of Superpositioner).** Some of the simplest superpositioners:
Single Node Superpositioner. This superpositioner has only one bit b, and thus only one Boolean function $f : B \to B$, with the reentry function $b = f(b)$. Note that there are only 4 such Boolean functions in total: $1, 0, b, \neg b$. Choosing $f = \neg b$ is the only reasonable choice, as the others don't really make sense. Therefore, we also call it the self-negating superpositioner. This superpositioner is very simple, but as we will see later, even such an extremely simple superpositioner can play an important role.

Yin-Yang Superpositioner. This superpositioner has only two nodes, with two reentry functions. The nodes are: b_1, b_2, and the reentry functions are:

$$b_1 = f_1(b_1, b_2) = b_1 \wedge b_2, \quad b_2 = f_2(b_1, b_2) = b1 \oplus b2$$

Similarly, with the same two nodes, different reentry functions can form different superpositioner, such as the Yang-Yang superpositioner, the Yin-Yin superpositioner, the negative Yin-Yang superpositioner, and so on. These superpositioner all have two nodes and two reentry functions, but their reentry functions are different. For example, the reentry functions of the Yang-Yang superpositioner are:

$$b_1 = f_1(b_1, b_2) = b_1 \wedge b_2, \quad b_2 = f_2(b_1, b_2) = b1 \wedge b2$$

And the reentry functions of the negative Yin-Yang superpositioner are:

$$b_1 = f_1(b_1, b_2) = b_1 \vee b_2, \quad b_2 = f_2(b_1, b_2) = b1 \oplus b2$$

We will mainly consider the Yin-Yang superpositioner later.

PQR Superpositioner. The PQR circuit we listed earlier is a simple superpositioner, with 3 nodes and 3 reentry functions: (1), (2), (3). We call this the PQR superpositioner.

Five Elements Superpositioner. This superpositioner has 5 nodes: b_1, b_2, b_3, b_4, b_5, and 5 reentry functions:

$$b_1 = sk(b_1, b_4, b_5)$$
$$b_2 = sk(b_2, b_5, b_1)$$
$$b_3 = sk(b_3, b_1, b_2)$$
$$b_4 = sk(b_4, b_2, b_3)$$
$$b_5 = sk(b_5, b_3, b_4)$$

Here sk is a Boolean function, $sk(x, y, z) = (y \wedge \neg z) \vee (x \wedge \neg(y \oplus z))$, we call sk as raise-press function. If one is familiar with traditional 5-elements thinking, the meaning is clear, and know why we call it as 5-elements superpositioner.

A most fundamental characteristic of the superpositioner is superposition, that is, function values reentry into variables, and then forming new function values, and this process can continue indefinitely. To help us see this more clearly, let's use the PQR superpositioner as an example. Let's assume the values at nodes P, Q, R are assigned as (1,1,1). If we do not consider the effect of the reentry functions, then when taking the values at these nodes, we would still get the values: (1,1,1). However, the function values reentry into the nodes, so the values at the nodes will be affected by the reentry functions. Because it is reentry, i.e. the values of the independent variables are the function values, and the function values are also the values of the independent variables, the effects of the reentry functions can be multiplicative. Not only that, but when considering the reentry functions, the order of the reentry is also very important. For example, if we first apply function f_1, then apply function f_3, and then take the values at the nodes, we would get the values: (1,1,0); whereas if we first apply function f_3, then apply function f_2, then apply function f_1, and then take the values at the nodes, we would get the values: (0,0,0). This means that if we want to take values at the nodes, we must consider the order and number of the reentry functions. This results in the phenomenon that only after clarifying the number and order of applying the reentry functions does discussing the values at the nodes become meaningful. However, in the PQR circuit, there are no limitations whatsoever on the number and order, meaning any number and order is allowed. Due to the superposition, the values at the nodes are linked head-to-tail: after being assigned a value by one function, it becomes the variable value for another function, and this process repeats endlessly, forming a fluctuation of values until the moment the value is taken. Therefore, in the superpositioner, unless the number and order of applying each reentry function is completely determined, the values at the nodes are not completely determined. This is a very meaningful fundamental property. Based on this consideration, we define the reentry configuration.

Definition 2 (Reentry Configuration and Intrinsic Function). *Assume the superpositioner C is composed of nodes $T = \{b_1, b_2, \dots, b_N\}$ and reentry functions $\{f_1, f_2, \dots, f_N\}$. A reentry function $f_j : B^N \to B, j = 1, \dots, N$, can form a mapping $F_j : B^N \to B^N$ of an N-dimensional Boolean space (composed of nodes) as follows:*

$$F_j(b_1, b_2, \dots, b_N) = (b_1, \dots, f_j(b_1, b_2, \dots, b_N), \dots, b_N)$$

That is to say, the other components remain unchanged, and only the jth component takes the value of the reentry function f_j. It can be seen that F_j is uniquely determined by f_j, so we can denote F_j as f_j. Therefore, in this understanding, f_j is both a reentry function and a mapping of an N-dimensional Boolean space. This is unambiguous. Additionally, for convenience, we define F_0 as the identity mapping of the N-dimensional Boolean space:

$$F_0 : B^N \to B^N, F_0(b_1, b_2, \dots, b_N) = (b_1, b_2, \dots, b_N)$$

And according to the same meaning, F_0 can also be denoted as f_0. Corresponding to a sequence of positive integers: $S = (j_1, \dots, j_K)$, where $j_1, \dots$ are numbers from 1 to N, and K is an integer, with no limitation on size, a mapping of an N-dimensional Boolean space can be formed:

$$h : B^N \to B^N, h(b_1, b_2, \dots, b_N) = f_{j_1} \cdots f_{j_K}(b_1, b_2, \dots, b_N)$$

Here, $f_j : B^N \to B^N$, as understood above, is a mapping of an N-dimensional Boolean space. We call such a sequence S a reentry configuration, and the corresponding mapping of the N-dimensional Boolean space h formed by the reentry configuration S is denoted as $h = C \diamond S$. Additionally, there is a special reentry configuration $S = (0)$, and the mapping corresponding to this feedback configuration is as above f_0. Note that a mapping h is composed of N Boolean functions, namely:

$$h(b_1, b_2, \dots, b_N) = (h_1(b_1, \dots, b_N), \dots, h_N(b_1, \dots, b_N))$$

We call these Boolean functions $h_1, \dots, h_N$ the Boolean functions formed by the reentry configuration S, and we also call these functions the intrinsic functions of the superpositioner C. ■

It is clear that the independent variables themselves are functions, and according to the above definition, the independent variable functions, such as $b_1, b_2, \dots$, are also inherent functions. We will discuss inherent functions more later. There are many reentry configurations, so although a superpositioner has only N reentry functions, there may be far more than N intrinsic functions in the superpositioner. Different reentry configurations may form the same function. In fact, there are infinitely many reentry configurations, but there can only be a finite number of intrinsic functions. Let's examine some examples of intrinsic functions in superpositioner.

Example 2 **(Single Node Superpositioner).** This superpositioner has only one node b, one reentry function f, $b = f(b) = \neg b$. This is the simplest superpositioner. The reentry configuration is also very simple, it is a sequence like this: $(1), (1,1), (1,1,1), ldots$. If the sequence has an odd length, then the intrinsic function formed is $\neg b$; if it has an even length, then the intrinsic function formed is b. The correspondence between the value at the node (only one node) and the reentry configuration can be seen in Table 1:

Table 1. Single Node Supoerpositioner - Reentry Configuration and Value

b	(1)	$(1,1)$	$(1,1,1)$	$(1,1,1,1)$	$(1,1,1,1,1)$
1	0	1	0	1	0
0	1	0	1	0	1

That is to say, the intrinsic functions of single node superpositioner are: $\{b, \neg b\}$, only 2 members.

Example 3 **(Yin-Yang Supoerpositioner).** This superpositioner has 2 nodes: b_1, b_2, and reentry functions are $b_1 = b_1 \wedge b_2$, $b_2 = b1 \oplus b2$, values and reentry sequences can be seen in Table 2:

Table 2. Yin-Yang Superpositioner - Reentry Configuration and Value

b_1, b_2	(1)	(2)	$(2,1)$	$(1,2)$	$(1,2,1)$	$(2,1,2)$
1, 1	1, 1	1, 0	1, 0	0, 0	0, 0	0, 0
1, 0	0, 0	1, 1	0, 0	1, 1	0, 0	1, 0
0, 1	0, 1	0, 1	0, 1	0, 1	0, 1	0, 1
0, 0	0, 0	0, 0	0, 0	0, 0	0, 0	0, 0

We can see that in the table above, continuing to increase the length of the reentry sequence does not bring about any more intrinsic functions. Therefore, the set of intrinsic functions for the Yin-Yang superpositioner is: $\{b_1, b_1 \wedge b_2, b_1 \wedge \neg b_2, 0, b_2, b_1 \oplus b_2, \neg b_1 \wedge b_2\}$, a total of 7 functions. Note that the superpositioner only has 2 reentry functions, but there are 7 intrinsic functions, while the total Boolean functions of the two variables is 16. Note that in the set of intrinsic functions, the first 4 are intrinsic functions evaluated at b_1, and the last 3 are intrinsic functions evaluated at b_2.

Note that in the Yin-Yang superpositioner, the reentry function "$\wedge$" plays a Yang role, i.e. a concentrating and converging role; while the reentry function "$\oplus$" plays a Yin role, i.e. a balancing and harmonizing role, hence this superpositioner is called the Yin-Yang superpositioner. It is easy to see that if both reentry functions are Yang ("$\wedge$", a so-called Yang-Yang superposition body), the behavior of the superpositioner becomes much simpler, with only 4 intrinsic functions. If both reentry functions are Yin (a Yin-Yin superpositioner), the behavior is also simple. Let's look at the PQR superpositioner next.

Example 4 **(PQR Superpositioner).** This superpositioner has 3 nodes and 3 reentry functions: b_1, b_2, b_3 (P,Q,R), $b_1 = f_1 = b_2 \vee b_3,\ b_2 = f_2 = b_3,\ b_3 = f_3 = b1 \oplus b2$. The value and reentry can see Table 3:

Table 3. PQR Superpositioner - Reentry Configuration and Value

b_1, b_2, b_3	(1)	(2)	(3)	(1, 3)	(3, 2)	(1, 2, 3)	(3, 1)	...
1, 1, 1	1, 1, 1	1, 1, 1	1, 1, 0	1, 1, 0	1, 1, 0	0, 0, 0	1, 1, 0	
1, 1, 0	1, 1, 0	1, 0, 0	1, 1, 0	1, 1, 0	1, 0, 1	0, 0, 0	1, 1, 0	
1, 0, 1	1, 0, 1	1, 1, 1	1, 0, 1	1, 0, 1	1, 1, 0	1, 1, 1	1, 0, 1	
1, 0, 0	0, 0, 0	1, 0, 0	1, 0, 1	1, 0, 1	1, 0, 1	1, 1, 1	0, 0, 0	
0, 1, 1	1, 1, 1	0, 1, 1	0, 1, 1	1, 1, 1	0, 1, 1	1, 1, 1	1, 1, 0	
0, 1, 0	1, 1, 0	0, 0, 0	0, 1, 1	1, 1, 1	0, 0, 0	1, 1, 1	1, 1, 0	
0, 0, 1	1, 0, 1	0, 1, 1	0, 0, 0	0, 0, 0	0, 1, 1	0, 0, 0	1, 0, 1	
0, 0, 0	0, 0, 0	0, 0, 0	0, 0, 0	0, 0, 0	0, 0, 0	0, 0, 0	0, 0, 0	

The PQR superpositioner has many reentry sequences, and in Table 3, we have only listed some of them, with many reentry sequences and corresponding evaluations not listed. We can look at one example: Let C be the PQR superpositioner, and $S = (1, 3)$ be a reentry configuration, then the mapping corresponding to S is: $f_1 f_3$, and it is not difficult to know that this mapping is $C \diamond S = (b_1 \vee b_2, b_2, b_1 \oplus b_2)$, here there are 3 Boolean functions: $b_1 \vee b_2, b_2, b_1 \oplus b_2$, which are all intrinsic functions of the PQR superpositioner. Furthermore, if $S = (3, 2)$ is another reentry configuration, then $C \diamond S = (b_1, b_3, b_1 \oplus b_3)$, therefore, $b_3, b_1 \oplus b_3$ are also intrinsic functions of the PQR superpositioner. On the other hand, if we consider the node b_1, then at this node the evaluation functions include at least these: $b_1, b_2 \vee b_3, b_2 \vee (b_1 \oplus b_2), \ldots$.

These 3 previous examples give us a lot of inspiration, revealing the richness of intrinsic functions in the superpositioner, as well as revealing the non-logicality and uncertainty of the superpositioner. Now let's consider how to deal with this non-logicality and uncertainty.

First, let's look at the non-logicality and uncertainty of the superpositioner. If we only look at the reentry functions in Definition 3.1, there is no non-logicality or uncertainty. The problem lies in the reentry, and the reentry configurations formed as a result. In the superpositioner, the output of the reentry functions is also the input (in contrast to feedforward circuits), and the input and output in the superpositioner do not have a clear boundary (in contrast to recurrent circuits) - this is the fundamental characteristic of the superpositioner. That is to say, if a reentry configuration is not forcibly imposed on the superpositioner, the superpositioner itself is ambiguous; if a reentry configuration is forcibly imposed on the superpositioner, the superpositioner degenerates into an ordinary mapping of the N-dimensional Boolean space. However, the reentry configuration is not unique - a superpositioner has many reentry configurations, and none of these reentry configurations has superiority or priority, all of these reentry configurations are possible. Even for a simple superpositioner like the single node superpositioner, this is the case. It is precisely the non-uniqueness of the reentry configurations that brings uncertainty to the superpositioner. This uncertainty does not come from the outside, but is inevitably formed by the internal structure. Therefore, we should consider that in the superpositioner, all the intrinsic functions formed by the reentry configurations coexist, and the evaluations they form also coexist, which is non-logical. To reiterate, the reentry functions inside the superpositioner follow strict logic and can be strictly computed, but due to the reentry, non-logical components are formed, which are non-removable non-logical components. If we want to eliminate the non-logical components, we need to forcibly impose a reentry configuration, but because of the non-uniqueness of the reentry configurations, uncertainty is introduced. This non-logicality and uncertainty are fundamental properties of the superpositioner. These properties are indeed non-classical and non-logical, but they can be said to be extremely useful, and we want to explore how to make the most of these properties.

The non-logicality and uncertainty of the superpositioner leads to the uncertainty of the evaluations at the nodes in the superpositioner. If we focus on a certain node of the superpositioner, we can see that the evaluation at that node is not determined, and can only be determined after the reentry sequence is determined. Moreover, this evaluation will change as the reentry sequence changes. For example, for the single node superpositioner, which has only one node, when the reentry sequence is odd, the evaluation is $\neg b$, and when the reentry sequence is even, the evaluation is b. That is, the evaluation of the node oscillates between 0 and 1, and cannot be determined. Only when the reentry sequence is determined, is this value determined. It is precisely this kind of superpositioner, with these properties, that is required by many applications and should be formed when dealing with many situations. We will see later that although the single node superpositioner is simple, it can be used to generate/describe that inherent hesitation, and even the simplest superpositioner can play a very important role.

As another example, the Yin-Yang superpositioner: If we consider the node b_1, then all the evaluation functions at this node are: $b_1, b_1 \wedge b_2, b_1 \wedge \neg b_2, 0$; If we consider the node b_2, then all the evaluation functions at this node are: b_2, $b_2, b_1 \oplus b_2, \neg b_1 \wedge b_2$. That is, at the node b_1, there are 4 evaluation functions, while at the node b_2, there are 3 evaluation functions. This is regardless of the length of the reentry sequence. That is, these are only these intrinsic functions.

Therefore, we see that the superpositioner is completely different from feedforward functions (feedforward circuits). The action in feedforward functions (circuits) is one-way, and therefore deterministic, with cause and effect clearly separated. However, the superpositioner is different: because of the feedback, cause and effect lose their clear boundary. The consequence is that in the superpositioner, many functions are superimposed, which is fundamentally inexpressible and indescribable in classical computation. Faced with such a situation, the approach we adopt is to introduce reentry sequences, and after imposing a reentry sequence on the superpositioner, it degenerates into the classical case, at which point classical computation can proceed. However, in the superpositioner there are many reentry sequences, and none of them has any priority.

But this is only the case inside the superpositioner. Outside the superpositioner, it is completely possible to generate a tendency for the reentry sequences inside the superpositioner, and to utilize this tendency in conjunction with the superpositioner to accomplish certain tasks. This is what we will discuss next: disposition and the tool capable of disposition, i.e. the dispositioner.

Definition 3 (Disposition and Dispositioner). *Assuming superpositioner C is formed by nodes $T = \{b_1, b_2, \ldots, b_N\}$ and reentry functions $\{f_1, f_2, \ldots, f_N\}$, and give one reentry configuration: $S = (j_1, \ldots, j_K)$, we will get one N-dim Boolean mapping $h : B^N \to B^N, h = C \diamond S = f_{j_1} \ldots f_{j_K}$, and the j_1 component of the mapping is one intrinsic function, i.e., $g : B^N \to B, g = (C \diamond S)_{j_1}$, and this function is taking value at b_{j_1}, and this value taking is completely certain. In this sense, S resolve C, so that C is no longer superposition, but is degenerated to a Boolean function. We call such a process as disposition.*

Since the reentry configuration is not unique, to choose reentry could have tendence. The dispositioner is such a device that can choose reentry configuration with certain tendence, and to disposition accordingly. ■

Example 5 **(Disposition of Single Node Superpositioner).** Single node superpositioner has only one node. As above, all intrinsic function of the superpositioner has only $\{b, \neg b\}$. Thus, the disposition is to choose b or $\neg b$ with certain tendence, or super+dis forms a random device that osilate between b or $\neg b$. Such osilation with randomness is a very basic component in information processing. This example shows that even this very simple superpositioner can play one important role.

Example 6 **(Disposition of Yin-Yang Superpositioner).** Yin-Yang superpositioner has 2 nodes. As above, it has 7 intrinsic functions: $\{b_1, b_1 \wedge b_2, b_1 \wedge \neg b_2, 0, b_2, b_1 \oplus b_2, \neg b_1 \wedge b_2\}$. Among them, 4 functions (at the front) are intrinsic functions taking value at b_1, 3 functions (at the end) are intrinsic functions taking value at b_2. If we consider b_1, there are 4 functions related to this node. That is to say, function b_1 could related to function 0. This is quite surprising. Such a relation means: if we adjust reentry configuration, the function will slide from one to another, and easily. This is one very useful feature. Dispositioner of Yin-Yang superpositioner could allow us to utilize these features.

Just from these 2 simple superpositioner, we can see super+dis form a new type of information processing, which is very different from classical computation.

4 Conceiving Space and Its Contents

The superpositioner, intrinsic functions, and dispositioner all need to exist within a container. Only in this way can they collaborate to perform appropriate computations, and only within the container can various operations be performed on them. This container is called conceiving space.

Definition 4 (Conceiving Space). *The conceiving space is a container comprising several bits and Boolean functions acting upon these bits. It serves as a workspace where these bits and Boolean functions can interact and operate.* ∎

Several years ago, we introduced the conceiving space [3]. Before this paper, we believed that the main elements in the conceiving space were feedforward networks and feedforward functions. After introducing the superpositioner, we now clearly see that the conceiving space can integrate and coordinate well with the superpositioner. The superpositioner needs conceiving space as a container for its existence, while conceiving space also needs the superpositioner as its content. Perhaps the most important component of the conceiving space is the superpositioner, with other components revolving around the superpositioner. There could be multiple superpositioners in a conceiving space, and they may interact with each other in complex ways. With the superpositioner, the conceiving space becomes richer and more substantive.

We have seen earlier that although a superpositioner has only N reentry functions, there may be a great many intrinsic functions. Here we restate the definition of intrinsic functions to highlight them:

Definition 5 (Intrinsic Function). *Suppose C is a superpositioner with a scale of N and nodes $T = \{b_1, b_2, \ldots, b_N\}$. Then, all of its reentry configurations form a set, denoted as W. It is important to note that W is an infinite set. Corresponding to a reentry configuration $S \in W$, assuming $S = (j_1, \ldots, j_K)$, where $j_i \in [1, N], i = 1, \ldots, K$, and K is an integer of unlimited size, there exists a function $g : B^N \to B$, given by $g = (C \diamond S)_{j_1}$. This function takes a value at the node b_{j_1}, and it is an intrinsic function of C, referred to as the intrinsic function taking value at node b_{j_1}, or it is formed by the reentry configuration S. Specifically, the functions with all independent variables, such as $b_1, b_2, \ldots, b_N$, are also intrinsic functions. The collection of all intrinsic functions forms the set of intrinsic functions of C.* ∎

Note that it is entirely possible for different reentry configurations to form the same Boolean function g (possibly evaluated at different nodes, but still the same function). It is also entirely possible for the same Boolean function g to be evaluated at different nodes. Note also that if we fix a node, e.g. b_1, then all reentry configurations ending with 1, such as $(1, 2), (1, 3, 2), (1, 1, 4, 3)$ etc., will form an intrinsic function evaluated at b_1. These intrinsic functions are superimposed on the node b_1.

All intrinsic functions of the superpositioner are members of the conceiving space, meaning that if there is a superpositioner in the conceiving space, there will also be many intrinsic functions as members. It can be easily seen that it is precisely because of the intrinsic functions that the superpositioner becomes the core of the conceiving space. Surrounding a superpositioner, a great many Boolean functions can be formed, forming a large group of Boolean functions.

Without the superpositioner, it would be very difficult to express such a scale of Boolean function groups. For a superpositioner C, which Boolean functions are intrinsic in C? At a node b_j of C, how many Boolean functions are superimposed? These questions are extremely important, and absolutely non-trivial, reflecting the fundamental properties of the superpositioner and determining its functionality.

Note that in defining intrinsic functions, we only used nodes and did not consider the source of the values at the nodes. We know that in the conceiving space there are many Boolean functions, so if we connect a Boolean function to each node of the superpositioner, and then let the reentry configurations take effect, this will form a Boolean function. This is using the superpositioner to construct Boolean functions, which is an important function of the superpositioner. We have the following definition:

Definition 6 (Boolean Function built on Superpositioner). *Assuming a superpositioner C is formed by nodes $T = \{b_1, b_2, \ldots, b_N\}$, and reentry functions $\{f_1, f_2, \ldots, f_N\}$, and assuming a group of Boolean function $g_i : B^M \to B, i = 1, \ldots, N$. We connect g_i to nodes $b_i, i = 1, \ldots, N$, i.e. make the values at b_i is $g_i(x_1, \ldots, x_M)$. For any reentry configuration, $S = (j_1, \ldots, j_K)$, we get one intrinsic function $g : B^N \to B,\ g = (C \diamond S)_{j_1}$, note that the variables of g are $b_1, \ldots, b_N$, i.e., $g(b_1, \ldots, b_N) = (C \diamond S)_{j_1}(b_1, \ldots, b_N)$, we use $g_i(x_1, \ldots, x_M), i = 1, \ldots, N$ to replace $b_i, i = 1, \ldots, N$, we will get a Boolean function:*

$$h : B^M \to B,\ h = (C \diamond S)_{j_1}(g_1(x_1, \ldots, x_M), \ldots, g_N(x_1, \ldots, x_M))$$

We call $g_1, \ldots, g_N$ feedin function, and function h as Boolean function constructed on C by S. We denote this function as $h = C \diamond S \diamond (g_1, \ldots, g_N)$. Note, M is different from N, often M is much larger. ■

We can see that $h = (C \diamond S)_{j_1}(g_1(x_1, \ldots, x_M)$ is an intrinsic function but with its independent variables substituted by feedin functions. It is easy to see that in this way, through a superpositioner, a great many Boolean functions can be constructed. This is a general way of constructing Boolean functions in the conceiving space. All of these constructed Boolean functions are connected through the superpositioner. Let's look at an example.

Example 7 **(Constructing Boolean Functions).** First consider the single node superpositioner. Suppose $f : B^M \to B$ is any Boolean function, then through the single node superpositioner we can construct f and $\neg f$. In this way, these two functions are connected through the superpositioner. Moreover, through the dispositioner, we can form a certain probability selection between these two Boolean functions (an innate hesitation), as well as slide to the other (change to the opposite).

For the Yin-Yang superpositioner, since its intrinsic functions are: $\{b_1, b_1 \wedge b_2, b_1 \wedge \neg b_2, 0, b_2, b_1 \oplus b_2, \neg b_1 \wedge b_2\}$, it is easy to construct these Boolean functions: Suppose $f, g : B^M \to B$ are two Boolean functions, then $\{f, f \wedge g, f \wedge \neg g, 0, g, f \oplus g, \neg f \wedge g\}$ are all Boolean functions constructed on the Yin-Yang superpositioner. These Boolean functions are all connected through the Yin-Yang superpositioner, and it is easy to form probabilistic selections and sliding between these functions.

Of course, the functions constructed in the example are all very simple, but as examples, they can help us clearly see the roles of the superpositioner and the constructed functions. As the scale and complexity of the superpositioner increases, the functions constructed become very rich, and these functions are connected through the superpositioner, and probabilistic selections and sliding between them can also be obtained through the dispositioner. Therefore, constructing functions in the conceiving space through the previous definition is an important tool. The Boolean functions constructed in this way are closely related to parameterized Boolean functions. Let's first look at the definition of parameterized Boolean functions.

Definition 7 (Boolean Function with Parameters). *One Boolean function $\varphi : B^N \times B^J \to B$ can be viewed as a function on B^N with J parameters. We often write as $\varphi(x, p) : B^N \to B,\ x \in B^N, p \in B^J$.* ■

Example 8 **(Boolean Function with Parameters).** $f : B^2 \to B, f(x_1, x_2) = x_1 \wedge x_2$ is a very simple Boolean function. This function has no parameter. We can see one function related to f but with parameter: $\varphi(x_1, x_2, s) = x_1 \wedge (x_2 \oplus s)$. It is easy to see, if $s = 0$, $\varphi(x_1, x_2, 0) = f(x_1, x_2) = x_1 \wedge x_2$, while $s = 1$, $\varphi(x_1, x_2, 1) = f(x_1, x_2) = x_1 \wedge \neg x_2$. That is to say, for different parameter values, we will have different functions.

Note that the parameterized Boolean functions in the previous example can be included in the Boolean functions constructed by the Yin-Yang superposition body. Specifically, it is like this: when the parameter $s = 0$, φ becomes $b_1 \wedge b_2$, which is the intrinsic function obtained when the reentry configuration is $S = (1)$; when $s = 1$, φ becomes $b_1 \wedge \neg b_2$, which is the intrinsic function obtained when the reentry configuration is $S = (1, 2)$. That is to say, the Boolean functions included in this parameterized Boolean function can actually all be constructed on the Yin-Yang superpositioner. We can also say that this parameterized Boolean function can be completely expressed by the Yin-Yang superpositioner. In fact, we will see that this is a general case, that is, any parameterized Boolean function can find a superpositioner to completely express it. The following lemma proves this point.

Lemma 1 (Complete Expression). *Assuming $\varphi(x, p) : B^M \to B,\ x \in B^M, p \in B^J$ is a parameterized Boolean function, then there is a superpositioner C, and a group of feedin function $g_i : B^M \to B, i = 1, \ldots, N$, and a reentry configuration S_p so that $\varphi(x, p) = C \diamond S_p \diamond (g_1, \ldots, g_N)$.*

Proof: This lemma has no any restriction on superpositioner, so the existence of superpositioner and reentry function is obvious. We only need to set $N = 2^J$, and to do a sorting on B^J: $p_i \in B^J, i = 1, \ldots, N = 2^J$, then for every $p \in B^J$, choose $g_i : B^M \to B, g_i(x) = \varphi(x, p_i), i = 1, \ldots, N = 2^J$, thus $\varphi(x, p_i) = C \diamond S_{p_i} \diamond (g_1, \ldots, g_N)$, here the reentry configuration is $S_{p_i} = (0)$. ■

Of course, the proof is only a simple demonstration of existence, showing that complete expression can be achieved. Ideally, the superpositioner used to construct parameterized Boolean functions should use the smallest possible N. This is a difficult problem that should be left for further discussion.

This lemma shows that for any parameterized Boolean function, we can find a superpositioner and a set of feedin functions, such that for each parameter value, the Boolean function using that parameter is expressed as a Boolean function constructed on that superpositioner. That is, we express a set of Boolean functions as content constructed by a superpositioner. Since the superpositioner can completely express any parameterized Boolean function, the superpositioner can express much more content than parameterized Boolean functions, and significantly more. More importantly, parameterized Boolean functions are imposed from the outside, and it is difficult to do much with them. However, for content constructed by the superpositioner, much can be done via sliding and selection through reentry configuration. This point is crucial. There is another critical difference: in parameterized Boolean functions, different Boolean functions are separate, but in the Boolean functions constructed by the superpositioner, different Boolean functions are superimposed together. This superposition will play an extremely important role.

Parameterized Boolean functions can play an important role in computation. In [4], we defined an operator on parameterized Boolean functions, which we call the trial-and-error operator, and with this operator, problems that are extremely difficult to express can be expressed very clearly and concisely. This demonstrates the important role of parameterized Boolean functions. In fact, for a computational case, if the parameters are known in advance, an exponential saving can often be achieved. But how could the parameters be known in advance? This is a big problem. In fact, Turing's oracle machine is precisely the kind of machine that can know the parameters in advance, and parameterized Boolean functions are very closely related to Turing's oracle machine.

For the oracle machine, it can be viewed as two parts: one part is the Turing machine T, and the other part is the oracle O. Since O is always imposed on T from the outside, T cannot do anything to O, it can only follow and execute accordingly. However, for the superpositioner, it is different: the functions constructed by the superpositioner are constructed from the inside, and can be adjusted based on experience and results. In this sense, the superpositioner is more powerful than the oracle machine. Even more importantly, even for the oracle, the functions formed by different parameters are still separate and isolated, while the functions constructed by the superpositioner are superimposed together.

Given a superpositioner, there will be a corresponding set of intrinsic functions. For example, the intrinsic function set of the signle node superpositioner has 2 members, and the intrinsic function set of the Yin-Yang superpositioner has 7 members. The intrinsic function set also has unique and interesting internal structures. All of these are determined by the reentry functions of the superpositioner. But how do the reentry functions determine this structure? And what is this structure? We believe that understanding these questions will play an important role in our understanding of the superpositioner. However, we are currently unable to explore these questions in depth, and we will continue to ponder them.

In this way, we can see the rich content in the conceiving space. First, in the conceiving space there are a large number of nodes, connected by a large number of Boolean functions. These Boolean functions can form feedforward networks, or possibly form recurrent networks, and more interestingly, these Boolean functions can form reentry, producing superpositioner. And because of the superpositioner, more functions can be constructed, and parameterized functions can be formed. There are also dispositioners and the dispositions formed by dispositioners. This makes the conceiving space even richer. We believe that in such a conceiving space, some computations that are difficult to realize in classical computation may become realizable (see next section).

5 Application and Realization

We believe that the superpositioner + dispositioner, as a new type of information processing model and computation model, will play a significant role. Now let's imagine some possible applications of the superpositioner + dispositioner.

Programming and Learning

By constructing Boolean functions on the superposition body as defined earlier, we actually form a new way of programming and learning. Suppose there is a superposition body C. If we choose reentry functions $g_i : B^M \to B, i = 1, \ldots, N$, and then select a reentry configuration $S = (j_1, \ldots, j_K)$, we obtain an intrinsic function $f = C \diamond S \diamond (g_1, \ldots, g_N)$. This process can be seen as a form of programming, achieved by selecting reentry functions and a reentry configuration. It's a novel programming approach. If we adopt a data-driven method to obtain reentry functions and a reentry configuration, this process can also be seen as learning. It's a novel learning method.

This usage, namely fixing the reentry configuration, reduces the superpositioner to a fixed Boolean function. This is a very powerful way to form new Boolean functions, with low cost, requiring only the selection of reentry functions and a reentry configuration. This can be compared to other programming and machine learning methods. Traditional manual programming requires expressing a Boolean function using logic gates and then writing it into a program; for machine learning, a large dataset (a suitable sample set) is needed, and then machine learning methods are used to form the Boolean function based on this data. Compared to these methods, programming and learning based on the superpositioner are much easier. In fact, a superpositioner itself includes some kind of inclination, making programming and learning consistent with this inclination easier. This programming and learning method is low-cost and can be used for very rapid programming or learning. Is it possible that programming and learning based on the superposition body are widely present in the human brain or animal brains? This idea is worth serious consideration.

Intrinsic Sensations
Referring to example 3.5, we can see that a reflexive superpositioner can be used to generate a simple but extremely important intrinsic sensation, namely hesitation. For more complex intrinsic sensations, more complex superpositioners are required. Forming various intrinsic sensations within an intelligent agent plays a very important role in the agent's subjectivity.

Analogy and Association
We hope to form analogy and association within intelligent agents, and we also hope to trigger, control, and utilize them. Classical computing does not provide a universal method to form analogy and association, let alone control and utilize them. From the preliminary discussion of the superpositioner, we see its potential capabilities. Analogy and association seem to exist within the superpositioner. Taking the Yin-Yang superpositioner as an example, as seen in example 3.6, at node b_1, there are 4 intrinsic functions, including $b_1 \wedge b_2$ and 0. These two functions are very different, but because they are connected through the superpositioner, sliding the reentry sequence also slides the intrinsic functions, and sliding the reentry sequence is very easy. Moreover, these two functions are superimposed. This is very close to our conception of analogy and association. Therefore, if we have some objects and want to achieve analogy and association between them, we need an appropriate superpositioner that connects the intrinsic functions related to these objects (how they are connected can vary widely). After achieving this, the analogy between objects becomes the sliding between two intrinsic functions, and the association between objects becomes the jumping from one intrinsic function to another. This is difficult to support with classical computing, but it can be easily supported by the superpositioner.

Analogy and association, especially how to implement them in artificial intelligence agents, have been long-standing issues in artificial intelligence and cognitive science. Now with the superpositioner, we see a new horizon, which is very meaningful.

Forming Understanding
What exactly is an intelligent agent's formation of understanding of something? What is understanding? For these questions, we provide a unique perspective here using the superpositioner. Typically, something in an intelligent agent will acquire some representation, which can be processed by the agent. However, even if this representation can undergo very comprehensive and accurate information processing, it is difficult to say that the agent understands this thing. This is because, for some reason, there may be slight changes in the representation within the agent, resulting in errors in information processing, which means the agent cannot be said to understand. In the usual sense, achieving understanding of something in an intelligent agent requires a high standard. However, let's imagine this scenario: the representation of something within an intelligent agent can reach a certain superpositioner, where the superpositioner integrates

information related to this thing, and then, in subsequent information processing, it is not the representations themselves that directly act, but rather the intrinsic functions in the superpositioner that act. In this case, the information processing of this thing by the agent becomes much more comprehensive. This is closer to our conception of understanding.

What understanding is, has also been a long-standing issue in artificial intelligence and cognitive science. With the superpositioner, we should be able to advance our understanding of understanding in intelligent agents.

Generating Initiative

The initiative of an intelligent agent is its ability to surpass predetermined programs and take new actions. If an intelligent agent is entirely based on classical computing, it's unlikely to generate initiative because everything in classical computing is predetermined. However, in the superpositioner, the situation is very different. In the superpositioner, all intrinsic functions are superimposed, so all intrinsic functions are possible, and the number of intrinsic functions may be very large. This creates the possibility for initiative. Of course, how initiative is achieved still requires further work, but the superpositioner allows for initiative, while classical computing excludes it, which is clear.

As mentioned earlier, it is precisely because of the pursuit of initiative within intelligent agents that we have come to the discussion of the superpositioner.

Participating in the Formation of Subjectivity

The subjectivity of an intelligent agent is its internal inclinations, various inclinations, such as intrinsic sensations and hesitation mentioned earlier, which may be numerous. It should be noted that without the superpositioner and relying entirely on classical computing, inclinations can still be formed. However, the superpositioner can greatly assist in this regard. For example, for a superpositioner, we know that a group of intrinsic functions is superimposed on certain nodes, forming a tendency, namely, the values of these nodes can only be determined by this group of intrinsic functions. Expressing this tendency using classical computing is quite difficult.

In addition to imagining some separate applications, we should also imagine the joint use of these applications within intelligent agents. It is very likely that in an intelligent agent, several superpositioners + dispositioners need to work together to achieve good results. In the conceiving space, there may be several super+dis pairs, some of which are used to form motivation, some are used to generate intrinsic sensations, some are used to form analogies and associations, some are used to generate initiative, some serve as execution parts, some are used for novel programming, and so on. These super+dis pairs working together can form a very capable intelligent agent. This is our basic idea.

We have discussed the potential applications of the superpositioner above. Now we will briefly discuss the physical implementation of the superpositioner. Both the superpositioner and the dispositioner are mathematical objects, so it is natural to start with mathematical discussions and then consider physical implementation. We already know that the superpositioner and the dispositioner cannot be perfectly described by classical computing, but we know that there are superpositioner in the brain (it is precisely the stimulation from neuroscience work that inspired us to form the concept of the superpositioner), and the superpositioners in the brain play an important role in information processing. Therefore, we have sufficient reason to believe that the physical implementation of the superpositioner can be achieved. There are two approaches to implementing the superpositioner and the dispositioner: hardware and software.

Let's first consider the software approach. Current computing software operates within the framework of classical computing, so it is not possible to fully implement arbitrary superpositioner and dispositioner with software. However, it is possible to use software to simulate superpositioner and dispositioner to some extent. The key here is the scale of the superpositioner. If the scale of the superpositioner is increased/increased the complexity of the reentry functions, there will be a very large number of intrinsic functions. At this point, it becomes practically impossible to simulate all intrinsic functions with random variables. Therefore, in practice, the simulated random variables can only cover some intrinsic functions (and the quantity is very small). This is feasible. However, the limitations of software simulation are evident. The superpositioner contains a rich set of intrinsic functions, but software simulation can only select a few to simulate. What to choose? This is a dilemma. This dilemma is the dilemma of classical computing. This is also why the superpositioner + dispositioner surpasses classical computing.

Now let's look at the hardware approach. The superposition body itself is non-logical, which makes it impossible to use existing hardware methods to implement a complete superpositioner, because existing hardware methods are still within the scope of classical computing. The superpositioner requires all intrinsic functions to be calculated simultaneously and superimposed, which is currently not possible with any hardware. This requires us to explore and utilize various physical properties, invent new physical devices, to implement the superpositioner concretely. However, one thing is certain: the capabilities of the human brain indicate that such hardware exists, and we need to invent and create it. When new hardware appears, matching software will also emerge. At that time, superpositioners can be implemented at a new level with software and hardware working together.

As neuroscience researchers have discovered, there is reentry in the human brain and animal brains, so there must be superpositioners. In the brain, the superpositioner must be a powerful information processing device, otherwise evolution would not allow such a device to exist. On the other hand, studying the superpositioner will further enhance the ability of information processing. Therefore, the achievements of neuroscience and consciousness science should be combined with the research on the superpositioner, which can greatly promote the development of both directions.

6 Comments

1. The preceding discussion indicates that the information processing formed by the super+dis possesses a more powerful information processing capability

than Turing computation. If resource consumption is not taken into account, Turing computation can also simulate the information processing formed by the super+dis to some extent. However, this is only a simulation and cannot be fully reproduced. Moreover, such simulation requires much higher resource consumption. Therefore, we should incorporate the computation formed by the super+dis into the framework of computation, which will greatly enhance the computational capability.

2. Turing proposed the oracle machine very early (within two or three years after proposing the Turing machine). The oracle machine model can explain many computational problems. However, the oracle machine is external to the Turing machine, so it is elusive within the computational model. In contrast, by using the super+dis, parameterized Boolean functions (oracle machines) naturally emerge within the model. Therefore, parameterized Boolean functions can develop, improve, and evolve within the model, bringing about significant capabilities.

3. Intelligent agents can be formed solely by Turing computation, meaning that all computational modules within the intelligent agent are Turing computational programs. Indeed, all intelligent agents to date have been like this. However, if an intelligent agent possesses one or more superpositioners, it can acquire stronger capabilities. We introduce the concept of a conceiving space, which contains superpositioners. It is conceivable that for certain difficult computational tasks (such as solving SAT, solving NPP, etc.), if we want to exceed computational complexity, we cannot use Turing computational programs (or algorithms) to process them. Instead, we should employ an intelligent agent with special capabilities. This intelligent agent contains a conceiving space with one or more superpositioners, which can generate good subjective and proactive abilities for the computational task, thereby enabling the intelligent agent to exceed computational complexity.

4. The computational model formed by the super+dis is very different from Turing computation. Turing computation is deterministic (although it can also simulate nondeterminism), while the superposition body is inherently nondeterministic. The two are fundamentally different. Due to the uncertainty introduced by the reentry function, the superpositioner must be intrinsically stochastic. However, the computation formed by the super+dis is very different from traditional methods of introducing randomness from the outside. Firstly, the randomness of such computation is determined by the structure of the reentry function, so it also has a clear structure. Secondly, it has a learning component that can be improved through learning. Therefore, such computation has the following characteristics: it has randomness, but it also has clear directionality, and this directionality can be adjusted through learning. It is difficult for traditional methods of introducing randomness from the outside to achieve these characteristics.

5. The super+dis appears to have a very close connection with quantum computation. From various aspects of these two computations, we can feel this connection. Exploring this direction should be very meaningful, and we will report our thoughts on this direction later.

6. The superpositioner has rich connotations. In this paper, we use reentry configurations to capture these connotations. However, it is certain that reentry configurations do not exhaust the connotations of the superpositioner; there must be many connotations that reentry configurations cannot touch upon. We believe that reentry configurations are first-order tools, and we should work on them first. We look forward to exploring higher-order tools and connotations after the success brought by reentry configurations.

7. In this paper, we only discussed the superpositioner based on Boolean functions. Boolean functions are only one kind of computation model. It is entirely believable that superpositioners can also be established on other computation models, that is to say, it is possible to build superpositioners using modern programming languages. Of course, this is only a kind of simulation-like expression because the superpositioner is non-logical, and its expression is not the kind that can be executed by a computer; it can only be partially simulated.

8. The superpositioner as a whole cannot be explained and described by classical logic, nor can it be handled by classical computation. However, parts inside the superpositioner, namely, the reentry functions, are completely in line with classical logic and classical computation. However, if we forcibly apply a reentry configuration from the outside, the superpositioner degenerates into classical logic. In this way, it actually provides a clue: Is classical logic imposing a configuration on complex things from the outside? Is classical logic absolutely superior to everything else? According to the capabilities of the superpositioner, it is very likely that the superpositioner is another kind of thinking tool, another kind of cognitive tool, complementary to classical logic. The Yin-Yang thinking and Five-Elements thinking in Chinese culture may be examples of applying the superpositioner (Yin-Yang superpositioner and Five-Elements superpositioner). These are very interesting trains of thought.

9. Based on the pursuit of surpassing computational complexity and inspired by consciousness science, we propose the superpositioer. This model currently exists as a mathematical model and has not yet formed a physical model, although we believe that a physical form of the superpositioner can be established. However, we still need to work further to demonstrate that this model can indeed be used to exceed computational complexity, at least in theory. We also need to work further to explain why this model can achieve functions such as categorization, association, understanding, and activity. In this way, the significance of this model will be demonstrated.

References

1. Xiong, C.: Exceeding Computational Complexity - Trial and Error, Dynamics and Intelligence (2022). https://www.researchgate.net/. (in Chinese)
2. Xiong, C.: Subjectivity and Dynamcis of Intelligent Agent (2023). https://www.researchgate.net/. (in Chinese)
3. Xiong, C.: Universal learning machine - principle, method, and engineering model. In: International Conference of Intelligence Science, Beijing (2018)

4. Xiong, C.: Sampling and Complexity of Partition Function. arxiv.org (2021)
5. Russel, P.N.S.: Artificial Intelligence: A Modern Approach, 3rd edn. Prentice Hall, Upper Saddle River (2020)
6. Findlay, G., Marshall, W., Albantakis, L., Mayner, W., Koch, C., Tononi, G.: Dissociating intelligence from consciousness in artificial systems - implications of integrated information theory (2019)
7. Koch, C.: The Feeling of Life Itself. The MIT Press, Cambridge (2019)

Factor Analog Reasoning Model and Its Solution Research

Tianyuan Wang(✉), Fanhui Zeng, and Sixing Ren

Liaoning Technical University, Fuxin 123000, China
954007684@qq.com

Abstract. Analogical reasoning is one of the most common forms of thinking that people use existing knowledge to reason, and it is a key phenomenon of human intelligence. However, when analogical reasoning is faced with simple reasoning tasks, the result is not accurate. Computationally complex problems arise when faced with complex inference tasks in big data. In order to solve the problem of analogical reasoning, based on the $[U, I]$ image matching principle in factor space theory, this paper proposes a factor analogical reasoning model, gives the steps of factor analogical reasoning algorithm, analyzes an example in UCI data set, and compares and analyzes the factor analogical reasoning algorithm proposed in this paper with the factor analysis algorithm. The results show that the factor analogy reasoning algorithm proposed in this paper can realize the effective reasoning of the analogy reasoning problem, and the algorithm has the advantages of accurate calculation results and short calculation time. The conclusion of analogical reasoning based on factor space expands the theory and application of factor space.

Keywords: Factor space theory · Analogical reasoning · $[U,I]$ image matching pair · Factor analysis algorithm

1 Introduction

This chapter will introduce the research status of analogical reasoning and factor space and lead to the core of this paper - factor analogical reasoning.

Factor space is a theory created by Professor Wang Peizhuang in the 1980s to solve the causal relationship and knowledge representation between things. At present, the research based on factor space theory has been widely used in different fields. Lu Jinhui, Guo Sicong et al. [1] applied factor space theory to decision making and put forward the expression form of concept interval set. He Ping [2] applied it to the mathematics of cybercrime, providing a quantitative analysis method for the study of cybercrime. Liu Haitao, Fu GUI et al. [3] applied the factor space theory to the prediction method of coal and gas outburst. Duan Yanlin [4] applied it to the comprehensive quality evaluation of college students.

In recent years, analogical reasoning has been paid more and more attention by researchers in cognitive science, artificial intelligence, philosophy and linguistics. At

Published by Springer Nature Switzerland AG 2025
Z. Shi et al. (Eds.): ICIS 2024, IFIP AICT 720, pp. 132–142, 2025.
https://doi.org/10.1007/978-3-031-71253-1_10

present, from the perspective of logic, the domestic research on analogical reasoning is mainly carried out from two aspects [5]: First, the study of analogical reasoning in ancient China. For example, Jin Rongdong [6] discussed the similarities and differences between the inference theory in ancient China and the analogical reasoning in Western logic. Ren Xiaoming et al. [7] analyzed the inductive characteristics of Chinese "class inference" logic, and pointed out the dilemma and solution strategy of the common sense model of analogical reasoning. XIE [8] systematically explained the analogy argumentation in ancient China. Second, combining the existing theories at home and abroad, further expand the theory of analogical reasoning. For example, Lu Yunrong [9] et al. discussed the argumentation and argumentation types of analogical reasoning. Hu Hao [10] analyzed Bartha's correlation model theory and summarized the characteristics and evaluation criteria of analogy demonstration. Jin Li et al.[11] conducted an in-depth discussion on the nature of analogical reasoning, argumentation schema and its application in the legal field. From the computer field, the research of analogical reasoning at home and abroad mainly focuses on how artificial intelligence simulates the process of human analogical cognitive mechanism. In China, Yibo et al. studied the automatic program of analogical reasoning [12]. Zhao Qinping et al. explained the calculation model of analogical reasoning in detail, divided analogical reasoning into four programs: association, refinement, matching and transformation, and gave the principles to be followed by each program [13].

The domestic research in the field of analogical reasoning is lack of theory and systematicness, and the result of simple analogical reasoning is not accurate when dealing with inference tasks. When dealing with large-scale data or complex inference tasks, computationally complex problems arise, and comprehensive and in-depth theoretical analysis and practice-oriented application attempts need to be carried out. However, factor space provides a unified reasoning problem solving platform for analog reasoning. Therefore, this paper will model and solve the analogical reasoning problem based on the factor space theory. The research of analog reasoning based on factor space theory will help people to solve problems and learn new knowledge by using specific knowledge, and can effectively solve problems such as inaccurate results and complicated calculation of analog reasoning.

2 Analogical Reasoning

This chapter will introduce the basic concepts and related knowledge of analogical reasoning.

Analogical reasoning is a method of solving a problem by mapping it to another known problem. It is based on the concept of similarity, the idea that if two problems are similar in some way, then the solution to one problem may also work for the other. Analogical reasoning is widely used in many fields, including science, engineering, business, decision making, etc. By connecting a problem to a known situation or experience, it can help people solve new problems more quickly and efficiently, while also facilitating the transfer of knowledge and the accumulation of experience.

The general model of analogical reasoning can be expressed as:

The general steps of analogical reasoning are as follows:

(1) Identify the problem: First identify what the current problem is.
(2) Look for analogies: Look for a known problem that is similar in some way to the problem at hand. This analogy problem is usually one that has already been solved with relevant experience.
(3) Analyze the similarities: Compare the current problem with the analogy problem and find the similarities between them. These similarities may include the structure of the problem, its characteristics, its solution, etc.
(4) Apply analogy: Apply the solution or strategy of analogy problem to the current problem. This may involve adapting or adapting the approach to the analogy problem to fit the specific needs of the problem at hand.
(5) Verification and adjustment: After applying the analogy method, it is necessary to verify its effectiveness and adjust or correct it as needed. This may require further experimentation, testing, or analysis.

Analogical reasoning is common in daily life. For example, I have a cat that loves to sleep. When I see a friend's cat at a friend's house, I may think that the friend's cat also loves to sleep. This leads to a simple reasoning structure: if one cat sleeps, then all cats do. This reasoning process is a common form of reasoning in everyday life, but obviously this reasoning process does not guarantee the accuracy of the results. The existence of one or more things with certain characteristics in common does not mean that all characteristics are the same between them. In order to make the results of analogical reasoning more convincing, the confirmed similarity gives us good reason to believe that there is further similarity between the two things, and this similarity helps to solve the unknown problem. Of course, the results of analogical reasoning are not always inaccurate.

Analogical reasoning, therefore, is based on previously acquired knowledge of a system as a means of conjecture about another similar system, the objective basis of which lies in the general connection between the elements of things, processes, and systems, as well as in the objective basis for comparison between these connections.

3 Factors and Factor Space

This chapter will introduce the basic concepts of factors and factor Spaces.

In 1982, Mr. Wang Peizhuang [14] founded "factor space" and proposed the term "factor". The "factor" defined in factor space is not consistent with the "attribute" proposed by German mathematician Wille [15] and Polish mathematician Pawlak [16]. Where Wille's "attribute" refers to the attribute value, Pawlak's "attribute" refers to the attribute name. A factor in a factor space is a mapping that maps an object to one of its attributes (or phase values).

Definition 1. Factor is a mapping

$$f : D \to I(f) \tag{1}$$

Here, D is called the domain of definition or discourse of f, and $I(f)$ is called the domain of phase or information of f.

When distinguishing between factors and attributes, it is necessary to clarify the qualitative differences between the two. Attributes are usually static statements that can directly ask yes or no, such as, "Is this car red?" Factors, on the other hand, are dynamic concepts that guide people's thinking and don't lend themselves to right and wrong descriptions, such as, "Is a car a color?" Although this distinction is not absolute, it will be transformed into a factor or attribute in different contexts. For example, the "evaluation criteria" as a factor to examine a garment, its phase can include color, style and price. These are static properties, but once we choose price as our focus and can subdivide it into cheap, moderate, and expensive, price becomes a derived evaluation factor with the phase domain {cheap, moderate, expensive}. Therefore, in order to accurately understand the factors, we need to clarify the phase domain of a given factor. When the phase domain of a given factor is defined, a clear distinction can be made between factors and attributes.

Factor space theory is a method of factor analysis of any object or behavior. It divides a thing into several dimensions, analyzes and measures each factor separately, and finally synthesizes each factor to form a factor space. Factor space is a coordinate frame with factor as the axis, and anything can be abstracted as a point on factor space. It is a universal framework for describing things.

Given a set of simple factors $\underline{F} = \underline{\{f_1, f_2, \cdots, f_n\}}$ defined on the domain U, the power $F = P(\underline{F})$ is the set of all subsets composed of simple factors, and any subset $\{f_{(1)}, f_{(2)}, \cdots, f_{(k)}\} \subseteq F$ is a complex factor defined on U, and they form a factor space.

Definition 2. $\underline{\phi} = (U, \underline{F}) = (U, \underline{f_1}, \underline{f_2}, \cdots, \underline{f_m})$ is called a element space on U, and if for any $\{\underline{f_{(1)}}, \underline{f_{(2)}}, \cdots, \underline{f_{(k)}}\} \subseteq F (0 \leq \overline{k} \leq m)$ there is

$$I(\{\underline{f_{(1)}}, \underline{f_{(2)}}, \cdots, \underline{f_{(k)}}\}) = I(\underline{f_{(1)}}) \times I(\underline{f_{(2)}}) \times \cdots \times I(\underline{f_{(k)}}) \tag{2}$$

$\underline{f_1}, \underline{f_2}, \cdots, \underline{f_m}$ is called element or simple factor; If $f_1, f_2, \cdots, f_n (n \leq 2^m)$ is a set of elements, then $\overline{\phi} = (U, f_1, f_2, \cdots, f_n)$ is called the $\underline{\phi}$-factor space.

4 Factor Analog Reasoning Model

This chapter will introduce the factor analog reasoning model.

Analogical reasoning model can help people solve new problems effectively, and also help to transfer knowledge and accumulate experience, but it also has some shortcomings. When dealing with simple analogical reasoning tasks, the result is not accurate. Computationally complex problems arise when dealing with large-scale data or complex inference tasks. Therefore, this paper puts forward the factor analog reasoning model, which can effectively solve the problems of inaccurate results and complicated calculation.

The general form of factor analogy reasoning model is:

Inference rule 1 If the conditional factor f_1是a_{11}且f_2是a_{12}且L 且f_n是a_{1n} of the object u_1, then the resulting factor g is b_1.

Inference rule 2 If the conditional factor f_1是a_{21}且f_2是a_{22}且L 且f_n是a_{2n} of the object u_2, then the resulting factor g is b_2.

Inference rule 3 If the conditional factor f_1是a_{31}且f_2是a_{32}且L 且f_n是a_{3n} of the object u_3, then the resulting factor g is b_3.

……

Inference rule *m* If the conditional factor f_1是a_{m1}且f_2是a_{m2}且L 且f_n是a_{mn} of the object u_m, then the resulting factor g is b_m.

Inference rules can be abbreviated as:

$$u_1 : a_{11} \wedge a_{12} \wedge \cdots \wedge a_{1n} \rightarrow b_1$$
$$u_2 : a_{21} \wedge a_{22} \wedge \cdots \wedge a_{2n} \rightarrow b_2$$
$$u_3 : a_{31} \wedge a_{32} \wedge \cdots \wedge a_{3n} \rightarrow b_3$$
$$\cdots\cdots$$
$$u_m : a_{m1} \wedge a_{m2} \wedge \cdots \wedge a_{mn} \rightarrow b_m$$

(Where "∧" stands for "conjunctive", conjunctive makes the division of factors superimposed and divided more finely.)

Factor analog reasoning rule 1 If the conditional factor of object A is most similar to that of object u_1 in inference rule 1, then the resulting factor g is b_1;

Factor analog reasoning rule 2 If the conditional factor of object B is most similar to that of object u_2 in inference rule 2, then the resulting factor g is b_2;

Factor analog reasoning rule 3 If the conditional factor of object C is most similar to that of object u_3 in inference rule 3, then the resulting factor g is b_3;

……

Factor analog reasoning rule *m* If the conditional factor of object Z is most similar to that of object u_m in inference rule m, then the resulting factor g is b_m.

The rule of factor analogy reasoning can be abbreviated as:

$$A \sim u_1 \rightarrow b_1$$
$$B \sim u_2 \rightarrow b_2$$
$$C \sim u_3 \rightarrow b_3$$
$$\cdots\cdots$$
$$Z \sim u_m \rightarrow b_m$$

5 Factor Analog Reasoning Algorithm

This chapter will introduce the principle and steps of factor analogical reasoning algorithm.

1) Algorithm principle:

Analogical reasoning is a process of reasoning based on the similarity between things and inferring that they are the same in other factors through comparison. In reasoning problems, the hierarchical difference between the factors will be reflected in the process of solving the problem. Factor space provides a unified platform for solving inference problems in analogical reasoning. The image matching pair $[U, I]$ and its focused truth matrix $\mathbf{T}$ are proposed as effective solving tools for analogical reasoning. Therefore, the definition of $[U, I]$ image matching pair and focusing truth matrix $\mathbf{T}$ is proposed as follows:

Definition 3. Given factor space (U, F), object set $U = \{u_1, u_2, \cdots, u_m\}(m \geq 1)$, factor set $F = \{f_1, f_2, \cdots, f_n\}(n \geq 1)$, if for any $j \in \{1, 2, \cdots, n\}$, f_j have the same form of phase domain

$$I = I(f_1) = I(f_2) = \cdots = I(f_n) = \{a_1, a_2, \cdots, a_k, \cdots, a_n\} \tag{3}$$

and have a common concern for one of the phases a_k, , then $[U, I]$ is called an image matching pair from U to I, referred to as pairing.

Definition 4. Let a_k be called the focused phase of $[U, I]$ image matching pair or the co-focused phase of F, referred to as the focused phase.

Definition 5. Let the matrix $\mathbf{T}$ be called the focused truth matrix on the $[U, I]$ image matching pairs.

$$t_{ij} = t(f_j(u_i) = a_k) \tag{4}$$

$t(f_j(u_i) = a_k)$ corresponds to the truth value of the proposition "$f_j(u_i) = a_k$". The focused truth matrix is a Boolean matrix composed of logical truth and logical false values.

The "image" in the image matching pair refers to the object in U, and the "phase" refers to the common focusing phase of F. The image matching pair distributes the human attention force from U to the focusing phase a_k, which is transformed into seeking the logical truth value of $x = a_k$, so that the factor analogical reasoning is transformed into the solution of the focused knitting matrix. This paper gives the following definition for the solving process of factor analog reasoning model:

Definition 6. Let $H^F = \{H^{f_1}, H^{f_2}, \cdots, H^{f_n}\}$ be called a partition over U determined by factor F, if $H^{f_1}, H^{f_2}, \cdots, H^{f_n}$ is a set of nonempty subsets of U and the following conditions are met:

(1) $H^{f_1} \cup H^{f_2} \cup \cdots \cup H^{f_n} = U$
(2) For any $i, j \in \{1, 2, \cdots, n\}$, if $i \neq j$, then $H^{f_i} \cap H^{f_j} = \emptyset$.

Definition 7. In a reasoning problem, $F = \{f_1, f_2, \cdots, f_n\}(n \geq 1)$ in factor set $f_1, f_2, \cdots f_n$ is a factor and $g = \{g_1 = 0, g_2 = 1\}$ is a phase domain of the same form that f_j both have, then the divisions determined by F and I on U are $H^F = \{H^{f_1}, H^{f_2}, \cdots, H^{f_n}\}$ and $H^g = \{H^{g_1}, H^{g_2}\}$ respectively, then $\mathbf{P}$ is a random truth matrix on $[U, I]$ pairing. Where

$$\mathbf{P} = \begin{bmatrix} p_{11}\ p_{12} \cdots p_{1n} \\ p_{21}\ p_{22} \cdots p_{2n} \\ p_{31}\ p_{32} \cdots p_{3n} \\ p_{41}\ p_{42} \cdots p_{4n} \end{bmatrix}_{4 \times n} \tag{5}$$

$p_{1j} = \frac{|H^{f_j} \cap H^{g_1}|}{|H^{f_j}|}$, $p_{4j} = \frac{|H^{f_j} \cap H^{g_2}|}{|H^{f_j}|}$, $p_{2j} = 1 - p_{1j}$ and $p_{3j} = 1 - p_{4j}$. That is, p_{1j} is the probability that factor f_j is false in the phase domain g_1.

Definition 8. In the inference problem, let W_j be the integrity of factor f_j, and the larger the value of W_j, the greater the influence of factor f_j on resulting factor g, where

$$W_j = \frac{1}{4}\sum_{i=1}^{4}\sum_{j=1}^{n} p_{ij}^2 \quad (6)$$

Definition 9. In inference problems, the importance of α_j as a factor or indicator relative to a thing is called weight, and it is also the result obtained after normalization of the integrity of factor f_j, where

$$\alpha_j = \frac{W_j}{\sum_{j=1}^{n} W_j}, j = 1, 2, \cdots, n, \quad (7)$$

And the linear combination $y = \sum_{j=1}^{n} \alpha_j f_j$ of weights and factors can be obtained.

Definition 10. Let $d(x_i, y_j)$ be the distance between the test sample result $x_i(i = 1, 2, \cdots, l)$ and the training sample result $y_j(j = 1, 2, \cdots, m)$, where

$$d(x_i, y_j) = \sqrt{(x_i - y_j)^2} \quad (8)$$

2) Algorithm steps:
Step 1. According to the given problem, determine the object set $U = \{u_1, u_2, \cdots, u_m\}(m \geq 1)$ and factor set $F = \{f_1, f_2, \cdots, f_n\}(n \geq 1)$ of the training sample, and find the phase domain $I = I(f_1) = I(f_2) = \cdots = I(f_n) = \{a_1, a_2, \cdots, a_k, \cdots, a_K\}$ of the same form that the factors f_j all have, and have common concern for a certain phase a_k. At this point, a_k (focused phase) can be written, and a $[U, I]$ image matching pair from U to I can be determined. By determining the matching pairs of a_k and $[U, I]$ images, we can write the focusing truth matrix $\mathbf{T}$ on the matching pairs of $[U, I]$ images.

Step 2. By dividing conditional factors and resulting factor, the random truth matrix $\mathbf{P}$ of $[U, I]$ image matching pair is determined.

Step 3. Calculate the integrity $W_1, W_2, \cdots, W_n$ of each conditional factor $f_1, f_2, \cdots, f_n$;

Step 4. Calculate the weight $\alpha_1, \alpha_2, \cdots, \alpha_n$ of each conditional factor $f_1, f_2, \cdots, f_n$;

Step 5. Calculate the result $x_i(i = 1, 2, \cdots, l)$ of the test sample and the result $y_j(j = 1, 2, \cdots, m)$ of the training sample, calculate the distance $d(x_i, y)$ between x_i and y, and find the y_j with the smallest distance from x_i; Then according to the calculated distance and the factor analog reasoning model, it can be inferred that the result factor g in the test sample is equal to the result factor b_i $(i = 1, 2, \cdots, m)$ in the training sample.

6 Example Analysis

The factor analogical reasoning algorithm was used to analyze the iris data in UCI database, and the algorithm was compared with the factor analysis algorithm.

1) Problem Description

The method proposed in this paper was used to analyze the Iris data set provided by UCI database. 10 data of Iris Setosa (mountain iris) and Iris Versicolour (color-changing iris) in the data set were randomly selected as training samples, and the remaining 80 data were used as test samples. The object set of the training sample is $U=\{u_1, u_2, \cdots, u_m\}(m = 20)$, factor set $F = \{f_1, f_2, \cdots, f_n\}(n = 4)$, f_1 = sepal length, f_2 = sepal width, f_3 = petal length, f_4 = petal width. Where, f_j represents the jth factor corresponding to all iris plants in object set U.

For factor analysis, f_1 represents the length of sepals corresponding to all iris plants in object set U, and the length of sepals of iris plants ranges from 4.3 to 7. The same attribute in factor "sepal length" is classified into one category, with a total of 16 categories. f_2 represents the sepal widths corresponding to all iris plants in object set U, and the sepal widths of iris plants range from 2.0 to 4.4. The same attribute in the factor "sepal width" is classified into one category, with a total of 13 categories. f_3 represents the corresponding petal length of all iris plants in object set U, and the petal length of iris plants ranges from 1.0 to 5.1. The same attribute in the factor "petal length" is classified into one category, with a total of 11 categories. f_4 represents the petal widths corresponding to all iris plants in object set U, and the petal widths of iris plants range from 0.1 to 1.8. The same attribute in the factor "petal width" is classified into one category, and there are 9 categories in total.

For factor analogical reasoning algorithm, f_1 = sepal length, $I(f_1)$ = sepal length = {long, short}, taking "long" as the focusing phase, then $I(f_1)$ can be simplified to {1 = long, 0 = short}; f_2 = sepal width, $I(f_2)$ = sepal width = {wide, narrow}, take "wide" as the focusing phase, then $I(f_2)$ can be simplified to {1 = wide, 0 = narrow}; f_3 = petal length, $I(f_3)$ = petal length = {long, short}, take "long" as the focused phase, so $I(f_3)$ can be simplified to {1 = long, 0 = short}; f_4 = petal width, $I(f_4)$ = petal width = {wide, narrow}, taking "wide" as the focused phase, then $I(f_4)$ can be simplified to {1 = wide, 0 = narrow}. For the above four factors, their phase domain can be unified as $I = I(f_1) = I(f_2) = I(f_3) = I(f_4) = \{1^*, 0\}$.

2) Problem model establishment.

The following rules can be deduced from the training sample:

Inference rule 1 If the conditional factor f_1是a_{11}且f_2是a_{12}且f_3是a_{13}且f_4是a_{14} of the object u_1, then the resulting factor g is b_1.

Inference rule 2 If the conditional factor f_1是a_{21}且f_2是a_{22}且f_3是a_{23}且f_4是a_{24} of the object u_2, then the resulting factor g is b_2.

……

Inference rule *m* If the conditional factor f_1是a_{m1}且f_2是a_{m2}且f_3是a_{m3}且f_4是a_{m4} of the object u_m, then the resulting factor g is b_m.

The following rules can be obtained by factor analogy reasoning between the test sample and the training sample:

Factor analogy inference rule: If the object $v_j (j = 1, 2, \cdots, 80)$ in the test sample is most similar to the object $u_i (i = 1, 2, \cdots, 20)$ in the training sample inference rule, then the resulting factor g is b_i.

3) Problem model solving

Step 1. According to the above information, it can be determined that the training sample is a space composed of 20 objects and 4 factors. If this problem is written in the form of $[U, I]$ image pairs, it is necessary to find the phase domain in which all factors have the same form and change it into two phases, close and determine the focused phase a_k. The image matching pair of $[U, I]$ can be written by the above method, and the focusing truth matrix **T** can be determined by the image matching pair of $[U, I]$, thus forming the image matching pair of $[U, I]$ and the focusing truth matrix **T** on it.

$$\mathbf{T} = \begin{bmatrix} 0\,1\,0\,0 \\ 0\,0\,0\,0 \\ \vdots\,\vdots\,\vdots\,\vdots \\ 1\,0\,1\,1 \end{bmatrix}_{20\times 4}$$

where t_{ij} represents the jth factor corresponding to the i iris plant;

Step 2. According to the focused truth matrix **T** calculated in step 1, the random truth matrix **P** of condition factor and result factor is calculated by dividing condition factor and result factor.

$$\mathbf{P} = \begin{bmatrix} 0.10\ 0.6364\ 0\ 0 \\ 0.90\ 0.3636\ 1\ 1 \\ 0.90\ 0.3333\ 1\ 1 \\ 0.10\ 0.6667\ 0\ 0 \end{bmatrix}$$

Step 3. According to the random truth matrix **P** calculated in Step 2 and the formula given in definition 8, the integrity w_j of the four factors is calculated.

$$w = [0.4100\ 0.2732\ 0.5000\ 0.5000]$$

Step 4. According to the integrity of each factor calculated in Step 3 and the formula given in definition 9, the weight value α_j of the four factors is calculated;

$$\alpha = [0.2436\ 0.1623\ 0.2971\ 0.2971]$$

Step 5. According to the weight values of the four factors calculated in Step 4 and the formula given in definition 10, the distance $d(x_i, y_j)$ between 80 test samples and 20 training samples can be calculated, and the results of 80 test samples can be deduced according to the distance between samples and the analogy reasoning rules of factors. The inference results are shown in Table 1.

In Table 1, inference result 0 represents Iris Setosa (mountain Iris) and inference result 1 represents Iris Versicolour (color-changing iris).

The comparison of iris data algorithms by factor analogy reasoning and factor analysis is shown in Table 2.

Based on the $[U, I]$ image matching principle, a factor analogy reasoning algorithm is proposed to analyze the iris plant data (20 training samples, 80 test samples) in UCI data set. The algorithm is compared with the factor analysis method. Factor analysis failed to reason the 16th data in the data set, and the whole operation took 0.032 s. The

Table 1. Inference results

U	Inference results				
	Similarity range with 20 rules	Maximum similarity	Maximum similarity rule	Inference result	Real result
1	0.0234–0.4426	0.0234	5	0	0
2	0.0011–0.4688	0.0011	8	0	0
3	0.0011–0.5117	0.0011	9	0	0
4	0.0338–0.5465	0.0338	9	0	0
5	0.0309–0.4351	0.0309	5	0	0
6	0.0172–0.3734	0.0172	6	0	0
⋮					
75	0.0149–0.3790	0.0149	20	1	1
76	0.0129–0.3770	0.0129	20	1	1
77	0.0138–0.3899	0.0138	16	1	1
78	0.0094–0.4131	0.0094	16	1	1
79	0.0097–0.2614	0.0097	18	1	1
80	0.0162–0.3803	0.0162	20	1	1

Table 2. Comparison of algorithms

Algorithm	Number of test samples	Number of training samples	Unidentified number	Accuracy rate
Factor analog reasoning algorithm	80	20	0	100%
Factor analysis	80	20	1	99%

factor analog reasoning algorithm successfully reasoned all the data sets, and the whole operation process took 0.02 s. For this data set, the inference rate of the proposed algorithm is 100%. This paper shows that the algorithm of factor analogy reasoning obtained by combining factor space with analogy reasoning is a good reasoning algorithm.

7 Conclusion

This chapter will summarize the article.

Based on the $[U, I]$ image matching principle under the factor space theory, this paper studies the factor analogy reasoning, constructs the factor analogy reasoning model, puts forward the factor analogy reasoning algorithm, and proves that the algorithm can solve the factor analogy reasoning model effectively. By comparing with the factor analysis algorithm, it is found that the algorithm proposed in this paper has shorter computing time. In this paper, the effectiveness of the algorithm is analyzed both theoretically and practically. In the future, the advantages of the factor analog reasoning algorithm will be further analyzed.

Acknowledgments. Here we need to thank: Liaoning Province "Xingliao Talent Plan" project support (XLYC2211085), Liaoning Province Department of Education project (JYTQN2023210; LJKZZ20220047) and Social Science Project of Fuxin City (2023Fsllx154; 2023Fsllx017; 2023Fsllx144).

Disclosure of Interests. The authors have no competing interests to declare that are relevant to the content of this article.

References

1. Lv, J., Guo, S.: Expression of interval sets of concepts in factor space and its application in decision making. Fuzzy Syst. Math. **32**(5), 143–150 (2018)
2. He, P.: Mathematical research of cybercrime based on factor space. J. Liaoning Police Univ. **19**(01), 1–8 (2017)
3. Liu, H., Hao, C., Gui, F.: Prediction method of coal and gas outburst under factor space. J. Heilongjiang Univ. Sci. Technol. **27**(04), 354–358 (2017)
4. Duan, Y.: Evaluation of college students' comprehensive quality based on fuzzy factor space Theory. J. Liaocheng Univ. (Nat. Sci. Ed.) **28**(02), 38–42 (2015)
5. Zhao, J.: Logic research on analogical reasoning in Artificial Intelligence. China-Arab States Sci. Technol. Forum **08**, 87–91 (2023)
6. Jin, R.: Is inference equal to analogical reasoning? J. Logic Res. **6**(4), 60–78 (2013)
7. Ren, X., Liu, C.: Analysis of inductive characteristics of Chinese "generalization" logic. Fujian Forum (Human. Social Sci. Ed.) **12**, 37–41 (2015)
8. Xie, Y.: Argument by analogy in ancient China. Argumentation **33**(3), 323–347 (2019)
9. Lu, Y., Zhu, J.: Argumentation types of analogical reasoning. J. Hengyang Normal Univ. **32**(1), 15–18 (2011)
10. Hu, H.: The characteristics and evaluation criteria of analogy argumentation. J. Chongqing Univ. Technol. (Social Sci.) **26**(1), 12–21 (2012)
11. Jin, L., Zhao, J.: Research on properties of analogical reasoning from the perspective of logic. J. Zhejiang Univ. (Human. Social Sci.) **45**(4), 42–51 (2015)
12. Yi, B., Xu, J.: Analog model and similar correspondence. Sci. China (Ser. A Math. Phys. Astron. Tech. Sci.) **01**, 87–93 (1992)
13. Zhao, Q., Li, B.: Computational model of analogical reasoning. J. Softw. (03), 156–162 (1996)
14. Wang, P., Sugeno, M.: Background structure of factor fields and fuzzy sets. Fuzzy Math. (2), 45–54 (1982)
15. Wille, R.: Restructuring lattice theory: an approach based on hierarchies of concepts. In: RIVAL I. Ordered Set, pp. 445–470. Springer, Dordrecht (1982)
16. Pawlak, Z.: Rough sets. Int. J. Comput. Inf. Sci. **11**(5), 341–356 (1982)

Research on Factor Support Vector Multi-classification Algorithm Based on Factor Space Theory

Kaijie Zhang[1,2], Fanhui Zeng[1,2], and Jiaxin Li[1,2](✉)

[1] College of Intelligent Engineering and Mathematics, Liaoning Technical University, Fuxin 123000, China
zfh3351@sina.com, 1120209952@qq.com

[2] College of Science, Liaoning Technical University, Fuxin 123000, China

Abstract. In order to solve the accuracy and complexity of multiple classification algorithms, on the basis of factor space theory, the divisibility measurement condition and the construction condition of binary tree are defined. On the basis of balanced binary tree, combining the relationship between class spacing and sample circle radius, a factor support vector multiple classification algorithm(M-FSV) is proposed by using recursion idea and the principle of "easy classification first". Experiments are done with one-to-one support vector machine and balanced binary tree support vector machine algorithm, and experimental comparison is made. The results of 8 data sets in UCI database show that the training time of M-FSV is less than that of SVM, and the algorithm accuracy is higher than that of SVM. The research results expand the theory and application of factor space, and provide a new idea and simple method for classification problems in machine learning.

Keywords: Factor space · M-FSV · Binary tree · Machine learning · Support vector machine

1 Introduction

In recent years, with the development of information technology, the scale of data sets is also increasing, and the multi-classification problem has become an important and urgent research topic. Multiple classification algorithms are often combined into multiple binary classification classifiers in some way, such as one-to-one [1], one-to-many [2], directed acyclic graphs [3], binary trees [4–9], fuzzy clustering methods [10–12], and so on. At present, the multi-classification algorithm is one-to-one, but it requires a lot of computation time and algorithm complexity, and most of the current multi-classification algorithms first classify the samples, and then perform one-to-one sample calculation, where the balanced binary tree requires the shortest time and the required algorithm complexity. However, the construction of the balanced binary tree algorithm is relatively complicated, and the balance of the binary tree needs to be precisely controlled. When the distribution range of class samples is wide in the eigenvector space, it is difficult to eliminate the influence on the distribution category of heterogeneous data.

Published by Springer Nature Switzerland AG 2025
Z. Shi et al. (Eds.): ICIS 2024, IFIP AICT 720, pp. 143–156, 2025.
https://doi.org/10.1007/978-3-031-71253-1_11

In order to solve the above problems, Based on the original balanced binary tree, this paper constructs a new classification metric condition between categories, uses recursion idea and the principle of "easy classification by first division" to construct a binary tree, and uses the factor support vector algorithm [13, 14] under the factor space theory to solve it, which is the factor support vector multi-classification algorithm (M-FSV). Finally, numerical experiments are carried out to verify it.

2 Multiple Classification Algorithm

This section analyzes the problems existing in current multi-classification methods, and analyzes the problems existing in the construction of binary trees and the problems existing in BDT-SVM [7] from the two aspects of solving class distance and class divisibility measure conditions.

At present, the one-to-many classification algorithm needs to train n optimal hyperplanes, and the training of each hyperplane needs to compute the whole data set; In the one-to-one multi-classification algorithm, although each hyperplane only needs to train two categories of data sets, it needs to train $n(n-1)/2$ hyperplanes, which takes too long in the training sample stage and the test stage of the data. The algorithm based on balanced binary tree only needs $n-1$ hyperplanes in the training stage and $\log 2n$ decision surfaces in the test stage, which is faster than the method of directed acyclic graph. The latter needs to train $n(n-1)/2$ hyperplanes in the training phase and traverse $n-1$ hyperplanes in the test phase.

(1) Divisibility measure analysis of classes

The distribution range of samples within the class has a great influence on the classification of samples. Therefore, the point set whose Euclidean distance between the middle point set and the center point is larger than the sample radius is selected to represent the distribution range of the sample. When the distribution of samples within the class is more concentrated, the sample points outside the circle in the class are less.

Suppose that given l classes, each class has n samples: $x_i(i = 1, 2, \cdots, n)$, the class center of a class is the average of all samples in the class, so the class center is defined as:

$$C_i = \frac{\sum_{i=1}^{n} x_i}{n} \quad (1)$$

The class radius of a class is the sum of the Euclidean distances between all samples in the class and the class center. The class center of each class is obtained by formula (1). The class radius R_i corresponding to the class center C_i of class i is calculated by formula (2):

$$R_i = \frac{\sum_{k=1}^{n} ||x_i - C_i||_2}{n} \quad (2)$$

The class-centric Euclidean distance for both classes is defined as follows:

$$\text{dis}_{ij} = ||C_i - C_j||_2 \tag{3}$$

In this case dis_{ij} represents the Euclidean distance between the class center of class i and class j.

The class spacing between classes i and j is defined as:

$$\text{cludis}_{ij} = \text{dis}_{ij} - R_i - R_j \tag{4}$$

Formula (4) shows that the larger cludis_{ij} is, the farther the distance between class i and class j is, and the higher the degree of separability between class i and class j is.

(2) Class distance analysis

Common sample classification methods include European distance classification, sphere structure classification and weighted European distance classification.

① Euclidean distance classification

Euclidean distance classification method obtains the center of the sample point set through formula (1), and further obtains the distance between the two class centers. The algorithm only considers the distance between the spherical centers and does not consider the specific distribution of the sample. The problem of Euclidean distance classification is shown in Fig. (1). The distance between the centers of Fig. 1(a) and Fig. 1(b) is equal, but the separability between the two categories in Fig. 1(b) is much greater than that of the two categories in Fig. 1(a).

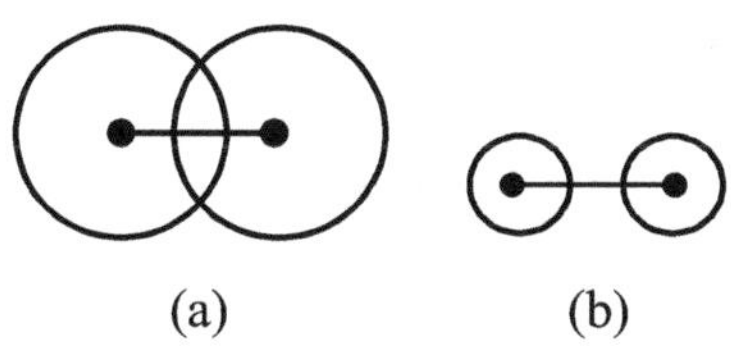

Fig. 1. Problems with Euclidean distance classification

② Spherical structure classification

By using the distance between the center of the sphere and the relationship between the two kinds of radii, the classification of spherical structure establishes the similarity measurement function. The similarity measurement function is established by using the center and radius of the hypersphere, and the calculation method is formula (2).When considering the sample distance between classes and sample distribution within classes, the algorithm can effectively avoid unbalanced sample data and reduce the error effect caused by misclassification of samples. As shown in Fig. (2), the sample distribution radius of a, b, d is equal, and the sample radius of class c is larger than that of class a, b, d. When the metric distance between categories a and b and categories c and d is equal, the separability of categories a and b is much greater than that of categories c and d due to the large sample distribution range of category c.

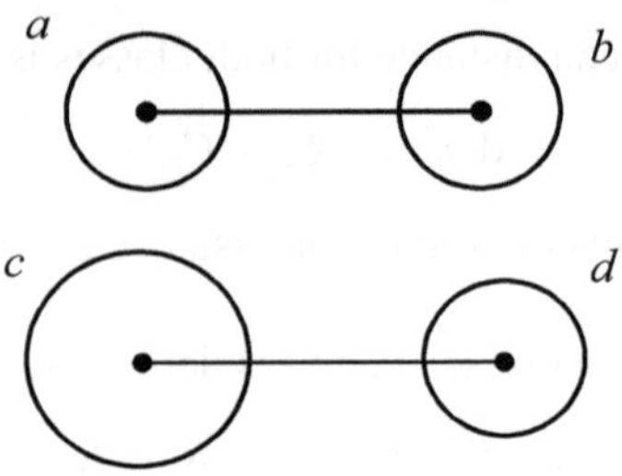

Fig. 2. Problems with the classification of spherical structures

③ Weighted Euclidean distance classification

On the basis of Euclidean distance, the weighted Euclidean distance classification method comprehensively considers the influence of inter-class sample distance and intra-class sample distribution, and uses weight K to combine them together to make them a divisibility measure between samples. However, this method ignores the influence of sample distribution region on sample separability, and for some samples with special distribution, the classification effect is not good, as shown in Fig. (3).

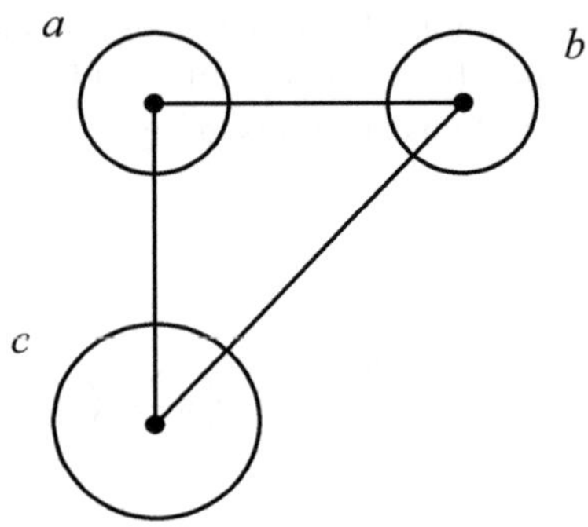

Fig. 3. The problems of weighted Euclidean distance classification

④ Problem analysis

When there are too many classes, the class center distance of two classes has little influence on the separability of the two classes. As shown in Fig. (2), when the class centers of the two categories are the same distance, the BDT-SVM algorithm selects sample points by class center distance, resulting in class misclassification, this results in errors caused by classification and affects the accuracy of the experimental results.

When the distribution range of category samples in the feature vector space is wide, the distribution structure of sample data often leads to the influence of category classification. In this case, it is difficult for the BDT-SVM algorithm to eliminate the influence on the distribution category of abnormal data in the process of building a binary tree, so the algorithm of the BDT-SVM algorithm is incomplete in the process of building a binary tree algorithm.

3 Factor Support Vector Multiple Classification Algorithm

This section introduces the concept and steps of factor support vector algorithm in factor space. On the basis of analyzing the problems existing in class distance and class separability measure in Sect. 1, it gives the class distance separability measure conditions of the binary tree constructed in this paper, and further proposes the classification and discrimination conditions with the same measurement conditions.

3.1 Factor Support Vector Algorithm

Definition 2.1. Given two kinds of sample data sets, positive class $S^+ = \{\boldsymbol{x}_1^+, \boldsymbol{x}_2^+, \cdots, \boldsymbol{x}_n^+\}$ and negative class $S^- = \{\boldsymbol{x}_1^-, \boldsymbol{x}_2^-, \cdots, \boldsymbol{x}_n^-\}$,the center of the positive class point set is $\boldsymbol{o}^+ = \sum_{i=1}^{n} \boldsymbol{x}_i^+/|S^+|$;The center of the negative class point set is $\boldsymbol{o}^- = \sum_{i=1}^{n} \boldsymbol{x}_i^-/|S^-|$,

$$\boldsymbol{w} = \boldsymbol{o}^+ - \boldsymbol{o}^- \tag{5}$$

It is called the sweeping class direction from positive class point set to negative class point set, where $|S|$ is the number of samples in the point set.

Definition 2.2. Let $\boldsymbol{w}^*$ be the projection direction that can separate the two classes(not necessarily optimal),and let $l^* = \max\{(\boldsymbol{x}_i^-, \boldsymbol{w}^*)\}$ be the maximum inner product of the negative class point set and the projection vector, and $u^* = \min\{(\boldsymbol{x}_i^+, \boldsymbol{w}^*)\}$ be the minimum inner product of the positive class point set and the projection vector.

Definition 2.3. Mark $o^* = (u^* + l^*)/2$ as the boundary wall of the positive and negative class samples, and the two parallel surfaces $(\boldsymbol{x}, \boldsymbol{w}^*) = o^* \pm r^*$ are called the supporting walls of the positive and negative class sample point set.

Definition 2.4. Let's call $f(\boldsymbol{x}) = \text{sign}[(\boldsymbol{x}, \boldsymbol{w}^*) - o^*]$ the decision function. Enter test point $\boldsymbol{x}$, which belongs to the positive sample point set if and only if $f(\boldsymbol{x}) > 0$.

Definition 2.5. Given a divisible 2-classification training dataset $S \times Y$ $(Y = \{+, -\})$ with $\boldsymbol{x}_i^*$ on the support wall,S is a base point in. Let S^* be a set composed of some base points, and if the supporting wall can be determined by it, it is said that S is a supporting set. The base point of the support set is also called the support point, also called the support vector.

Definition 2.6. There are t points in the support set S_t^*,whose coordinates are taken as columns to form a matrix A_t,which is called the construction matrix.

Definition 2.7. Denote $\boldsymbol{w}_t^*$ as the projection vector, and solving the $\boldsymbol{w}_t^*$ system can be expressed as $\boldsymbol{w}_t^* A_t = \mathbf{1}_t$, with $\mathbf{1}_t = (1, 1, \cdots, 1)$.To solve this system, we have.

$$w_t^* = \mathbf{1}_t A_t^{-1} \tag{6}$$

(1) Algorithm step

Input 2 classification sample point sets in n-dimensional space, positive class $S^+ = \{x_1^+, x_2^+, \cdots, x_n^+\}$ and negative class $S^- = \{x_1^-, x_2^-, \cdots, x_n^-\}$;
empty set;
Step 0 The direction of the sweeping class is obtained according to Eq. (5).
$t = 1; S_1^* = \{x_{(1)}^-\}$;among them,$(1) = \arg\max_i\{(x_i^-, w)\}; S^- = S^- \backslash \{x_{(1)}^-\}$;
Step 1 $t = t + 1; S_t^* = S_{t-1}^* + \{x_{(t)}^-\}$;among them,

$$(t) = \arg\max_i\{(x_i^-, w_{t-1}) | x_i^- \in S^-\} \tag{7}$$

Step 2 The t-dimensional square array A_t is formed by taking the coordinates of the t points before the negative class points in S_t^* as columns. Find the inverse matrix $A_t^{-1}; w_t^* = \mathbf{1}_t A_t^{-1}$ is obtained according to formula (2.2).
Step 3 Find the lowest positive class point $x_{(t)}^+$, where

$$(t) = \arg\min_i\{(x_i^+, w_t) | x_i^+ \in S^+\} \tag{8}$$

Put the point into S_t^*:$S_t^* = S_t^* + \{x_{(t)}^+\}$; (The reduced support set consists of t negative class boundary points and one positive class point).

Step 4 The highest point $x_{(t)}^-$ in S^- and the lowest point $x_{(t)}^+$ in S^+ are substituted into the equation $(x, w_t) = b$ to find b, and b^- and b^+ are obtained.

①If $b^- > b^+$,then the test fails, delete $(1) = \arg\max_i\{(x_i^-, w)\}$ in the negative class point set, and re-find $S_{t+1}^* = S_t^* + \{x_{(t+1)}^-\} \backslash \{x_{(1)}^-\}$ as the pre-t site set of negative class points in the support set S_t^* and return to step 2.
② If there is a point $x_i \in S$ that breaks into the isolation zone and $b^- < (x_i, w_t) < b^+$ is present, the experiment also fails. Collect $S_t^* = S_{t-1}^*$ and the inner product of the maximum negative point in the isolation zone (x_i, w_t) as the pre-t-site set of negative class points in S_t^* and return to step 2. Otherwise, step t is successful, stop, output $S^* = S_t^*$.
(2) Kernel function theory

In order to solve the problem of factor support vector algorithm effectively processing linear non-fractional data sets, the kernel function theory is given in this section: Add + 1 and-1 respectively to the positive and negative class samples, thereby raising the positive and negative class samples by 1 dimension. In order to reduce the classification accuracy caused by data samples after dimensional upgrade, therefore, on the basis of the 1-dimensional increase of positive and negative samples, the hyperparameter $r, q (0 < r, q \leqslant 1)$ is introduced to adjust the accuracy rate of the algorithm test of the dimensional increase algorithm and reduce the experimental error. In order to speed up the algorithm's processing of sample points and avoid the increase of algorithm complexity caused by excessive data in high-dimensional space, this section gives the corresponding calculation method of kernel function inner product of positive and negative class samples.

Given two types of sample data sets, positive class $S^+ = \{x_1^+, x_2^+, \cdots, x_n^+\}$ and negative class $S^- = \{x_1^-, x_2^-, \cdots, x_n^-\}$,the expression of sample kernel function and calculation expression of positive and negative class are as follows:

The expression for dimensionality upgrading of positive samples is as follows:

$$\Phi(x_i^+) = (1, rx_{i1}^+, rx_{i2}^+, \cdots, rx_{in}^+) \tag{9}$$

The expression when the negative class sample is upgraded is:

$$\Phi(x_i^-) = (-1, qx_{i1}^-, qx_{i2}^-, \cdots, qx_{in}^-) \tag{10}$$

The expression for solving the swept class vector is:

$$w = \frac{1}{n}\sum_{i=1}^{n}\Phi(x_i^+) - \frac{1}{m}\sum_{j=1}^{m}\Phi(x_i^-)$$

The inner product of the swept class vector and the positive class sample is calculated as follows:

$$K(w, x_i^+) = 1 + rw(x_i^+)^{\mathrm{T}} \tag{11}$$

The inner product of swept class vector and negative class sample is calculated as follows:

$$K(w, x_i^-) = 1 + qw(x_i^-)^{\mathrm{T}} \tag{12}$$

3.2 Factor Support Vector Multiple Classification Algorithm

(1) Principle of algorithm

In view of the problems existing in the construction of a binary tree in Sect. 1, formulas (14) and (14) are used as the metric conditions for the construction of a normal binary tree to complete the construction process of a normal binary tree.

On the basis of formula (4), the divisibility measurement conditions between categories are given.

The expression for the calculation of separability between class i and other classes is:

$$D_i = \sum_{i=1}^{l} \mathrm{cludis}_{ij} \tag{13}$$

l represents the number of categories, and the higher the D_i value, the higher the degree of separation between class i and other classes, and the easier it is to divide.

In the process of classification, when D_i values of two or more categories are the same, the class radius obtained according to formula (2), when there are k samples outside the circle of class center C_i,the distribution error distance of sampling points for each class is:

$$AC_i = \frac{\sum_{k=1}^{k} (||x_i - C_i||_2 - R_i)}{k} \tag{14}$$

According to formula (14), a smaller AC_i indicates that the sample points of this class are more concentrated and the distribution range of sample points is smaller. In this case, the sample point set with a smaller AC_i value can be selected first, and vice versa.

(2) Algorithm steps

For the classification problem of the given l class samples, each class of samples is numbered and classified first, the numbered samples are put into the empty set S, and the empty sets S1 and S2 are taken as backup.

Step 1 In the set S, select the most easily divided class, that is, the class with the largest median value of D_i value, and put them into S1 respectively; Take the least indivisible class of the set S, that is, the smallest class of D, and put it into S2.If there are only two classes in a certain set, it is divided into left and right leaves according to Q value, and the small Q value is left, and the other is right;
Step 2 Find the largest class in set S that is equal to D_i in set S1 and put it in S1,S = S-S1;
Step 3 Find the largest class in set S that is equal to D_i in set S2 and put it in S2,S = S-S2;
Step 4 Repeat steps 2–3 until all sample classes are placed in S1 or S2;
Step 5 Let the set S equal to S1 or S equal to S2,and repeat the process of steps 1 to 4 until all samples are classified.

At this time, the construction of the normal binary tree is completed, and each fulcrum of the binary tree is obtained by using the factor support vector algorithm, so as to complete the solution of the classification sample.

The flow of factor support vector multi-classification algorithm is shown in Fig. (4).

(3) Algorithm complexity analysis

The algorithm complexity analysis in this paper is based on examples, as shown in Fig. (5). The classification of the literature [8] in Fig. (5) requires repeated calculation of the category of $n-1$ class. The classification algorithm in this paper firstly classifies class c into S1 and class a into S2. At this time, when the spacing between class b and class d is the same, b is classified into S2 and a is classified into S1 according to the size of the separation factor. Compared with literature [8], under the same classification, the classification of this paper only needs to calculate the computation amount of class n-2 each time, so the algorithm complexity of this paper is lower than that of literature [8]. However, it can be seen from the reference [8] that the algorithm complexity of the reference [8] is almost the same as that of the BDT-SVM algorithm, so the complexity of the proposed algorithm is lower than that of the BDT-SVM algorithm.

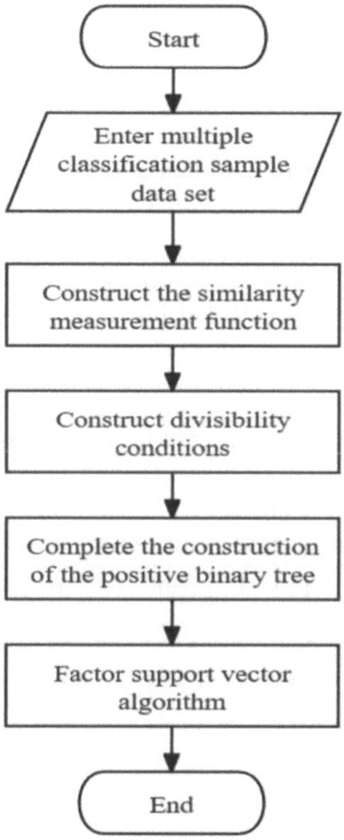

Fig. 4. Normal binary tree factor support vector multi-classification algorithm flow

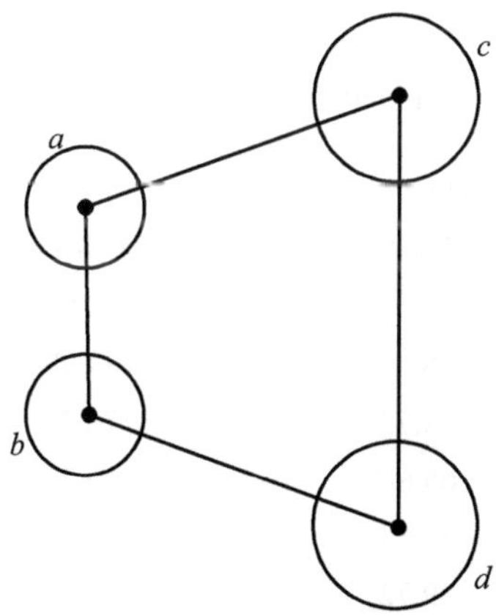

Fig. 5. Multi-class example

4 Numerical Experiment

The experimental data in this paper comes from the data set of UCI database, and the machine environment is Intel CORE i5 7th Gen. In the experiment, eight multi-classification datasets, including Iris, Balance Scale, Yeast, NPHA, Wine, Cirrhosis, Exasens and Image Segmentation, were selected from the UCI database, using Matlab2018a, the proposed algorithm was experimentally compared with BDT-SVM [7] and one-to-one support vector machine multiple classification algorithm (OVO-SVM). 80% of the sample data sets were selected for training, and the remaining 20% were tested and verified (Table 1).

Table 1. Properties of the eight data sets.

Data set	Sample size	Training sample	Test sample	Number of classes	Characteristic number
Iris	150	120	30	3	4
Balance Scale	625	500	125	3	5
Yeast	1429	1143	286	7	9
NPHA	714	572	142	3	14
Wine	178	142	36	3	13
Cirrhosis	418	335	83	3	3
Exasens	399	320	79	4	3
Image Segmentation	2310	1848	462	7	19

Table 2. Comparison of algorithm training time

Data set	Time/ms		
	BDT-SVM	OVO-SVM	M-FSV
Iris	33.03	303.99	1.45
Balance Scale	66.49	34.77	2.56
Yeast	328.72	1776.24	13.44
NPHA	65.88	66.77	5.06
Wine	47.14	60.51	5.48
Cirrhosis	49.72	50.41	3.57
Exasens	69.21	13.23	2.97
Image Segmentation	305.64	1870.86	64.14

In the experimental process, SVM of BDT-SVM algorithm and OVO-SVM algorithm uses RBF kernel function to improve the classification accuracy of the algorithm, while

Table 3. Accuracy comparison of algorithms

Data set	Accuracy%		
	BDT-SVM	OVO-SVM	M-FSV
Iris	100	100	100
Balance Scale	94.8	91.2	96
Yeast	80.79	55.09	95
NPHA	70.83	52.11	68.4
Wine	62.31	60.71	88.56
Cirrhosis	80.43	65.06	85.85
Exasens	78.74	62.03	83.99
Image Segmentation	85.95	88.42	89.29

the algorithm in this paper uses kernel function to accelerate the data processing ability of the algorithm and the accuracy of the algorithm. The following is the binary tree generated by the BDT-SVM algorithm and the algorithm in this paper for some data sets.

For the Iris and Balance Scale datasets, there are three categories. Due to the small number of categories, there is little difference between the binary tree formed by the proposed algorithm and the BDT-SVM algorithm according to each category and classification step. The constructed binary tree model is shown in Figs. (6) and (7).

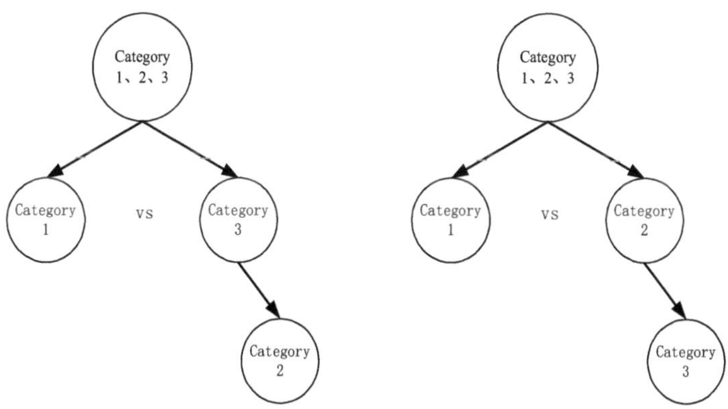

BDT-SVM algorithm M-FSV algorithm

Fig. 6. Comparison of binary tree models in Iris dataset

For the Yeast dataset, there are seven categories. The binary tree formed by the yeast algorithm and the BDT-SVM algorithm according to each category and classification step is shown in Fig. (7).

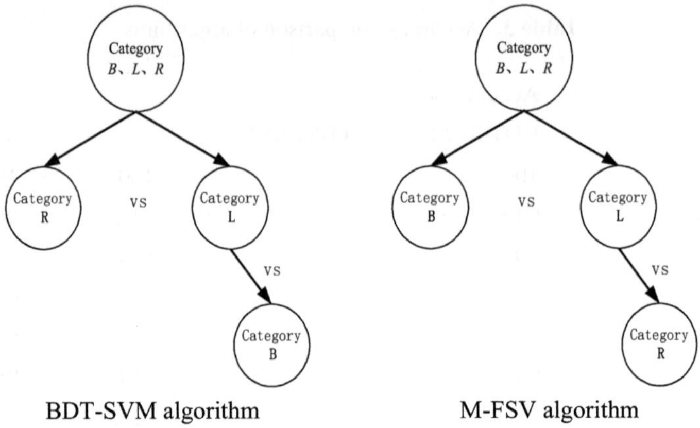

Fig. 7. Comparison of binary tree models in the Balance Scale dataset

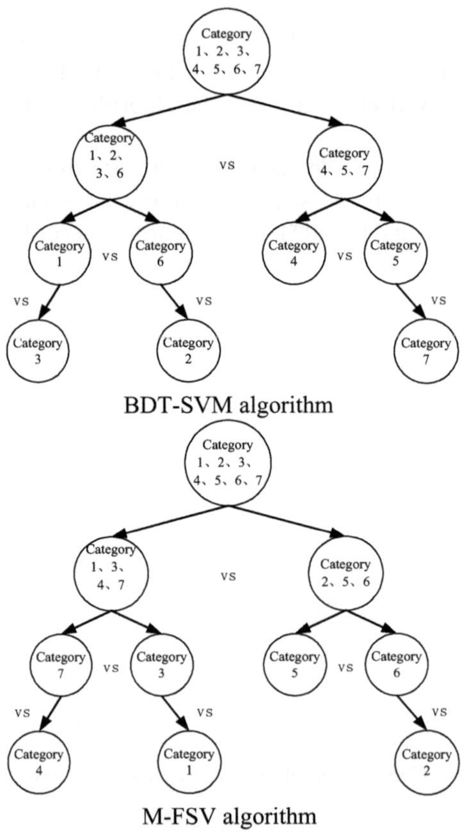

Fig. 8. Comparison of binary tree model in Yeast data set

It can be seen from Fig. (7) that the binary trees generated by the proposed algorithm and BDT-SVM algorithm in the Balance Scale data set are the same, but as shown in Figs. (6) and (8), there are obvious differences in the binary trees generated by the proposed algorithm and BDT-SVM algorithm in the Iris and Yeast data sets.

The following conclusions can be drawn from Tables 2 and 3:

① Based on the experimental results of Iris, Balance Scale, Yeast, NPHA, Wine, Cirrhosis, Exasens, Image Segmentation and other data sets, if the training sample and test sample are the same, The proposed algorithm is shorter than the BDT-SVM algorithm and OVO-SVM algorithm.

② Based on the experimental results of Iris, Balance Scale, Yeast, NPHA, Wine, Cirrhosis, Exasens, Image Segmentation and other data sets, if the training sample and test sample are the same, the recognition rate of the proposed algorithm, BDT-SVM algorithm and OVO-SVM algorithm in Iris data set is the same; In terms of Balance Scale, Yeast, Wine, Cirrhosis, Exasens and Image Segmentation data set, the sample recognition accuracy of the proposed algorithm is higher than that of the BDT-SVM and OVO-SVM algorithms; In the NPHA data set, the recognition rate of the proposed algorithm is lower than that of the BDT-SVM algorithm, but the gap is smaller, and the recognition rate of the proposed algorithm is higher than that of the OVO-SVM algorithm. Through the above experiments, the superiority and feasibility of the proposed algorithm are illustrated.

③ The algorithm in this paper fully considers the influence of sample data structure on sample classification in the construction process of binary tree, so as to reduce the influence of uneven sample point set on sample separability, and reduce the sample recognition rate of categories caused by uneven distribution of sample point set.

5 Conclusion

Aiming at the problems faced by classification algorithms in machine learning, improving classification accuracy and reducing algorithm complexity, this paper proposes factor support vector algorithm on the basis of factor space theory, and studies the multi-classification application of factor support vector algorithm:

① This paper analyzes the problems of one to one, one to many and other multiple classification algorithms, and analyzes the problems of Euclidean distance classification, ball structure classification, weighted Euclidean distance classification,, BDT-SVM algorithm to establish similarity measurement classification conditions.

② In order to solve the above problems, this paper establishes the similarity measurement condition of classification through the relationship between class spacing and the circle radius formed by samples, and solves the problem that multiple classification algorithms affect the classification results of abnormal data structures.

③ In this paper, a new binary tree method is constructed on the basis of constructing the similarity measurement condition, using the idea of recursion and the classification principle of first division and easy division. Finally, factor support vector algorithm is used to solve the problem.

The experimental results show that the multi-classification algorithm of factor support vector can effectively reduce the errors caused by classification errors and improve the classification accuracy of the multi-classification algorithm under the condition of low complexity of binary tree construction. Factor support vector multi-classification algorithm has a profound mathematical theory foundation, which provides a new idea and simple method for solving classification problems in machine learning, and expands the theoretical and applied research of factor space.

Acknowledgments. This study is supported by the "Xingliao Talent Program" project of Liaoning Province (XLYC2211085); Project of Education Department of Liaoning Province, No.JYTQN2023210; Supported by Fuxin Social Science Project (2023Fsllx144).

Disclosure of Interests. It is now necessary to declare any competing interests or to specifically state that the authors have no competing interests.

References

1. Shan, Y., Wang, H., Dong, S.: Improved multi-classification algorithm of one- against-one SVM. Comput. Eng. Des. **33**(5), 1837–1841 (2012)
2. Hsc, C., Lin, C.: A comparison of methods for multiclass support vector machines. IEEE Trans. Neural Netw. **13**(2), 415–425 (2002)
3. Platt, J., Cristianini, N., Shawetaylor, J.: Large margin DAGs for multiclass classification. Adv. Neural. Inf. Process. Syst. **12**(3), 547–553 (2000)
4. Wu, Y., Lv, J.: Research on multi-class classification algorithm of support vector machine. J. Chongqing Normal Univ. (Nat. Sci. Edn.) **33**(3), 102–106 (2016)
5. Pu, Q.: One kind research on improved sphere-structured partial binary SVM multi-class classification algorithm. Autom. Instrum. **37**(01), 71–75 (2022)
6. Pan, Y., Zheng, Y.: Improved binary tree support vector machine multi-class classification algorithm. In: 2011 International Conference on Computational Science and Applications (ICCSA 2011), pp. 121–125 (2011)
7. Leng, Q., Liu, F., Qin, Y.: Multi-class classification algorithm for SVM based on hybrid binary tree structure. Comput. Sci. **45**(5), 220–237 (2018)
8. Lin, Z., Yu, C.: An improved support vector machines with balanced binary decision tree for multi-class classification. Small Microcomput. Syst. **35**(5), 1128–1132 (2014)
9. Haiyang, Z., Minqiang, X., Dongqiang, W.: An improved binary tree SVM and application for fault diagnosis. J. Vibrat. Eng. **5**, 765–770 (2013)
10. Zhang, Z., et al.: Research of multi-class algorithm based on fuzzy support vector machine. Comput. Appl. **2008**(7)
11. Wu, L., et al.: Adaptive fuzzy clustering algorithm for high resolution remote sensing image segmentation. Beijing Survey. Mapp. **33**(04), 438–442 (2019)
12. Shen, Y., Dai, M.: Binary tree multi-classification algorithm based on weighted fuzzy membership. Comput. Appl. Res. **37**(11), 3281–3286 (2020)
13. Zhang, K., et al.: Research on factor support vector machine algorithm based on factor space theory. J. Intell. Syst. (2024). (Have contributed)
14. Peizhuang, W., Fanhui, Z.: Factor Space Theory-Mathematical Basis of Unified Intelligence Theory. Science Press, Beijing (2024)

Large Language Model

Improve LLM Inference Performance with Matrix Decomposition Strategies

Jiyuan Shi[1(✉)] and Chunqi Shi[2]

[1] The Hong Kong University of Science and Technology (Guangzhou), No.1 Duxue Road, Nansha District, Guangzhou 511400, China
jshi365@connect.hkust-gz.edu.cn

[2] China Pacific Insurance (Group) Co., Ltd.,, No.1 Zhongshan South Road, Huangpu District, Shanghai 200010, China

Abstract. Large Language Models (LLMs) are highly effective in various applications but are often limited by their performance (both efficiency and accuracy) during the inference stage. This paper introduces a novel compression technique that leverages Singular Value Decomposition (SVD) and Non-negative Matrix Factorization (NMF) within the MLP layers of transformer-based LLMs. By incorporating adaptive batch sizing and various initialization methods, our method significantly enhances the inference efficiency of these models without compromising their accuracy. We present empirical evidence showing that our method improves both model efficiency and accuracy during inference stage. Specifically, with SVD decomposition, we achieve a 1.6x speedup in inference tokens processing while retaining over 95% of the original model's accuracy. Additionally, through NMF decomposition, we observe up to a 7% improvement in model accuracy compared with the original model, while maintaining or slightly enhancing tokens processing efficiency. These observations suggest that different matrix decomposition techniques can be strategically employed depending on the application requirements-SVD decomposition to boost efficiency, and NMF decomposition to enhance accuracy.

Keywords: Large Language Models · Model Compression · Singular Value Decomposition · Non-negative Matrix Factorization · Low_Rank Reduction

1 Introduction

LLMs (Large Language Models) based on transformer architecture have proven to be remarkably effective for many downstream tasks related to machine learning. Such as natural language understanding [1], text classification [2], and computer vision [3].

The powerful reasoning power of LLMs has been well studied. While LLMs has demonstrated such powerful capabilities, its transformer-based architecture

Published by Springer Nature Switzerland AG 2025
Z. Shi et al. (Eds.): ICIS 2024, IFIP AICT 720, pp. 159–171, 2025.
https://doi.org/10.1007/978-3-031-71253-1_12

results in the need for tremendous computing resources in both the training and reasoning phases. For large language models, deeper organization often leads to better performance, giving researchers an intuition that the more parameters, the better performance [4,5].

However, recent research has shown that transformer-based large language models do not always require an enormous number of parameters to maintain their superior capabilities. This insight has led many researchers to explore various large language model compression techniques. Techniques based on quantization [6–8], parameter pruning [9,10], and knowledge distillation [11,12] have been intensively studied. In comparison, the Singular Value Decomposition (SVD) technique, based on low-rank approximation, is noteworthy for further exploration due to its hardware independence and efficient inference capabilities. In addition, Non-negative Matrix Factorization (NMF), as an auxiliary matrix decomposition technique, not only maintaining the non-negativity of the data but also helping to enhance the interpretability of the model. [23]

This paper proposes examine the input of the large language model from a batch perspective and to employ methods of low-rank approximation, including both Singular Value Decomposition (SVD) and Non-negative Matrix Factorization (NMF), to achieve truncation of large lanuage models. We analyze the relationship between batch size and the change in reasoning ability for specific layers of matrix decomposition truncation within the transformer architecture of large language models. Our study finds that optimizing the combination of selected batch size and the appropriate matrix decomposition not only maintains the performance of the large language model but also enhances inference efficiency. By integrating both SVD and NMF techniques, we aim to demonstrate a balanced approach to model compression that leverages the unique strengths of each method, potentially leading to a more robust model that does not compromise on computational efficiency.

2 Related Work

Large Language Model Compression. In the domain of Large Language Models (LLMs) compression, much of the focus has been on alleviating the large computational and memory requirements that these models impose. Various innovative techniques have been employed to address these challenges, which generally fall into three main categories: weight quantization, network pruning, and knowledge distillation.

Weight Quantization has emerged as a prominent method due to its effectiveness in reducing the memory occupancy of LLMs, where models like GPT-Q utilize layer-wise quantization updating weights with inverse Hessian information, although this method provides only a limited range of compression options, typically from 3 to 8 bits [13–15].

Network Pruning techniques, encompassing both unstructured and structured variants, refine the network architecture by eliminating superfluous weights or entire components. Unstructured pruning, exemplified by Sparse-GPT, targets minimally important weight elements through the inversion of the Hessian matrix, yet it often faces hardware-specific performance constraints. Conversely, structured pruning, as implemented in LLM-Pruner, can significantly affect model accuracy, particularly under high compression ratios [16,17].

Knowledge Distillation involves training a smaller model (student) to mimic the behavior of a larger pre-trained model (teacher), preserving the performance while significantly reducing the size of the model [18,19].

Moreover, the recent introduction of a novel low-rank decomposition method tailored for LLMs presents a training-free approach for decomposing weight matrices, exploiting the untapped potential of low-rank factorization in this domain, which has not been extensively explored yet [15].

These methods collectively represent the forefront of research in LLM compression, each offering unique advantages and facing distinct challenges, as the field continues to evolve towards more efficient and effective solutions for managing the demands of large-scale models.

Low-Rank Decomposition. Low-rank decomposition is a pivotal technique in the field of neural network compression, particularly for Large Language Models (LLMs), which are notorious for their extensive computational and storage requirements. This method leverages Singular Value Decomposition (SVD) and Non-negative Matrix Factorization (NMF) to effectively reduce the dimensionality of weight matrices, thereby decreasing model size while striving to maintain performance integrity.

SVD decomposes a matrix W into three matrices: U, S, V_k^{T}, where U and V are orthogonal matrices, and S is a diagonal matrix containing the singular values of W. The approximation of W can be expressed as:

$$W \approx U_k S_k V_k^{\mathrm{T}}$$

NMF, on the other hand, decomposes the weight matrix W into two non-negative matrices $W \approx HK$, where H and K are constrained to have non-negative entries. This decomposition is particularly useful for data that contains inherent non-negativity, such as pixel values or word frequencies, allowing for a more interpretable compression:

$$W \approx H_k K_k$$

In the LLM compression context, traditional SVD has been utilized to compress weight matrices straightforwardly. However, this approach often overlooks the significance of individual parameters, potentially leading to notable compression errors. Enhanced methods like Fisher Weighted SVD (FWSVD) address this by incorporating Fisher information to evaluate parameter importance, thereby refining the compression process [20]. Although FWSVD offers improved accuracy, it demands intensive computations due to its complex gradient calculations. Another advanced adaptation, Adaptive SVD (ASVD), modifies traditional SVD by scaling the weight matrix with a diagonal matrix that reflects the impact of input channels on the weights. This method aims to optimize the compression process by adjusting to the activation distribution within the network, which can significantly influence compression accuracy [21]. Similarly, while NMF offers a potentially more interpretable model compression by preserving data's non-negativity, it too faces challenges in balancing compression with maintaining the fidelity of model predictions, particularly in complex tasks performed by LLMs.

These SVD- and NMF-based approaches illustrate the delicate balance between achieving substantial model size reduction and retaining the predictive accuracy of LLMs. Future research in this area could potentially focus on more dynamic and intelligent strategies for determining decomposition ranks that can adapt based on operational demands, thereby paving the way for more efficient and scalable neural network models.

3 Methodology

Low-Rank Decomposition in MLP Layers. We give a primary introduction to the large language model based on transformer: The structure of these models (*e.g.,* LLAMA2, GPT-J) is usually a stack of transformer architectures. Take the popular large language model LLAMA2-7B for example, LLAMA2-7B is a stack of 32 transformer architectures. Transformer architecture is often a combination of attention layer and MLP layer, according to previous studies, it is more meaningful to carry out rank reduction decomposition on the MLP layer, so we use l to represent the mlp layer number, then the MLP layer can be expressed as $l_1, \ldots, l_t$, then the MLP layer after rank reduction can be expressed as $l'_1, \ldots, l'_t$.

The rank reduction process of the MLP layer matrix can be concretely expressed as: **1.** The matrix W in the MLP layer which shape is R*R (*e.g.,* 4096 × 4096 matrices are ubiquitous in LLaMA2-7b [22]) **2.** According to Pratyusha Sharma [23], While it is clear that eliminating the higher-order components "denoises" the model and helps recover "hidden", less-frequent information. And the higher-order components often encode multiple conflicting responses, and that when all components are used they clash to produce a generic token. Removing the higher-order components, which anecdotally appear to often capture incorrect responses of the correct type, resolves this internal conflict and allows the model to respond accurately. In this way, the appropriate method can be used to reduce the rank of the matrix W, and the matrix W whose MLP layer is originally $R{*}R$ can be reduced to the matrix $r{*}r$ $(R > r)$ (Figs. 1, 2).

Using Batch as Input Dimension. In this section, we explore the strategy of incorporating batch size as a critical input dimension in large language model inference, which significantly impacts model throughput and memory resource usage.Utilizing larger batches enhances the utilization of hardware resources such as GPUs, leveraging their parallel computational capabilities.

However, increasing batch size also presents challenges. Larger batches can lead to increased memory usage, especially when dealing with large models.

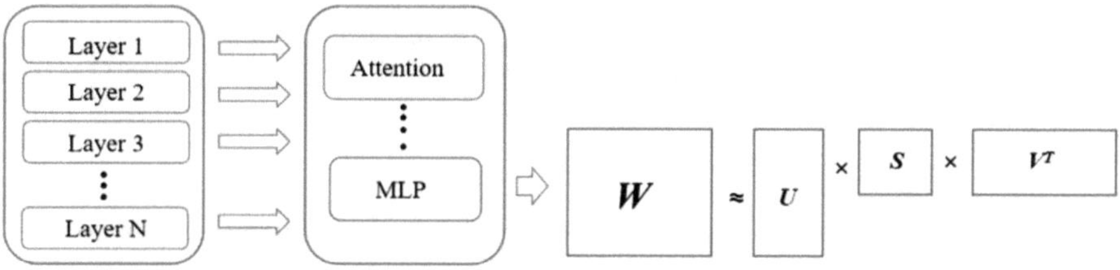

Fig. 1. The figure of the flowchart of using Singular Value Decomposition (SVD) in matrix W (whose dimension is R) to get matrix W'(whose dimension is r).

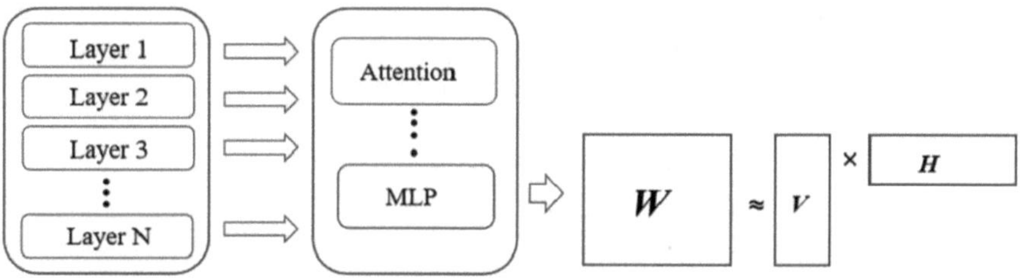

Fig. 2. The figure of the flowchart of using Non-negative Matrix Factorization (NMF) in matrix W (whose dimension is R).

Moreover, processing large batches may extend processing time per batch, potentially affecting responsiveness in real-time applications.

After the introduction of batch size as the input dimension of large language model inference, we can alleviate the obstacle of memory usage to a certain extent, and improve the efficiency of inference at the same time.

Combine Batch and Low-Rank Decomposition to Compress Large Language Models. We suppose that appropriate parameters can be found in both batchsize and decomposition of mlp layer of the large language model at the same time, then the model inference efficiency can be improved without affecting the accuracy of the model.

Our motivations mainly come from two observations: (1) Selecting appropriately LLM's MLP layers with low-rank approximation, characterized by rank r, leads to only trivial performance degradation. (2) The use of batch input can greatly improve the reasoning efficiency of large language models. Thus, we hypothesize that: 1. We can find the right rank r for low-rank approximation in the large language model, leading to significant efficiency gains with only trivial performance degradation. 2. If we can establish a relationship between batch size B and reduction in MLP layers Δm through low-rank approximation, then the efficiency of inference can be improved without affecting the accuracy of large language models.

Let r represent the compression ratio of the large language model, ϵ be the threshold for performance degradation (a very small ratio), B denote the batch size, and Δm represent the reduction in MLP layers. The hypotheses can be mathematically expressed as:

1. There exists a compression ratio r so that the performance degradation $\delta \leq \epsilon$ while maximizing efficiency gains. This can be mathematically expressed as:

$$\max_r \text{Efficiency}(r) \quad \text{with} \quad \text{Performance Degradation}(r) \leq \epsilon$$

2. Establish a relationship between the batch size B and the reduction in MLP layers Δm so that inference efficiency can be improved without affecting the accuracy of large language models. This involves finding a function f, such that:

$$\begin{cases} \text{Inference Efficiency}(B, \Delta m) = f(B, \Delta m), \\ \text{Accuracy}(B, \Delta m) \approx \text{Accuracy(original)} \end{cases}$$

Algorithm 1. Optimal Rank Reduction Parameters for SVD Decomposition

Input: Initial max rank reduction $r_{\max}$
Input: Performance degradation threshold ϵ
Initialize: $r \leftarrow r_{\max}$
Initialize: Best efficiency max_efficiency $\leftarrow 0$
Initialize: Optimal rank $r_{\text{opt}} \leftarrow r$
Initialize: Best method best_method
while $r \geq 1$ **do**
  for each method in {SVD} **do**
    Choose Decomposition: SVD or NMF with selected method
    Run model with chosen decomposition, obtain performance perf and efficiency eff
    if perf $\geq (1 - \epsilon)$ and eff $>$ max_efficiency **then**
      max_efficiency $\leftarrow$ eff
      $r_{\text{opt}} \leftarrow r$
      best_method $\leftarrow$ method
    end if
  end for
  $r \leftarrow r - 32$
end while
Output: Optimal rank r_{opt}, best decomposition method best_method

Representation of NMF decomposition algorithm Where W is the weight matrix of layer i, and H_i is the basis matrix obtained through the NMF algorithm.

$$W \approx H_i H_i^T$$

where $f(M, D)$ denotes the performance evaluation function of model M on dataset D, which could be accuracy, loss value, etc.

$$\text{OriginalPerformance} = f(\text{Model}, \text{DataSet})$$

$$\text{UpdatedPerformance} = f(\text{updatedModel}, \text{DataSet})$$

Algorithm 2. Update Model Layers Using NMF Decomposition

Input: Model, NumLayers, DataSet
$originalPerformance \leftarrow$ Evaluate original model on specified datasets
for $i = 0$ **to** $numLayers - 1$ **do**
    Start timer
    $updatedModel \leftarrow$ Update model layer i using NMF decomposition
    Record elapsed time
    $updatedPerformance \leftarrow$ Evaluate updated model layer on specified datasets
    if $updatedPerformance > originalPerformance$ **then**
        Record improvement: layer i and $updatedPerformance$
        Save evaluation results to $outputDir$
    end if
end for
Output: Updated model with optimal layer settings, record of improvements

4 Experiments

In this section, we will introduce our experiments, using our methods on large language models. In Sect. 4.1, we introduced the setup of our experiment, including model selection, dataset selection, hardware used in the experiment, etc. In Sect. 4.2, we evaluated the effect of the rank-reduction method on the reasoning ability of large language models, presenting results on various tasks, such as accuracy in WIKI and MMLU. In Sect. 4.3, we carry out analysis of Throughput in large language model. To demonstrate the efficiency advantages of our approach.

4.1 Experiments Setups

In this section, we assess the effectiveness of our method by conducting experiments on LLaMA-2-7b [22]. Under our two methods, SVD decomposition method and NMF decomposition method, We selected the experimental datasets of WIKI and MMLU to analyze the accuracy and confusion index of inference of large language model. In addition, in order to further verify the rationality of the nmf decomposition method, we also tested the model loss on CounterFact to verify the model performance. All of our experiments are conducted on An Nvidia 3080ti GPU.

4.2 Inference Accuracy Analysis

Table 1. Performance of Inference Accuracy, Rank (r) represents the rank retained after SVD decomposition, MMLU results are 5-shot results.

Model	Dataset	Method	Rank ($0 < r < 4096$)	Acc (Perplexity)
LLaMA2-7b	MMLU	FULL	4096	44.5
LLaMA2-7b	MMLU	SVD	2944	42.8
LLaMA2-7b	WIKI	FULL	4096	5.48
LLaMA2-7b	WIKI	SVD	3072	7.26

According to the experimental data presented in Table 1, a suitable rank reduction strategy achieves about a 30% parameter reduction in the MLP layer while maintaining roughly 95% of the original LLM accuracy. Specifically, SVD with a rank of 2944 on the MMLU dataset slightly increases the LLaMA2-7b model's perplexity from 44.5 to 42.8, indicating a 5% loss in accuracy. For the WIKI dataset, retaining a rank of 3072 increases perplexity from 5.48 to 7.26.

Specfic MLP layer analysis of llama-2-7b with NMF. From previous studies [22], it can be found that in a large language model, matrix decomposition at different layers of MLP has different impacts on the model, the impact of SVD decomposition on different layers of MLP in large language models has been carefully studied. Follow this view, we hope to study whether it has the same effect through NMF decomposition, so as to further improve the performance of LLMs through NMF decomposition.

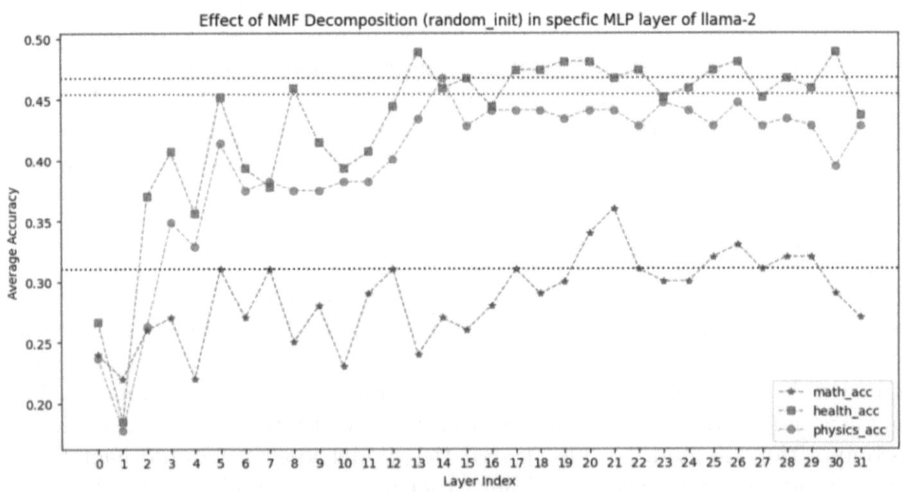

Fig. 3. NMF Decomposition (rand_init) in specfic MLP layer of llama-2-7b

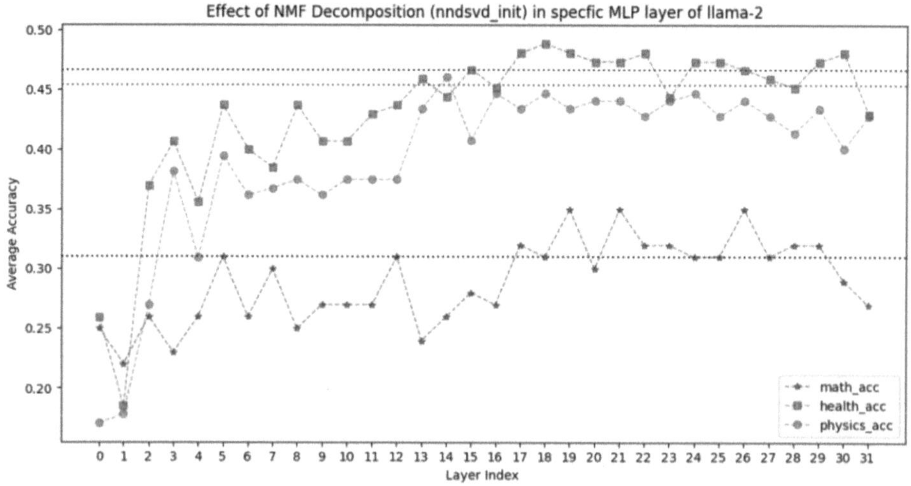

Fig. 4. NMF Decomposition (nndsvd_init) in specfic MLP layer of llama-2-7b

According to Fig. 3 and 4, we selected three subdatasets in the MMLU dataset to test the inference performance of the model. We can find that whether random_init or nndsvd_init method is used after NMF decomposition between about 17–30 layers of MLP layer of LLMs, it will have a certain positive effect on the inference performance of the model (Figs. 5, 6 and 7).

In order to further verify the above idea, we evaluated the performance of the model with loss data on the counterfact dataset. According to Pictures 5 and 6, it can be seen that the loss of MLP layers from 17–30 after nmf decomposition has decreased to a certain extent, which supports the above idea (Table 2).

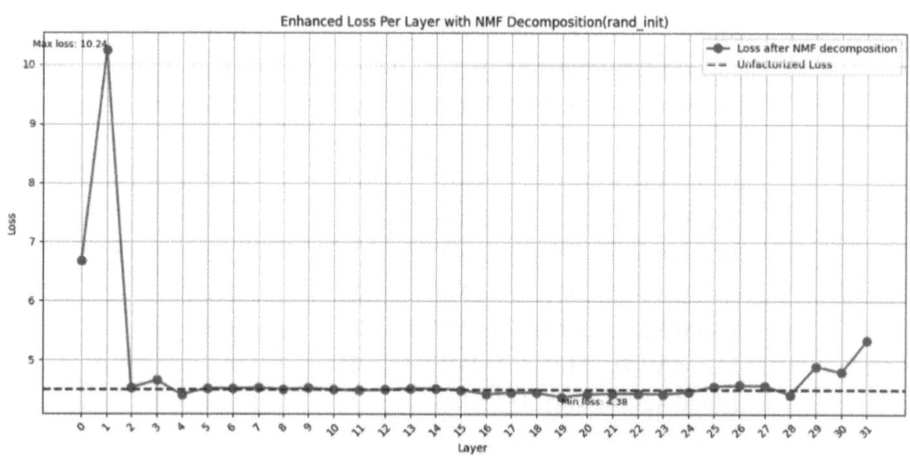

Fig. 5. Enhanced Loss Per Layer with NMF Decomposition (rand_init)

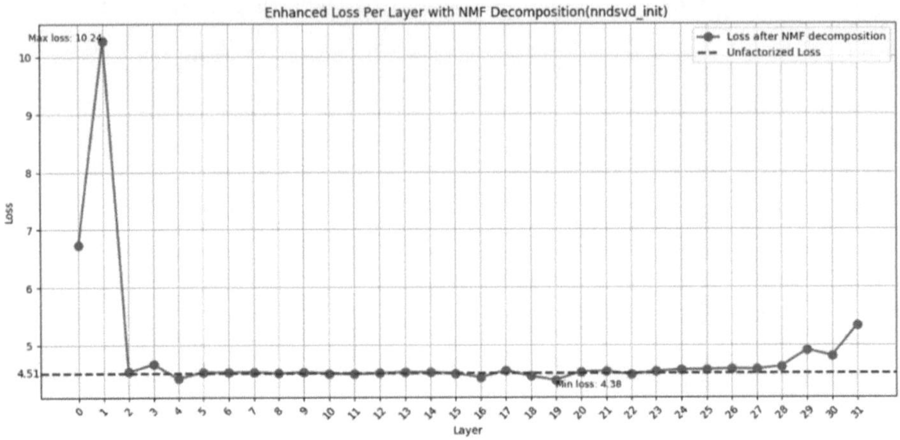

Fig. 6. Enhanced Loss Per Layer with NMF Decomposition (nndsvd_init)

According to the data presented in the table, it's evident that the application of NMF method to the MLP layers of the LLaMA2-7b model on the MMLU dataset significantly enhances model performance. Notably, improvements are observed in the layers with Layer_id 18, 19, 22, 23, and 24, where the accuracy rates compared to the baseline (*44.5%* when no NMF is applied) demonstrate substantial increases. The most notable enhancement reaches 47.6%, an approximate 7% increase from the baseline.

Table 2. The accuracy of the MLP-specific layer in the llama-2-7b model after NMF decomposition on the MMLU

Model	Dataset	Method	Layer_id	Acc
LLaMA2-7b	MMLU	NO–NMF		44.5
LLaMA2-7b	MMLU	NMF	17	43.8
LLaMA2-7b	MMLU	NMF	18	45.2 ↑
LLaMA2-7b	MMLU	NMF	19	47.6 ↑
LLaMA2-7b	MMLU	NMF	20	43.7
LLaMA2-7b	MMLU	NMF	21	42.1
LLaMA2-7b	MMLU	NMF	22	45.2 ↑
LLaMA2-7b	MMLU	NMF	23	46.3 ↑
LLaMA2-7b	MMLU	NMF	24	45.7 ↑
LLaMA2-7b	MMLU	NMF	25	44.1

4.3 Inference Speedup

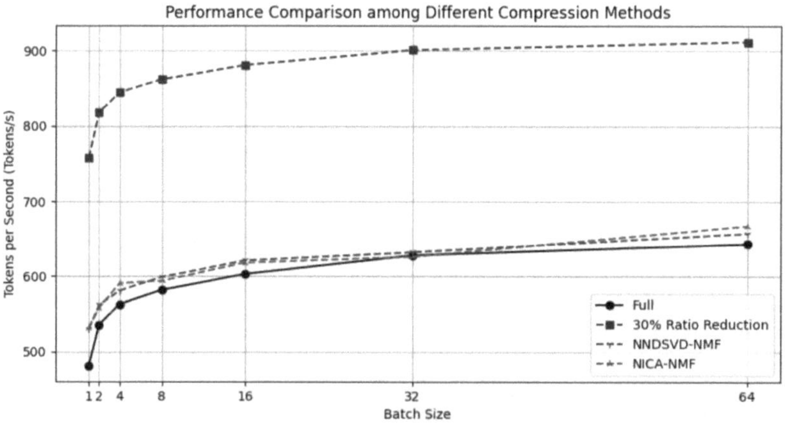

Fig. 7. Tokens processing efficiency of different matrix decomposition strategies

According to the data in the figure, we can find that under the compression efficiency of 30%, the speed of the model processing tokens will be much faster, close to 1.6×. The other two strategies of matrix decomposition also have some benefits for the speed for model processing tokens.

5 Limitation and Future Work

Our study has two limitations. First, our idea of considering batch size in combination with the MLP layer of the large language model did not improve the inference accuracy of the large language model. In addition, the current rank reduction method is still relatively fixed, and it is not possible to conduct different quantitative rank reduction according to different situations. In the future, we hope to explore more dynamic implementations of rank reduction.

6 Conclusion

In this paper, we give an analysis of compressing Large Language Models (LLMs) MLP layers using Singular Value Decomposition (SVD) and Non-negative Matrix Factorization (NMF), coupled with adaptive batch sizing, can significantly enhance computational efficiency without severely compromising accuracy. In addition, the NMF method can improve the model inference precision while slightly improving the model inference efficiency. Our findings are promising; however, the fixed nature of rank reduction and the lack of accuracy improvement with batch size adjustments highlight areas for further research. Future research will focus on more dynamic compression methods that adapt to varying operational demands and refine accuracy.

References

1. Zhao, W.X., et al.: A survey of large language models. CoRR, abs/2303.18223 (2023)
2. Wang, A., Singh, A., Michael, J., Hill, F., Levy, O., Bowman, S.R.: Glue: a multi-task benchmark and analysis platform for natural language understanding. arXiv preprint arXiv:1804.07461 (2018)
3. Dosovitskiy, A., et al.: An image is worth 16x16 words: transformers for image recognition at scale. arXiv preprint arXiv:2010.11929 (2020)
4. Brown, T., et al.: Language models are few-shot learners. In: Advances in Neural Information Processing Systems, vol. 33, pp. 1877–1901 (2020)
5. Touvron, H., et al.: Llama: open and efficient foundation language models. arXiv preprint arXiv:2302.13971 (2023)
6. Frantar, E., Ashkboos, S., Hoefler, T., Alistarh, D.: GPTQ: accurate post-training quantization for generative pre-trained transformers. CoRR, abs/2210.17323 (2022)
7. Lin, J., Tang, J., Tang, H., Yang, S., Dang, X., Han, S.: AWQ: activationaware weight quantization for LLM compression and acceleration. CoRR, abs/2306.00978 (2023)
8. Xiao, G., Lin, J., Seznec, M., Wu, H., Demouth, J., Han, S.: Smoothquant: accurate and efficient post-training quantization for large language models. In: Proceedings of Machine Learning Research, vol. 202, pp. 38087–38099. ICML, PMLR (2023)
9. Ma, X., Fang, G., Wang, X.: On the structural pruning of large language models. In: NeurIPS, Llm-pruner (2023)
10. Frantar, E., Alistarh, D.: Sparsegpt: massive language models can be accurately pruned in one-shot. In: ICML, vol. 202, pp. 10323–10337. PMLR (2023)
11. Gu, Y., Dong, L., Wei, F., Huang, M.: Knowledge distillation of large language models. CoRR, abs/2306.08543 (2023)
12. Hsieh, C-Y., et al.: Distilling step-by-step! outperforming larger language models with less training data and smaller model sizes. In: ACL (Findings), pp. 8003–8017. Association for Computational Linguistics (2023)
13. Courbariaux, M., Bengio, Y., David, J.-P.: Binaryconnect: Training deep neural networks with binary weights during propagations. In: Advances in Neural Information Processing Systems, vol. 28 (2015)
14. Dettmers, T., Lewis, M., Belkada, Y., Zettlemoyer, L.: Llm. int8 (): 8-bit matrix multiplication for transformers at scale. arXiv preprint arXiv:2208.07339 (2022)
15. Zhu, X., Li, J., Liu, Y., Ma, C., Wang, W.: A survey on model compression for large language models. arXiv preprint arXiv:2308.07633 (2023)
16. LeCun, Y., Denker, J., Solla, S.: Optimal brain damage. In: Advances in Neural Information Processing Systems, vol. 2 (1989)
17. Hinton, G., Vinyals, O., Dean, J.: Distilling the knowledge in a neural network. arXiv preprint arXiv:1503.02531 (2015)
18. Agarwal, R., Vieillard, N., Stanczyk, P., Ramos, S., Geist, M., Bachem, O.: Gkd: generalized knowledge distillation for auto-regressive sequence models. arXiv preprint arXiv:2306.13649 (2023)
19. Hsu, Y-C., Hua, T., Chang, S., Lou, Q., Shen, Y., Jin, H.: Language model compression with weighted low-rank factorization. In: ICLR. OpenReview.net (2022)
20. Yuan, Z., Shang, Y., Song, Y., Wu, Q., Yan, Y., Sun, G.: ASVD: activation-aware singular value decomposition for compressing large language models. CoRR, abs/2312.05821 (2023)

21. Touvron, H., et al.: Llama 2: open foundation and finetuned chat models. arXiv preprint arXiv:2307.09288 (2023b)
22. Sharma, P., Ash, J.T., Misra, D.: The Truth is in there: improving reasoning in language models with layer-selective rank reduction. arXiv preprint arXiv:2312.13558 (2023)
23. Wang, J., Zhang, X.-L.: Deep NMF topic modeling. arXiv preprint arXiv:2102.12998

Intelligent Robot

Trajectory Prediction of Unmanned Surface Vehicle Based on Improved Transformer

Zhipeng Cheng[1], Jian Yu[2], Junyu Chen[2], Jihuan Ren[1], and Xiang Wu[1(✉)]

[1] Nanjing University of Science and Technology, Nanjing 210094, China
{rjhuan,wuxiang1}@njust.edu.cn
[2] China Ship Development and Design Center, Wuhan 430064, China

Abstract. In recent years, the significance of applying Unmanned Surface Vehicles (USVs) in coastal defense has been progressively increasing. Precise prediction of USV trajectories plays a vital role in the decision-making of coastal defense, anti-privacy, and so on. However, the intricate nature of USV trajectories, characterized by high maneuverability and sudden motion pattern changes, poses great challenges for accurate prediction. To address these issues, this paper proposes a trajectory prediction model based on an improved Transformer with sparse self-attention and physical rule constraints. Focus on designing the "Max-Mean" sparse self-attention mechanism to streamline computational demands and memory usage, and the physical loss function to improve the accuracy and robustness of predictions. Moreover, a generative decoder is included to improve the model's ability to process long sequence data and the inference efficiency. To verify the prediction effect of the proposed method, we construct a USV simulation trajectory dataset based on the ship kinematic model for trajectory prediction experiments. The simulation results illustrate that the proposed model surpasses existing trajectory prediction models and fulfills the stringent requirements for precise and rapid USV trajectory predictions.

Keywords: Unmanned Surface Vehicle · trajectory prediction · trajectory generation · transformer · self-attention mechanism

1 Introduction

Since the 20th century, the rapid advancements in Artificial Intelligence (AI) technology have greatly propelled the development of unmanned systems [1]. As a branch of unmanned systems, Unmanned Surface Vehicles (USVs) have garnered significant attention in various fields due to their compact size, high concealability, and exceptional maneuverability. In maritime operations, USVs play important roles in reconnaissance, tracking, and target acquisition under central command, and can often cooperate with other unmanned platforms such

Published by Springer Nature Switzerland AG 2025
Z. Shi et al. (Eds.): ICIS 2024, IFIP AICT 720, pp. 175–189, 2025.
https://doi.org/10.1007/978-3-031-71253-1_13

as drones to achieve comprehensive integration across land, sea, air, and space domains [2]. Consequently, timely and effective interception and neutralization of enemy USVs are imperative to our coastal defense.

Accurate prediction of USV trajectories is vital to improve the efficacy of interception and targeting efforts. Unlike traditional sailing vessels, predicting the trajectories of USVs presents unique challenges. Firstly, their high maneuverability results in intricate and rapidly changing motion patterns. Furthermore, the trajectory data of non-cooperative USVs obtained from satellites, radars, and other sensors, are susceptible to interference and loss, which increases the difficulty of trajectory prediction using existing methods. Therefore, we propose a trajectory prediction model to address these challenges effectively. Initially, a highly realistic simulation model of USV motion is performed to generate a comprehensive trajectory dataset. Subsequently, leveraging Transformer architecture which can mitigate short-distance dependency issues, we design multiple refinements to construct a precise and efficient USV trajectory prediction model. The prediction model undergo rigorous training on simulation data followed by comprehensive testing for demonstration.

The key contributions of this paper include:

1) Propose a USV trajectory prediction model based on an improved Transformer. Specifically, we devised a "Max-Mean" sparse self-attention mechanism to reduce computational complexity and storage requirements. Then, domain-specific knowledge is embedded into the model through a physical rule-tailored loss function, facilitating faster convergence during training and improving prediction accuracy.
2) Design a USV trajectory simulation model. We design a dynamic ship kinematics model for the generation of simulated USV trajectories, which can simulate USV motion behaviors in a near-realistic manner, such as simple "M-shaped" motions as well as complex looping and continuous turning behaviors.
3) Conduct comparative experiments. We use an established dataset to train and test the proposed model and compare it with LSTM, Transformer, and Informer. Results demonstrate the superior predictive capabilities of the proposed model over existing approaches.

The remaining content of the paper is organized as follows: Sect. 2 provides an overview of relevant research about ship trajectory prediction. Section 3 introduces the USV trajectory simulation model and the trajectory prediction model designed in this paper. Section 4 presents the experimental configuration, results, and corresponding analysis. Finally, Sect. 5 summarizes this paper.

2 Related Work

In recent years, researchers worldwide have extensively explored ship trajectory prediction. These prevalent prediction methods are typically categorized into physics-based, traditional machine learning, and deep learning approaches.

The physics-based method utilized mathematical and physical equations to establish a motion model describing ship movement [3]. Zhang et al. [4] developed a dynamic equation model focusing on speed and course prediction, while another study [5] integrated behavior recognition and curvature constraints. Some researchers have also incorporated Kalman Filtering (KF) to address noise, with Perera et al. [6] applying Extended Kalman Filtering (EKF) and Nurhadi et al. [7] utilizing Square Root Ensemble Kalman Filter (EnSRKF) for accurate predictions. However, these methods face challenges in complex environments despite offering interpretable predictions rooted in actual motion states. In the maritime battlefield, the lack of trajectory data for USV affects the predictive accuracy, particularly for long-term predictions in practical applications.

Machine learning-based trajectory prediction diverges from physics-based approaches by relying on statistical probability. Gaussian Process (GP) model, favored by some researchers [8,9], leverages Bayesian reasoning to predict ship trajectories, yet their accuracy diminishes with higher-dimensional data. Support Vector Machine (SVM), while applicable, exhibits limited effectiveness in trajectory prediction [10,11] due to its classification-focused nature. Conversely, the Hidden Markov Model (HMM) shows significant improvement when coupled with wavelet analysis, as demonstrated by Zhang et al. [12]. However, these methods often neglect environmental interactions during prediction. Jansen et al. [13] propose Dynamic Bayesian Networks (DBN), which model context as latent variables to predict future positions. However, this approach's generalization ability may falter in complex scenarios with nonlinear, high-dimensional data, restricting its applicability and hindering its capacity to capture intricate trajectory patterns and dynamic changes.

Recently, deep learning-based trajectory prediction methods have gained popularity for their ability to comprehensively account for various relevant factors and dynamically adapt to complex scenarios. These methods primarily involve converting historical trajectory data into time series data, establishing correlations between past and predicted trajectory points, and ultimately achieving accurate trajectory prediction. Xu et al. [14] introduced a trajectory prediction model based on a three-layer Back Propagation neural network (BPNN). Considering the limitation that BPNN cannot memorize, some scholars use Recurrent Neural Networks (RNN) for trajectory prediction. Hu et al. [15] developed a data preprocessing technique based on symmetric segmented path distance, utilizing RNN for trajectory prediction. Notably, RNN's advantage lies in its ability to retain past and current input information within each hidden layer, facilitating accurate time-series predictions. However, limitations in remembering distant historical information led to the introduction of Long Short-Term Memory (LSTM) networks, which can address gradient vanishing issues and excel in processing long sequences [16]. Nguyen [17] divided the navigation sea area into spatial grids, transforming Automatic Identification System (AIS) data into a sequence-to-sequence format and proposing an LSTM-based prediction model for real-time ship trajectory prediction. Despite its efficacy, further enhancements are needed for prediction accuracy. The transformer's powerful self-attention mechanism can extract features of input data in a parallel manner, with a more enhanced ability to capture long-range dependencies and better prediction accuracy. While many researchers [18–20] have applied the Transformer to ship trajectory prediction, solely relying on data-driven models may limit effectiveness and overlook the physical laws of USV movements, potentially leading to oscillatory prediction results. Additionally, the model's computational complexity and storage requirements increase substantially with larger datasets, posing practical deployment challenges.

Given the challenges above, this paper proposes a more efficient USV trajectory prediction model based on an improved Transformer. First, we improve the self-attention mechanism to reduce the computational complexity and memory usage. Secondly, we design a physical loss function to improve the robustness and prediction accuracy of the model. Finally, a generative decoder is introduced to improve the reasoning efficiency of the model.

3 USV Trajectory Prediction Model Based on Improved Transformer

We propose an improved Transformer-based model for USV trajectory prediction, which can adeptly handle USV trajectory data samples, enabling precise, efficient, and long-term trajectory predictions.

3.1 Problem Formulation

The USV trajectory prediction task can be described as estimating future trajectories using historical trajectory data. Radar systems capture the USV trajectory and promptly feed the detected trajectory data into the prediction model. Subsequently, the model generates a projected trajectory based on the input sequence to support subsequent tasks.

The trajectory data detected by the radar system can be viewed as a chronological sequence:

$$\mathcal{L} = \{P_1, P_2, P_3, ..., P_T\} \tag{1}$$

where P_T is the corresponding trajectory data tuple of USV at timestamp t, which is specifically expressed as follows:

$$P_t = (x_t, y_t, z_t, \varphi_t, \theta_t, \psi_t, \nu_t, c_t) \tag{2}$$

where x_t, y_t, z_t denote the three-dimensional coordinates, φ_t denotes roll angle, θ_t denotes pitch angle, ψ_t denotes yaw angle, ν_t denotes speed, c_t denotes heading of the USV at time t. These eight selected features comprehensively describe the USV's motion status. The three-dimensional trajectory conveys spatial position information, while the roll, pitch, and yaw angles depict the unmanned boat's movement attitude. Speed and heading parameters are utilized explicitly in formulating the physical loss function.

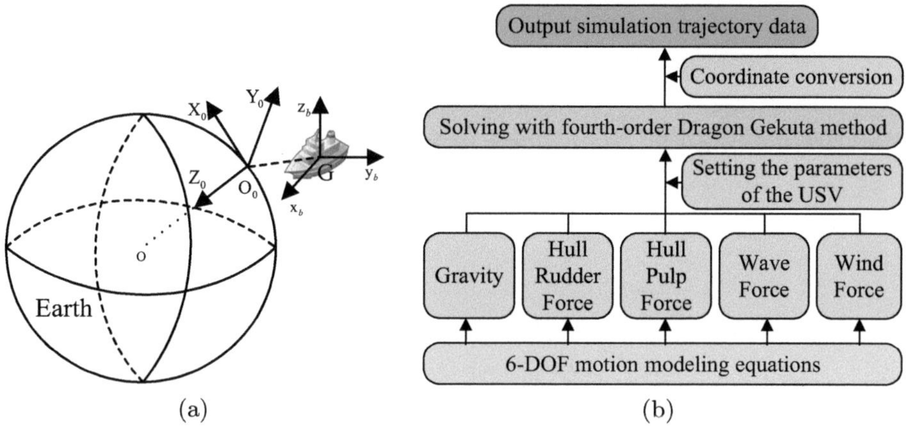

Fig. 1. (a)Ship's 6-DOF motion coordinate system. (b)USV trajectory simulation model.

Based on the previously given USV trajectory data, the trajectory prediction model predicts future position using the following formula:

$$y = \{p_{T+1}, \dots, p_{T+L}\} = f_p\left(p_1, \dots, p_T\right) \tag{3}$$

where f_p means that the model outputs predicted trajectory data of length L based on historical trajectory data of length T.

3.2 USV Trajectory Simulation Model

Ship Kinematics Model. Due to the challenge of obtaining the actual trajectory of the USV, we utilize the ship's kinematic model to generate realistic USV trajectory data for subsequent trajectory prediction experiments. Ship kinematic models predominantly based on the Mathematical Model Group (MMG) [21].

To obtain the realism of the USV trajectory data, we conducted trajectory simulations using the ship's Six Degrees of Freedom (6-DOF) model [22] based on the MMG model. The 6-DOF model accounts for the ship's motion in two coordinate systems (see Fig. 1(a)): the inertial coordinate system $\mathrm{O_0} - \mathrm{X_0 Y_0} Z_0$ and the body coordinate system $\mathrm{G} - \mathrm{x}_b \mathrm{y}_b z_b$. By modeling the characteristics of each USV component, this model accurately simulates changes in angles and speeds influenced by external factors such as currents, waves, and wind. The following differential equations can be established for 6-DOF motion in the two coordinate systems:

$$\begin{pmatrix} \dot{x} \\ \dot{y} \\ \dot{z} \\ \dot{\varphi} \\ \dot{\theta} \\ \dot{\psi} \end{pmatrix} = \begin{pmatrix} c\psi c\theta & -s\psi c\phi + c\phi s\theta s\phi & s\phi s\psi + c\psi c\phi s\theta & 0 & 0 & 0 \\ s\psi c\theta & c\psi c\phi + s\psi s\theta s\phi & -c\psi c\phi + s\theta s\psi s\phi & 0 & 0 & 0 \\ -s\theta & c\theta s\phi & c\theta c\phi & 0 & 0 & 0 \\ 0 & 0 & 0 & 1 & s\phi t\theta & c\phi t\theta \\ 0 & 0 & 0 & 0 & c\phi & -s\theta \\ 0 & 0 & 0 & 1 & \frac{s\phi}{c\theta} & \frac{c\phi}{c\theta} \end{pmatrix} \begin{pmatrix} u \\ v \\ w \\ p \\ q \\ r \end{pmatrix} \tag{4}$$

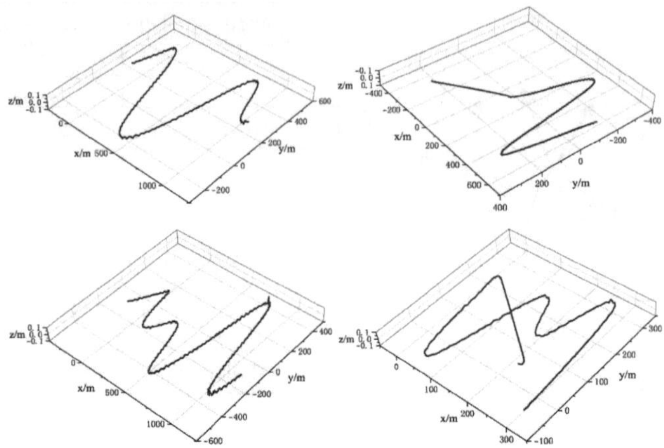

Fig. 2. Examples of partial trajectories.

where $x, y, z, \phi, \theta, \psi$ respectively represent the three-dimensional coordinates, the angle of roll, pitch and heading in the inertial coordinate system, u, v, w, p, q, r respectively represent the speed of forward, swaying, heave, rolling angular, pitching angular and heading angular in the body coordinate system. c represents cos, s represents sin, and t represents tan.

USV Simulation Trajectory Generation. In the simulation of ship trajectories, under the assumption of infinite water depth as per Newton's motion theorem and the MMG model definition, the 6-DOF motion model of the USV in the body coordinate system can be articulated as follows:

$$\begin{cases} \dot{\eta} = J(\eta)\upsilon \\ M\dot{\upsilon} + C(\upsilon)\upsilon + D(\upsilon)\upsilon + g(\eta) = \tau + \omega \end{cases} \tag{5}$$

In the equation, $\eta = [x, y, z, \phi, \theta, \psi]^\top$ denotes the position and direction vector in the inertial coordinate system, while $n = [u, v, w, p, q, r]^\top$ signifies the velocity state vector in the body coordinate system. Additionally, $M \in \mathbb{R}^{6\times6}$, $C(\nu) \in \mathbb{R}^{6\times6}$ and $D(\nu) \in \mathbb{R}^{6\times6}$ represent the inertia matrix, the Coriolis matrix and the hydrodynamic damping matrix respectively. $g(\eta) \in \mathbb{R}^6$ encapsulates the combined effects of gravity and buoyancy. Notably, $\tau \in \mathbb{R}^6$ embodies the force and moment vector or generalized force within the 6-DOF model, with $\omega \in \mathbb{R}^6$ encompassing external forces such as wind and waves. $J(\eta) \in \mathbb{R}^{6\times6}$ symbolizes the transformation matrix bridging the inertial and attached coordinate systems.

During USV trajectory simulation, modules for gravity, hull paddle force, hull rudder force, wave force, and wind force are established based on Eq. 5 (see Fig. 1(b)). We use the fourth-order Runge-Kutta method [23] to solve the Eq. 4, and coordinate transformation is executed to derive three-dimensional coordinates, roll angle, pitch angle, and heading angle of the USV in the inertial coordinate system. Then we calculate the speed and heading based on the simulation step size to form the entire trajectory data set. Table 1 illustrates the parameter settings for the unmanned boat in the trajectory simulation model, with a portion of the simulated trajectory visualized in Fig. 2.

Table 1. Parameters related to USV.

Parameter name	Value	Description
rho_w	1025.0(kg/m^3)	Density of water
l	2.38(m)	Length of USV
m	100(kg)	Quality of USV
F_max	440(N)	Maximum limiting value of external forces on USV
M_max	440(N·m)	Maximum limiting value of external moments to which the USV is subjected
delta_max	25(°)	Maximum limit values for rudder angles of USV

3.3 Improved Transformer Model

The model proposed in this paper (see Fig. 3) mainly consists of two parts: an encoder and a decoder. The encoder features a Multi-Head "Max-Mean" Self-attention layer alongside a Conv-pooling layer, which processes the input sequence into high-dimensional hidden state vectors. The "Max-Mean" self-attention layer refines the traditional self-attention mechanism, while the Conv-pooling operation streamlines data complexity, minimizing memory usage. The decoder primarily employs self-attention layers to map hidden states, feeding the output to a fully connected feed-forward network for trajectory prediction. Furthermore, prior to feeding the data into the encoder and decoder, we enhance the model's comprehension of the motion patterns of USV by incorporating absolute positional information using a trigonometric function position encoding mechanism.

Before the encoder and decoder obtain the input sequence, the model maps the input trajectory sequence into embedding vectors. At time t, the input x_t can be expressed as

$$x_t = \text{Embed}(p_t) \quad 1 \leqslant t \leqslant N \tag{6}$$

Subsequently, the model transforms the input sequence $(x_1, x_2, ..., x_T)$ into a hidden state vector $\boldsymbol{h} = (h_1, h_2, ..., h_T)$ through the encoder, which is then processed by the decoder to generate the predicted trajectory sequence $y = \{p_{T+1}, \dots, p_{T+L}\}$ in a forward step.

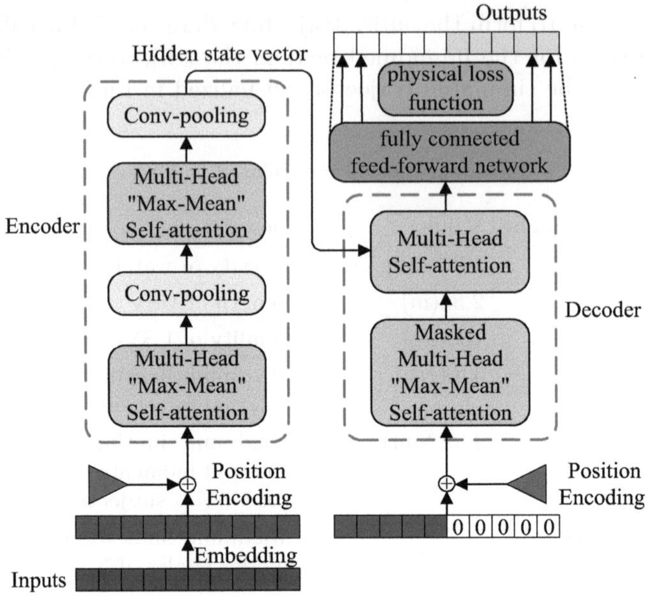

Fig. 3. The structure of the model.

"Max-Mean" Self-attention Mechanism. The encoder receives the input sequence and transforms it into a sequence of high-dimensional hidden state vectors. The scaled dot-product of the self-attention mechanism in the Transformer model performs as

$$\mathrm{Att}(\mathbf{Q}, \mathbf{K}, \mathbf{V}) = \mathrm{softmax}\left(\frac{\mathbf{Q}\mathbf{K}^{\mathbf{T}}}{\sqrt{d}}\right)\mathbf{V} \tag{7}$$

where $\mathbf{Q} \in \mathbb{R}^{L_Q \times d}$, $\mathbf{K} \in \mathbb{R}^{L_K \times d}$ and $\mathbf{V} \in \mathbb{R}^{L_V \times d}$ denote the Query, Key and Value respectively, while L_Q, L_K, L_V represent the lengths of matrices $\mathbf{Q}$, $\mathbf{K}$, and $\mathbf{V}$ respectively, with d representing the word embedding dimension. Utilizing $\mathbf{q}_i$, $\mathbf{k}_i$, and $\mathbf{v}_i$ to stand for the i-th row of the $\mathbf{Q}$, $\mathbf{K}$ and $\mathbf{V}$, the i-th query's attention calculation is as follows:

$$\mathrm{Att}\left(\mathbf{q}_i, \mathbf{K}, \mathbf{V}\right) = \sum_j \frac{k\left(\mathbf{q}_i, \mathbf{k}_j\right)}{\sum_l k\left(\mathbf{q}_i, \mathbf{k}_l\right)} \mathbf{v}_j = \mathbb{E}_{p(\mathbf{k}_j|\mathbf{q}_i)}\left[\mathbf{v}_j\right] \tag{8}$$

where $p(\mathbf{k}_j|\mathbf{q}_i) = k(\mathbf{q}_i, \mathbf{k}_j)/\sum_l k(\mathbf{q}_i, \mathbf{k}_l)$, $k(\mathbf{q}_i, \mathbf{k}_j) = \exp(\mathbf{q}_i\mathbf{k}_j^\top/\sqrt{d})$. Although the self-attention mechanism can address the challenge of long dependencies in conventional sequence modeling, it requires the quadratic times dot-product computation and $O(L^2)$ memory usage to acquire outputs.

Previous studies have indicated that the self-attention probability distribution is a long-tailed distribution suggesting that only a tiny fraction of dot products significantly influence the attention score. Consequently, we design a "Max-Mean" self-attention mechanism to identify critical elements in $\mathbf{q}_i$ that strongly impact the attention score. We define the i-th query's attention calculation as

$$\mathrm{M}\left(\mathbf{q}_i, \mathbf{K}\right) = \max_u \left\{ \frac{\mathbf{q}_i \mathbf{k}_j^\top}{\sqrt{d}} \right\} - \frac{1}{L_K} \sum_{L_K}^{j=1} \frac{\mathbf{q}_i \mathbf{k}_j^\top}{\sqrt{d}} \tag{9}$$

where $\max_u\{\cdot\}$ means the sum of the largest u elements in the set of $\mathbf{q}_i \mathbf{k}_j^\top / \sqrt{d}$. When $\mathbf{q}_i$ gets a higher M, the attention probability $p(\mathbf{k}_j \mid \mathbf{q}_i)$ of the $\mathbf{q}_i$ is more likely to include dominant dot product pairs in the head field of the long-tailed self-attention distribution. By selecting the u $\mathbf{q}_i$ with the highest M value and filling other pairs with zero, we construct a new query matrix $\bar{\mathbf{Q}}$ to obtain the new sparse attention calculation formula as follows:

$$\overline{\mathrm{Att}}(\mathbf{Q}, \mathbf{K}, \mathbf{V}) = \mathrm{Softmax}\left(\frac{\overline{\mathbf{Q}} \mathbf{K}^\top}{\sqrt{d}} \right) \mathbf{V} \tag{10}$$

where $u = c \cdot \ln L_Q$, c is a very small constant sampling factor.

Introducing the "Max-Mean" self-attention mechanism reduces both the time and space complexity from $O(L^2)$ to $O(L \ln L)$, enhancing the model's practicality and the efficiency of trajectory prediction.

Physical Loss Function. The Transformer, as a data-driven model, may not be able to understand the motion laws of the target well. Some scholars have found that the average parameter model can effectively describe the motion state of surface ships. When a surface ship is in motion, it satisfies the following formula:

$$x_{n+1} = x_n + v \cdot \Delta t \cdot \sin c \tag{11}$$

where x_n and x_{n+1} represent the x-axis coordinate position of the surface vessels at the current moment and the next moment, v and c represent the speed and the heading angle of the surface ship at the current moment, Δt indicates the time difference between these two moments. Therefore, we propose to integrate this formula as physical knowledge into the data-driven model and design a physical loss function to enable the model to comprehend certain physical principles behind the operational state of USV. This approach aims to expedite model convergence during training and enhance the accuracy and smoothness of trajectory prediction. Specifically, we select the Mean Squared Error (MSE) function as the loss function and the designed physical loss function encompasses the following two components:

$$\begin{aligned} \mathrm{MSE} &= \mathrm{MSE}_{pred} + \mathrm{MSE}_{phy} \\ &= \frac{1}{n} \sum_{i=1}^{n} \left[y_{pred} - y_i \right]^2 + \frac{1}{m} \sum_{j=1}^{m} \left[\frac{dx_j}{dt} - \nu \cdot \sin c \right]^2 \end{aligned} \tag{12}$$

where MSE_{pred} and MSE_{phy} represent the primary MSE and the physical loss incorporated as expert knowledge, y_{pred} and y_i represent the model's output value and the observed value, n and m represent the prediction length and the last m state vectors of x_{starttok} .

The selection method considers the sequential timing of the data, emphasizing a more substantial influence among closely related data points. Specifically, the m height values closest in time to the predicted value within the time series are considered. The physical loss (see Fig. 4(a)) involves predicting the trajectory over L time steps, with each step comprising eight dimensions of data. The proposed model utilizes the x-coordinate, speed (v), and heading (c) from the last m time steps to calculate the physical information loss, highlighted within the red box in the figure. Further experiments have shown that when predicting the USV trajectory, additional physical knowledge enhances the accuracy and smoothness of model predictions.

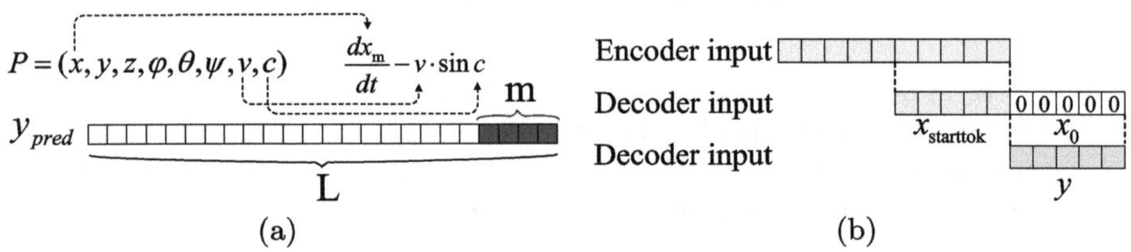

Fig. 4. (a)Physical loss. (b)Input and output of the decoder an encoder.

Generative Decoder. The model we proposed introduces a generative decoder to replace the Transformer's original auto-regressive decoder to solve problems such as error accumulation and low inference efficiency (see Fig. 4(b)). This generative decoding mechanism feeds vectors into the decoder in the following manner:

$$x_{\text{dec}} = \text{Concat }(x_{\text{starttok}}, x_0) \in \mathbb{R}^{(L_{\text{startok}}+L_y)\times d} \tag{13}$$

where x_{starttok} represents the flag bit denoting the start of the vector, x_0 serves as a placeholder typically set to 0. The final output data length of the model matches that of x_0, both being L_y. Through the generative decoding mechanism, the model can efficiently infer and predict state sequences of length L_y for target in a single iteration. For instance, considering target trajectory sequence data spanning 128 time steps, generative decoding accomplishes this task in just one iteration. In contrast, traditional auto-regressive decoding necessitates repeated calculations and iterations 128 times for completion.

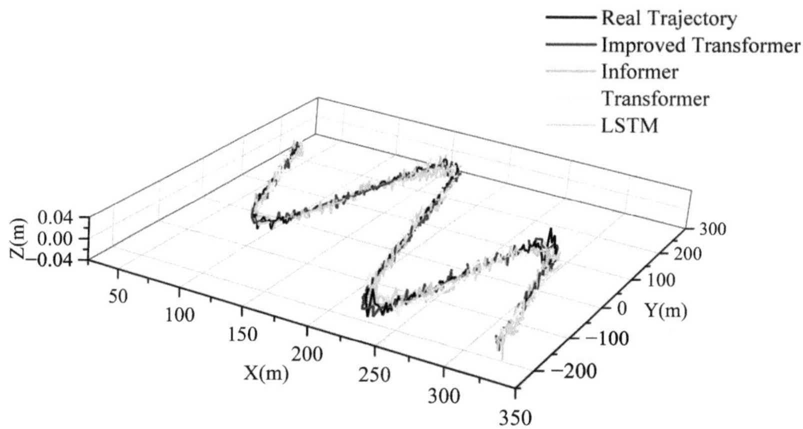

Fig. 5. 3-D Presentation of prediction results.

4 Experiment and Result Analysis

In this section, we use the previously established USV trajectory simulation model to create the USV trajectory dataset and then conduct trajectory prediction experiments, followed by experimental verification analysis.

4.1 Dataset Preparation and Model Setup

The dataset used for simulation verification comprises 930 USV trajectories, totaling 754,887 timestamp data points. Each trajectory includes eight characteristics of the USV: three-dimensional coordinates, roll angle, pitch angle, yaw angle, speed, and heading. Figure 2 illustrates a segment of the simulation, showcasing various types of maneuvers, including simple "M"-shaped movements as well as more intricate maneuvers such as "swing" and "multi-bend" types. Around 75% of the dataset focuses on trajectories with complex maneuvers to ensure the model meets more complex scenarios. Then the dataset is divided into training (80%), validation (10%), and test (10%) sets.

The model is implemented using the PyTorch library, with six self-attention modules included in the encoder and four self-attention modules in the decoder. We use the physical loss function delineated in Sect. 3.3 and the Gaussian error linear units (GELU) [24] activation function to expedite model convergence. We train the model 600 epochs with Adam optimizer to update the parameters according to the error gradient. The batch size is 32 which enhances the model's generalization capabilities and mitigates the risk of overfitting. The learning rate starts at 0.001 and decreases by a factor of 0.5 for each epoch, which aims to reduce fluctuations in the latter stages of training, facilitating an optimal solution.

The MSE and mean absolute error (MAE) are selected as an evaluation criterion, and lower MSE and MAE indicate that the predicted trajectory is closer to the real trajectory.

4.2 Simulation Results and Analysis

After training the model, the test set is utilized for evaluation. Three popular trajectory prediction models-LSTM, Transformer, and Informer-are selected for comparative analysis to compare the predictive performance.

A random trajectory is chosen for assessment, and the prediction results of the four models on this trajectory are presented in Fig. 5. Given that the USV primarily navigates on the water surface, a trajectory (L=320) is visualized in a two-dimensional plane (see in Fig. 6). Additionally, two partially enlarged views of the trajectory are presented on the left side of Fig. 6, offering a more detailed comparison of prediction accuracy among the models.

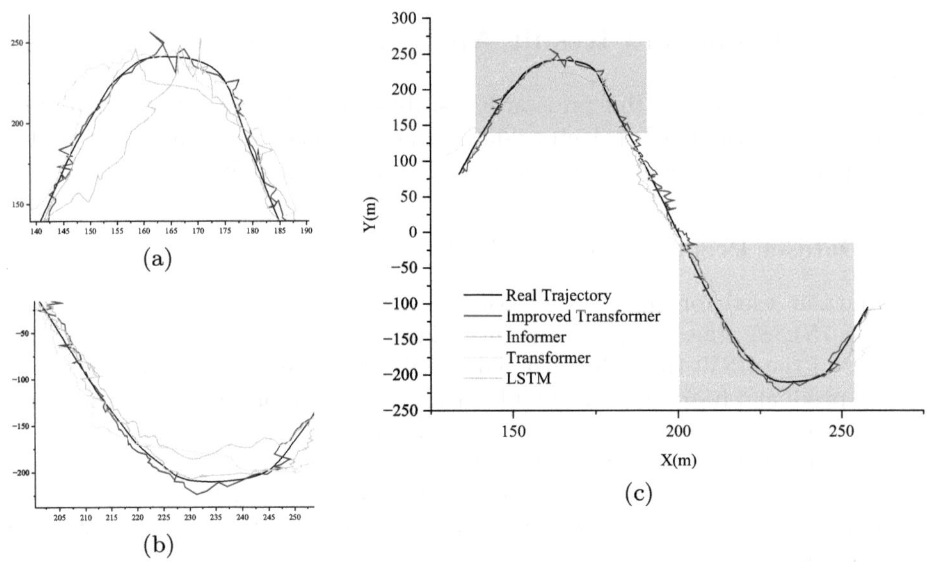

Fig. 6. 2-D Presentation of prediction results. (a) Local magnification from the gray box. (b) Local magnification from the orange box. (c) Selected from the Fig. 5 (Color figure online).

The partial enlargement shows that during a turning maneuver of the USV, the LSTM model exhibits the poorest performance, manifesting noticeable oscillations in the predicted trajectory. It underscores a limitation: while LSTM excels in processing long-term sequences, it struggles to capture dependencies and spatio-temporal features within such data sequences effectively. In contrast, both the Transformer and Informer models exhibit comparatively minimal oscillations. This can be attributed to the self-attention mechanism's robust spatio-temporal feature extraction capability. Notably, the improved Transformer model proposed in this study demonstrates the most favorable prediction efficacy, characterized by minimal trajectory oscillation closely mirroring the original trajectory. This underscores the significant enhancement in trajectory prediction accuracy facilitated by the "Max-Mean" sparse self-attention mechanism designed in this study, complemented by a physical loss function designed to ensure smoother predicted trajectories.

To ensure robust evaluation, each model undergoes five repeated experiments using the same dataset, with the average MSE/MAE calculated across different prediction lengths, as detailed in Table 2.

It can be seen that the MSE and MAE of the improved Transformer model are both the most minor with three different prediction lengths, indicating that the prediction accuracy of the model we proposed is higher than that of other mainstream models. Compared with LSTM, when $L=64$, the MAE and MSE of the model proposed in this paper are reduced by 56.3% and 46.1% respectively. As the prediction length increases, when $L=320$, the MAE and MSE decrease by 64.2% and 56.7% respectively, indicating that the proposed model can more effectively handle long sequence data and obtain better long-term prediction results. Our model also outperforms the most related work Transformer and Informer. When $L=192$, MAE is 25.7% lower than the Transformer and 16.9% lower than the Informer. When $L=320$, MSE also decreased by 23.2% and 10.8%, respectively. It shows that the generative decoder performs much better than the Transformer's auto-regressive decoder in long-term prediction. Moreover, compared with Informer, the introduction of the physical loss function enables the model to learn additional physical knowledge. At the same time, the "Max-Mean" sparse self attention mechanism designed in our model can effectively make the model pay more attention to the key information in the trajectory data, thereby making more accurate predictions.

Table 2. MSE and MAE for different models.

Modle	Evaluation	Length(L) of Prediction		
		64	192	320
LSTM	MSE	0.0768	0.1343	0.3094
	MAE	0.1633	0.2367	0.3571
Transformer	MSE	0.0543	0.1100	0.1918
	MAE	0.1292	0.2031	0.2324
Informer	MSE	0.0513	0.1109	0.1651
	MAE	0.1089	0.1817	0.2195
Improved Transformer	MSE	0.0336	0.0634	0.1113
	MAE	0.0881	0.1170	0.1547

5 Conclusion

This paper presents a comprehensive ship motion analysis, culminating in the development of a trajectory simulation model for USV. Subsequently, an improved Transformer-based USV trajectory prediction model is proposed. The model incorporates a novel "Max-Mean" sparse self-attention mechanism and a trigonometric function position encoding technique to extract trajectory features, thereby enhancing prediction accuracy effectively. A physical loss function is also devised to bolster model robustness, resulting in smoother and more accurate trajectory predictions. Furthermore, a generative decoder enhances the model's reasoning efficiency. Experimental validations affirm that the efficacy of the proposed model is better than that of existing mainstream trajectory prediction models. In the future, to further enhance the model's predictive accuracy for USV trajectories, several avenues are proposed:

1)Experimentation with real-world USV trajectories.

2)Structural optimizations are envisaged to enhance the model's adaptability across diverse trajectory prediction scenarios.

3)Additional physical variables augment the model's capacity to glean underlying physical insights from trajectories, thus enhancing prediction accuracy.

References

1. Wu, C., Zhang, T.: Intelligent unmanned systems: important achievements and applications of new generation artificial intelligence (2020)
2. Specht, C., Świtalski, E., Specht, M.: Application of an autonomous/unmanned survey vessel (ASV/USV) in bathymetric measurements. Pol. Marit. Res. **24**(3), 36–44 (2017)
3. Wang, Y., Perera, L.P., Batalden, B.-M.: Kinematic motion models based vessel state estimation to support advanced ship predictors. Ocean Eng. **286**, 115503 (2023)
4. Zhang, Y., Gao, S., He, W., Cai, J.: Navigation trajectory prediction method of inland ships based on multi-model fusion. China Mech. Eng. **33**(10), 1142 (2022)
5. Xie, F., Lou, J., Zhao, K., Qi, Y.: A research on vehicle trajectory prediction method based on behavior recognition and curvature constraints. Automot. Eng. **41**(9), 1036–1042 (2019)
6. Perera, L.P., Soares, C.G., et al.: Ocean vessel trajectory estimation and prediction based on extended Kalman filter. In: The Second International Conference on Adaptive and Self-Adaptive Systems and Applications, pp. 14–20. Citeseer (2010)
7. Nurhadi, H., Herlambang, T., Adzkiya, D.: Trajectory estimation of autonomous surface vehicle using square root ensemble Kalman filter. In: 2019 International Conference on Advanced Mechatronics, Intelligent Manufacture and Industrial Automation (ICAMIMIA), pp. 325–328. IEEE (2019)
8. Rong, H., Teixeira, A.P., Guedes Soares, C.: Ship trajectory uncertainty prediction based on a gaussian process model. Ocean Eng. **182**, 499–511 (2019)
9. Chenchen, M., Chen, P., Bo, Y., Yining, L., Xunqi, X.: Ship trajectory prediction based on gaussian process regression. Technol. Innovation Appl. **31**, 28–29 (2017)
10. Jiao, L., Guoyou, S., Xueqian, Y., Kaige, Z.: Ship track prediction model based on DE-SVM. J. Shanghai Marit. Univ. **41**(01), 34–39 (2020)

11. Liu, X., He, W., Xie, J., Chu, X.: Predicting the trajectories of vessels using machine learning. In: 2020 5th International Conference on Control, Robotics and Cybernetics (CRC), pp. 66–70. IEEE (2020)
12. Zhang, X., Liu, G., Hu, C., Ma, X.: Wavelet analysis based hidden Markov model for large ship trajectory prediction. In: 2019 Chinese Control Conference (CCC), pp. 2913–2918. IEEE (2019)
13. Jansen, L., Pavlin, G., Atamas, A., Mignet, F.: Context-based vessel trajectory forecasting: a probabilistic approach combining dynamic bayesian networks with an auxiliary position determination process. In: 2020 IEEE 23rd International Conference on Information Fusion (FUSION), pp. 1–10. IEEE (2020)
14. Tingting, X., Xiaoming, L., Xin, Y.: Real time prediction of ship track based on BP neural network. J. Dalian Marit. Univ. **38**(01), 9–11 (2012)
15. Yuke, H., Xia Wei, H., Xiaoxuan, S.H., Yunhui, W.: Ship track prediction based on recurrent neural network. Syst. Eng. Electron. Technol. **42**(4), 7 (2020)
16. Park, J., Jeong, J., Park, Y.: Ship trajectory prediction based on bi-LSTM using spectral-clustered AIS data. J. Marine Sci. Eng. **9**(9), 1037 (2021)
17. Nguyen, D-D., Le Van, C., Ali, M I.: Vessel trajectory prediction using sequence-to-sequence models over spatial grid. In: Proceedings of the 12th ACM International Conference on Distributed and Event-Based Systems, pp. 258–261 (2018)
18. Jiang, D., Shi, G., Li, N., Ma, L., Li, W., Shi, J.: TRFM-ls: transformer-based deep learning method for vessel trajectory prediction. J. Marine Sci. Eng. **11**(4), 880 (2023)
19. Nguyen, D., Fablet, R.: A transformer network with sparse augmented data representation and cross entropy loss for AIS-based vessel trajectory prediction. IEEE Access (2024)
20. Xue, H., Wang, S., Xia, M., Guo, S.: G-trans: a hierarchical approach to vessel trajectory prediction with GRU-based transformer. Ocean Eng. **300**, 117431 (2024)
21. Yoshimura, Y.: Mathematical model for manoeuvring ship motion (MMG Model). In: Workshop on Mathematical Models for Operations involving Ship-Ship Interaction, pp. 1–6 (2005)
22. Ömer Sinan Şahin: Mathematical modeling of the ships' six-degree-of-freedom motions. Gemi ve Deniz Teknolojisi **209**, 5–18 (2017)
23. Kutta, W.: Beitrag zur näherungsweisen Integration totaler Differentialgleichungen. Teubner (1901)
24. Hendrycks, D., Gimpel, K.: Gaussian error linear units (gelus). arXiv preprint arXiv:1606.08415 (2016)

Deep Neural Network Based Relocalization of Mobile Robot in Visual SLAM

Azhar Muhammad Hamza[1], Chaoxia Shi[1], and Yanqing Wang[2(✉)]

[1] Nanjing University of Science and Technology, Nanjing 210094, China
{mian.hamza,scx}@njust.edu.cn
[2] Nanjing Xiaozhuang University, Nanjing 211171, China
wyq0325@126.com

Abstract. Relocalization after track loss in Visual Simultaneous Localization and Mapping (Visual SLAM) is a critical challenge in robotics, especially for autonomous mobile robots navigating dynamic environments. This paper introduces a deep learning approach that employs Deep Neural Networks (DNNs), particularly VGG16 and ResNet34, to reorient and relocalize robots effectively. Trained on a vast repository of indoor images from the Multimodal Indoor Simulator (MINOS) and Matterport3D dataset, the DNN models discern the most viable direction for movement be it translation or rotation based on the robot's current visual input in relation to its last known position within the ORB-SLAM2 generated map. The methodology involves real-time data exchange between MINOS and the ORB-SLAM2 system via a dedicated ROS node, facilitating the recovery process. Extensive testing shows that our proposed model successfully predicts the appropriate recovery action in over 90% of track loss instances, substantiating its efficacy and potential for deployment in real-world applications. This research contributes to the advancement of robust relocalization strategies in Visual SLAM, enhancing the autonomous capabilities of mobile robotics.

Keywords: Mobile Robot Relocalization · Tracking Failure · Visual SLAM · Deep Neural Networks

1 Introduction

Simultaneous Localization and Mapping (SLAM) enables robots to determine their location, navigate autonomously, and map their surroundings. Visual SLAM faces challenges like localization loss, cumulative errors, and high computational demands. Using cameras on mobile robots introduces variability, limited by their visual range and factors like Wi-Fi interference, affecting perception, control, localization, and remote operation. Thus, advanced algorithms are essential for consistent performance and environmental comprehension. SLAM integrates data from various sensors to create a coherent spatial understanding for autonomous decision-making, crucial for real-time navigation. The rise in autonomous vehicle technology increases interest in tracking and re-localizing outdoor mobile robots in urban settings. Conversely, indoor re-localization exploration

Published by Springer Nature Switzerland AG 2025
Z. Shi et al. (Eds.): ICIS 2024, IFIP AICT 720, pp. 190–203, 2025.
https://doi.org/10.1007/978-3-031-71253-1_14

remains limited [1], posing significant challenges due to uniform, feature-sparse environments, and transient object layouts. Visual SLAM begins by capturing visual input through cameras, extracting features to identify unique scene elements, matching, and tracking these features to discern the robot's path. This process involves optical flow or advanced feature matching techniques, incrementally building a 3D environmental map updated with incoming data. Central to Visual SLAM is localization, pinpointing the robot's exact location within the evolving map, crucial for effective navigation and environmental interaction [2]. Optimization strategies like loop closure detection aid in correcting movement and map accuracy (Fig. 1).

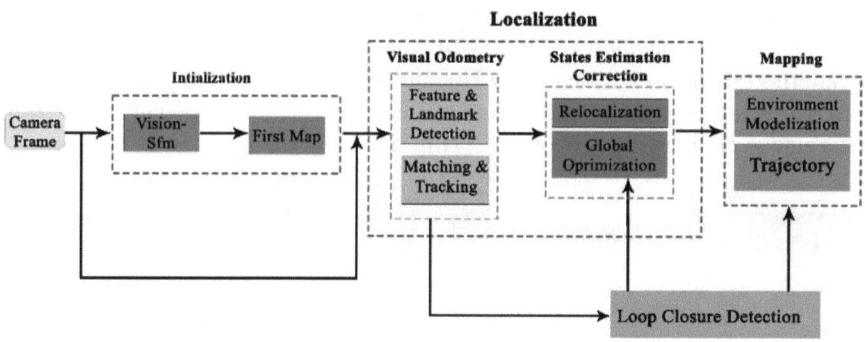

Fig. 1. Visual SLAM Framework

The applications of SLAM are vast, particularly in autonomous navigation for robotics, autonomous vehicles, and drone mapping. It enables robots to perform tasks like obstacle avoidance, path planning, and exploration in unstructured environments. Visual SLAM also propels innovations in augmented reality, enhancing human-machine interaction by enabling immersive virtual experiences [3]. Indoor environments pose significant challenges for SLAM algorithms, prompting ongoing research to refine precision and dependability. This burgeoning interest has led to the exploration of deep neural networks for addressing tracking failures and relocalization in Visual SLAM, particularly for indoor mobile robots.

Visual SLAM initiates with capturing visual input through cameras, which vary from single-lens monocular types offering one viewpoint, to stereo cameras providing depth details, to RGB-D cameras that deliver both color and depth data [4]. The system then performs feature extraction, pinpointing unique, identifiable elements within the scene, like specific spots or contours. After this extraction, the system proceeds to match and track these features.

As the robot moves through its surroundings, it maintains a continuous observation of these features over successive video frames, crucial for discerning the robot's path by recognizing and aligning the same features across different frames [5]. Visual SLAM has diverse applications in the field of robotics, playing a pivotal role across various domains. It is crucial for autonomous vehicles, aiding in navigation and the comprehension of their surroundings to ensure safe operations [6]. Drones, especially in areas where GPS is unavailable, depend on Visual SLAM for accurate flight control. In industrial environments, robots leverage this technology for improved navigation and task efficiency, enhancing overall safety and productivity [3].

1.1 Problem Statement

This research addresses challenges within the MINOS indoor simulated environment [4]. The objective is to develop a sophisticated path planning algorithm for mobile robots operating in MINOS, ensuring efficient navigation through intricate spaces. Subsequently, the research integrates the MINOS simulator with ORB-SLAM2 within a ROS framework, managing data streams effectively and maintaining real-time performance. This integration allows operating SLAM in any indoor environment provided in the Matterport3D dataset, tested using Ubuntu 16 for the first time. The field of Visual SLAM has advanced with the integration of Deep Neural Networks (DNNs), marking a transformative era in mobile robotics [7] (Fig. 2).

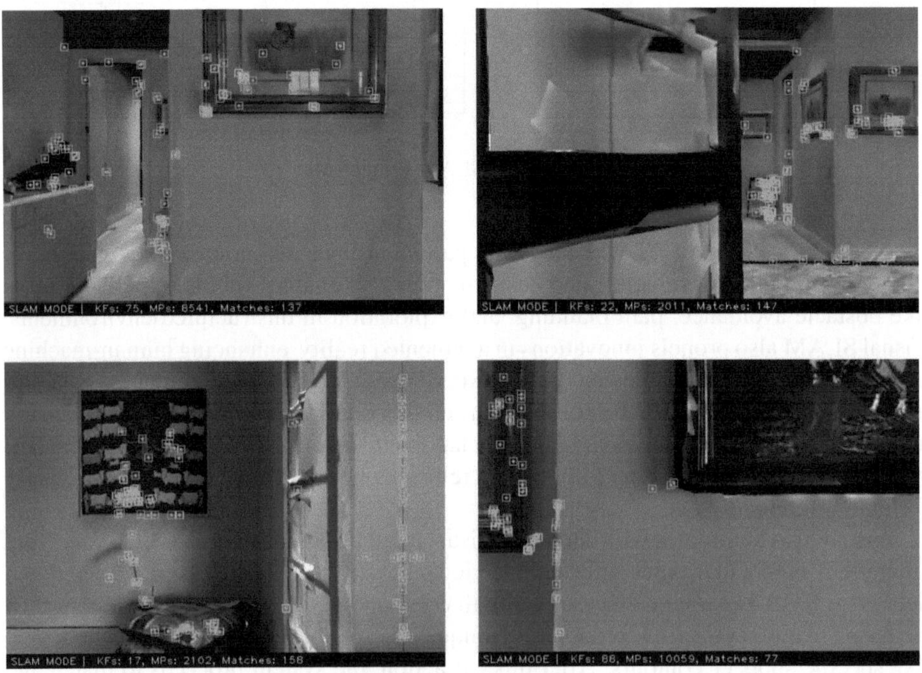

Fig. 2. Track Failure Cases

Another critical aspect involves structuring data from the MINOS environment for input into deep neural network classifiers, crucial for preparing the dataset for machine learning algorithms. An extensive evaluation of different deep neural network models identifies the most efficient classifier [8]. The proposed solution culminates in deploying the optimized image classifier within the MINOS virtual environment, ensuring the trained model performs accurately within the simulation, providing reliable real-time decision-making capabilities for the mobile robot. This approach enhances navigation, data processing, and machine learning integration for autonomous and efficient robot operation.

1.2 Research Contributions

- **Integration with MINOS Simulator:** Evaluate the enhancement of real-time ORB-SLAM2 navigation in complex, dynamic indoor simulations.
- **Enhanced Robustness to Track Loss:** Identify innovative deep recovery network strategies for ORB-SLAM2's tracking resilience in challenging visual environments.
- **Autonomous Recovery and Relocalization:** Evaluate the capability for autonomous tracking recovery and relocalization in unpredictable indoor settings.

The landscape of Visual SLAM, deep learning, and robotics is rich with diverse methodologies and groundbreaking research. The introduction of the dataset provides a robust platform for evaluating SLAM systems under varied conditions [9]. Notable contributions include MapNet for refining spatial mapping and memory, self-aware robots with introspection in navigation, and fortifying deep learning models against adversarial attacks. Integrating object detection in dynamic environments enhances relocalization capabilities, contributing to the robustness of Visual SLAM systems. The comprehensive review highlights the ongoing evolution and application scope of SLAM systems, showcasing the potential of deep learning in transforming this field.

This extensive array of research underscores ongoing innovation in Visual SLAM and robotics, showcasing the potential deep learning holds in enhancing the capabilities of autonomous systems.

2 Methodology

This section details our novel system model leveraging deep learning to enhance re localization of mobile robots in Visual SLAM, focusing on integration with the MINOS simulator and the Matterport 3D dataset. Figures 6 and 7 illustrate data flow between the MINOS simulator and ORB-SLAM2, managed through ROS topics, enabling real-time mapping and localization. Rectangular boxes represent system components, while arrows indicate data flow.

The MINOS simulator generates simulated sensor data, including images and depth information, transmitted via ROS topics to the ORB SLAM system. ORB SLAM processes this data for simultaneous mapping and localization, generating an environmental map and estimating the robot's pose. Bidirectional arrows between the MINOS simulator and ORB SLAM signify dynamic mapping and localization information exchange.

This integration through ROS topics facilitates efficient communication, enabling the system to adapt to real-time environmental changes. The architecture depicted in Fig. 6 shows the interplay between various components enhancing the Visual SLAM framework. The MINOS environment provides diverse datasets, incorporating textured 3D meshes and panoramic views, crucial for the path re-planning module, which adjusts navigation based on real-time feedback. Central to this setup is ROS, ensuring seamless communication between the simulation environment and the ORB SLAM system. ORB SLAM provides continuous tracking information, contributing to spatial awareness. Figure 7 outlines the autonomous navigation system's operational sequence, starting from the robot's journey initiation. The process begins with the MINOS environment, where movement is controlled through standard keyboard navigation commands processed by ROS nodes, facilitating communication with the ORB SLAM system. ORB SLAM performs real-time mapping and tracking, ensuring the robot follows the planned path. If tracking is lost, indicating deviation or obstacles, the system halts movement. An image classifier, trained for such scenarios, suggests recovery actions based on visual input. This sequence ensures the robot can autonomously navigate and recover within the environment (Fig. 3).

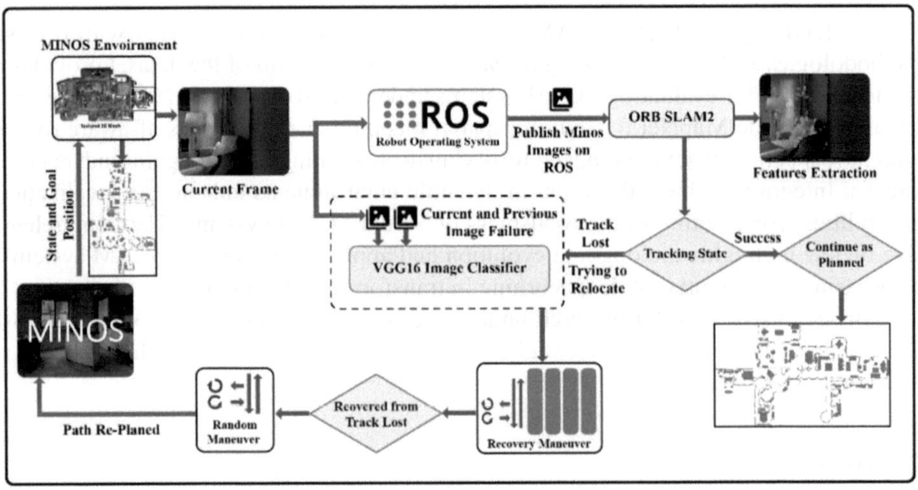

Fig. 3. Integrated system architecture for enhanced Visual SLAM

2.1 Active Vision Dataset

We used the Active Vision Dataset [10] to train our image classifier, essential for relocalization. This dataset includes over 30,000 indoor scene images, capturing 12 images at each location, spaced 30° apart. Comprehensive annotations were pivotal for sorting images into specific classes pertinent to our system's requirements (Fig. 4).

Images were categorized into six classes: Clockwise (CW), Counter-Clockwise (CCW), Left, Right, Forward, and Backward. The classifier, utilizing VGG16 and ResNet34 architectures, was trained on the last two frames of the dataset sequences, optimizing for precise classification tasks (Fig. 5).

RGB images were transformed into grayscale, concatenated, and a dummy channel was added for ConvNet architectures. This preprocessing-maintained network input

Fig. 4. Active Vision Dataset.

Fig. 5. Classification of data into six actionable classes.

structure while simplifying the dataset's complexity. The Active Vision Dataset significantly enhances our SLAM system's adaptability and accuracy in various indoor settings, reinforcing autonomous navigation and re-localization capabilities.

2.2 Image Classification

We trained ResNet34 and VGG-16 models using the Active Vision Dataset to determine the most effective model for our MINOS ORB-SLAM2 framework. The dataset's extensive indoor images facilitated comprehensive training. Using PyTorch and Jupyter Notebook, we split the data into 115,925 training images and 16,457 testing images, maintaining uniform class distribution. Training parameters included a 20% validation split, capped at 10 epochs, with a learning rate of 0.00001 and a batch size of 8. VGG-16 demonstrated superior performance, with precision, recall, and accuracy rates surpassing 90%.

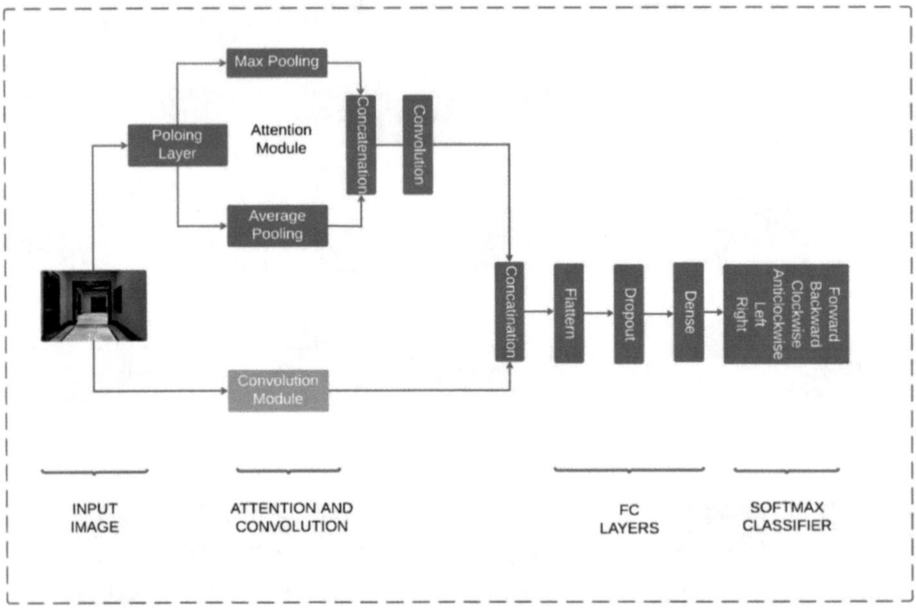

Fig. 6. The VGG16 neural network architecture employed in our system.

We tested the models in the MINOS ORB-SLAM2 framework, assessing their accuracy in re-localizing after track loss incidents. VGG-16 outperformed ResNet34 in making real-time decisions for autonomous re-localization, especially in scenarios requiring specific actions like identifying doors.

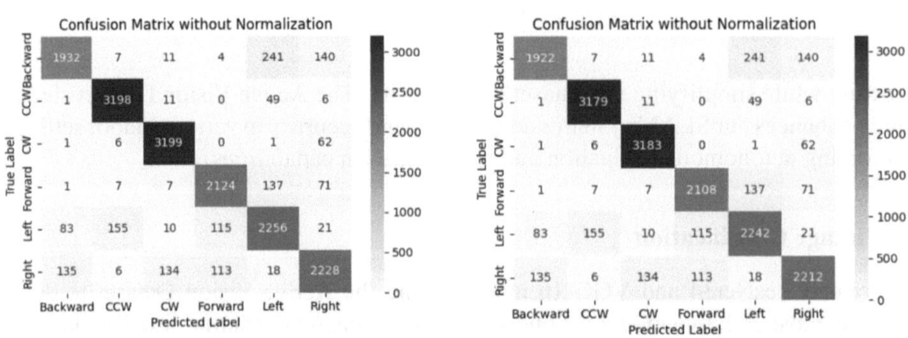

Fig. 7. Confusion matrices for VGG16 and ResNet34 models.

The confusion matrices provide a quantitative evaluation of each model's classification performance. VGG16 shows a high degree of correct predictions, particularly for

'Right' and 'Left' movements, while ResNet34, although commendable, lags slightly in overall predictive accuracy (Fig. 8).

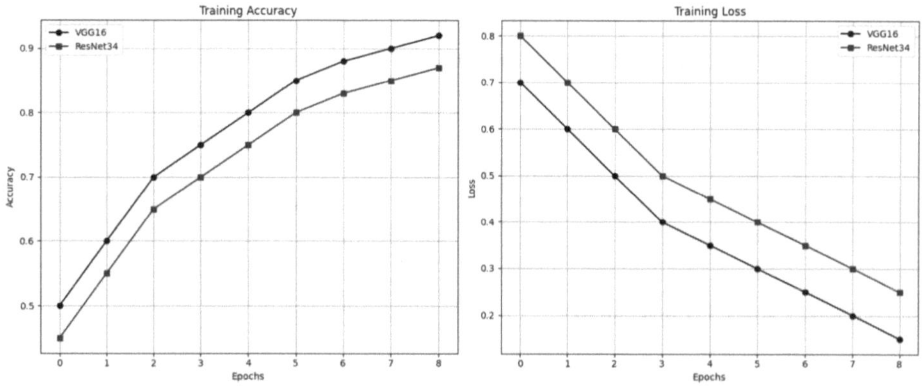

Fig. 8. Training accuracy and loss comparison for VGG16 and ResNet34 models.

The graph compares training accuracy and loss for VGG16 and ResNet34 models. Both models show effective learning and convergence, with ResNet34 generally out-performing VGG16 in accuracy while maintaining comparable loss reduction. The loss function used to evaluate the performance of our model is Root Mean Square Error.

$$RMSE = \sqrt{\frac{1}{n}\sum_{i=1}^{n}(y_i - y_i)^2} \quad (1)$$

2.3 Environmental Setup

We discuss the ORB-SLAM2, MINOS Simulator with Matterport 3D dataset, and ROS. Our controlled experimental setup utilized the MINOS Simulator, equipped with the Matterport 3D Dataset, integrated with ROS to manage data flow and synchronization. The ORB-SLAM2 framework enabled real-time 3D mapping and navigation. This setup provided a stable platform for sophisticated experiments in Visual SLAM (Fig. 9).

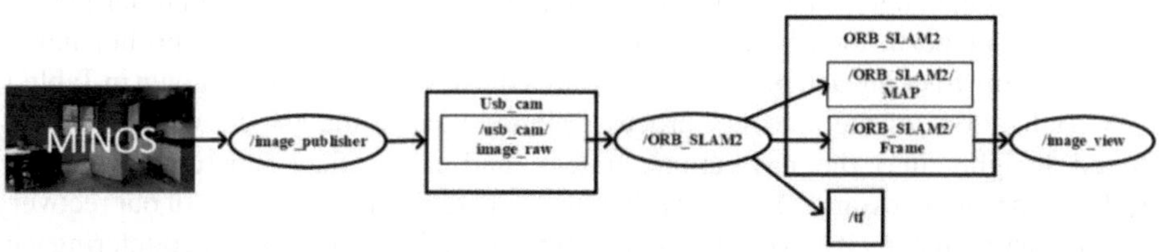

Fig. 9. Schematic of data flow between the MINOS simulator and ORB-SLAM2 managed through ROS topics.

Algorithm performs the navigational process, considering collision status, direction, and distance to the target. The logic navigates potential collisions with intelligent decision-making, opting for random actions upon collision detection, and adjusting orientation based on the angle relative to the desired direction.

This configuration is instrumental for intricate algorithmic experimentation and evaluation within a controlled virtual environment.

$$X_{t+1} = \mathrm{f}(\mathrm{X}_t,\mathrm{U}_t,\mathrm{Z}_t) \tag{2}$$

where X_{t+1} represents the state vector at the next time step, X_t the current state, U_t the control input, and Z_t the observation at time t. This model optimizes the SLAM process, ensuring system responsiveness to dynamic complexities of virtual environments.

3 Results and Discussion

This section discusses the experimental outcomes centered on the recovery method's efficacy across five house IDs in the MINOS simulator and how it compares with other approaches in terms of track loss recovery.

3.1 Track Loss Recovery in Different Episodes

A SLAM robot localizes itself and builds a map simultaneously since it does not know its environment in advance and must explore its surroundings later, which represents the renowned SLAM problem. A disadvantage of ORB-SLAM is that after track loss, it causes a loss of map data. ORB-SLAM2 fails to localize itself and starts a relocalization loop unless it cannot identify a previously visited place. Incoming images are not used for improving the map, only for relocalization.

As soon as ORB-SLAM2 is unable to determine its current position due to track loss, its only goal is to relocalize itself in previously recorded map keypoints with current camera frames. If a relocalization attempt fails, the current frame is discarded without being saved or processed, resulting in a full loss of map information during this period of track loss. In this paper, two approaches, Reverse Replay and Parallel Tracking, were derived as extensions of the SLAM system to avoid loss of time and data after track loss. We conducted a series of experimental episodes across various simulated house environments, identified by unique IDs, to evaluate the efficacy of our track loss recovery method in Visual SLAM systems. Each episode introduced common navigational challenges leading to tracking failures. The results reveal that our method consistently outperformed baseline approaches, displaying remarkable proficiency in re-establishing tracking and progressing towards the designated goal as shown in Table 1.

Visualizations of the recovery process, plotted against the respective house maps, offered insights into the navigation strategy and the critical junctures where relocalization was necessary. These experiments underscored the reliability of our recovery method, distinguishing it as a robust solution for Visual SLAM systems encountering varied and unpredictable environmental conditions. Across different house IDs, our method demonstrated an ability to cope with track loss efficiently, minimizing the distance traveled before regaining tracking capabilities. This contrasts with other tested methods, such

Table 1. Comparison of recovery times using ORB-SLAM2 with DNN and random movements.

Trial #	House ID	Points	ORB-SLAM2 with DNN (Our Method)		Random Movements	
			Recovered (Yes/No)	Recovery Time	Recovered (Yes/No)	Recovery Time
1	1pXnuDYAj8r	1	Yes	6s	Yes	1s
2	1pXnuDYAj8r	1	Yes	12s	No	Infinite
		2	Yes	5s	-	-
		3	Yes	4s	-	-
		1	Yes	5s	Yes	2s
		2	Yes	5s	No	Infinite
3	17DRP5sb8fy	3	Yes	4s	-	-
		4	Yes	5s	-	-
		5	Yes	5s	-	-
		1	Yes	5s	Yes	4s
		2	Yes	12s	Yes	2s
		3	Yes	15s	No	Infinite
4	JeFG25nYj2p	4	Yes	5s	-	-
		5	Yes	11s	-	-
		6	Yes	10s	-	-
		7	Yes	-	-	-

as ORB-SLAM2 with DON, SLAM2-SAFE, and standard ORB-SLAM2 implementations, which exhibited varying degrees of delay and less consistency in track recovery. By integrating deep learning with traditional SLAM techniques, our approach proved to be a significant advancement in autonomous navigation, ensuring reliable tracking and accurate localization in environments that previously posed substantial challenges to baseline systems.

3.2 Total Distance Covered and Goal Reached or not

A comprehensive comparative analysis was conducted between our recovery method and several baseline systems to highlight enhanced performance. The total distance covered by each method was meticulously recorded, revealing significant improvements in navigation efficiency with our approach. The system's ability to successfully reach the designated goal after recovery was evaluated, emphasizing the practical benefits of our method in real-world scenarios. Each row corresponds to a specific episode and house ID, while the columns represent different methods used for track loss recovery. Our method, ORB SLAM with DNN, consistently achieves recovery within a few seconds, showcasing superior performance compared to other methods such as ORB SLAM with

DQN, ORB-SLAM2 with SLAM SAFE, Random Recovery Method, Standard ORB-SLAM2, ORB-SLAM2 with CNN, and ORB-SLAM2 with SVM. The total distance to the goal for each episode is also provided, indicating the efficiency of each method in reaching the designated goal. These results underscore the effectiveness of our proposed method in improving navigation efficiency and achieving successful recovery in real-world scenarios (Table 2).

Table 2. Distance covered comparison across various episodes and enhancements of ORB-SLAM2

Methods	HouseID				
	Episode 1	Episode 2	Episode 3	Episode 4	Episode 5
	JeFG25nYj2p	q9vSo1VnCiC	2azQ1b91cZZ	1pXnuDYAj8r	PuKPg4mmafe
Total Distance to Goal	17.94	20.92	12.43	8.55	30.39
ORB SLAM with DQN	10.02	17.85	10.5	5.05	12.91
ORB-SLAM2 with SLAM SAFE	9.89	6.54	5.98	4.90	2.39
Random Recovery Method	9.81	4.70	5.90	4.02	3.78
Standard ORB-SLAM2	9.35	4.3	5.75	2.57	1.84
ORB-SLAM2 with CNN	10.23	5.33	6.00	3.90	3.66
ORB-SLAM2 with SVM	10.10	5.08	5.90	2.60	2.97
ORB-SLAM2 with DNN (Our Method)	**10.95**	**20.92**	**12.43**	**8.55**	**15.51**

Our method, ORB-SLAM2 with DNN, consistently outperformed other methods, achieving recovery within a minimal distance, and successfully reaching the intended goal in a significant majority of tested episodes. This efficiency demonstrates the practical viability of integrating DNN into the ORB-SLAM2 framework, marking a substantial progression towards more resilient and dependable Visual SLAM systems. The integration of deep learning enhances the system's capability to recover from track losses more efficiently and improves overall navigation accuracy, as evidenced by the improved goal-reaching performance. Thus, our study presents compelling evidence supporting the adoption of deep learning techniques in the development of advanced Visual SLAM solutions, paving the way for more autonomous and reliable robotic navigation in complex environments (Table 3).

Table 3. Comparison of goal-reaching capability across various episodes for different ORB-SLAM2 enhancements

Method	HouseID				
	Episode 1	Episode 2	Episode 3	Episode 4	Episode 5
House ID	JeFG25nYj2p	q9vSo1VnCiC	2azQ1b91cZZ	1pXnuDYAj8r	PuKPg4mmafe
Total Distance to Goal	17.94	20.92	12.43	8.55	30.39
ORB SLAM with DQN	N	N	N	Y	N
ORB-SLAM2 with SLAM SAFE	N	N	N	N	N
Standard ORB-SLAM2	N	N	N	N	N
ORB-SLAM2 with DNN (Our Method)	**Y**	**Y**	**Y**	**Y**	**N**

This table presents a comparison of the goal-reaching capability across various episodes for different enhancements of the ORB-SLAM2 system. Our proposed method (ORB-SLAM2 with DNN) achieved the goal in most episodes, demonstrating its effectiveness in real-world scenarios. Conversely, the standard ORB-SLAM2 and other enhancement methods showed varying degrees of success in reaching the goal across different episodes. This comparison underscores the superior performance of our proposed method in terms of goal-reaching capability, suggesting its suitability for practical applications in autonomous navigation (Fig. 10).

In scenarios where the robot encounters an unexpected change in the environment, it may lose track, necessitating a relocalization process. This process is critical to ensure that the robot can successfully recover its intended trajectory and continue towards its goal. Our findings suggest that with the implementation of advanced neural network architectures such as.

VGG16 and ResNet34, the system exhibits robust track recovery capabilities, leading to successful goal attainment even after significant deviations.

3.3 Discussion

Our method effectively addresses track loss in autonomous navigation. Experiments in the MINOS environment showed significant improvements in relocalization speed and

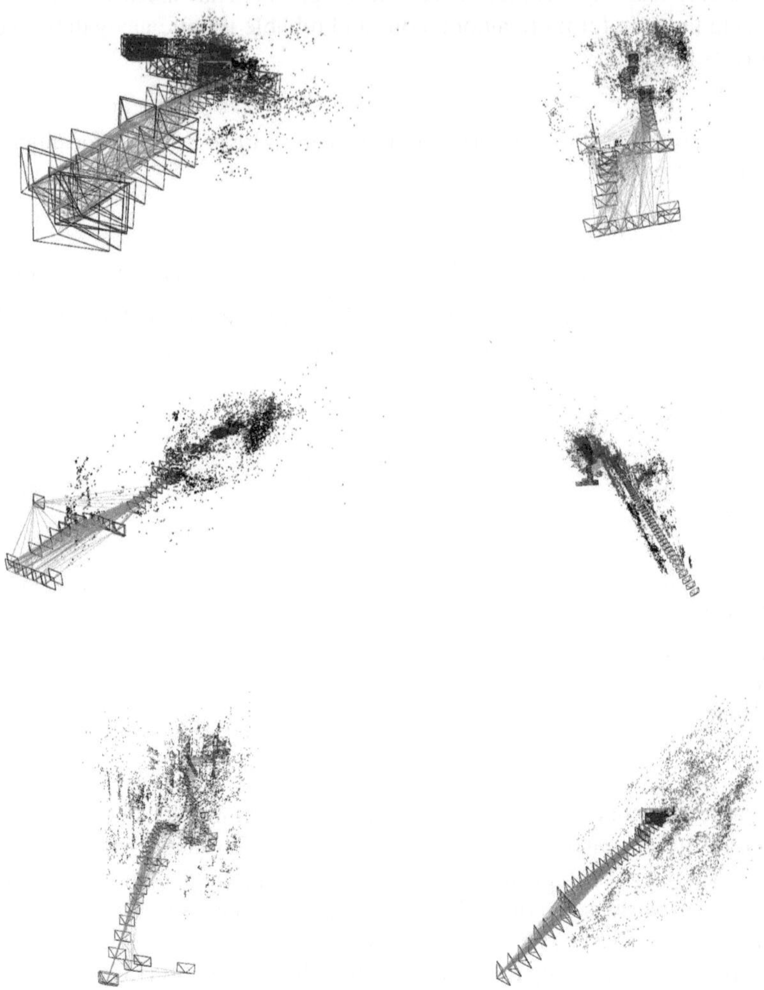

Fig. 10. House ID Map Results

trajectory precision, reducing time spent disoriented. Our system accurately retraces its trajectory and resumes operation, minimizing disruptions. Visualizations and analyses demonstrated our method's superiority across different house IDs, consistently outperforming others in minimizing distance traveled before regaining tracking. Comparative analysis highlighted our approach's efficiency, recovering within seconds compared to delayed and inconsistent random movements. VGG16 and ResNet34 models showed high accuracy in motion prediction, validated by training data. Integrating advanced recovery strategies with traditional SLAM enhances autonomous navigation, ensuring reliable tracking and accurate localization in challenging environments, promising more resilient robotic systems for real-world scenarios.

4 Conclusion

In conclusion, robust Visual Simultaneous Localization and Mapping (Visual SLAM) is a significant challenge in robotics, especially regarding track loss during autonomous navigation. Our study proposes a deep learning-based relocalization strategy using VGG16 and ResNet34 neural networks, enabling mobile robots to recover from track loss effectively. Through experiments within the MINOS simulator and integrating an ROS node for data transmission to ORB-SLAM2, we demonstrated our method's superiority. Our system improves recovery from track losses in various simulated environments, minimizing post-recovery distance traveled and maintaining efficiency. Integrating our method into existing SLAM frameworks promises more resilient robotic systems. Our findings, including training accuracy and loss improvements and successful track loss recovery, enhance robotic navigation knowledge. Our approach highlights the potential of deep neural networks to augment traditional robotic systems, paving the way for fully autonomous robots with navigation capabilities akin to human intelligence.

References

1. Koide, K., Miura, J., Yokozuka, M., Oishi, S., Banno, A.: Interactive 3D graph SLAM for map correction. IEEE Robot. Autom. Lett. **6**(1), 40–47 (2020)
2. Sidaoui, A., Zein, M.K., Elhajj, I.H., Asmar, D.: A-slam: human in-the-loop augmented slam. In: 2019 International Conference on Robotics and Automation (ICRA), pp. 5245–5251. IEEE (2019)
3. Chaplot, D.S., Gandhi, D., Gupta, S., Gupta, A., Salakhutdinov, R.: Learning to explore using active neural SLAM (2020). http://arxiv.org/abs/2004.05155
4. Sattler, T., Zhou, Q., Pollefeys, M., Leal-Taixe, L.: Understanding the limitations of CNN-based absolute camera pose regression. In: Proceedings of the IEEE/CVF Conference on Computer Vision and Pattern Recognition, pp. 3302–3312 (2019)
5. Savva, M., et al.: Habitat: a platform for embodied AI research. In: Proceedings of the IEEE/CVF International Conference on Computer Vision, pp. 9339–9347 (2019)
6. Lin, H.Y., Yeh, M.C.: Drift-free visual slam for mobile robot localization by integrating UWB technology. IEEE Access **10**, 93636–93645 (2022)
7. Zafar, M.M., Anjum, M.L., Hussain, W.: LTA*: local tangent based A* for optimal path planning. Auton. Robots. **45**(2), 209–227 (2021). https://doi.org/10.1007/s10514-020-09956-3
8. Heo, S., Mun, J., Choi, J., Park, J., Matson, E.T.: Outdoor visual SLAM and path planning for mobile-robot. In: 2022 Sixth IEEE International Conference on Robotic Computing (IRC), pp. 296–301. IEEE (2022)
9. Ahmad, H., Usama, S.M., Hussain, W., Anjum, M.L.: A sketch is worth a thousand navigational instructions. Auton. Robots. **45**, 313–333 (2021). https://doi.org/10.1007/s10514-020-09965-2
10. Ammirato, P., Poirson, P., Park, E., Kosecka, J., Berg, A.C.: A dataset for developing and benchmarking Active Vision (2017). http://arxiv.org/abs/1702.08272, https://doi.org/10.48550/arXiv.1702.08272

A Vision-Based Method for UAV Autonomous Landing Area Detection

Qiutong Zhang[1], Qingyuan Xia[1(✉)], Lisheng Wei[2], and Bohai Deng[2]

[1] School of Computer Science and Engineering, Nanjing University of Science and Technology, Nanjing, China
{zhangqiutong,xqy}@njust.edu.cn

[2] National Key Laboratory of Rotorcraft Aeromechanics, Nanjing University of Aeronautics and Astronautics, Nanjing, China
dengbohai@nuaa.edu.cn

Abstract. Automatic identification of the landing area is crucial for UAV (Unmanned Aerial Vehicles) to land correctly and safely. Using passive vision sensors to achieve this objective is a very promising avenue due to their low cost and the potential they provide for performing simultaneous terrain analysis. In this paper, a computer vision method is proposed using an improved U-Net based architecture on UAV imagery to assess the safe landing area. Contrary to past methods, which little attention has been paid to the whole landing process with multiple descending altitude, experiment involves evaluating the landing area by analyzing visual images obtained from different descending heights. In the initial stage of landing, separation was made between water and land, guiding the flight to the land. As descending, classification was applied on images captured near ground into safe/unsafe landing areas and then mapped to the safety score for selection. Experiments on public datasets have shown promising results.

Keywords: UAV · Autonomous Landing · Computer Vision · Detection

1 Introduction

Unmanned Aerial Vehicles, also known as drones, have witnessed a surge in popularity and applications in various industries [1]. Recently UAVs have found widespread applications in areas such as surveillance, monitoring, inspection, delivery, and entertainment. To support this capabilities, it is imperative to develop automatic precision landing detection technology, enabling an accurate landing process and ensuring the safety and efficiency of the system.

While GPS is widely used in autonomous landing of UAV, it is not sufficient for precise and reliable landing, especially in GPS-denied situations [2]. The integration of camera-based computer vision techniques enables UAV to overcome the limitations of GPS and accurately detect safe landing areas [3, 4]. Computer vision based algorithms can help analyze various factors, such as terrain stability, obstruction presence, and

Published by Springer Nature Switzerland AG 2025
Z. Shi et al. (Eds.): ICIS 2024, IFIP AICT 720, pp. 204–213, 2025.
https://doi.org/10.1007/978-3-031-71253-1_15

proximity to humans or infrastructure, to rank the safety level and suitability of the potential landing locations.

UAV landing area detection involves separating the water surface from the land and analyzing various factors such as topography, ground texture, and specific ground types. Generally, Flat, spacious and uncrowded areas are generally preferred, with paved ground and hard land being prioritized. Grass surfaces and sand areas may also be considered depending on the circumstances. Avoiding obstacles and assessing terrain priorities based on the UAV capabilities are essential for ensuring safe and successful UAV landings. Furthermore, the process of UAV landing requires the methods tailored to different descending heights.

Previous works on vision-based landing area detection exemplify the diverse range of techniques employed to improve the accuracy and reliability of UAV landings. By combining different vision methods, leveraging stereo cues, semantic segmentation, and deep learning models, these approaches contribute to enhancing the safety and efficiency of UAV landing operations [5, 6]. Previous research on vision-based landing area detection has explored various techniques with the aim of improving the accuracy and reliability of UAV landings. In [7], the authors conducted a comprehensive literature review, categorizing the techniques into three main categories: camera-based, LiDAR-based, and their combination. In [8], researchers proposed a pipeline for vision-based UAV landing area detection, focusing on generating UAV trajectories in different landing scenarios. This method provides a systematic approach to analyzing and planning UAV landings, considering factors such as obstacle avoidance and safe descent paths. Semantic segmentation was utilized in [9] to identify a safe zone around the target delivery area, enabling the UAV to descend from higher altitudes. This method demonstrates the effectiveness of semantic segmentation in identifying suitable landing areas, particularly in complex and dynamic environments. In [10], researchers use of Gabor filters to detect flat regions, which are crucial for identifying suitable landing zones. This approach emphasizes the importance of texture-based analysis in detecting safe landing areas. Similarly, [11] implemented an onboard landing areas detection system by extracting differences between image segmentation outputs in video frames. This technique focuses on real-time analysis and decision-making, enabling the UAV to rapidly identify suitable landing areas. More recently, [12] proposed a visual-based method specifically designed for landing UAVs in crowded areas. By utilizing a deep learning model, an occupancy map is estimated to assess the availability of landing spaces. However, researches seldom focused on evaluation and image types based on different descending heights.

In our work, a Vision-Based Method is proposed for UAV Autonomous Landing Area Detection using a U-Net based architecture on UAV imagery to assess the safe landing area. Unlike previous works, with little attention paid to the multiple descending altitude. Our experiment involves evaluating the landing area by analyzing visual images obtained from different descending heights.

This paper is organized as follows: In Sect. 2, this paper present the proposed methodology for landing area detection. In Sect. 3, we present experimental results for evaluating our approach. Then end the paper with a conclusion and future work perspectives.

2 Methodology

In the process of UAV landing, utilizing image information from remote sensing images to terrain information near the ground. An improved U-Net based architecture is used on UAV imagery to assess the safe landing area. And then size flatness and obstacle distribution are weighted to make an assessment and decision-making process. Based on the output of the selection, the identified landing area is selected as the initial tracking target and then track the landing area as the UAV descends.

2.1 Landing Area Evaluation

The whole landing process involves multiple descending altitude. In the initial stage, the task is to separate the water from land, instructing the UAV to descend on the land. As the UAV descends, the images captured will contain more detailed surface texture information. At this stage, segmentation techniques is applied to identify areas that are suitable for landing.

2.1.1 High Altitude

Our model still adopts the classic U-shaped symmetrical structure [13], with the encoder section on the left, the decoder section on the right and a feature pyramid module [14] added in the middle to extract the features as shown in Fig. 1.

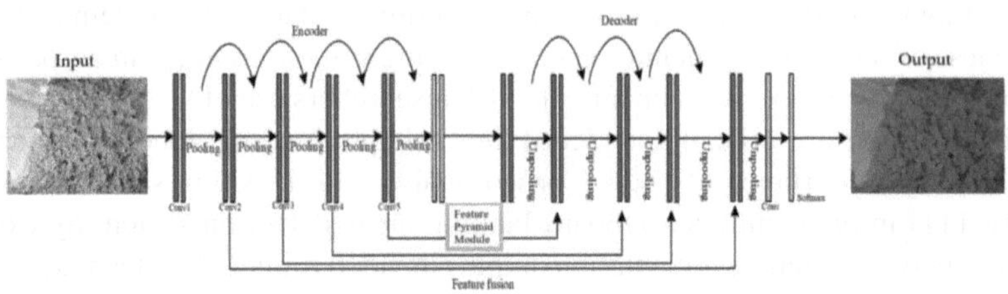

Fig. 1. The structure of our improved U-Net segmentation

The feature information of the last convolutional layer in the Conv1 and Conv2 stages of the encoder and all of the convolutional layers in the Conv3, Conv4, and Conv5 stages were extracted. A feature pyramid module was used to extract the features in the Conv5 stage, and then the features were fused into the corresponding layers of the decoder in a pixel-by-pixel manner. Integrating the features of the encoder into the decoder could provide more information for the decoding process and make the segmentation results smoother.

The Feature Pyramid Module, as shown in Fig. 2 first, with the application of a 3 $\times$ 3 and 5 $\times$ 5 convolutional kernel (conv5) to capture context information at different scales and then gradually integrated to achieve the purpose of combining adjacent scale context features. The original input feature map (conv5) was then convolved 1 $\times$ 1 and multiplied with multi-scale features in pixels. Finally, global pooling information was integrated to improve the performance of the Feature Pyramid Module. The Feature Pyramid Module operates in the conv5 stage and, due to the lower resolution of deeper advanced feature maps, using a larger convolutional kernel will not bring too much computational burden. In addition, the Feature Pyramid Module aggregates multi-scale information in a gradual pixel by pixel manner. This approach takes into account the hierarchical dependencies of features at different scales and maintains local consistency of feature information.

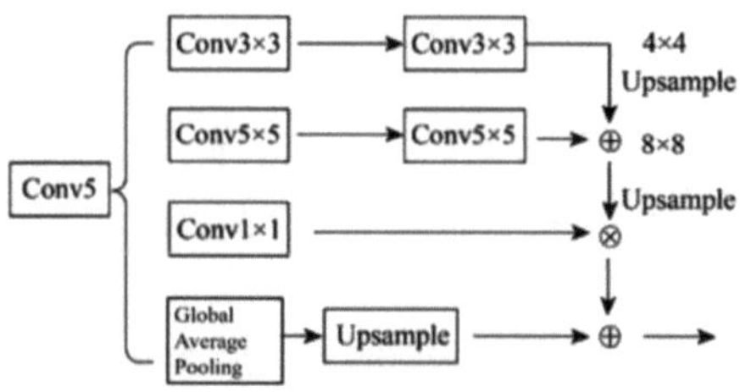

Fig. 2. Feature pyramid module

2.1.2 Low Altitude

Contrary to segmentation that assigns categorical labels for thematic classes [15–17], we generate safety values around two grades: Low risk and High-risk, which reflect the safety potential of each location we converted the dataset by labeling paved area, gravel, dirt, and grass as of low risk, while the remaining classes as considered of high risk. In our framework, since the model needs to run on UAV with small computing power, network based on the Resnet101 as backbone which has been pretrained on the ImageNet dataset [18] is used.

2.2 Landing Area Selection

Selection of landing areas for UAVs involves factors such as size, flatness, and obstacle distribution. These parameters are weighted to make an assessment and decision-making process.

2.2.1 Size

Assuming that the landing UAV is a cuboid, L and S are the length and width respectively ($L \geq S$). Calculate the point where the distance to the contour line of the obstacle area is greater than the threshold value. The threshold is usually set with reference to the focal length of the camera, the vertical distance of drone from the ground, and the size of the lander, The threshold can be referred to as:

$$L' = |\lambda t f L / d| \quad (1)$$

L' is the threshold; f is the focal length of camera, d is the vertical distance of camera from the ground, and L and S are the length and width of the drone respectively, t represent the number of in the length of one meter, and λ is set to refine the size of the obstacle cannot be greater than λLS, or it can be ignored. According to [19], λ is set 10 in our work.

2.2.2 Flatness

Among the obstacles that pose a threat to landing safety, such as Continuities, slope and rock will have strong contrast between light and dark under the light [20]. We use D(i, j) to represent the flatness of landing area.

$$D(i,j) = \frac{1}{(2\omega+1)^2}\left\{\sum_{p=i-w}^{p=i+w}\sum_{q=j-w}^{q=j+w} I(p,q)^2 - \frac{1}{(2\omega+1)}\left[\sum_{p=i-w}^{p=i+w}\sum_{q=j-w}^{q=j+w} I(p,q)\right]^2\right\} \tag{2}$$

where I(p, q) is the value of each pixel of the image, and the window size is: $(2\omega + 1) \times (2\omega + 1)$. In general, the initial value of the monitor depends on descending height and the Field of View (FOV) of the camera. It is generally believed that areas with low values are relatively flat, so in order to quickly obtain safe landing area.

2.2.3 Obstacles Distribution

Obstacles such as trees, buildings, power lines, or structures can pose hazards to the UAV. In this section, the distribution of obstacles [20] within the landing area is proposed.

Assuming that the position relation ωP between point P in the image and an obstacle in the image is calculated. If there are N obstacle objects in the image, and the Euclidean distance between point P and the center of gravity of these N obstacles is expressed as $d_i(i = 1, 2, \ldots, N)$, The size of an obstacle is expressed as $\omega_i(i = 1, 2, \ldots, N)$, then The position relationship between P and image obstacle is expressed as:

$$\omega P = \sum_{i=0}^{N} \omega_i/d_i \tag{3}$$

2.2.4 Score

According to size, flatness and obstacle, this paper use a calculation to select the landing area. The steps are as follows.

Step1, Calculate the average of each indicator, $\overline{D} = \frac{1}{T}\sum_{i=0}^{T} D_i$, $\overline{\omega P} = \frac{1}{T}\sum_{i=0}^{T} \omega p_i$, T is the number of alternate landing areas.

Step2, The score for each alternate landing circle is calculated based on the average of the indicators.

$$score_i = \sum_{i=0}^{T} D_i + \omega p_i, (i = 1, 2, \cdots, T) \tag{4}$$

2.3 Landing Area Tracking

Based on the output of the method presented in Sect. 2, the identified landing area is selected as the initial tracking target. This area serves as a reference for subsequent tracking. In the subsequent frames of the continuous image sequence, The tracking algorithm compares each frame with the initial area and identifies the region with the highest similarity. This region is then considered as the landing area in the subsequent frame.

3 Experimentation and Evaluation

This experiment was carried out on the Linux operating system Ubuntu 18.04, implemented in Visual Studio Code with python. The entire dataset is resized to a size of 512×512 pixels we compared our approach with a U-Net segmentation method where we trained both datasets to have segmentation outputs using the categorical loss function. Our results for segmentation are presented as follows.

3.1 Dataset

Experimental data are collected from the ICG dataset, MidAir dataset, Massachusetts dataset and FloodNet dataset [21–24] height ranging from 100–500 m. The original different classes are recategorized into 2 levels of risk. Safe classes consist of road, ground and grass, and other classes are categorized as of high risk. In our evaluation, quantitative metrics that can be used are the Mean Absolute Error (MAE) and Mean Squared Error (MSE), which reflect the average deviation of the prediction.

Table 1 presents the values for the two metrics obtained for our datasets. For the ICG dataset, The MAE and MSE is 0.104 and 0.065. For the MidAir dataset, these errors are 0.154 and 0.113, respectively. With regard to the Massachusetts and, produced an average of 0.088 and 0.050, respectively. For the FloodNet, the values are 0.076 and 0.039. For our datasets, adding the safety margins improved the results both in training and test images, as presented in Table 1.

Table 1. Experiment Results.

Dataset	MAE	MSE
ICG dataset	0.104	0.065
MidAir dataset	0.154	0.113
Massachusetts dataset	0.088	0.050
FloodNet dataset	0.076	0.039

3.2 Evaluation

After 100 epochs of training, the models start to predict the safety maps in the range associated with a specific region. The improved model is compared with classical semantic segmentation models such as U-Net and Deeplabv3 in Accuracy, Precision, Recall and F1, as shown in Table 2.

Table 2. Experiment Results.

Model	Accuracy/%	Precision/%	Recall/%	F1/%
U-Net	96.26	80.36	81.43	82.09
Deeplabv3	96.41	80.91	81.52	82.22
Our Model	96.45	81.06	81.49	82.26

The separation of water and land from images obtained in high altitude are presented in Fig. 3(left) and images closer to ground in Fig. 3(right) respectively. The ground truth are represented using only two grades (Low and High risk), the predictions have classification into safe/unsafe landing areas on images. For a visual representation, we converted the prediction into a green (safe) and red (unsafe).

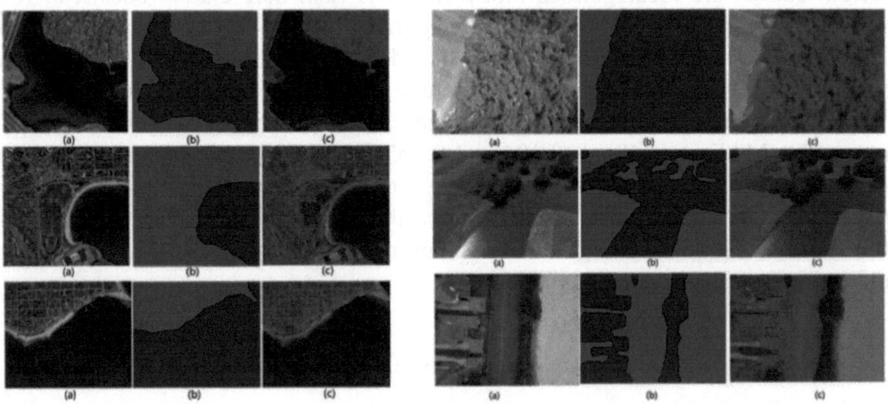

Fig. 3. Predictions on the test samples. (a) Input image (b) Ground truth (2 categories) (c) prediction (Color figure online)

3.3 Selection

Figure 4 shows the landing circle with the highest score in Sect. 2. The vertical distance of the camera from the ground is about 120 m, f is 2 cm, the L and S of the lander are both 0.5 m, and λ is 10. The size of the pixels is 54 μm, where $t = 1\,00 \times 1\,00/54 = 185$. Landing circles No. 2 and No. 3 are in the same connected area, and the area of landing circle No. 1 is larger than the connected area of landing circles No. 2 and No. 3 and The ω p value of No. 1 landing circle is the higher, and the Di value of No. 2 is higher which indicates that the ground characteristics of No. 2 landing circle are the most complex among the three. Since the radius of landing circle No. 1 is the largest among the three, it is concluded that landing circle No. 1 is the best landing circle.

Fig. 4. Landing area selection

The method has been tested on video recordings of camera capture from a height of 120 m, the average processing speed is 4 frames per second.as shown in Fig. 5.

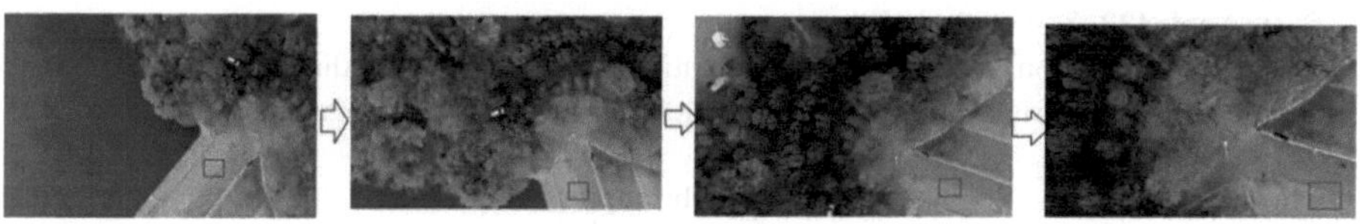

Fig. 5. Tracking

4 Conclusion

In this paper, a visual approach is presented aimed to detect landing areas for an UAV. Instead of following the classical approach of segmentation, this paper proposed an algorithm that involves images obtained from different descending heights to evaluate the landing area. Our approach to landing involves the separation of water from land during the initial stage, followed by classification of landing areas into safe or unsafe based on images captured near the ground and then map the classification results to a safety score to prioritize safe landing areas and make informed decisions during the selection process. Once a suitable landing area has been selected, we track the movement of the target during the landing process to ensure consistent guidance. It has been tested on video capture from 120 m by DJI. This research still has limited datasets because UAV has a wide area coverage, as well as datasets adapted to UAV operation. Therefore, this research will need development and many challenges.

References

1. Mu, J., et al.: UAV meets integrated sensing and communication: challenges and future directions. IEEE Commun. Mag. **61**(5), 62–67 (2023)
2. Shi, Z., et al.: Autonomous security evaluation model for UAV based on airborne information. In: 2023 6th International Conference on Information Communication and Signal Processing (ICICSP). IEEE (2023)
3. Kakaletsis, E., et al.: Computer vision for autonomous UAV flight safety: an overview and a vision-based safe landing pipeline example. ACM Comput. Surv. **54**(9), 1–37 (2022). https://doi.org/10.1145/3472288
4. Yan, C., Fu, L., Luo, X., Chen, M.: A brief overview of waveforms for UAV air-to-ground communication systems. In: Proceedings of the 3rd International Conference on Vision, Image and Signal Processing, Vancouver BC Canada, pp. 1–7 (2019). https://doi.org/10.1145/3387168.3387203
5. Mejias, L., Fitzgerald, D.: A multi-layered approach for site detection in UAS emergency landing scenarios using geometry-based image segmentation. In: 2013 International Conference on Unmanned Aircraft Systems (ICUAS). IEEE (2013)
6. Zhu, Y., et al.: Trajectory design for 3D UAV localization in UAV based networks. In: GLOBECOM 2023–2023 IEEE Global Communications Conference. IEEE (2023)
7. Alam, M.S., Oluoch, J.: A survey of safe landing zone detection techniques for autonomous unmanned aerial vehicles (UAVs). Expert Syst. Appl. **179**(115091), 1–12 (2021)
8. Garg, R., Yang, S., Scherer, S.: Monocular and stereo cues for landing zone evaluation for micro UAVs, arXiv preprint arXiv:1812.03539 (2018)
9. Kaljahi, M.A., et al.: An automatic zone detection system for safe landing of UAVs. Expert Syst. Appl. **122**, 319–333 (2019)
10. Kinahan, J., Smeaton, A.F.: Image segmentation to identify safe landing zones for unmanned aerial vehicles. In: Irish Conference on Artificial Intelligence and Cognitive Science, pp. 235–247 (2021)
11. Mitroudas, T., et al.: Embedded light-weight approach for safe landing in populated areas. arXiv preprint arXiv:2302.14445 (2023)
12. González-Trejo, J., et al.: On the visual-based safe landing of UAVs in populated areas: a crucial aspect for urban deployment. IEEE Robot. Autom. Lett. **6**(4), 7901–7908 (2021)
13. Yin, X.-X., et al.: U-net-based medical image segmentation. J. Healthc. Eng. **2022** (2022)
14. Seferbekov, S., et al.: Feature pyramid network for multi-class land segmentation. In: Proceedings of the IEEE Conference on Computer Vision and Pattern Recognition Workshops (2018)
15. Yuan, X., Shi, J., Gu, L.: A review of deep learning methods for semantic segmentation of remote sensing imagery. Expert Syst. Appl. **169**, 114417 (2021)
16. Hossain, M.D., Chen, D.: Segmentation for object-based image analysis (OBIA): a review of algorithms and challenges from remote sensing perspective. ISPRS J. Photogramm. Remote Sens. **150**, 115–134 (2019)
17. Kotaridis, I., Lazaridou, M.: Remote sensing image segmentation advances: a meta-analysis. ISPRS J. Photogramm. Remote Sens. **173**, 309–322 (2021)
18. Krizhevsky, A., Sutskever, I., Hinton, G.E.: Imagenet classification with deep convolutional neural networks. In: Advances in Neural Information Processing Systems, vol. 25 (2012)
19. 万文辉, 等. 基于降落图像匹配的嫦娥三号着陆点位置评估. 航天器工程 **23**(4), 5–12 (2014)
20. 丁萌,曹云峰和吴庆宪. 月球探测器着陆中基于被动图像的着陆场搜索及斜坡估计. 宇航学报 **6**, 2258–2264 (2009)

21. Institute of Computer Graphics and Vision (ICG). Graz University of Technology (TU Graz). http://dronedataset.icg.tugraz.at. Accessed 31 Jan 2021
22. Fonder, M., Droogenbroeck, M.V.: Mid-air: a multimodal dataset for extremely low altitude drone flights. In: Conference on Computer Vision and Pattern Recognition Workshop (CVPRW), pp. 553–562 (2019)
23. Mnih, V.: Machine Learning for Aerial Image Labeling. Citeseer, Princeton (2013)
24. Rahnemoonfar, M., et al.: Floodnet: a high resolution aerial imagery dataset for post flood scene understanding. IEEE Access **9**, 89644–89654 (2021)
25. Kannan, S.S., Min, B.-C.: Autonomous Drone Delivery to Your Door and Yard. arXiv, 10 May 2022. http://arxiv.org/abs/2104.05503. Accessed 09 June 2022

Perceptual Intelligence

Research on Object Detection for Intelligent Sensing of Navigation Mark in Yangtze River

Taotao He[1], Pinfu Yang[2], Xiaofeng Zou[3], Shengli Zhang[3], Shuqing Cao[3], and Chaohua Gan[1](✉)

[1] School of Resources and Environmental Sciences, Wuhan University, Wuhan, China
sinoward.gan@whu.edu.cn
[2] Yangtze River Waterway Bureau, Wuhan, China
[3] Changjiang Waterway Survey Center, Wuhan, China

Abstract. The maintenance and management of navigation marks are essential for ensuring the safety of transportation on the Yangtze River. Considering the current inspection and management approaches, this paper introduces an intelligent method for inspecting inland river navigation marks using **U**nmanned **A**erial **V**ehicles (UAVs). The method enables real-time monitoring of navigation marks using UAV video inspection. A UAV data acquisition platform captures video images of these marks. We have developed the ED-YOLOv5s object detection algorithm to detect and classify navigation marks. Building on this, the system can automatically assess the light quality and status of navigation marks at night. The ED-YOLOv5s algorithm is an enhancement of the YOLOv5s model, incorporating the ECA mechanism and DFFN structure, which are based on the ResNet principle. This modification enhances the model's capability for network feature fusion. Experimental results indicate improvements in navigation mark detection with the ED-YOLOv5s. Although precision decreased by 1.76% when compared to the YOLOv5s model, recall and mAP@0.5 increased by 3.59% and 2.97%, respectively. The detection results for light quality state from video images of navigation marks at night accurately reflect actual conditions. We have developed an intelligent sensing scheme for navigation marks on the Yangtze River based on the improved model. This scheme has been implemented in the Yichang section of the Yangtze River, significantly reducing the cost of daily inspections, enhancing cruise monitoring effectiveness, facilitating intelligent maintenance decisions for navigation marks, and further ensuring the navigational safety of the Yangtze River.

Keywords: Navigation Mark · Object Detection · ED-YOLOv5s · UAV

1 Introduction

The Yangtze River is the world's largest inland waterway by cargo volume. The increasing demand for cargo transport on the Yangtze has heightened require-

Z. Shi et al. (Eds.): ICIS 2024, IFIP AICT 720, pp. 217–231, 2025.
https://doi.org/10.1007/978-3-031-71253-1_16

ments for its efficient and safe operation. Navigation marks play a crucial role in enhancing the capacity and operational efficiency of the water transport infrastructure. According to the IALA [1], navigation marks, including buoys and beacons, guide vessels along safe routes.

The examination of navigational markers along the Yangtze Waterway is primarily conducted through on-site and electronic inspections [2]. On-site inspection focuses on assessing the visual integrity, stability, fastening condition of connecting components, and water depth indication of the channel's navigational marks. Electronic inspection primarily involves remote monitoring and management of navigation marks' status via telemetry and remote control functions through a business system or platform. Electronic examination focuses on analyzing electronic data such as signal characteristics, operational current and voltage, and configuration parameters. Currently, traditional on-site inspections predominantly rely on regular vessel inspections of navigation marks, which are hindered by water conditions, resulting in low efficiency and high labor costs. However, the electronic inspection method is plagued by numerous alarm errors. According to statistics from the second half of 2019 from the Changjiang Wuhan Waterway Bureau [3], 884 telemetry remote control terminals were installed for navigation marks, generating a total of 120,000 alarms due to drift, abnormal navigation mark lights, abnormal voltage of navigation mark lights, etc., with 87.6% of these being false alarms. The abundance of false alarms significantly increases the number of invalid voyages, thereby dampening staff morale to some extent. This issue stems from the limited monitoring data in electronic inspections and a lack of effective means to monitor the external characteristics of navigation marks.

To address these challenges, researchers have turned their attention to navigation mark imagery for exploring the application of vision-based target detection in navigation mark maintenance. However, in the realm of inland water transportation, object detection predominantly revolves around identifying and tracking waterborne entities like ships [4–6], with scant literature available on this subject. Ni [7] devised the Cascade-RCNN network based on the Faster-RCNN model to facilitate the detection, identification, and classification of navigation marks. Du [8] and Pan [9] amalgamated the contour emphasis algorithm with a navigation mark classification model employing a multi-scale attention mechanism to establish the **R**esnet-**M**ultiscale-**A**ttention (RMA) model, enabling precise classification of navigation marks. Han [10] developed the NMLNet model to discern the color and flashing frequency of mark lights during nocturnal hours. While these studies predominantly concentrate on the classification and recognition of navigation mark images, aiding statistical analysis of navigation marks, they offer limited assistance for navigation mark patrolling and fail to provide real-time monitoring of the external features of navigation marks.

The rise of information technology alongside the growing prevalence of UAVs (Unmanned Aerial Vehicles) has elevated the significance of UAV aerial photography in various domains, including industrial inspection [11], traffic management [12], and emergency rescue [13], owing to its wide imaging coverage and freedom from geographical constraints. Inland waterway navigation mark maintenance stands to benefit from the integration of UAVs and deep learning-based target detection technology. Thus, this paper proposes a target detection model tailored for inland waterway navigation marks from a UAV perspective, named ED-YOLOv5s. Building upon the YOLOv5s (You Only Look Once-v5s) model, it incorporates a novel ECA-DFFN structure to enhance feature extraction capabilities of the convolutional layer, broaden the perceptual field, and address the issue of feature variability inherent in small and blurred navigation marks captured in UAV aerial images. Compared to the original model, the enhanced ED-YOLOv5s model achieves a 2.97% improvement in map@0.5 and successfully detects the flashing state of navigation mark lights during night-time. By devising an intelligent identification scheme for navigation marks on a UAV platform, this study demonstrates the practical application of UAVs and target identification technology along the Yichang segment of the Yangtze River, validating the feasibility of intelligent inspection of inland waterway navigation marks. The primary contributions of this paper are outlined below:

(1) Due to the varying sizes of navigation marks and the loss of small target details after multiple convolutions in UAV aerial photography datasets, the ECA-DFFN module is developed to enhance the YOLOv5s algorithm's network structure. This module effectively widens the perceptual field and improves feature fusion across different scales.
(2) Building upon navigation mark target detection, the system achieves night-time identification of navigation mark light color, flashing frequency, and flashing period measurement. The testing results are compared with the actual navigation mark light quality to ensure consistency.
(3) A UAV platform-based intelligent identification program for navigational markers is proposed and executed. This program is demonstrated and implemented at the Changjiang Yichang Waterway Bureau to enhance navigation mark maintenance efficiency and uphold navigation safety standards.

2 Related Work

2.1 Object Detection

The architecture of the YOLOv5s network comprises four main components: the input network, backbone network, neck network, and prediction network. The backbone network is tasked with extracting essential features from the input image, while the neck network utilizes a feature pyramid network to integrate these extracted image features. Finally, the prediction layer generates anchor frames with feature mappings and outputs bounding boxes containing detection category names and probabilities.

Currently, deep learning-based object detection algorithms are extensively applied across various domains such as traffic management and life scenarios. In 2012, Hinton [14] introduced AlexNet, a convolutional neural network (CNN), demonstrating its superiority over traditional detection algorithms using the ImageNet dataset, thus establishing CNN as a pivotal tool in computer vision.

As deep learning has evolved, existing object detection models can broadly be categorized into two-stage and single-stage structural models [15].

The two-stage structural model includes the R-CNN [16], Fast-CNN [17], and Faster-RCNN [18] series. During the detection process, the object candidate box is initially generated, and the image undergoes oversegmentation to partition it into multiple small regions. These regions are compared and merged based on their similarity, consolidating them into larger areas. Subsequently, the classifier discriminates and classifies the selected regions within the box. Finally, the results are refined using a regression model to align with the measurement standard. Although this type of object detection model offers high accuracy, its method of extracting and classifying global features at each position results in relatively slow detection speeds, rendering it unsuitable for real-time small object detection requirements.

The single-stage structural model includes YOLO [19] and SSD [20]. During the detection process, it solely utilizes an end-to-end full convolutional neural network. This approach allows for direct acquisition of the final result through feature learning from the original data, eliminating the need for separate intermediate processing steps. In terms of real-time detection, it outperforms the two-stage structural model, striking a better balance between accuracy and speed.

Within the single-stage structural model, the SSD model exhibits slight inferiority to YOLO in terms of speed and the detection of very small objects. Presently, the fifth-generation YOLOv5 model stands as the most commonly utilized within the YOLO family. Notably, the previous YOLOv4 [21] incorporated mosaic data augmentation and focus network structures, leading to significant enhancements in detection speed and accuracy. Additionally, YOLOv5 [22] integrates multi-scale framework detection, effectively covering targets of various scales. With its lightweight design and efficient detection speed, YOLOv5 has become one of the most prevalent object detection models. The YOLOv5 detection network offers four models: YOLOv5s, YOLOv5m, YOLOv5l, and YOLOv5x. Notably, among these, the YOLOv5s model stands out as the smallest and fastest option [23]. Therefore, this paper opts for YOLOv5s as the fundamental model for inland waterway navigation mark detection.

2.2 ED-YOLOv5s

Analysis of the UAV aerial photography dataset reveals that UAVs predominantly capture navigation marks from a top angle at long distances, resulting in small and blurred images. Additionally, the features of the targets undergo changes due to water reflections, further complicating target detection. The ED-YOLOv5s model is an enhancement of the YOLOv5s base model specifically tailored to address these challenges inherent in UAV aerial photography datasets. It incorporates **E**fficient **C**hannel **A**ttention (ECA) and **D**eep **F**eature **F**usion **N**etwork (DFFN) modules into the backbone of YOLOv5s to optimize feature utilization during the fusion stage.

Attention mechanisms are crucial for enhancing target detection performance and are widely employed in various mainstream detection algorithms. The ECA

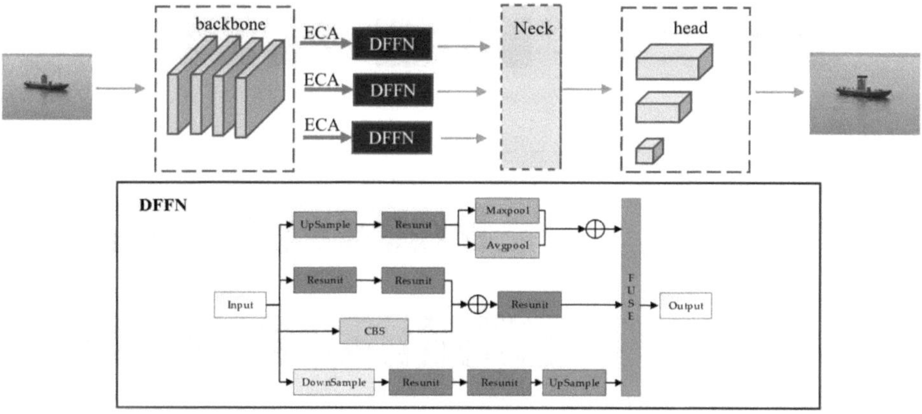

Fig. 1. Architecture of ED-YOLOv5s network.

mechanism reduces model complexity while enhancing feature expression, ultimately improving model accuracy [24–26].

The **D**eep **F**eature **F**usion **N**etwork (DFFN) adopts the residual structure concept from ResNet [27], with its network structure depicted in Fig. 1. DFFN primarily comprises a pooling layer, sampling layer, and Resunit. It features three branches: Branch 1 undergoes upsampling, batch normalization, and activation function before entering Resunit. Following the enhancement of local features, branch 1's weights are obtained through superposition after both maximum pooling and average pooling, respectively. Branch 2 traverses two layers of Resunit and a CBS module before merging the results back into Resunit to determine the weights of branch 2. Branch 3 undergoes downsampling, batch normalization, and activation function before entering the Resunit module in two layers, ultimately obtaining branch 3's weights through upsampling. During model training, the DFFN module utilizes various pooling methods and Resunit quantities across its multiple branches to acquire distinct receptive fields. This approach enables the fusion of information from diverse receptive fields to bolster feature extraction. The multiple residual structures within the DFFN module act akin to multiple gradient propagation paths, effectively simulating the training of multiple networks concurrently and enhancing the efficiency of feature information extraction.

2.3 Navigation Mark Light Quality Inspection

For the nighttime navigation mark light flashing video images in inland waterway scenarios, this study proposes a method for detecting navigation mark light quality based on target behavior, as illustrated in Fig. 2. Navigation mark light quality detection encompasses identifying the color of navigation mark lights, measuring their flashing frequency, and determining the flashing period. Video images captured by UAVs are processed using OpenCV to extract the video frames, each containing time series and navigation mark light behavior data.

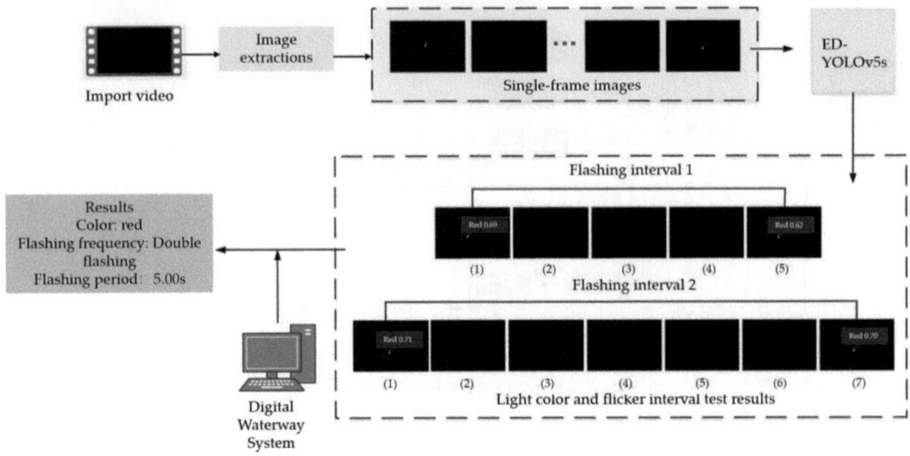

Fig. 2. Technical roadmap of navigation mark light quality inspection.

The ED-YOLOv5s network is employed to detect the flickering state of navigation mark lights in each frame, providing output for navigation mark light color detection, alongside recording time series and target behavior information in each frame. The video stream for each flashing starting sequence of navigation mark lights is determined based on adjacent frame detection results. Subsequently, the flashing interval is utilized to ascertain the frequency and calculate the flashing period of the navigation mark lights. Concurrently, utilizing UAV position information and navigation mark detection classification results from the digital navigation system, the detected navigation mark light results are compared with the original information to facilitate real-time monitoring of nighttime navigation mark lights.

3 Experimental Results and Analysis of Navigation Mark

3.1 Production of Data Sets

The algorithm in this study utilizes navigation mark image datasets captured by UAVs in the Wuhan section of the Yangtze River. Commonly encountered buoys in this area include the Right Bank Tank-type Side Buoy (RTB), Left Bank Conical Side Buoy (LCB), Yellow Conical Special Buoy (YCB), Side Buoy of Left Bank Light Boat (LLB), Side Buoy of Right Bank Light Boat (RLB), and Left and Right Navigation Buoys (LRLB). Samples are collected under varying weather conditions, including sunny and cloudy skies. During data acquisition, the UAV camera's attitude and azimuth are adjusted to capture images from different angles around the mark, providing a comprehensive view of its real state in the channel. Figure 3 illustrates an example of training samples, comprising a total of 2000 pictures. The navigation marks are annotated using the LabelImg software, and the dataset is formatted according to the VOC dataset standards, with a division ratio of training set:test set:verification set = 8:1:1.

Fig. 3. Samples example of navigation mark.

3.2 Model Training

The algorithm described in this paper is constructed using the PyTorch 1.11 framework. The graphics card utilized is the NVIDIA GeForce RTX 2080Ti, and the operating system employed is Windows. Both the labeled source domain dataset and the target domain dataset comprise the training set input into the model. These datasets undergo Mosaic data augmentation, adaptive filling, and scaling processes, resulting in all images being standardized to dimensions of 640×640 pixels. The initial learning rate of the algorithm is set at 0.01, which is subsequently adjusted to 0.002 after 200 iterations. The training process consists of a total of 300 rounds. A batch size of 8 is employed, meaning that each batch comprises 8 image data inputs. Additionally, the number of data loading threads is set to 4.

3.3 Evaluation Criteria

In evaluating object detection results, three key metrics are employed: Mean Average Precision (MAP), Precision (P), and Recall (R), which serve as indicators of algorithmic detection accuracy [28]. Precision (P) denotes the proportion of accurately predicted positive results among all samples classified as positive, while Recall (R) signifies the ratio of correctly predicted positive results

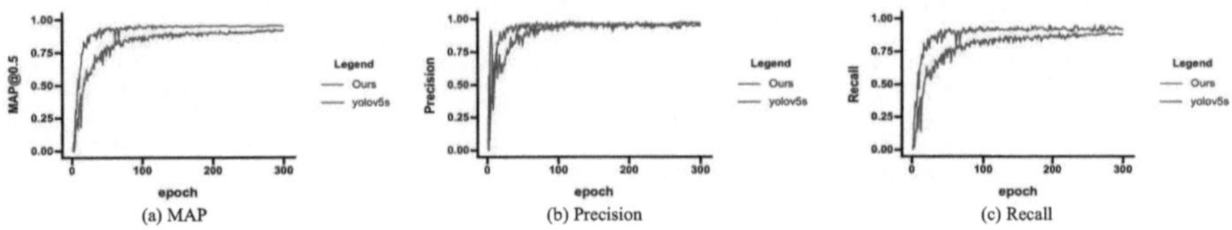

Fig. 4. MAP, precision and recall ratio comparison diagram.

among all actual positive samples. MAP represents the average accuracy across all detection categories. The calculation formulas for these evaluation metrics are as follows:

$$P = \frac{TP}{TP+FP} \tag{1}$$

$$R = \frac{TP}{TP+FN} \tag{2}$$

$$MAP = \frac{1}{n}\sum\nolimits_{i=1}^{n} \left(\int_0^1 P(R)dR\right)_i \tag{3}$$

In the context of evaluation metrics for classification tasks, TP (True Positives) refers to positive samples correctly classified by the model, FP (False Positives) indicates negative samples erroneously classified as positive, and FN (False Negatives) represents positive samples mistakenly classified as negative.

3.4 Result Analysis

Test Results. The comparison results with the training data curve of the original YOLOv5s algorithm are depicted in Fig. 4. It's evident that the algorithm proposed in this paper exhibits improvements in both **M**ean **A**verage **P**recision (MAP) and recall rate. Specifically, the MAP@0.5 is 95.02%, compared to YOLOv5s' 92.06%, indicating an increase of 2.97%. Similarly, the final recall rate rises from 88.08% to 91.68%, reflecting a 3.59% enhancement. Despite a decrease in precision to 95.23% (versus YOLOv5s' 96.99%), representing a decline of 1.76%, both recall and MAP@0.5 demonstrate improvement. Additionally, the convergence rate of each index surpasses that of the YOLOv5s algorithm notably. By approximately the 40th iteration, all indexes in the training data curve converge, highlighting the efficacy of the proposed algorithm's enhancements.

Ablation Experiments. In order to further investigate the impact of the enhanced measures on the model, an ablation experiment was conducted, and the results are presented in Table 1. A checkmark (✓) in the table denotes the incorporation of the improved method during training. As seen from Table 1, while the YOLOv5s algorithm exhibits the highest precision among all algorithms, it is only 1.76% lower than that of the proposed algorithm. However, its recall and

Table 1. Comparative experiments.

DFFN	ECA	YOLOv5s	MAP@0.5/%	Precision/%	Recall/%
		✓	92.06	96.99	88.08
	✓	✓	92.30	95.23	89.00
✓		✓	93.28	96.26	90.97
✓	✓	✓	95.02	95.23	91.68

Table 2. Comparison of object detection algorithms.

Method	MAP@0.5	Precision/%	Recall/%
SSD	75.4	71.8	54.5
Faster-RCNN	76.3	73.6	62.1
YOLOv4	85.5	83.5	79.5
YOLOv5s	92.1	97.0	88.1
Ours	95.0	95.2	91.7

MAP @ 0.5 are the lowest. Upon integrating ECA and DFFN, noticeable enhancements are observed in the recall and MAP @ 0.5 of the algorithm compared to YOLOv5s. Comparing the ECA algorithm with the original YOLOv5s, a decrease of 1.76% in precision is noted, while the recall and MAP @ 0.5 increase by 0.92% and 0.24%, respectively, affirming the efficacy of the ECA mechanism. Similarly, upon adding DFFN, the precision rate of the algorithm decreases by 0.73% compared to the original YOLOv5s, whereas the recall and MAP @ 0.5 increase by 2.89% and 1.22%, respectively, further confirming the effectiveness of DFFN. This algorithm enhances the efficiency of feature information extraction and expands the receptive field through the ECA and DFFN modules.

Comparison of Different Algorithms. To demonstrate the superiority of the proposed algorithm over other object detection algorithms, we employed the same dataset used in this paper to train commonly used object detection models such as YOLOv4, Faster-RCNN, and SSD. Subsequently, their results were summarized and compared, as presented in Table 2. The proposed algorithm exhibits significantly higher average accuracy and recall rates compared to SSD and Faster-RCNN. Moreover, the performance of YOLOv4 is inferior to both YOLOv5s and the enhanced algorithm proposed in this study. This comparison, along with the earlier evaluation against the original YOLOv5s algorithm, highlights the significant superiority of the proposed algorithm in object detection overall.

4 Experimental Results and Analysis of Navigation Mark Light

4.1 Dataset and Experimental Environment

The experimental dataset consists of 50 video clips, each lasting 60 s, capturing the nighttime flashing of navigation mark lights collected via UAV. To mitigate

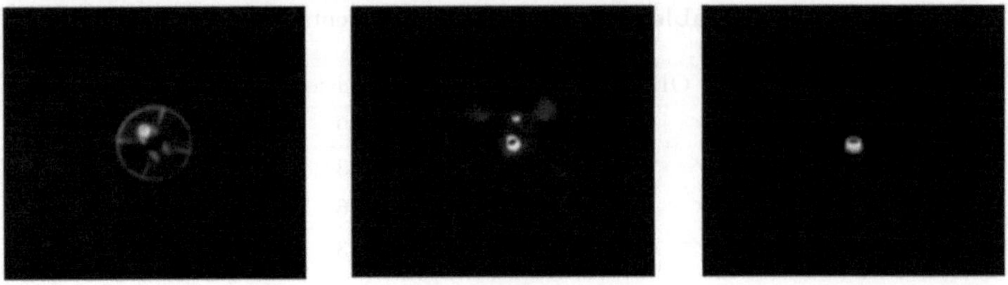

Fig. 5. Training samples of the aids to navigation light quality detection. a: green light b: red light c: yello light. (Color figure online)

interference from coastal city lights, the UAV navigation route was strategically planned. By controlling the camera angle, the UAV captured lateral and overhead views of various types of navigation mark lights flashing. Typically, nighttime navigation mark lights exhibit colors such as red, green, and yellow. Each frame of the video was converted into an image for frame-by-frame labeling using video frame extraction techniques, as illustrated in Fig. 5, depicting a training sample example. For labeling the flashing status of navigation mark lights, the data labeling tool Labelimg was employed. The labeling method and experimental environment mirrored those of inland waterway navigation mark detection experiments, with 500 training rounds spanning approximately 7 h.

4.2 Navigation Marks Light Quality Testing and Evaluation Indicators

This experiment employs two criteria to evaluate algorithm detection accuracy: the period detection error rate (FT) and the video stream detection rate (V). FT represents the ratio of the algorithm's detected period to the predefined period in the Digital Waterway System, while V indicates the average time taken to detect each image frame within the video stream. The formulation of these evaluation indexes is as follows:

$$F_T = \frac{T_0 - T_1}{T_1} \tag{4}$$

The variable T_0 represents the algorithm used to detect the flashing period of the navigation mark light, while T_1 denotes the digital channel system recording the actual flashing period of the navigation mark light.

4.3 Navigation Mark Light Quality Testing Experimental Results and Analysis

The ED-YOLOv5s algorithm was utilized to train the model using video images capturing flickering navigation mark lights obtained by a custom-made nighttime UAV. A video analysis method based on target behavior and time series

Table 3. Comparative experiments.

Navigation mark	Light color	Flash Frequency	$T_0(s)$	$T_1(s)$	F_T	V (ms/frame)
LLB	green	double flashing	5.04	5.00	0.008	5.7
YCB	yellow	single flashing	4.00	4.00	0	5.4
RLB	red	double flashing	5.00	5.00	0	5.4
RTB	red	single flashing	4.04	4.00	0.01	4.9
LCB	green	double flashing	5.02	5.00	0.002	5.6

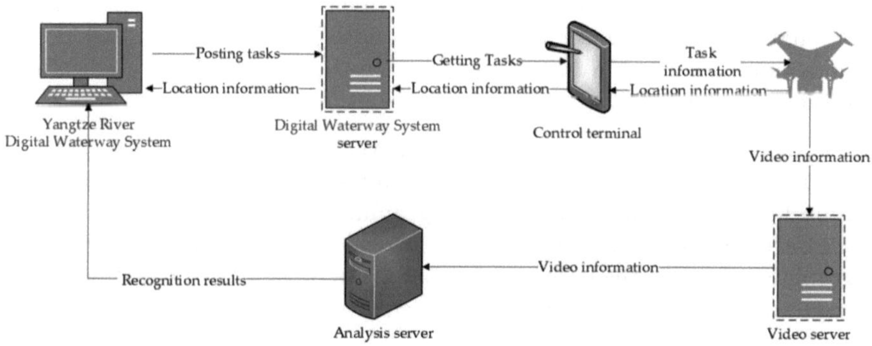

Fig. 6. Intelligent sensing of Yangtze River navigation mark.

information was employed to derive the detection outcomes. Select video samples from the test set were utilized for evaluation, and the obtained results were compared with data from the digital navigation system, as illustrated in Table 3. Across various navigation marks with different light colors and flicker frequencies, the algorithm demonstrated commendable detection accuracy, aligning well with actual navigation mark light quality. During testing, it was observed that the primary source of errors stemmed from interference caused by other lights in the vicinity, such as ship lights and coastal city lights. In practical applications, meticulous attention to UAV route planning is essential.

5 Intelligent Sensing Scheme for Navigation Mark of the Yangtze River

After achieving the aforementioned improvements, the ED-YOLOv5s model underwent deployment for a demonstration at the Changjiang Yichang Waterway Bureau. Equipped with a high-definition camera, a UAV captured images and videos of navigational markers along the Yangtze River. These visual data were transmitted using video image data transmission technology to an AI-powered identification application system running in the background. Leveraging AI intelligent identification technology, the system identified, detected, and analyzed navigational markers within the image and video data, culminating in the establishment of a digital waterway navigational markers video inspection system. The fundamental workflow is illustrated in Fig. 6.

5.1 Perceptual Process

Step 1 Data Transmission. The Changjiang Yichang Waterway Bureau employs the DJI Matrice 300 RTK UAV model. Leveraging the DJI SDK package, a data connectivity route has been established between the UAV and the digital waterway system of the Yangtze River. This infrastructure facilitates the transmission of both structural and video data captured by the UAV. Additionally, it enables task assignment for aerial photography missions and provides real-time monitoring of UAV operations within the Yangtze River digital waterway production service system.

Step 2 Route Planning. The Yangtze River region exhibits diverse terrain characteristics, featuring a zonal topography aligned parallel to the river's course. Based on field surveys and existing topographic data, the UAV flight path and coverage area are meticulously planned, considering both the precision of the topographic maps and the endurance capabilities of the UAV. Careful attention is given to designing flight courses with adequate heading and lateral overlap to prevent any gaps in aerial coverage.

Step 3 Object Recognition. The UAV captures video data, which is then transmitted to the AI analysis server via the video server. Employing the OpenCV video frame extraction technique, the video is converted into individual images. These images undergo preprocessing before being subjected to recognition using the ED-YOLOv5s algorithm. Post-processing steps follow, facilitating the detection of the navigation mark's appearance and position. Additionally, the identification results are accessible through the Yangtze River Digital Waterway production service system [29].

Step 4 Early Warning and Display. Using message flow push and data subscription mode technology, along with AI targeting, warning norms and levels are established based on predefined rules and alarm conditions. Relevant warning information corresponding to the determined levels is then automatically distributed to the respective recipients. The production service system interface of the Yangtze River facilitates simultaneous real-time display of navigation mark identification from UAV aerial videos and the operating route of the UAV on the Changjiang Electronic Navigational Chart [30], as illustrated in Fig. 7.

5.2 Application Effects

The implementation of an intelligent sensing scheme for the navigation marks along the Yangtze River by the Changjiang Yichang Waterway Bureau has yielded significant benefits: (1) Cost Reduction: UAV cruises now require only 2 to 3 staff members, half the number needed for traditional cruises. This reduction not only lowers labor costs but also lightens the workload. (2) Enhanced

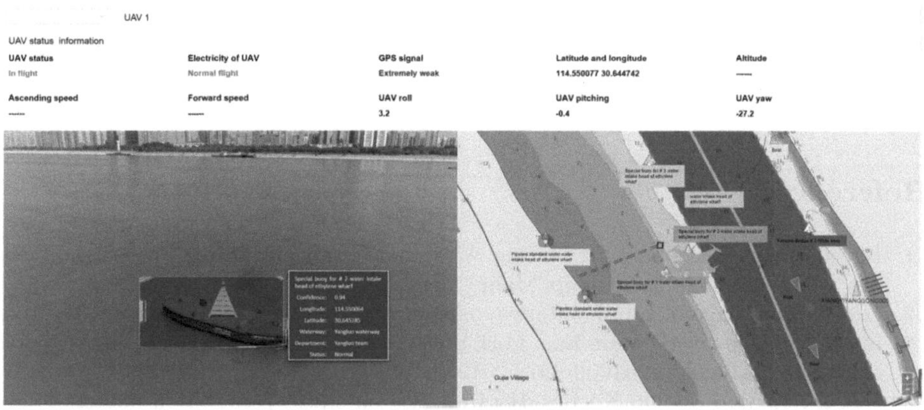

Fig. 7. Real-time identification interface of navigation marks. Left: Recognition results of aerial navigation marks of UAV. Right: Position of Operational UAV in Yangtze River Electronic Channel Map.

Monitoring: With UAVs operating at approximately 100 m altitude, they offer a high vantage point and wide field of view. This enables clear observation of waterway details, adaptable shooting angles as per operational requirements, and comprehensive monitoring of navigation mark conditions. Such monitoring eliminates factors influencing human judgment, thereby improving the effectiveness of cruises. (3). Intelligent Decision-Making: Artificial intelligence identification results aid in the detection, enumeration, and analysis of navigation markers. These results are swiftly integrated with real-time digital navigation channel monitoring data in the database. This integration facilitates cruise monitoring for navigation channel management departments, enhances the real-time efficiency of data necessary for digital navigation channel decision-making, improves the accuracy of decision analysis, and optimizes intelligent navigation channel management and maintenance.

6 Conclusion

To develop an intelligent detection model for aerial marker video inspection from a UAV perspective, we constructed the ED-YOLOv5s model based on the YOLOv5s algorithm. This model enhances the fusion of navigation mark target features, making it more suitable for UAV aerial photography datasets. Across the dataset, the mAP@0.5 reached 95.02%, marking a 2.97% improvement over the original model. We designed a detection scheme for night navigation mark lights, with experiments confirming excellent quality detection. To assess the practical application of the improved model, we implemented an intelligent identification scheme for navigation marks at the Changjiang Yichang Waterway Bureau. Results indicate significant cost reductions in daily inspections, enhanced navigation mark maintenance effectiveness, and improved decision-making. However, the improved model was not tested under low visibility conditions, limiting its verification for foggy environments. Future research will address this scenario.

References

1. International Dictionary of Marine Aids to Navigation. https://www.iala-aism.org/wiki/dictionary/index.php/Main_Page
2. Lv, Y.: Key technology of waterway elements perception and interaction system in the Yangtze river's main line. Port Waterw. Eng. (09), 153 (2012). https://doi.org/10.16233/j.cnki.issn1002-4972.2012.09.011
3. Nie, Z., Jiang, Z., Chu, X., Liu, H.: Research on status recognition model of aids to navigation based on BP-DS evidence theory. Port Waterw. Eng. **01**, 150–156 (2022). https://doi.org/10.16233/j.cnki.issn1002-4972.20211227.036
4. Yu, M., Han, S., Wang, T., Wang, H.: An approach to accurate ship image recognition in a complex maritime transportation environment. J. Mar. Sci. Eng. **2022**, 10 (1903). https://doi.org/10.3390/jmse10121903
5. Ma, R., Bao, K., Yin, Y.: Improved ship object detection in low-illumination environments using RetinaMFANet. J. Mar. Sci. Eng. **2022**, 10 (1996). https://doi.org/10.3390/jmse10121996
6. Shao, Z., et al.: Multi-scale object detection model for autonomous ship navigation in maritime environment. J. Mar. Sci. Eng. **10**, 1783 (2022). https://doi.org/10.3390/jmse10111783
7. Ni, H., Chu, X., Zhang, B., Jiang, Z.: Inland navigation mark detection algorithm based on improved cascade RCNN. Navig. China **03**, 99–105 (2022)
8. Du, Y., Sun, S., Qiu, S., Li, S., Pan, M., Chen, C.-H.: Intelligent recognition system based on contour accentuation for navigation marks. Wirel. Commun. Mob. Comput. **2021**, 6631074 (2021). https://doi.org/10.1155/2021/6631074
9. Pan, M., Liu, Y., Cao, J., Li, Y., Li, C., Chen, C.-H.: Visual recognition based on deep learning for navigation mark classification. IEEE Access **8**, 32767–32775 (2020). https://doi.org/10.1109/ACCESS.2020.2973856
10. Han, X., et al.: Multilabel video classification model of navigation mark's lights based on deep learning. Comput. Intell. Neurosci. **2021**, 6794202 (2021). https://doi.org/10.1155/2021/6794202
11. Nikolic, J., Burri, M., Rehder, J., Leutenegger, S., Huerzeler, C., Siegwart, R.: A UAV system for inspection of industrial facilities. In: Proceedings of the 2013 IEEE Aerospace Conference, pp. 1–8 (2013)
12. Samir Labib, N., Danoy, G., Musial, J., Brust, M.R., Bouvry, P.: Internet of unmanned aerial vehicles-a multilayer low-altitude airspace model for distributed UAV traffic management. Sensors **19**, 4779 (2019). https://doi.org/10.3390/s19214779
13. Liu, C., Szirányi, T.: Road condition detection and emergency rescue recognition using on-board UAV in the wildness. Remote Sens. **14**, 4355 (2022). https://doi.org/10.3390/rs14174355
14. ImageNet Classification with Deep Convolutional Neural Networks | Communications of the ACM. https://dl.acm.org/doi/abs/10.1145/3065386. Accessed 16 Dec 2022

15. Guo, Y., Liu, Y., Oerlemans, A., Lao, S., Wu, S., Lew, M.S.: Deep learning for visual understanding: a review. Neurocomputing **187**, 27–48 (2016). https://doi.org/10.1016/j.neucom.2015.09.116
16. Deep Learning Techniques-R-CNN to Mask R-CNN: A Survey | SpringerLink. https://link.springer.com/chapter/10.1007/978-981-13-9042-5_56. Accessed 16 Dec 2022
17. Girshick, R.: Fast R-CNN, pp. 1440–1448 (2015). https://proceedings.neurips.cc/paper/2015/hash/14bfa6bb14875e45bba028a21ed38046-Abstract.html. Accessed 16 Dec 2022
18. Faster R-CNN: Towards Real-Time Object Detection with Region Proposal Networks. https://pesquisa.bvsalud.org/global-literature-on-novel-coronavirus-2019-ncov/resource/pt/covidwho-994115. Accessed 16 Dec 2022
19. Jiang, P., Ergu, D., Liu, F., Cai, Y., Ma, B.: A review of yolo algorithm developments. Procedia Comput. Sci. **199**, 1066–1073 (2022). https://doi.org/10.1016/j.procs.2022.01.135
20. Liu, W., et al.: SSD: single shot MultiBox detector. In: Leibe, B., Matas, J., Sebe, N., Welling, M. (eds.) ECCV 2016. LNCS, vol. 9905, pp. 21–37. Springer, Cham (2016). https://doi.org/10.1007/978-3-319-46448-0_2
21. Bochkovskiy, A., Wang, C.-Y., Liao, H.-Y.M.: YOLOv4: Optimal Speed and Accuracy of Object Detection (2020)
22. Mahendrakar, T., White, R.T., Wilde, M., Kish, B.: Real-Time Satellite Component Recognition with YOLO-V5 (2021)
23. Liu, Y., Lu, B., Peng, J., Zhang, Z.: Research on the use of YOLOv5 object detection algorithm in mask wearing recognition. World Sci. Res. J. **6**(11), 276–284 (2020). http://arxiv.org/abs/1807.06521
24. Woo, S., Park, J., Lee, J.-Y., Kweon, I.S.: CBAM: Convolutional Block Attention Module (2018). http://www.springer.com/lncs
25. Roy, A.G., Navab, N., Wachinger, C.: Concurrent spatial and channel 'squeeze & excitation' in fully convolutional networks. In: Frangi, A.F., Schnabel, J.A., Davatzikos, C., Alberola-López, C., Fichtinger, G. (eds.) MICCAI 2018. LNCS, vol. 11070, pp. 421–429. Springer, Cham (2018). https://doi.org/10.1007/978-3-030-00928-1_48
26. Wang, Q., Wu, B., Zhu, P., Li, P., Zuo, W., Hu, Q.: ECA-net: efficient channel attention for deep convolutional neural networks. In: Proceedings of the IEEE/CVF Conference on Computer Vision and Pattern Recognition, pp. 11534–11542 (2020)
27. He, K., Zhang, X., Ren, S., Sun, J.: Deep residual learning for image recognition. In: 2016 IEEE Conference on Computer Vision and Pattern Recognition (CVPR), Las Vegas, NV, USA, pp. 770–778 (2016). https://doi.org/10.1109/CVPR.2016.90
28. CVPR 2016 Open Access Repository
29. Xue, L.: Summary and prospect of the technology of inland digital waterway. In: Proceedings of the 2017 4th International Conference on Transportation Information and Safety (ICTIS), pp. 163–171 (2017)
30. Yang, B., Zhang, Q., Li, L., Xu, S., Yang, P.: The production and service technologies of changjiang electronic navigational chart. J. Geomatics **01**, 51–55 (2022). https://doi.org/10.14188/j.2095-6045.2021647

Cascaded Sliding-Window-Based Relativistic GAN Fusion for Perceptual and Consistent Video Super-Resolution

Dingyi Li(✉)

PCA Lab, Key Lab of Intelligent Perception and Systems for High-Dimensional Information of Ministry of Education, and Jiangsu Key Lab of Image and Video Understanding for Social Security, School of Computer Science and Engineering, Nanjing University of Science and Technology, Nanjing 210094, China

lidingyi@njust.edu.cn

Abstract. Perceptual video super-resolution aims at converting low-resolution videos to visually appealing high-resolution ones. It may lead to temporal inconsistency due to the drastically changing outputs. In this paper, we propose cascaded sliding-window-based relativistic GAN (Generative Adversarial Network) fusion for perceptual and consistent video super-resolution (PC-VSR). Firstly, cascaded sliding-window-based relativistic GAN is designed to extract more useful information. It enlarges the temporal receptive field of sliding-window-based model in each step. It is able to enhance perceptual quality and compensate temporal consistency progressively and sufficiently. The trained separate refinement generator networks are fused into a final refinement generator. The final refinement generator can be calculated recursively at the testing stage. With our generator fusion, the parameter number is reduced and good quality is maintained. Extensive experimental results demonstrate that our approach outperforms state-of-the-art super-resolution methods in terms of perceptual quality. Our method also achieves good temporal consistency and per-pixel accuracy, compared with other perceptual approaches.

Keywords: Video Super-Resolution · Perceptual Quality · Temporal Consistency · Information Science · Intelligent Information Processing

1 Introduction

Video super-resolution [40,43] aims at converting low-resolution videos to visually appealing and realistic high-resolution ones. The accuracy of video super-resolution has been increased by per-pixel loss guided Convolutional Neural Networks (CNNs) [11,37,44,51,52,57]. However, per-pixel accuracy-oriented video

This work was supported by the National Natural Science Foundation of China under Grant 62002168.

Published by Springer Nature Switzerland AG 2024
Z. Shi et al. (Eds.): ICIS 2024, IFIP AICT 720, pp. 232–247, 2024.
https://doi.org/10.1007/978-3-031-71253-1_17

super-resolution methods may generate over-smoothed results. Perceptual loss and Generative Adversarial Networks (GANs) have been widely employed in single-image super-resolution [18,25,53,63]. Perceptual loss [18] can help to generate visually appealing results. Ledig *et al.* [25] designed SRGAN (Super-Resolution GAN) which is based on perceptual loss and adversarial loss. GAN can improve the visual quality of the super-resolution results.

For GAN-based video super-resolution, the major problem is how to obtain good perceptual quality and temporal consistency for the results at the same time. Different from single-image super-resolution, video super-resolution approaches capture the motion information in consecutive frames either explicitly or implicitly. There is motion compensation error generated in the process of extracting motion details, causing temporal inconsistency. For the results of GAN-based video super-resolution methods, the problem is more obvious. There is flickering artifact due to the unreasonable utilization of inter-frame information caused by GAN. To deal with this problem, some methods design new loss functions for the models of GAN-based video super-resolution [6,42,46]. These algorithms are either sliding-window-based or recurrent. In sliding-window-based methods [42], more precise frame or feature alignment is conducted in the window to make the results accurate. However, the sliding window limits the extraction of useful information from long range. Recurrent methods [6,46] utilize the super-resolved previous frames or features to restore the following frames. Long-term dependency can be employed. The disadvantage of recurrent methods is that there is less alignment information from multiple local frames. Also, the processing is performed in a single forward pass, which limits the performance of visual quality and temporal coherence.

In view of the above situation, we establish cascaded sliding-window-based relativistic GAN fusion for video super-resolution. The motivation of our method is enhancing the perceptual quality and temporal consistency in a progressive manner. Our method is named PC-VSR (perceptual and consistent video super-resolution). It adopts multiple stacked sliding-window-based relativistic GANs for the upsampling and gradual restoration of videos. In each GAN, the information in the neighboring window of each frame is incorporated into the original information in the frame. With cascaded GANs, the temporal receptive field of our structure is enlarged step by step. The perceptual quality and temporal consistency are improved progressively. At the testing stage, we fuse multiple refinement generator networks into a final one which can be performed recursively, to reduce parameter number and keep good performance.

The main contributions of this work are listed as follows.

1. We design cascaded sliding-window-based relativistic GANs for video super-resolution. Our framework can improve perceptual quality and temporal consistency progressively and sufficiently.
2. We adopt refinement generator network fusion. The fusion can reduce parameter number and maintain good quality.
3. Our method outperforms state-of-the-art approaches in terms of visual quality, and is of better temporal consistency and per-pixel accuracy compared with other perceptual approaches.

The remainder of the paper is organized as follows. Section 2 describes about the related work. In Sect. 3, the details of our video super-resolution method, are illustrated. The experiments are shown and discussed in Sect. 4. In Sect. 5, we draw a conclusion.

2 Related Work

2.1 Perceptual Single-Image Super-Resolution

Perceptual super-resolution includes perceptual single-image super-resolution and perceptual video super-resolution. Perceptual video super-resolution algorithms are motivated by the successful employment of perceptual loss and adversarial loss in single-image super-resolution. Previous single-image super-resolution methods which are based on per-pixel accuracy loss tend to generate over-smoothed results. Researchers found that if perceptual loss and adversarial loss are involved in the training of single-image super-resolution networks, perceptually pleasant results can be obtained. Johnson *et al.* [18] utilized perceptual loss for single-image super-resolution. Perceptual loss differs from per-pixel accuracy loss, and can help to generate visually appealing results. Ledig *et al.* [25] designed SRGAN (Super-Resolution GAN) which is based on perceptual loss and adversarial loss. SRGAN can improve the visual quality of the super-resolution results. Sajjadi *et al.* [47] proposed the texture matching loss and combined it with pixel-wise loss, perceptual loss and adversarial loss. The PIRM (Perceptual Image Restoration and Manipulation) challenge [1] aims at improving the visual quality of single-image super-resolution results. Wang *et al.* [53] proposed ESRGAN (Enhanced Super-Resolution GANs) and won the first place in the perceptual track. They modified the basic module of the generator network of SRGAN, introduced the relativistic GAN and changed the strategy of perceptual feature extraction. Zhang *et al.* [63] proposed RankSRGAN (Super-Resolution GANs with Ranker). They trained a ranker to guide the generator network to produce results with better perceptual metrics.

In single-image super-resolution, temporal information in videos is not considered. It is not optimal to apply single-image super-resolution to video super-resolution.

2.2 Perceptual Video Super-Resolution

Recently some researchers designed generator networks and trained them with per-pixel accuracy loss to reach good PSNR (peak signal to noise ratio) values [7, 10, 22, 23, 36, 39, 49, 50, 53, 64, 65]. Others tried to improve visual quality by using these powerful generator nets and adversarial training. Plain GANs for video super-resolution tend to generate flickering artifact in complex motion scenes. In order to solve the problem, Li and Wang [30] proposed a GAN-based face video super-resolution method with the guidance of identity features. Lucas *et al.* [42] designed a video super-resolution approach based on pixel-wise loss, perceptual loss and adversarial loss. They used LPIPS (Learned Perceptual Image Patch

Similarity) [62] as the perceptual quality metric. LPIPS was designed by Zhang *et al.* [62]. This metric is the similarity calculated by using neural network structures and can be applied to evaluate perceptual quality in image and video processing tasks. Chu *et al.* [6] and Pérez-Pellitero *et al.* [46] designed new loss functions for temporal consistency. They also used LPIPS as the perceptual metric. Chen *et al.* [5] presented a high-order relational GAN for video super-resolution. Xu *et al.* proposed a new GAN for video super-resolution based on GigaGAN [20]. Those models are either sliding-window-based [2,5,11,15,17,21,26–28,33–35,38,51,52,54,59–61] or recurrent [3,4,8,9,12–14,16,29,31,32,41,48,55,56,58]. Sliding-window-based methods are limited by the small temporal window. Recurrent network-based algorithms are less effective in motion compensation among multiple local neighboring frames.

Different from those approaches, our method enlarges the temporal receptive field of sliding-window-based model step by step. It can progressively improve the perceptual quality and temporal stability.

3 Our Method

3.1 Overview

We establish cascaded sliding-window-based relativistic GAN fusion for video super-resolution. Our method is named PC-VSR (perceptual and consistent video super-resolution). The overview of our framework is illustrated in Fig. 1. Because of the limit of sliding window, it is difficult for plain sliding-window-based perceptual video super-resolution methods to achieve good perceptual quality and temporal consistency at the same time. We aim at reducing the difficultly of video super-resolution and enhancing consecutive frames progressively. Firstly, we train a coarse relativistic GAN and multiple refinement relativistic GANs with per-pixel accuracy loss, perceptual loss and relativistic adversarial loss. At the testing stage, the refinement generators are fused into a final refinement one. The final refinement generator is employed recursively to generate the final results. Refinement generator network fusion can reduce parameter number and maintain good quality.

3.2 Cascaded Sliding-Window-Based Relativistic GANs for Video Super-Resolution

We train a coarse GAN and multiple refinement GANs for video super-resolution in our PC-VSR. Firstly, the coarse generator network upsamples the frames and generates the coarse super-resolution results. Then the results are modified by the stacked refinement networks. Sliding-window-based video super-resolution model regards multiple images as the inputs and generates one super-resolved frame (usually the centering frame) at each step. With cascaded sliding-window-based relativistic GANs, the temporal receptive field is gradually enlarged. The video super-resolution results are also refined progressively.

We adopt the per-pixel accuracy loss, perceptual loss and relativistic adversarial loss for all steps. The relativistic discriminator net [19] is utilized to

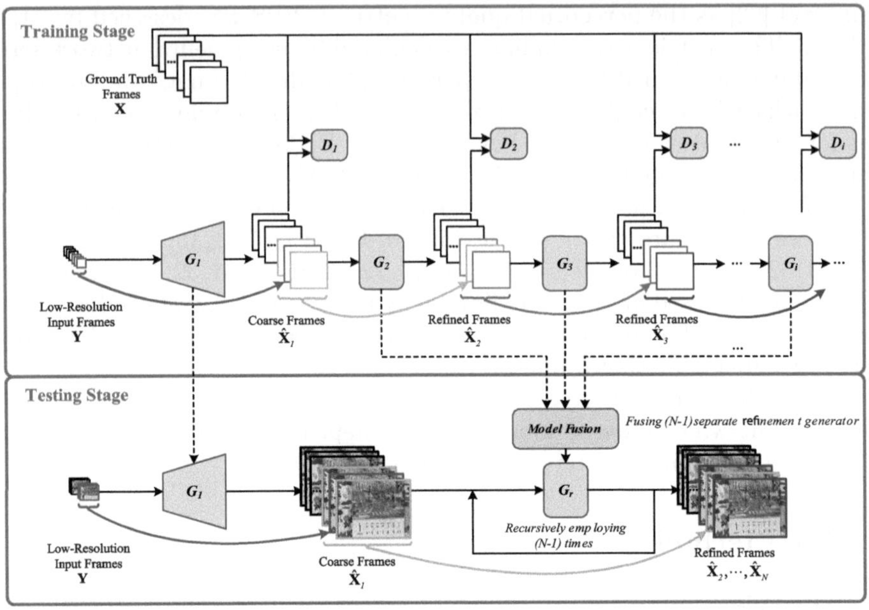

Fig. 1. Overview of the proposed video super-resolution method PC-VSR (perceptual and consistent video super-resolution). In this figure, we let the temporal length of the sliding window to 3 frames at each step for an illustration. In the experiments, we use longer window (5 or 7 frames). The sliding-window-based video super-resolution model regards multiple (3 for here) images as the inputs and generates one centering super-resolved frame at each step. With cascaded sliding-window-based relativistic GAN fusion, the temporal receptive field is gradually enlarged (3, 5, 7, 9, $\cdots$ for each step here). The perceptual quality and temporal consistency of the video super-resolution results are also refined progressively.

calculate the relativistic adversarial loss. All loss functions are calculated by using the super-resolved frames and ground truth frames. The total loss for the training of the ith generator network G_i is defined as

$$L_{G_i} = \lambda_{Acc} L^i_{Acc} + \lambda_{Per} L^i_{Per} + \lambda_{Adv} L^i_{Adv}, i = 1, 2, \cdots, N \tag{1}$$

where N is the total number of relativistic GANs. λ_{Acc}, λ_{Per} and λ_{Adv} are the weights of the per-pixel accuracy loss, perceptual loss and relativistic adversarial loss, respectively. We have

$$L^i_{Acc} = \mathbb{E}_{\hat{\mathbf{X}}_i} ||\hat{\mathbf{X}}_i - \mathbf{X}||_1, i = 1, 2, \cdots, N \tag{2}$$

$$L^i_{Per} = \mathbb{E}_{\hat{\mathbf{X}}_i} ||P(\hat{\mathbf{X}}_i) - P(\mathbf{X})||_1, i = 1, 2, \cdots, N \tag{3}$$

and

$$\begin{aligned} L^i_{Adv} = &- \mathbb{E}_{\mathbf{X}}[log(1 - D_i(\mathbf{X}, \hat{\mathbf{X}}_i))] \\ &- \mathbb{E}_{\hat{\mathbf{X}}_i}[log(D_i(\hat{\mathbf{X}}_i, \mathbf{X}))], i = 1, 2, \cdots, N \end{aligned} \tag{4}$$

where P is the function of the perceptual net. $\hat{\mathbf{X}}_i$ is the estimated result at the ith stage. $\mathbf{X}$ is the ground truth. The functions of the ith discriminator network D_i are

$$D_i(\mathbf{X}, \hat{\mathbf{X}}_i) = \sigma(N_i(\mathbf{X}) - \mathbb{E}_{\hat{\mathbf{X}}_i}[N_i(\hat{\mathbf{X}}_i)]), i = 1, 2, \cdots, N \tag{5}$$

and

$$D_i(\hat{\mathbf{X}}_i, \mathbf{X}) = \sigma(N_i(\hat{\mathbf{X}}_i) - \mathbb{E}_{\mathbf{X}}[N_i(\mathbf{X})]), i = 1, 2, \cdots, N \tag{6}$$

where σ is the sigmoid function, N_i is the output of the ith discriminator network before the sigmoid transformation. $\mathbb{E}_{\hat{\mathbf{X}}_i}[N_i(\hat{\mathbf{X}}_i)]$ and $\mathbb{E}_{\mathbf{X}}[N_i(\mathbf{X})]$ is the averaged non-transformed output of the ith discriminator network in a mini-batch for the super-resolution result at the ith stage and ground truth, respectively. The loss of the ith discriminator net is

$$L_{D_i} = -\mathbb{E}_{\mathbf{X}}[log(D_i(\mathbf{X}, \hat{\mathbf{X}}_i))] - \mathbb{E}_{\hat{\mathbf{X}}_i}[log(1 - D_i(\hat{\mathbf{X}}_i, \mathbf{X}))], i = 1, 2, \cdots, N \tag{7}$$

3.3 Refinement Generator Network Fusion

At the testing stage, we fuse the separately trained refinement generator networks to get a final refinement generator. The separate refinement generators are the generators those are not the first one (the coarse generator). The structure of the separate refinement networks is the same but the parameters are different. The separate refinement networks are trained for enhancing the results at different levels. We can fuse the separate networks in order to get a unified one for all levels to reduce parameter number. Suppose that the function of the ith generator network is G_i and there are N generators. We have

$$\theta_{G_r} = \frac{1}{N-1} \sum_{i=2}^{N} \theta_{G_i} \tag{8}$$

where θ_{G_r} and θ_{G_i} are the parameters of the final refinement generator and ith separate generator, respectively.

As shown in Fig. 1, at the testing stage, firstly the low-resolution video frames $\mathbf{Y}$ are fed into the coarse generator network to generate the coarsely super-resolved video frames. Then the final refinement generator is applied $(N-1)$ times recursively to get the final result $\hat{\mathbf{X}}_N$. The function of the coarse generator network is G_1. We have

$$\hat{\mathbf{X}}_N = G_r(\cdots(G_r(G_1(\mathbf{Y})))) \tag{9}$$

where G_r is employed $(N-1)$ times.

4 Experiments

Extensive experiments are conducted to show the effectiveness of the proposed approach and its important modules. Our method is compared with state-of-the-art super-resolution algorithms. The experimental results demonstrate that our approach outperforms other methods in terms of visual quality, and reaches good temporal consistency and per-pixel accuracy compared with other perceptual models.

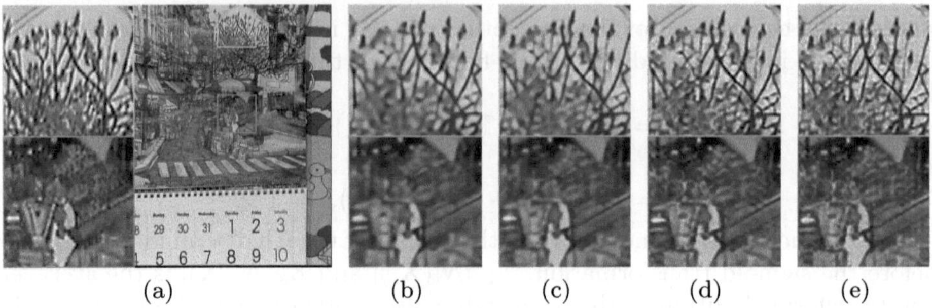

Fig. 2. The super-resolution results and LPIPS values of the generator networks at different steps (from step 1 to step 4) for one frame on Vid4 testing dataset. (a) Ground Truth. (b) Step 1/0.1971. (c) Step 2/0.1727. (d) Step 3/0.1501. (e) Step 4/0.1464. The red values are the best results. The images are better viewed by zooming. (Color figure online)

4.1 Datasets and Implementation Details

In our experiments, the REDS [44] and Vimeo90K training dataset [57] are used for training. We have 3 testing datasets, including the REDS4 [44], Vid4 [37] and SPMCS-32 testing dataset [11,51]. We downsample each ground truth video frame by a scale factor of 4 with bicubic interpolation to generate the low-resolution images on all datasets.

In our method, all sliding-window-based video super-resolution structures can be selected as the generators. In our experiments, we apply EDVR as the basic generator. Note that there is no perceptual loss or GAN involved in the original PSNR-oriented EDVR. There are two stages for the original EDVR. The stage 1 and stage 2 models are used for coarse upsampling and further refinement, respectively. The stage 1 model trained on REDS training dataset are used to test on REDS4 testing dataset. The stage 1 model for testing on Vid4 and SPMCS-32 testing dataset, are trained on Vimeo90K training dataset. Since the length of each video clip on Vimeo90K is only 7, the stage 2 model is trained on REDS (100 frames for each clip) to introduce long-range information. We follow these settings of EDVR. Firstly two coarse relativistic GANs are trained on REDS and Vimeo90K training dataset respectively. Then we train multiple refinement GANs on REDS. The models trained on REDS and Vimeo90K employ 5 and 7 input frames separately, to restore the centering frame in each process. For the coarse generator network and multiple refinement generators, the parameters of the pretrained stage 1 and stage 2 models of EDVR are employed for initialization, respectively.

Adam [24] is the optimization method that we utilize. The size of ground truth training patches is 128×128. The learning rate for training all the generator networks and discriminator networks, is 1e-4. For the training of the coarse generator and separate refinement generators, the batch sizes are 16 and 8, respectively. The refinement networks need larger memory. We train the coarse GAN and the first refinement GAN with 50000 and 100000 iterations, separately. The weights of the per-pixel accuracy loss, perceptual loss and relativistic

Table 1. The LPIPS, tOF, PSNR (dB) values of the generator networks at different steps (from step 1 to step 4) on three testing datasets including REDS4, Vid4 and SPMCS-32. The red values are the best results among all steps on the corresponding dataset. The running time for Step 1–4 on one 1280×720 image with an NVIDIA 2080 Ti GPU is 0.199 s, 0.487 s, 0.775 s and 1.063 s, separately.

Dataset	Metric	Step 1	Step 2	Step 3	Step 4
REDS4	LPIPS↓	0.1389	0.1118	0.0847	0.0813
	tOF↓	0.6249	0.6014	0.5350	0.5211
	PSNR↑	32.02	32.22	31.75	31.47
Vid4	LPIPS↓	0.2028	0.1667	0.1297	0.1258
	tOF↓	0.1427	0.1239	0.1225	0.1250
	PSNR↑	26.95	27.00	26.52	26.34
SPMCS	LPIPS↓	0.1467	0.1241	0.1040	0.1043
	tOF↓	0.1572	0.1328	0.1252	0.1240
	PSNR↑	31.26	31.29	30.87	30.63

Table 2. The LPIPS, tOF, PSNR (dB) and parameter numbers of the models with separate refinement generators and fused refinement generator, on REDS4, Vid4 and SPMCS-32. The red values are the best results on the corresponding dataset.

Dataset	Metric	Separate	Fused
REDS4	**Params**↓	50.7 M	35.7 M
	LPIPS↓	0.0847	0.0831
	tOF↓	0.5350	0.5466
	PSNR↑	31.75	31.61
Vid4	**Params**↓	50.7 M	35.7 M
	LPIPS↓	0.1297	0.1277
	tOF↓	0.1225	0.1194
	PSNR↑	26.52	26.51
SPMCS-32	**Params**↓	50.7 M	35.7 M
	LPIPS↓	0.1040	0.1052
	tOF↓	0.1252	0.1228
	PSNR↑	30.87	30.86

adversarial loss at the first 2 training stages, are 1e-2, 1e-4 and 5e-7, respectively. The 3rd and the following GANs can be quickly trained with only 3325 iterations (1 epoch) with larger weights for perceptual loss and adversarial loss. The weights of the per-pixel accuracy loss, perceptual loss and adversarial loss at these steps, are 1e-2, 1e-3 and 5e-6, separately. The program is based on PyTorch [45]. An NVIDIA 2080 Ti GPU is employed to train the networks.

LPIPS [62], tOF [6] and PSNR are selected as the metrics for perceptual quality, temporal consistency and per-pixel accuracy, respectively. Lower LPIPS values represent better perceptual quality. Lower tOF values are of better temporal consistency. Higher PSNR values indicate better per-pixel accuracy. All metrics are calculated with the codes provided by Chu *et al.* [6].

4.2 The Effects of Cascaded Sliding-Window-Based Relativistic GANs

We show the qualitative and quantitative effectiveness of cascaded sliding-window-based relativistic GANs in Fig 2 and Table 1, respectively. In Fig. 2, the

Fig. 3. The super-resolution results and LPIPS values of different methods for one frame on REDS4 testing dataset. (a) Ground Truth. (b) Bicubic/0.4412. (c) RBPN/0.2402. (d) EDVR-S2/0.1696. (e) BasicVSR++/0.1250. (f) SSL/0.1972. (g) ESRGAN/0.1263. (h) RankSRGAN/0.1278. (i) TecoGAN/0.1557. (j) Our PC-VSR/0.0769. The red value is the best result. The images are better viewed by zooming. (Color figure online)

super-resolution results of different steps for one frame on Vid4 testing dataset are shown. It can be observed that with the increase of step number, the details on the leaves and fruit shelf are enhanced by using cascaded generator networks. At the highest step (step 4), there is some noise on the background of the tree, which demonstrates that we should limit the step number in order to reduce noise and maintain good visual quality.

The quantitative results of different steps on 3 testing datasets, are shown in Table 1. The trend is that the LPIPS and tOF values are gradually decreased with the growth of step number. The PSNR values are firstly increased from step 1 to 2 and then reduced on all datasets. The results demonstrate that perceptual quality and temporal consistency can be greatly enhanced by using cascaded sliding-window-based relativistic GANs. Step 3 and 4 achieve similar performance on different metrics. For the balance between performance and efficiency, we choose step 3 as the final model for the following experiments.

4.3 The Effects of Refinement Generator Network Fusion

In Table 2, we compare the fused refinement generator with the separate refinement generator at step 3. The LPIPS, tOF and PSNR values of the results

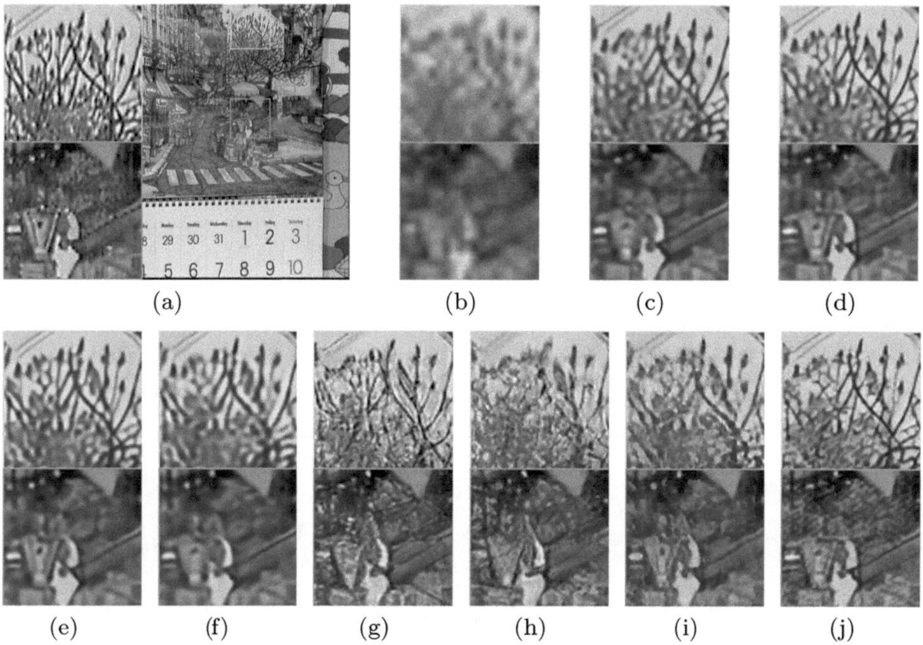

Fig. 4. The super-resolution results and LPIPS values of different methods for one frame on Vid4 testing dataset. (a) Ground Truth. (b) Bicubic/0.5611. (c) RBPN/0.2698. (d) EDVR-S2/0.2122. (e) BasicVSR++/0.2408. (f) SSL/0.2818. (g) ESRGAN/0.1908. (h) RankSRGAN/0.1960. (i) TecoGAN/0.1679. (j) Our PC-VSR/0.1562. The red value is the best result. The images are better viewed by zooming. (Color figure online)

for the fused generator network and the separate one are similar. However, the parameter numbers of the fused recursive network are much smaller. As a result, we employ the fused refinement network recursively for refinement.

4.4 Comparison with State-of-the-Art Methods

We compare our method PC-VSR with state-of-the-art single-image and video super-resolution algorithms. Among these methods, RBPN [11], EDVR-S2 [52], BasicVSR++ [4] and SSL [55] are per-pixel accuracy-based video super-resolution algorithms. EDVR-S2 denotes the second stage of EDVR. It achieves better performance than the stage 1 model. ESRGAN [53] and RankSRGAN [63] are GAN-based perceptual single-image super-resolution methods. TecoGAN [6] is a perceptual video super-resolution approach.

Some of the super-resolution results of different algorithms are shown in Fig. 3 and 4. It can be seen that our PC-VSR can restore more details on edges and textures, and generate visually appealing and natural results those are more similar to the ground truth images. The results also demonstrate that our method

Table 3. The LPIPS, tOF and PSNR (dB) values of different super-resolution methods on REDS4, Vid4 and SPMCS-32 testing dataset. The red and blue values are the first and second place results on the corresponding dataset, respectively.

Dataset	Metric	Bicubic	Per-pixel accuracy-based methods				Perceptual methods			
			RBPN	EDVR-S2	BasicVSR++	SSL	ESRGAN	RankSRGAN	TecoGAN	PC-VSR
REDS4	LPIPS↓	0.4550	0.2305	0.1612	0.1290	0.1816	0.1222	0.1309	0.1614	0.0831
	tOF↓	2.6018	1.0561	0.7391	0.6449	0.7787	0.8536	0.8655	1.4022	0.5466
	PSNR↑	27.41	31.19	32.75	33.81	32.44	27.66	27.54	29.32	31.61
Vid4	LPIPS↓	0.5008	0.2500	0.2193	0.2350	0.2549	0.1933	0.1994	0.1668	0.1277
	tOF↓	0.4420	0.1485	0.1218	0.1133	0.1367	0.4670	0.4626	0.1813	0.1194
	PSNR↑	23.76	27.02	27.42	27.74	27.11	22.95	23.05	25.98	26.51
SPMCS-32	LPIPS↓	0.4114	0.1799	0.1588	-	-	0.1414	0.1629	0.1337	0.1052
	tOF↓	0.4475	0.1611	0.1264	-	-	0.2656	0.2974	0.1790	0.1228
	PSNR↑	27.19	31.72	32.00	-	-	27.37	27.08	29.51	30.86

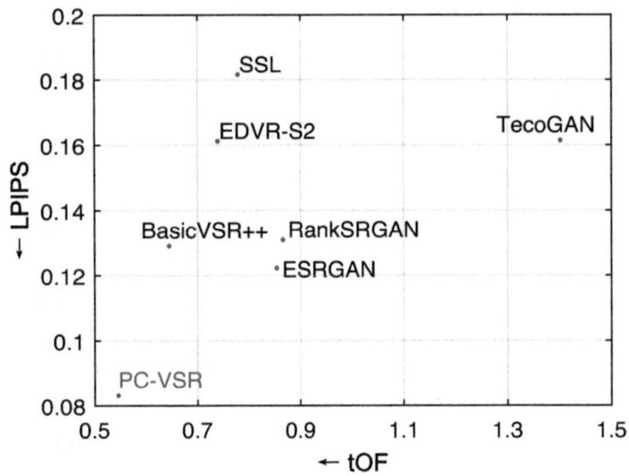

Fig. 5. The LPIPS and tOF values of different methods on REDS4 testing dataset. The lower the better.

performs well in each region while other approaches may fail to restore some contents. In Fig. 3, our PC-VSR is able to restore the details of the leaves and signs at the same time. The results of RBPN, EDVR-S2, BasicVSR++, SSL and TecoGAN are over-smoothed. The results of ESRGAN and RankSRGAN are pleasant on the leaves, but are distorted on the sign and have noticeable noise. In Fig. 4, the results of RBPN, EDVR-S2, BasicVSR++ and SSL are quite smooth. The leaves and fruit shelf are unnatural for ESRGAN, RankSRGAN and TecoGAN, but are well recovered by our PC-VSR.

The LPIPS, tOF and PSNR values of different approaches on the 3 testing datasets are provided in Table 3. It is shown that our PC-VSR outperforms state-of-the-art super-resolution methods in terms of LPIPS by a large margin on all datasets, demonstrating that the visual quality of our results is better than other approaches. Our PC-VSR achieves the best temporal consistency metric (tOF) under all circumstances except for BasicVSR++ on Vid4. Since our method is not per-pixel accuracy-based, the PSNR values of our PC-VSR are lower than per-pixel accuracy-based methods including RBPN (on Vid4 and SPMCS-32), EDVR, BasicVSR++ and SSL. But they are much higher than other perceptual super-resolution approaches.

In Fig. 5, the LPIPS and tOF values of different approaches on REDS4 testing dataset are illustrated. It can be found that the LPIPS and tOF values of our PC-VSR are much smaller than other methods, showing that our approach is better than other methods in terms of perceptual quality and temporal consistency. It takes about 0.775 s to process one frame with 1280×720 resolution using an NVIDIA 2080 Ti GPU.

5 Conclusion

In this paper, we have presented cascaded sliding-window-based relativistic GAN fusion for perceptual and consistent video super-resolution. Multiple sliding-window-based relativistic GANs are stacked to enhance perceptual quality and temporal coherence progressively. The temporal receptive field is gradually enlarged in each step. We also fuse the multiple refinement generators and get the fused recursive refinement generator which can reduce parameter number and maintain good performance. Our method outperforms state-of-the-art super-resolution algorithms in terms of visual quality. It reaches good temporal consistency and per-pixel accuracy compared with other perceptual approaches. It is readily applicable to other video processing tasks such as video denoising and debluring.

References

1. Blau, Y., Mechrez, R., Timofte, R., Michaeli, T., Zelnik-Manor, L.: The 2018 PIRM challenge on perceptual image super-resolution. In: Proceedings of the European Conference on Computer Vision Workshops, pp. 1–22 (2018)
2. Caballero, J., et al.: Real-time video super-resolution with spatio-temporal networks and motion compensation. In: Proceedings of the IEEE Conference on Computer Vision and Pattern Recognition, pp. 4778–4787 (2017)
3. Chan, K.C., Wang, X., Yu, K., Dong, C., Loy, C.C.: Basicvsr: the search for essential components in video super-resolution and beyond. In: Proceedings IEEE Conference on Computer Vision and Pattern Recognition, pp. 4947–4956 (2021)
4. Chan, K.C., Zhou, S., Xu, X., Loy, C.C.: Basicvsr++: improving video super-resolution with enhanced propagation and alignment. In: Proceedings of IEEE Conference on Computer Vision and Pattern Recognition, pp. 5972–5981 (2022)
5. Chen, R., Mu, Y., Zhang, Y.: High-order relational generative adversarial network for video super-resolution. Pattern Recog. **146**, 110059 (2024)
6. Chu, M., Xie, Y., Mayer, J., Leal-Taixé, L., Thuerey, N.: Learning temporal coherence via self-supervision for GAN-based video generation. ACM Trans. Graphics **39**(4), 1–13 (2020)
7. Dong, C., Loy, C.C., He, K., Tang, X.: Image super-resolution using deep convolutional networks. IEEE Trans. Pattern Anal. Mach. Intell. **38**(2), 295–307 (2016)

8. Fuoli, D., Gu, S., Timofte, R.: Efficient video super-resolution through recurrent latent space propagation. In: Proceedings of IEEE International Conference on Computer Vision Workshop, pp. 3476–3485 (2019)
9. Guo, J., Chao, H.: Building an end-to-end spatial-temporal convolutional network for video super-resolution. In: Proceedings of the AAAI Conference on Artificial Intelligence, pp. 4053–4060 (2017)
10. Haris, M., Shakhnarovich, G., Ukita, N.: Deep back-projection networks for super-resolution. In: Proceedings of the IEEE Conference on Computer Vision and Pattern Recognition, pp. 1664–1673 (2018)
11. Haris, M., Shakhnarovich, G., Ukita, N.: Recurrent back-projection network for video super-resolution. In: Proceedings of IEEE Conference on Computer Vision and Pattern Recognition, pp. 3897–3906 (2019)
12. Huang, Y., Wang, W., Wang, L.: Bidirectional recurrent convolutional networks for multi-frame super-resolution. In: Proceedings of Advances in Neural Information Processing Systems, pp. 235–243 (2015)
13. Huang, Y., Wang, W., Wang, L.: Video super-resolution via bidirectional recurrent convolutional networks. IEEE Trans. Pattern Anal. Mach. Intell. **40**(4), 1015–1028 (2018)
14. Isobe, T., Jia, X., Gu, S., Li, S., Wang, S., Tian, Q.: Video super-resolution with recurrent structure-detail network. In: Vedaldi, A., Bischof, H., Brox, T., Frahm, J.-M. (eds.) ECCV 2020. LNCS, vol. 12357, pp. 645–660. Springer, Cham (2020). https://doi.org/10.1007/978-3-030-58610-2_38
15. Isobe, T., et al.: Video super-resolution with temporal group attention. In: Proceedings of IEEE Conference on Computer Vision and Pattern Recognition, pp. 8008–8017 (2020)
16. Isobe, T., Zhu, F., Jia, X., Wang, S.: Revisiting temporal modeling for video super-resolution. In: Proceedings of British Machine Vision Conference, pp. 1–12 (2020)
17. Jo, Y., Wug Oh, S., Kang, J., Joo Kim, S.: Deep video super-resolution network using dynamic upsampling filters without explicit motion compensation. In: Proceedings of the IEEE Conference on Computer Vision and Pattern Recognition, pp. 3224–3232 (2018)
18. Johnson, J., Alahi, A., Fei-Fei, L.: Perceptual losses for real-time style transfer and super-resolution. In: Leibe, B., Matas, J., Sebe, N., Welling, M. (eds.) ECCV 2016. LNCS, vol. 9906, pp. 694–711. Springer, Cham (2016). https://doi.org/10.1007/978-3-319-46475-6_43
19. Jolicoeur-Martineau, A.: The relativistic discriminator: a key element missing from standard GAN. arXiv preprint arXiv:1807.00734 (2018)
20. Kang, M., et al.: Scaling up GANs for text-to-image synthesis. In: Proceedings of IEEE Conference on Computer Vision and Pattern Recognition, pp. 10124–10134 (2023)
21. Kappeler, A., Yoo, S., Dai, Q., Katsaggelos, A.K.: Video super-resolution with convolutional neural networks. IEEE Trans. Comput. Imag. **2**(2), 109–122 (2016)
22. Kim, J., Lee, J.K., Lee, K.M.: Accurate image super-resolution using very deep convolutional networks. In: Proceedings of the IEEE Conference on Computer Vision and Pattern Recognition, pp. 1646–1654 (2016)
23. Kim, J., Lee, J.K., Lee, K.M.: Deeply-recursive convolutional network for image super-resolution. In: Proceedings of the IEEE Conference on Computer Vision and Pattern Recognition, pp. 1637–1645 (2016)
24. Kingma, D., Ba, J.: Adam: a method for stochastic optimization. arXiv preprint arXiv:1412.6980 (2014)

25. Ledig, C., et al.: Photo-realistic single image super-resolution using a generative adversarial network. In: Proceedings of the IEEE Conference on Computer Vision and Pattern Recognition, pp. 4681–4690 (2017)
26. Li, D., Liu, Y., Wang, Z.: Video super-resolution using motion compensation and residual bidirectional recurrent convolutional network. In: Proceedings of IEEE International Conference on Image Processing, pp. 1642–1646 (2017)
27. Li, D., Wang, Z.: Video super-resolution via motion compensation and deep residual learning. IEEE Trans. Comput. Imag. **3**(4), 749–762 (2017)
28. Li, D., Liu, Y., Wang, Z.: Video super-resolution using non-simultaneous fully recurrent convolutional network. IEEE Trans. Image Process. **28**(3), 1342–1355 (2019)
29. Li, D., Liu, Y., Wang, Z., Yang, J.: Video rescaling with recurrent diffusion. IEEE Trans. Circuits Syst. Video Technol. 1–14 (2024)
30. Li, D., Wang, Z.: Face video super-resolution with identity guided generative adversarial networks. In: Yang, J., et al. (eds.) CCCV 2017. CCIS, vol. 772, pp. 357–369. Springer, Singapore (2017). https://doi.org/10.1007/978-981-10-7302-1_30
31. Li, D., Wang, Z., Yang, J.: Video super-resolution with inverse recurrent net and hybrid local fusion. Neurocomputing **489**, 40–51 (2022)
32. Li, F., Zhang, L., Liu, Z., Lei, J., Li, Z.: Multi-frequency representation enhancement with privilege information for video super-resolution. In: Proceedings of IEEE International Conference on Computer Vision, pp. 12814–12825 (2023)
33. Li, F., Bai, H., Zhao, Y.: Learning a deep dual attention network for video super-resolution. IEEE Trans. Image Process. **29**, 4474–4488 (2020)
34. Liang, J., et al.: VRT: a video restoration transformer. arXiv preprint arXiv:2201.12288 (2022)
35. Liao, R., Tao, X., Li, R., Ma, Z., Jia, J.: Video super-resolution via deep draft-ensemble learning. In: Proceedings of the IEEE International Conference on Computer Vision, pp. 531–539 (2015)
36. Lim, B., Son, S., Kim, H., Nah, S., Lee, K.M.: Enhanced deep residual networks for single image super-resolution. In: Proceedings of the IEEE Conference on Computer Vision and Pattern Recognition Workshops, pp. 136–144 (2017)
37. Liu, C., Sun, D.: On Bayesian adaptive video super resolution. IEEE Trans. Pattern Anal. Mach. Intell. **36**(2), 346–360 (2014)
38. Liu, D., et al.: Robust video super-resolution with learned temporal dynamics. In: Proceedings of the IEEE International Conference on Computer Vision, pp. 2507–2515 (2017)
39. Liu, D., Wang, Z., Wen, B., Yang, J., Han, W., Huang, T.S.: Robust single image super-resolution via deep networks with sparse prior. IEEE Trans. Image Process. **25**(7), 3194–3207 (2016)
40. Liu, H., et al.: Video super-resolution based on deep learning: a comprehensive survey. Artif. Intell. Rev. **55**(8), 5981–6035 (2022)
41. Liu, M., Jin, S., Yao, C., Lin, C., Zhao, Y.: Temporal consistency learning of inter-frames for video super-resolution. IEEE Trans. Circuits Syst. Video Technol. **33**(4), 1507–1520 (2023)
42. Lucas, A., Lopez-Tapia, S., Molina, R., Katsaggelos, A.K.: Generative adversarial networks and perceptual losses for video super-resolution. IEEE Trans. Image Process. **28**(7), 3312–3327 (2019)
43. Moser, B.B., Raue, F., Frolov, S., Palacio, S., Hees, J., Dengel, A.: Hitchhiker's guide to super-resolution: introduction and recent advances. IEEE Trans. Pattern Anal. Mach. Intell. **45**(8), 9862–9882 (2023)

44. Nah, S., et al.: NTIRE 2019 challenge on video deblurring and super-resolution: dataset and study. In: Proceedings of IEEE Conference on Computer Vision and Pattern Recognition Workshops, pp. 1–11 (2019)
45. Paszke, A., et al.: Pytorch: an imperative style, high-performance deep learning library. In: Proceedings of Advances in Neural Information Processing Systems, pp. 8024–8035 (2019)
46. Pérez-Pellitero, E., Sajjadi, M.S., Hirsch, M., Schölkopf, B.: Perceptual video super resolution with enhanced temporal consistency. arXiv preprint arXiv:1807.07930 (2018)
47. Sajjadi, M.S., Scholkopf, B., Hirsch, M.: Enhancenet: single image super-resolution through automated texture synthesis. In: Proceedings of the IEEE International Conference on Computer Vision, pp. 4491–4500 (2017)
48. Sajjadi, M.S., Vemulapalli, R., Brown, M.: Frame-recurrent video super-resolution. In: Proceedings of the IEEE Conference on Computer Vision and Pattern Recognition, pp. 6626–6634 (2018)
49. Tai, Y., Yang, J., Liu, X.: Image super-resolution via deep recursive residual network. In: Proceedings of the IEEE Conference on Computer Vision and Pattern Recognition, pp. 3147–3155 (2017)
50. Tai, Y., Yang, J., Liu, X., Xu, C.: Memnet: a persistent memory network for image restoration. In: Proceedings of the IEEE International Conference on Computer Vision, pp. 4539–4547 (2017)
51. Tao, X., Gao, H., Liao, R., Wang, J., Jia, J.: Detail-revealing deep video super-resolution. In: Proceedings of the IEEE International Conference on Computer Vision, pp. 4472–4480 (2017)
52. Wang, X., Chan, K.C., Yu, K., Dong, C., Change Loy, C.: EDVR: video restoration with enhanced deformable convolutional networks. In: Proceedings IEEE Conference on Computer Vision and Pattern Recognition Workshops, pp. 1–10 (2019)
53. Wang, X., et al.: ESRGAN: enhanced super-resolution generative adversarial networks. In: Proceedings of the European Conference on Computer Vision Workshops, pp. 1–16 (2018)
54. Wang, Z., et al.: Multi-memory convolutional neural network for video super-resolution. IEEE Trans. Image Process. **28**(5), 2530–2544 (2019)
55. Xia, B., et al.: Structured sparsity learning for efficient video super-resolution. In: Proceedings of IEEE Conference on Computer Vision and Pattern Recognition, pp. 22638–22647 (2023)
56. Xu, Y., et al.: Videogigagan: towards detail-rich video super-resolution. arXiv preprint arXiv:2404.12388 (2024)
57. Xue, T., Chen, B., Wu, J., Wei, D., Freeman, W.T.: Video enhancement with task-oriented flow. Int. J. Comput. Vis. **127**(8), 1106–1125 (2019)
58. Yang, W., Feng, J., Xie, G., Liu, J., Guo, Z., Yan, S.: Video super-resolution based on spatial-temporal recurrent residual networks. Comput. Vis. Image Understanding **168**, 79–92 (2018)
59. Yi, P., Wang, Z., Jiang, K., Jiang, J., Lu, T., Ma, J.: A progressive fusion generative adversarial network for realistic and consistent video super-resolution. IEEE Trans. Pattern Anal. Mach. Intell. **44**(5), 2264–2280 (2020)
60. Yi, P., Wang, Z., Jiang, K., Jiang, J., Ma, J.: Progressive fusion video super-resolution network via exploiting non-local spatio-temporal correlations. In: Proceedings of IEEE International Conference on Computer Vision, pp. 3106–3115 (2019)

61. Yi, P., Wang, Z., Jiang, K., Shao, Z., Ma, J.: Multi-temporal ultra dense memory network for video super-resolution. IEEE Trans. Circuits Syst. Video Technol. **30**(8), 2503–2516 (2019)
62. Zhang, R., Isola, P., Efros, A.A., Shechtman, E., Wang, O.: The unreasonable effectiveness of deep features as a perceptual metric. In: Proceedings of the IEEE Conference on Computer Vision and Pattern Recognition, pp. 586–595 (2018)
63. Zhang, W., Liu, Y., Dong, C., Qiao, Y.: Ranksrgan: generative adversarial networks with ranker for image super-resolution. In: Proceedings of IEEE International Conference on Computer Vision, pp. 3096–3105 (2019)
64. Zhang, Y., Li, K., Li, K., Wang, L., Zhong, B., Fu, Y.: Image super-resolution using very deep residual channel attention networks. In: Proceedings of the European Conference on Computer Vision, pp. 286–301 (2018)
65. Zhang, Y., Tian, Y., Kong, Y., Zhong, B., Fu, Y.: Residual dense network for image super-resolution. In: Proceedings of the IEEE Conference on Computer Vision and Pattern Recognition, pp. 2472–2481 (2018)

Integration of Raman Spectroscopy, On-Line Microscopic Imaging and Deep Learning-Based Image Analysis for Real-Time Monitoring of Cell Culture Process

Xiaoli Wang, Guangzheng Zhou(✉), and Xue Zhong Wang(✉)

Beijing Key Laboratory of Enze Biomass Fine Chemicals, College of New Materials and Chemical Engineering, Beijing Institute of Petrochemical Technology, Beijing 102617, China
{zhouguangzheng,wangxuezhong}@bipt.edu.cn

Abstract. Traditionally, condition monitoring of mammalian cell culture processes is based on sampling and off-line analysis, which is labour intensive, time consuming, and causes time delays. In this work, in situ microscope and on-line Raman spectroscopy are investigated for simultaneous measurement of multiple properties of the cell growth state and biochemical indices of suspended animal cells. The focus is on investigation of deep learning-based Mask R-CNN algorithm for image analysis. The model is trained by 184 images with 183,040 cells using data augmentation methods and transfer learning technique. Mask R-CNN segments the clustered cells more effectively than the conventional one combining edge detection, intensity thresholding, and advanced watershed method. The evolution of geometrical features of cells is further analyzed, including equivalent diameter, circularity, and aspect ratio. It demonstrates the great potential of deep learning in the analysis of on-line images for control of the cell culture process.

Keywords: Image Analysis · Deep Learning · Process Analytical Technology · Cell Culture · Raman Spectroscopy

1 Introduction

During the culture process, the mammalian cells modified via genetic engineering could produce biopharmaceuticals, such as recombinant proteins [1]. The current practices of understanding cell information during the cultivation process rely largely on off-line analysis, such as using biochemical analyzers for biochemical indices, automated counting devices for cell number, and inverted microscopes for cell size/morphology. These methods are labour intensive, and introduce time delays and the risk of contamination. Monitoring of mammalian cell culture processes using process analytical technology (PAT) is significant for their optimization and control, and thus contributes to the improvement of the productivity and product quality of biopharmaceuticals [2]. PAT recommends on-line real-time observations and analyses of multiple process parameters and product quality properties to guarantee consistent product quality and efficiency

Published by Springer Nature Switzerland AG 2025
Z. Shi et al. (Eds.): ICIS 2024, IFIP AICT 720, pp. 248–256, 2025.
https://doi.org/10.1007/978-3-031-71253-1_18

while reducing costs [3]. Among various PAT tools, the in situ microscopic imaging technique and Raman spectroscopy are two typical methods for the monitoring of mammalian cell culture processes [4]. The in situ microscopic imaging technique coupled with image analysis offer information concerning cell number densities, dimensions, and geometrical morphologies. The cell number is closely related to the productivity and quality of cell expression products. Size distribution reveals the cell ages, while the cell morphology provides information about cell age, division state, and virus infection to some extent. On the other hand, Raman spectroscopy could provide quantitative information about the concentrations of nutrients and metabolites, such as glucose, lactate, glutamine, and ammonium in bioreactors.

Data analysis plays a crucial role in PAT technology [5]. For mammalian cell culture processes, PLS (partial least squares) is usually employed as the chemometric method to build the prediction model of Raman spectroscopy, revealing high accuracy for some important biochemical indices [6]. As for the analysis of images from in situ microscopy, the classical methods generally require some pre-processing steps, and their accuracies largely depend on several factors, including image quantifications, cell size distribution, cell number density, and cell clusters. There frequently exist obvious cell clusters at high-density cultivation scenarios, while the segmentation of cell individuals from clusters is commonly rather challenging for traditional image analysis approaches. Fortunately, the deep learning technique based on convolutional neural networks (CNN) has been successfully applied in a variety of computer vision tasks, where the precision achieved outperformed most traditional methods, including human observation [7]. Based on the strategies of local connectivity and weight sharing, CNN algorithms with advanced combinations of many convolutional layers are feasible for solving complex image analysis problems.

There have been some reports about cell image analysis based on deep learning methods, focusing on different aspects of cell information. Some researches employed the regression algorithm for the direct output of cell counting results, but its accuracy was often affected by the complexity of image content [8]. There also exists some work depicting the distribution of cell number density, neglecting information about cell sizes and morphologies [9]. As for the task of cell segmentation, the algorithm category of "semantic segmentation" generates the exact domain of cells without distinguishing the interior individuals within cell clusters, and thus fails to provide the exact cell number [10]. It is usually difficult to obtain a large number of annotated images in the biomedical field. U-Net is a representative segmentation algorithm for that filed, which is based on fully convoluted network (FCN) with a symmetric U-shaped structure [11]. Falk et al. [12] developed a software plug-in for convenient applications of U-Net algorithm, where the pre-trained model could be transferred into a new segmentation task. Isensee et al. [13] further proposed nnU-Net, which automatically configured network architecture and displayed strong generalization characteristics. Whole-slide blood cell segmentation was carried out through a novel convolutional encoder-decoder framework and pixel-level feature extraction model, and high class-wise accuracies were achieved [14]. Besides, most researches tackled off-line images with dyeing pretreatment to enlarge the color discrepancies between cells and their background. Regarding the cell images from in situ microscope, the color differences between the cells and their background are not obvious, those natural cells in the bioreactor typically have some extent of clusters, and their movements agitated by the stirring bars negatively influence the image quality.

On-line in situ monitoring of the mammalian cell culture process is of vital importance for its optimization and control, but the accurate image analysis of clustered cells at high concentrations should be solved in the first place. This study specifically investigates a deep learning-based instance segmentation algorithm for cell image analysis, which could give the exact pixel-level domain of each cell, facilitating the statistics of cell number and distributions of cell size and morphology. In view of the limited number of raw images, some data enhancement methods and the transfer learning technique are utilized to enhance model performance. The results of deep learning-based algorithm are compared with the advanced conventional one combining edge detection, intensity thresholding, and watershed method in terms of many evaluation metrics. Eventually, important geometrical characteristics of cells are analyzed from the statistics of segmented cells.

2 Methodology

2.1 PAT System for Cell Culture Monitoring

The Chinese hamster ovary (CHO) cell is one type of most typical engineering cells for recombinant proteins in practices, which is widely utilized in a number of biopharmaceutical applications, such as antibody, genetic recombination, and vaccine [15]. Figure 1 illustrates the in situ monitoring platform of CHO cell culture, where the imaging probe and Raman probe are connected to the on-line microscopic imaging system and Raman spectrometer, respectively. The volume of culture media inside the bioreactor is around 5 L, and the ends of these two probes are immersed in the culture media with a depth about half of total liquid height. The results of these two monitoring tools are displayed on the computers, while the resolutions of images are 1600×1200 with the camera magnification of 6 times. The control station adjusts the temperature, pH value, dissolved oxygen, and stirring speed of bioreactor, which are 37 °C, 7.2, 50%, and 100 revolutions/min, respectively. The CHO-K1 cell line is adopted for the suspension culture with an initial seeding density of 2.5×10^5 cells/ml. The cell culture process lasts about 11 days, beyond which the cell density could not be effectively enhanced due to the high consumption of nutrients and accumulation of metabolites.

2.2 Deep Learning-Based Image Segmentations

As a well-known deep learning-based algorithm of instance segmentation, Mask R-CNN displayed good performance in many scenarios [16], and thus it is examined for the cell images from in situ observations of cell culture. Figure 2 illustrates the network architecture of Mask R-CNN algorithm. To enhance the analysis accuracy, this algorithm adopts the bilinear interpolation in the module of ROI Align for accurate pixel information after rescaling image dimensions, and introduces the extra Mask branch for the prediction of binary mask of each class. The output of this algorithm is three aspects of target information, including class, bounding box, and mask (specific pixels

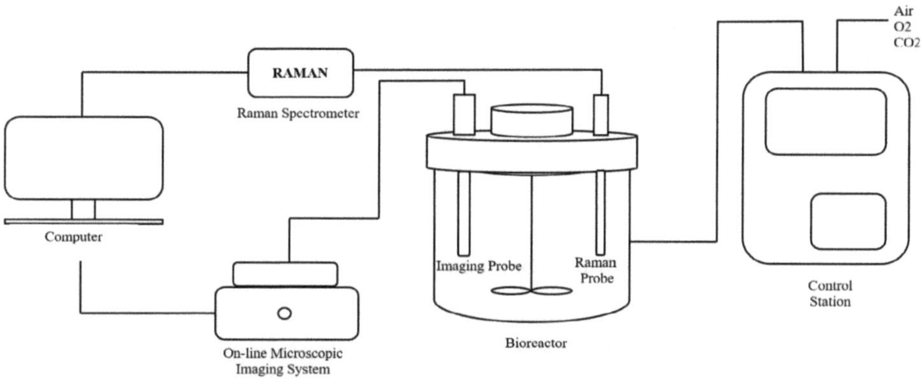

Fig. 1. On-line monitoring system for cell culture processes.

covering the object inside the box). The model training requires image files together with their annotation files. For instance segmentation, the annotation files give lots of discrete coordinate points depicting the border of all cells in every image. There are 45,760 labelled cells for all 46 images.

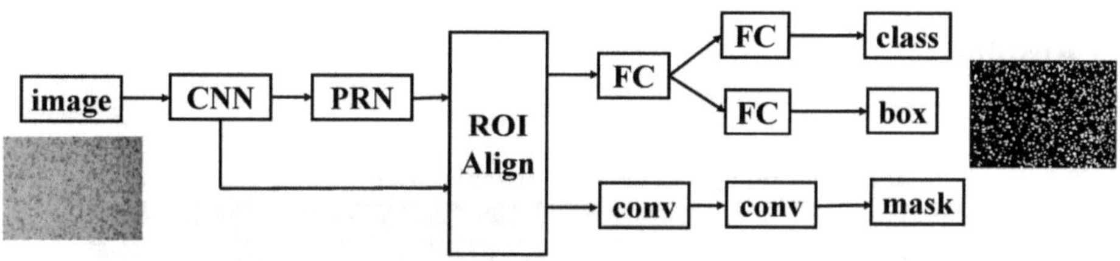

Fig. 2. Network architecture of Mask R-CNN algorithm.

Deep learning-based algorithms commonly have huge number of parameters, and thus the increase of training data amount contributes to the sufficient learning of target features. For those scenarios with only limited data, the strategy of data augmentation could be applied to enhance the data quantity, which generates new images through the artificial operations on existing raw images. The relatively simple approaches of flipping and rotating images are used in this work, including horizontal flip, vertical flip, and rotation of 180°. The new images and their annotation files are simultaneously generated through computer codes based on the raw images as well as their annotation files. The above three techniques of data augmentation are implemented for all 46 images, leading to the image number of 184 and the corresponding cell amount of 183,040.

Moreover, the transfer learning technology is also adopted in the present study to alleviate the problem of insufficient training data and accelerate the model training process as well. Specifically, a pre-trained model from a similar computer vision task is designated as the initial model for a new relevant issue. The model parameters of feature extract are frozen for the new model, while those parameters in the last layers of network are retrained based on some data of the target scenario. Due to the powerful capability of feature extract proportion, the strategy of transfer learning has been demonstrated to be effective for different kinds of computer vision tasks [17, 18]. To train the Mask R-CNN model for the cell analysis of in situ images, the values of algorithm parameters learned from the Microsoft COCO (benchmark dataset) with eighty classes are employed as the base ones. Those network parameters in the part of feature extract are directly frozen for the present task, and only other parameters of Mask R-CNN are readjusted.

2.3 Traditional Method of Image Segmentation

To comprehensively assess the performance of Mask R-CNN algorithm, a recent conventional approach combining edge detection, intensity thresholding, and advanced watershed method [19] is also investigated for the segmentation of in situ cell images. For brevity, this image analysis approach is referred to as "multiple processing method" below. Its operations include pre-processing, segmentation, and post-processing. A background image obtained from the rolling ball method is used for the background subtraction of raw image. Some subsequent pre-processing approaches are separately carried out for the two segmentation algorithms in parallel, i.e., Canny edge detection and intensity thresholding. The two results further merges, while watershed irregular feature with a convexity threshold splits those cells within clusters ultimately.

3 Results

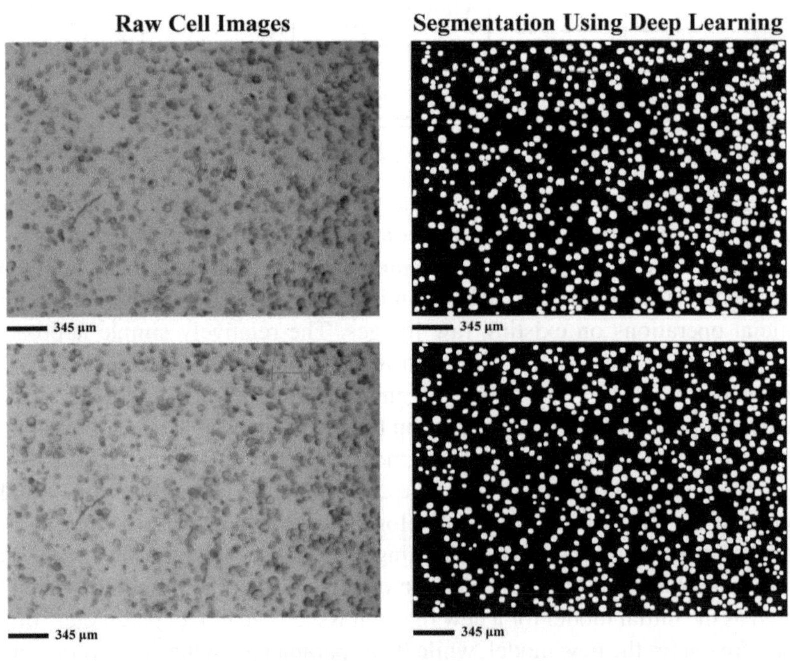

Fig. 3. Deep learning-based image segmentation.

Figure 3 displays the raw images and their segmentation results from Mask R-CNN algorithm. Notice that there exist some cell clusters in the images due to relatively high cell densities. The exact cell numbers of the upper and lower rows are 713 and 754, respectively. The counterparts from the Mask R-CNN algorithm are 719 and 743. According to pixel-level evaluations, the precision, sensitivity, and F1 score reach 0.901, 0.827, and 0.862, respectively. Generally, the deep learning method well recognizes those individual cells discretely distributed across the space, and successfully segments those cells in the form of clusters.

In contrast, Fig. 4 presents the segmentation results from multiple processing method together with their raw images. For both two images with different cell numbers and dimensions, the multiple processing method effectively separates a majority of clustered cells, but there still exist many cells not correctly segmented. Moreover, it is found that some cells are over-split by this approach, i.e., the number of segmented cells is larger than the exact number in some domains. Consequently, the results from Mask R-CNN outperform those counterparts from multiple processing method by a large margin.

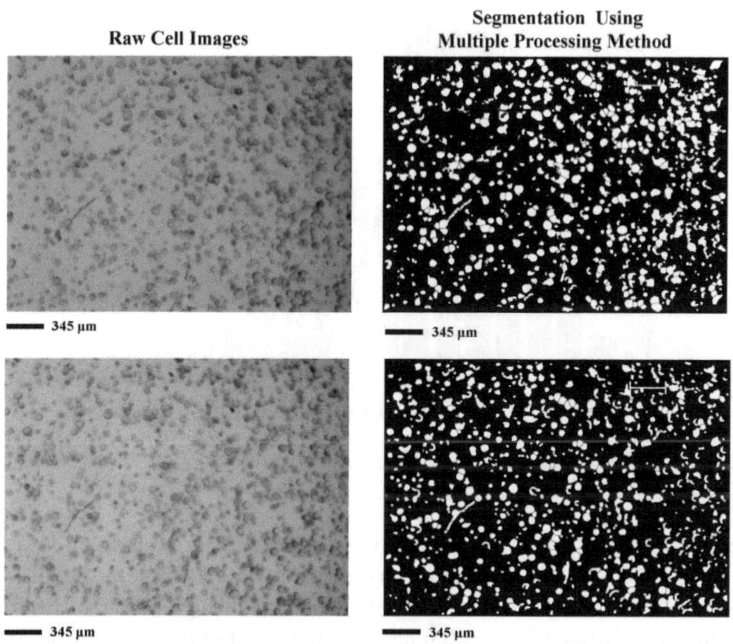

Fig. 4. Segmentation result from multiple processing method.

The cell dimensions and morphologies directly reflect the proliferation and growth behaviors of cell population. Therefore, they are quite relevant to the productivity and quality of cell expression products. Due to the sufficiently high accuracy of Mask R-CNN algorithm, its segmentation results are adopted for the analysis of cell states. With the assumption of a spherical shape for all cells, the equivalent diameter is employed to describe the cell dimensions. The diameters are between 10.33 μm and 27.03 μm with an average of 16.13 μm for the 11th day of cell culture process. For those cells from in situ images of the 3rd day, the equivalent diameters range from 7.2 μm to 24.94 μm, while the average is 9.94 μm. Therefore, the cell size remarkably increases during the culture process. Figure 5 displays the histogram of equivalent diameter distribution of cells on the 11th day. Those cell diameters are approximately in normal distribution. The region with maximum number percent is 16–17 μm, taking up 14.05% of all cells, and the equivalent diameters ranging from 11 to 21 μm account for 94.07%.

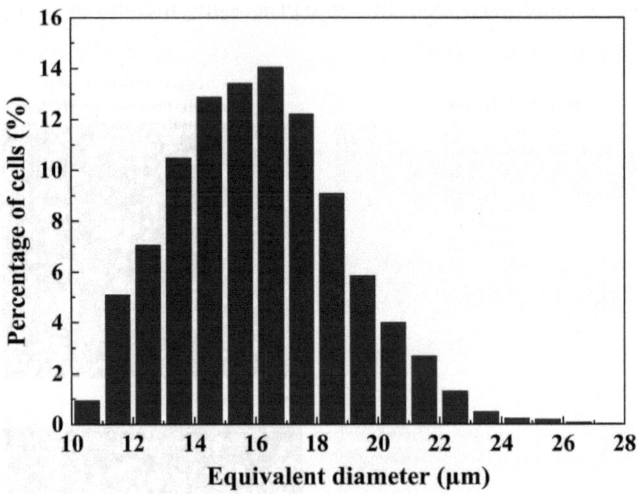

Fig. 5. Histogram of equivalent diameter distribution of cells.

The circularity and aspect ratio are utilized to characterize the cell morphologies. Figure 6 gives the histogram of circularity distribution of cells on the 11th day. The circularity is smaller than 1.0 for convex cells, and becomes greater than 1.0 for concave ones. For the circularities between 0.9 and 1.1, the number percentages are 92.53% for the 11th day. The domain of aspect ratios with maximum cell number ranges from 1.0 to 1.1, and the corresponding cell percentage is 70.60%. Therefore, although the cell shapes evolve throughout the culture process, a majority of them are approximately spherical all the time.

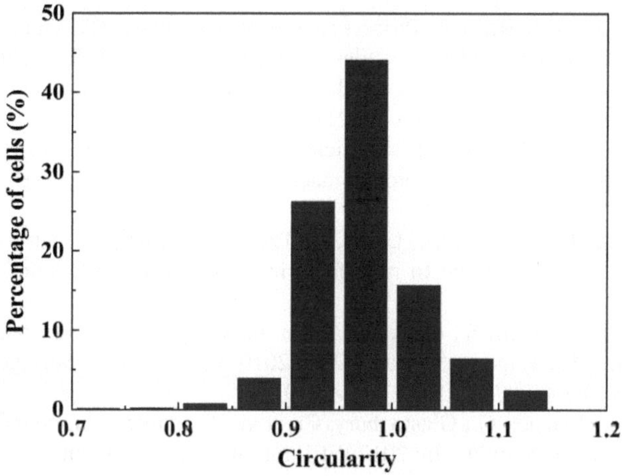

Fig. 6. Histogram of circularity distribution of cells.

4 Concluding Remarks

The deep learning-based Mask R-CNN algorithm is investigated for cell segmentation of in situ microscopic images from the mammalian cell culture process. With the strategies of data augmentation and transfer learning, the Mask R-CNN model well recognizes those cells within the clusters, and its accuracy outperforms some other processing methods. Based on the segmented result, the dimensions and morphologies of cells are assessed by the distributions of their equivalent diameters, circularities, and aspect ratios, revealing that the overwhelming majority of cells are approximately spherical. This study demonstrates the potential of in situ microscope with deep learning-based image analysis method for monitoring mammalian cell culture processes, while integration of in situ microscope and Raman spectroscopy could provide more comprehensive information.

Acknowledgments. The authors gratefully acknowledge the funding from the Beijing Natural Science Foundation (IS23033), the Beijing Municipal Education Commission, China (22019821001), and the National Natural Science Foundation of China (61633006).

Disclosure of Interests. The authors have no competing interests to declare that are relevant to the content of this article.

References

1. O'Flaherty, R., Bergin, A., Flampouri, E., et al.: Mammalian cell culture for production of recombinant proteins: a review of the critical steps in their biomanufacturing. Biotechnol. Adv. **43**, 107552 (2020)
2. Wasalathanthri, D., Rehmann, M., Song, Y., et al.: Technology outlook for real-time quality attribute and process parameter monitoring in biopharmaceutical development—a review. Biotechnol. Bioeng. **117**(10), 3182–3198 (2020)

3. Read, E., Park, J., Shah, R., et al.: Process analytical technology (PAT) for biopharmaceutical products: part I. concepts and applications. Biotechnol. Bioeng. **105**(2), 276–284 (2010)
4. Reardon, K.: Practical monitoring technologies for cells and substrates in biomanufacturing. Curr. Opin. Biotechnol. **71**, 225–230 (2021)
5. Rolinger, L., Rüdt, M., Hubbuch, J.: A critical review of recent trends, and a future perspective of optical spectroscopy as PAT in biopharmaceutical downstream processing. Anal. Bioanal. Chem. **412**(9), 2047–2064 (2020)
6. Esmonde-White, K., Cuellar, M., Lewis, I.: The role of Raman spectroscopy in biopharmaceuticals from development to manufacturing. Anal. Bioanal. Chem. **414**(2), 969–991 (2022)
7. O'Mahony, N., Campbell, S., Carvalho, A., et al.: Deep learning vs. traditional computer vision. In: Arai, K., Kapoor, S. (eds.) CVC 2019, pp. 128–144. Springer, Cham (2020). https://doi.org/10.1007/978-3-030-17795-9_10
8. Paul Cohen, J., Boucher, G., Glastonbury, C., et al.: Count-ception: counting by fully convolutional redundant counting. In: 2017 IEEE International Conference on Computer Vision Workshops (ICCVW), New York, pp. 18–26. IEEE (2017)
9. Xie, W., Noble, J., Zisserman, A.: Microscopy cell counting and detection with fully convolutional regression networks. Comput. Methods Biomech. Biomed. Eng. Imaging Vis. **6**(3), 283–292 (2018)
10. Asgari Taghanaki, S., Abhishek, K., Cohen, J.P., et al.: Deep semantic segmentation of natural and medical images: a review. Artif. Intell. Rev. **54**, 137–178 (2021)
11. Ronneberger, O., Fischer, P., Brox, T.: U-Net: convolutional networks for biomedical image segmentation. In: Navab, N., Hornegger, J., Wells, W., Frangi, A. (eds.) MICCAI 2015. LNCS, vol. 9351, pp. 234–241. Springer, Cham (2015). https://doi.org/10.1007/978-3-319-24574-4_28
12. Falk, T., Mai, D., Bensch, R., et al.: U-Net: deep learning for cell counting, detection, and morphometry. Nat. Methods **16**(1), 67–70 (2019)
13. Isensee, F., Jaeger, P.F., Kohl, S.A., et al.: NnU-Net: a self-configuring method for deep learning-based biomedical image segmentation. Nat. Methods **18**(2), 203–211 (2021)
14. Shahzad, M., Umar, A.I., Khan, M.A., et al.: Robust method for semantic segmentation of whole-slide blood cell microscopic images. Comput. Math. Methods Med. **2020**(1), 4015323 (2020)
15. Hunter, M., Yuan, P., Vavilala, D., et al.: Optimization of protein expression in mammalian cells. Curr. Protoc. Protein Sci. **95**(1), e77 (2019)
16. He, K., Gkioxari, G., Dollár, P., et al.: Mask R-CNN. In: Proceedings of the 2017 IEEE International Conference on Computer Vision, pp. 2961–2969 (2017)
17. Zhuang, F., Qi, Z., Duan, K., et al.: A comprehensive survey on transfer learning. Proc. IEEE **109**(1), 43–76 (2020)
18. Zong, S., Zhou, G., Li, M., et al.: Deep learning-based on-line image analysis for continuous industrial crystallization processes. Particuology **74**, 173–183 (2023)
19. Vancleef, A., Maes, D., Van Gerven, T., et al.: Flow-through microscopy and image analysis for crystallization processes. Chem. Eng. Sci. **248**, 117067 (2022)

DRL-SLAM: Enhanced Object Detection Fusion with Improved YOLOv8

Farooq Usman[1], Chaoxia Shi[1(✉)], and Yanqing Wang[2(✉)]

[1] Nanjing University of Science and Technology, Nanjing 210094, China
{usman,scx}@njust.edu.cn
[2] Nanjing Xiaozhuang University, Nanjing 211171, China
wyq0325@126.com

Abstract. Simultaneous Localization and Mapping (SLAM) technologies are pivotal in advancing robotics and autonomous navigation, particularly within challenging indoor environments. These systems face significant challenges due to dynamic variables such as fluctuating lighting, occlusions, and the presence of moving objects. In response, this paper introduces a novel integration of Deep Reinforcement Learning (DRL) with the advanced object detection capabilities of YOLOv8 within a SLAM framework, termed DRL-SLAM YOLOv8. This integration enhances object detection by leveraging DRL's ability to learn from environmental interactions and YOLOv8's precise and efficient real-time object recognition. Our experiments demonstrate the superiority of DRL-SLAM YOLOv8 over traditional methods, with marked improvements in detection accuracy and system reliability under diverse conditions. Notably, our approach significantly improves navigational effectiveness, as evidenced by increased distance coverage and goal achievement compared to standard SLAM techniques, validating its potential in real-world applications.

Keywords: Deep Reinforcement Learning · DRL-SLAM · Robot Navigation · MINOS Simulator · Object Detection · YOLOv8 · Depth Information Fusion

1 Introduction

The integration of robotics into everyday scenarios from domestic assistance to complex industrial applications has been significantly enhanced by advancements in technology [12]. At the forefront of these advancements are sophisticated navigational systems that allow robots to interpret and interact with their environments in unprecedented ways [1]. Among the key technologies driving these capabilities is Visual Simultaneous Localization and Mapping (Visual SLAM), which empowers robots to simultaneously map their environment and pinpoint their location within it using visual data from onboard cameras [16]. Visual SLAM has been critical in extending the operational range of robots

Z. Shi et al. (Eds.): ICIS 2024, IFIP AICT 720, pp. 257–272, 2025.
https://doi.org/10.1007/978-3-031-71253-1_19

beyond controlled settings, enabling navigation in unpredictable urban environments [2]. The adaptation and integration of ORB-SLAM2, a well-known SLAM framework, have further refined these capabilities by enhancing the precision and speed of the mapping process, even in dynamic settings where changes occur in real time [3]. Alongside these spatial awareness advancements, Deep Reinforcement Learning (DRL) has emerged as a transformative approach by integrating learning-based strategies with traditional SLAM [15]. DRL allows robotic systems to learn and adapt from their environmental interactions, optimizing their decision-making processes over time through a trial-and-error approach akin to human learning [4]. This integration not only enhances the adaptability of Correspondence should be addressed to autonomous systems but also enables them to perform under a variety of environmental conditions with increased autonomy.

Moreover, object detection stands as a crucial component in the enhancement of Visual SLAM [11]. The incorporation of object detection algorithms enables robots to identify and track objects within their operational environments [5]. The advent of Improved YOLOv8 has set a new standard in this domain by achieving real-time detection with heightened accuracy, thereby significantly boosting the performance of SLAM systems [6]. This version of YOLO, an evolution of the "You Only Look Once" framework, combines deep learning algorithms to process visual data faster and with more reliability [7]. To further support the development and testing of these sophisticated systems, the MINOS Simulator offers a controlled yet realistic virtual testing ground [16]. This simulator is instrumental in providing diverse scenarios, which help in refining the algorithms and ensuring their robustness across various real-world-like conditions [8]. Another pivotal technology in the robotics landscape is the Robot Operating System (ROS), which provides a flexible framework for writing robot software. ROS has been instrumental in managing the complex data and control pipelines necessary for modern robotic systems. It supports the integration of hardware and software in an accessible manner, allowing for the effective implementation of advanced techniques like DRL and object detection within Visual SLAM [10]. Depth information fusion also plays a vital role in enriching the data available to robotic navigation systems, providing a layer of depth to the visual information captured [9]. This technique merges depth data obtained from various sensors with traditional imagery, enhancing the robot's understanding of its three-dimensional environment [19]. Such depth-enhanced data facilitates more accurate object detection, navigation, and interaction with the surroundings, enabling robots to perform more complex tasks such as precise manipulation and obstacle avoidance [13]. This paper presents a comprehensive overview of these technologies and discusses the challenges and limitations inherent in existing approaches. We propose an innovative solution that integrates DRL with an improved version of YOLOv8 for object detection within the Visual SLAM framework. This integrated approach aims to significantly enhance the robustness and efficiency of SLAM systems, particularly in indoor environments characterized by varying lighting conditions, occlusions, and dynamic changes. By addressing these challenges, our proposed methodology not only enhances the operational efficacy of robotic systems but also paves the way for more accurate and reliable autonomous navigation and mapping in complex environments.

2 Methodology

The integration of (VSLAM) systems with YOLOv8 object detection algorithm with the ORB-SLAM2 framework, focusing particularly on dynamic indoor environments. The integration of YOLOv8 enables real-time detection and classification of objects, which is crucial for effective navigation in environments characterized by dynamic elements such as moving people and changing lighting conditions. Training and validation data are sourced from the Matterport 3D dataset, renowned for its detailed representations of indoor settings that closely mimic real-world complexities. This dataset is instrumental in fine-tuning YOLOv8, where images are annotated with precise object labels and depth information, enhancing the detection accuracy vital for robust VSLAM performance These tests assess key performance metrics such as detection accuracy, map robustness, and localization continuity, ensuring the system's effectiveness across a variety of settings. The fused VSLAM algorithm, termed DRL-SLAM, incorporates these advancements into the ORB-SLAM2 framework.

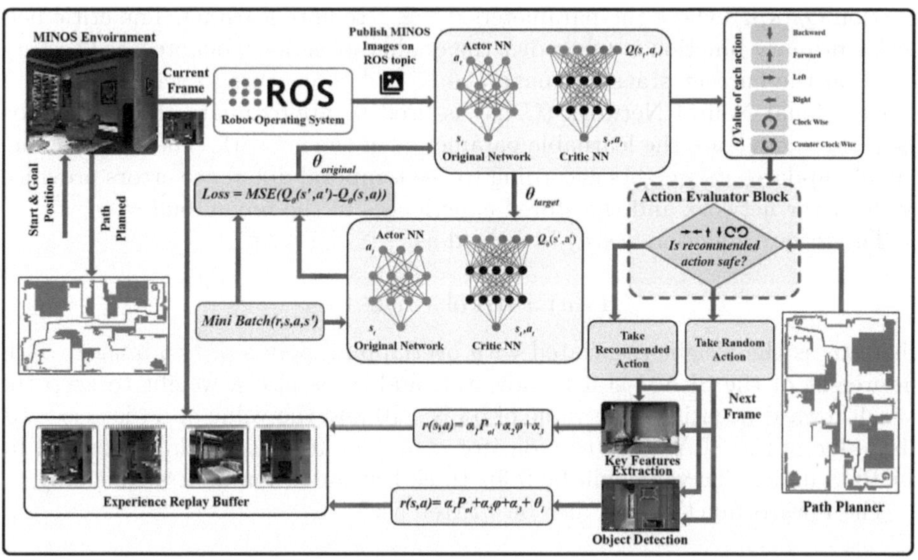

Fig. 1. Our DRL-SLAM Model Architecture)

2.1 Actor-Critic Framework with ORB-SLAM2

The system evaluates the safety of each proposed action before execution. Safe actions are processed by the ORB-SLAM2 system, which extracts features from the current frame and feeds this information into the actor-network. The actor-network calculates the Temporal Difference (TD) error and passes it to the critic network, simultaneously storing the image data in the experience replay buffer

[17]. This process is repeated until the agent either reaches its goal or experiences a tracking loss, facilitating continuous learning and adaptation to evolving environmental conditions [18]. This methodology emphasizes a systematic approach to integrating advanced object detection technologies within VSLAM systems, enhancing navigational precision and interactive capabilities through sophisticated machine learning algorithms and real-time data processing. If the action is safe, the recommended action is taken. After taking the action, ORB-SLAM2 extracts the features of that frame and feeds them to the actor-network. The actor-network calculates the TD error and feeds it to the critic network while also saving the information of the image in the experience replay buffer.

2.2 Critic Network and Reward Function

The objective of the Critic Network is to forecast the quality, represented as $Q_\theta(s, a)$, of a given action $a \in A$, as directed by the path planner, through an examination of the current state (image) denoted as $s \in \mathbb{R}^{80\times80\times3}$. To achieve this, we employ a Convolutional Neural Network (CNN) to approximate the Q function $Q_\theta(s, a)$ where the parameters $\theta \in \mathbb{R}^N$ require learning. The critic network's primary function is to predict the quality of actions, denoted as $Q_\theta(s, a)$, based on the current state or image $s \in \mathbb{R}^{80\times80\times3}$ captured by the system. A Convolutional Neural Network (CNN) is used to approximate the Q function $Q_\theta(s, a)$, where θ are the learnable parameters of the network. The network continually updates its weights according to the temporal difference errors provided by the actor network and the stored experiences in the replay buffer.

The reward function $r(s, a)$ is defined as:

$$r(s, a) = \alpha_1 \text{Pol} + \alpha_2 \varphi + \alpha_3 \tag{1}$$

where α_1 is the weight associated with overlapping points of two images, α_2 is the weight of the SLAM status indicator, and α_3 is also a weight to keep the overall reward negative. The value of α_2 is -10 and the value of α_3 is also -10. The value of the SLAM status indicator φ may be 0 or 1, which is provided by our ROS node. The value will be 0 for track lost and 1 for the tracking stage.

The reward function can also be written as:

$$r(s, a) = \alpha_1 \text{Pol} + \alpha_2 \varphi + \alpha_3 + \Theta_i \tag{2}$$

where:

- α_1Pol: This term represents the reward based on the overlap of point clouds or images between consecutive frames. α_1 is the weighting factor for this overlap, where a higher overlap suggests better continuity in mapping, enhancing the stability and accuracy of the SLAM process.
- $\alpha_2 \varphi$: Adjusts the reward based on the SLAM system's tracking status. φ is a binary indicator where 1 represents successful tracking and 0 represents a tracking loss. The negative weight α_2 penalizes the loss of tracking, encouraging the system to maintain robust tracking capabilities.

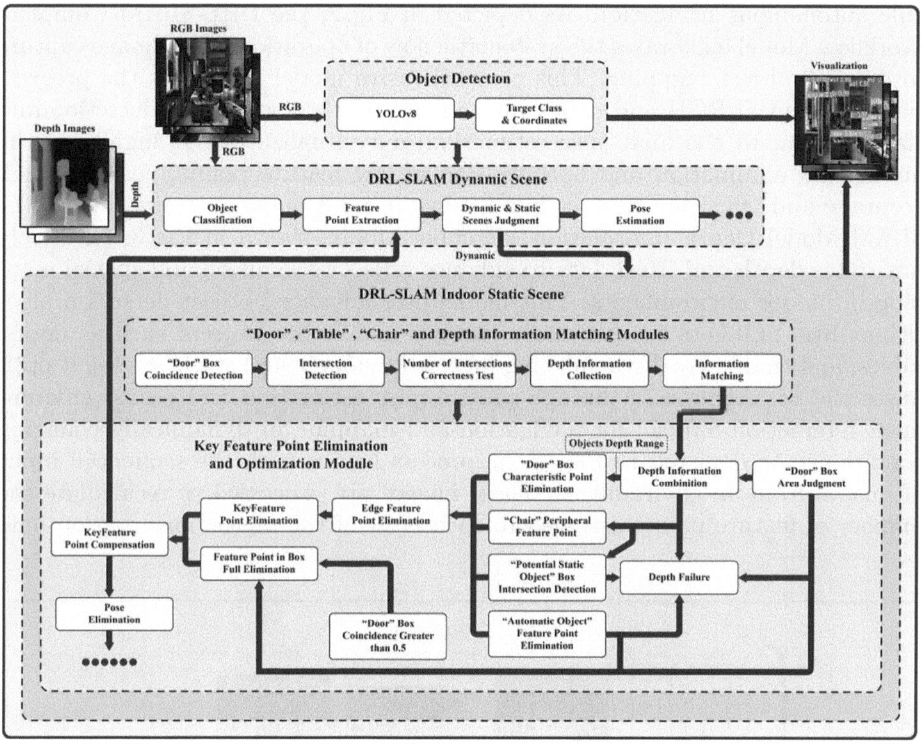

Fig. 2. DRL-SLAM Complete Work Flowchart Model

- α_3: A constant negative reward to promote proactive error avoidance by the system.
- Θ_i: Represents the detection of objects within the frame. This term is critical for object-oriented tasks in SLAM, as detecting and correctly identifying objects can be crucial for both navigation and interaction in dynamic environments.

The architecture of our DRL-SLAM model, depicted in Fig. 1, integrates various sophisticated components for autonomous navigation in the MINOS environment. This system leverages the Robot Operating System (ROS) for publishing images and managing communications between components. At the heart of the architecture are the neural networks, specifically the Actor and Critic networks, which process state and action pairs to produce optimal navigation commands. The system also features an Action Evaluator Block, which assesses the safety of recommended actions, enhancing the decision-making process. Key features extraction and object detection are implemented in real time to dynamically adjust the path based on environmental feedback. The model uses an Experience Replay Buffer to refine its decision process, while the path planner develops efficient routes from start to goal positions, ensuring robust and reliable autonomous navigation. As depicted in Fig. 2, the DRL-SLAM Complete Workflow Model elaborates the systematic flow of operations from image capture to detailed object mapping. This comprehensive model showcases the progression from initial RGB and depth image capture, through object detection and classification, to the final pose estimation and visualization. It highlights the methodical elimination and optimization of key feature points, ensuring high accuracy and efficiency in real-time navigation and mapping tasks. The DRL-SLAM Model Depth Information Matching Model, shown in Fig. 3, effectively integrates depth and RGB data to enhance object recognition and spatial mapping in indoor environments. This model uses advanced object detection algorithms like YOLOv8 to accurately identify and locate objects such as doors, tables, and chairs. By distinguishing between dynamic and static scenes, it optimizes the SLAM process through precise pose estimation and robust environment interaction, crucial for navigation and mapping in dynamically changing conditions. As depicted in Fig. 4, the process begins with the sequential input of images from an environment. These images are processed to recalculate the number of feature points assigned to each layer of the image, ensuring optimal

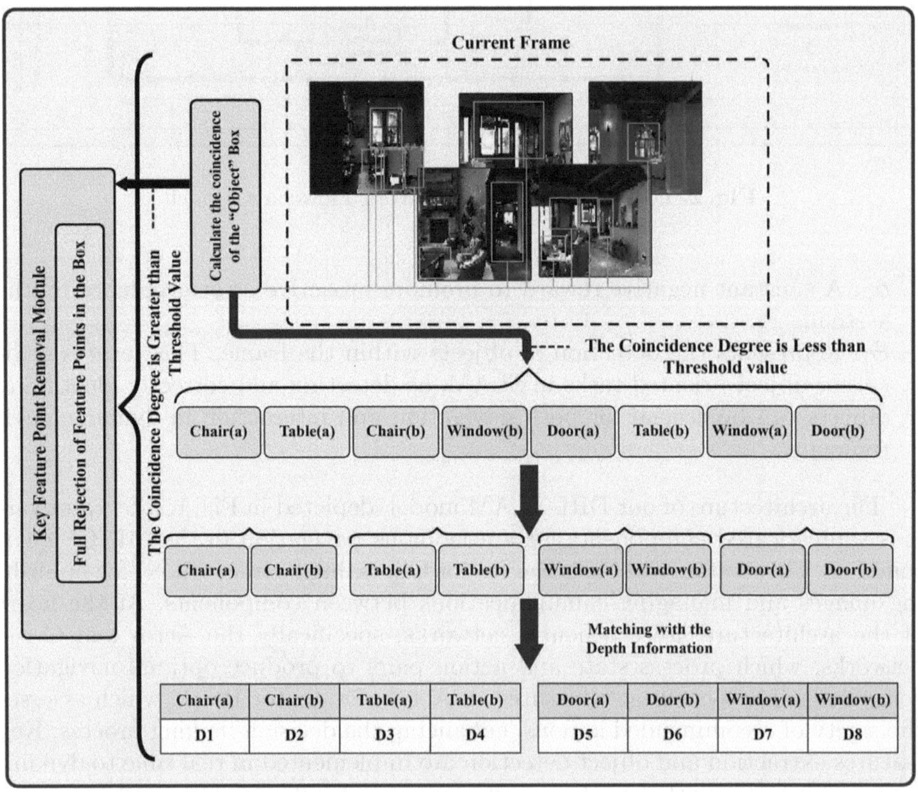

Fig. 3. DRL-SLAM Model Depth Information Matching Model

coverage and detail. The ORB (Oriented FAST and Rotated BRIEF) algorithm extracts key feature points, which are essential for the SLAM's understanding of the environment's structure. Following extraction, a critical assessment is conducted where feature points that do not meet specific criteria, such as stability or matchability, are rejected. This rejection is quantified by calculating the ratio of rejected to extracted feature points, providing a metric for the efficiency and quality of the feature extraction process. The recalculated feature point assignments for subsequent frames are adjusted based on this ratio, optimizing the process for continuous and dynamic environmental understanding.

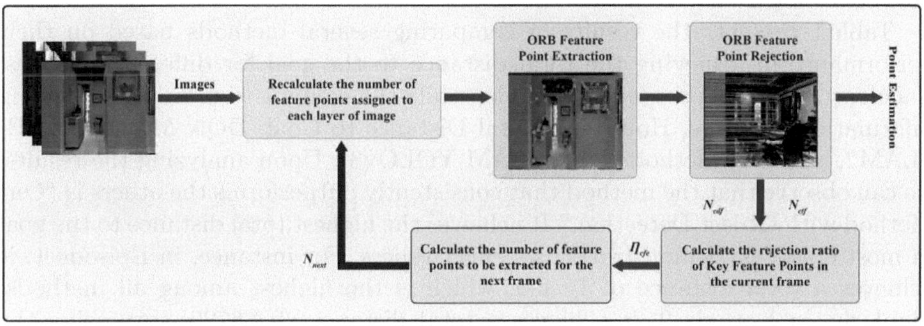

Fig. 4. DRL-SLAM Feature Extraction and Rejection Model

3 Experimental Results and Analysis

To ensure effective sensing and observation in the environment and smooth navigation, our agent needed to be equipped with a robust multisensory system. However, training such an agent posed significant challenges due to the high perceptual complexity involved. Pre-recorded and static datasets were deemed inadequate due to their passive nature. Although active vision datasets were available, they were not suitable for our purposes as ORB-SLAM2 could not be initialized on them due to their large step size. Real-world datasets also presented challenges, leaving simulation data as the most viable option.

3.1 Experimental Setup and Results

For our experiments, we utilized the MINOS simulator, which is designed for goal-oriented navigation in indoor environments. MINOS leverages datasets like Matterport3D, providing a virtual yet realistic environment ideal for training and experimenting with ORB-SLAM2. This environment enables learning in cluttered scenes, contributing to the robustness of our system. MINOS offers various realistic environments, a dataset with over 45,000 3D indoor models, and the Matterport3D dataset with reconstructed indoor scenes. After calibrating the MINOS camera according to ORB-SLAM2 specifications, our agent navigated within the MINOS environment. The agent captured and saved images of the current view, which were then processed by ORB-SLAM2 to initialize the mapping and tracking process once the feature reached its threshold value. The map generated by ORB-SLAM2 could be visualized using a map viewer.

Our integration, DRL-SLAM, was compared against standard versions of the YOLO algorithm to highlight the improvements brought about by our modifications, particularly for dynamic environments. The results indicate significant improvements in the detection accuracy and reliability of the system under variable conditions.

Table 1 presents the results of comparing several methods based on their performance in achieving the total distance to the goal for different episodes. Each row represents a specific episode, while the columns contain the following information: Episode, House ID, Total Distance to Goal, DQN Method, ORB-SLAM2, and Our Method (DRL SLAM YOLOv8). Upon analyzing the results, we can observe that the method that consistently outperforms the others is "Our Method with Object Detection." It achieves the highest total distance to the goal in most episodes, demonstrating its effectiveness. For instance, in Episode 1, it achieves a total distance of 18.459, which is the highest among all methods. Similarly, in Episode 2, it achieves a total distance of 4.6729, surpassing the other methods. This pattern continues throughout the table, with Our Method with Object Detection consistently achieving competitive results. This analysis provides an overview of the performance of different methods in achieving the goal. Further analysis and investigation may be required to gain deeper insights into the specific strengths and weaknesses of each method.

As depicted in Fig. 5, we present a comparative analysis of the total distances covered by different autonomous navigation methods across various simulated environments, represented by House IDs. Total distance, DQN Method, ORB-SLAM2, and Our Method (DRL SLAM YOLOv8) are represented by blue squares, red triangles, green stars, and black diamonds, respectively.

The methods compared include a standard approach (Total Distance), a Deep Q-Network (DQN) based method, the ORB-SLAM2 algorithm, and our proprietary method which integrates DRL-SLAM with YOLOv8 for object detection. The plot clearly illustrates that our method consistently achieves comparable or superior performance in terms of total distance traveled, suggesting improved efficiency in navigation tasks. Notably, in environments represented by House IDs 4 and 14, our method matches or slightly outperforms the standard total distance, highlighting its robustness in complex scenarios. Conversely, the ORB-SLAM2 method shows varied performance, excelling in less complex environments (House ID 15) but falling short in more challenging settings (House ID 4). The DQN method demonstrates strong performance in mid-complexity environments (House ID 7), but it exhibits limitations in simpler scenarios (House ID 2), which could be attributed to its learning-based nature that may require a diversity of training scenarios to generalize effectively. Thus, the analysis underscores

Table 1. Comparison of different methods

Episode #	House ID	Total Distance	DQN Method	ORB-SLAM2	Our Method (DRL SLAM YOLOv8)
1	2azQ1b91cZZ	18.45969	8.58985	2.25	**18.459**
2	2t7WUuJeko7	6.42842	2.38995	2.74853	**4.6729**
3	2t7WUuJeko7	7.08406	6.6598	5.42842	**7.08406**
4	uNb9QFRL6hY	20.54507	4.37279	0.67573	**12.365**
5	ac26ZMwG7aT	11.35685	7.09411	1.84	**11.35685**
6	1pXnuDYAj8r	11.97695	11.97	4.13137	**11.97695**
7	1pXnuDYAj8r	18.38708	18.38	18.38708	**18.38708**
8	PuKPg4mmafe	16.74264	16.01	12.82134	**16.74264**
9	PuKPg4mmafe	16.90832	15.97	3.34142	**16.14264**
10	2t7WUuJeko7	9.27695	7.64	0.90997	**9.27**
11	2n8kARJN3HM	15.50121	15.5	6.64142	**15.5**
12	ZMojNkEp431	18.33969	13.5434	12.22132	**18.33**
13	YmJkqBEsHnH	16.39827	15.14975	0.50711	**16.39827**
14	ZMojNkEp431	18.59827	18.59827	0.1	**18.59827**
15	ac26ZMwG7aT	11.35685	3.5923	0.79706	**7.59411**

the potential of integrating deep reinforcement learning and advanced object detection techniques to enhance the adaptability and efficiency of autonomous navigation systems. In Table 2, we present a comparative success rate across fifteen episodes involving various methods.

Our method, DRL-SLAM YOLOv8, outperforms other techniques, achieving success ('Y') in a majority of the scenarios where others (DQN Method and ORB-SLAM2) often fail ('N'). This underscores the robustness and efficiency of our approach, particularly in complex environments, as indicated by successful outcomes in challenging House IDs like 1pXnuDYAj8r and ZMojNkEp431.

Figure 6 depicts the training results of an object detection model's performance throughout its training and validation phases. Analyzing the metrics, we see a consistent theme across both training and validation loss graphs for bounding box (box_loss), detection (cls_loss), and deformation or other adjustments (df_loss). Each starts with a steep decline, indicating rapid learning in early epochs, which gradually plateaus as the model starts to converge and incremental learning diminishes. Figure 7 showcases YOLOv8's object detection capabilities in an indoor scene. Objects such as walls, a pillar, vases, and a sofa are identified with high confidence scores, outlined by bounding boxes with the confidence level noted above each box. The precision of the model is evident as it discriminates between closely placed and visually similar objects.

The performance of the DRL-SLAM Object Detection system is also noteworthy. This visualization captures the system's ability to identify and classify objects within a dynamic environment accurately. The method utilizes deep reinforcement learning combined with simultaneous localization and mapping to enhance detection reliability and spatial awareness. The enhanced object detec-

[title=Comparison of Total Distance Covered by Different Methods, xlabel=House IDs, ylabel=Total Distance, legend pos=outer north east, ymajorgrids=true, grid style=dashed, nodes near coords, every node near coord/.append style=font=, anchor=north, point meta=explicit symbolic, clip marker paths=true,] [color=blue, mark=square,] coordinates (1,18.45969) [18.46] (2,6.42842) [6.43] (3,7.08406) [7.08] (4,20.54507) [20.55] (5,11.35685) [11.36] (6,11.97695) [11.98] (7,18.38708) [18.39] (8,16.74264) [16.74] (9,16.90832) [16.91] (10,9.27695) [9.28] (11,15.50121) [15.50] (12,18.33969) [18.34] (13,16.39827) [16.40] (14,18.59827) [18.60] (15,11.35685) [11.36] ; Total Distance

[color=red, mark=triangle,] coordinates (1,8.58985) [8.59] (2,2.38995) [2.39] (3,6.6598) [6.66] (4,4.37279) [4.37] (5,7.09411) [7.09] (6,11.97) [11.97] (7,18.38) [18.38] (8,16.01) [16.01] (9,15.97) [15.97] (10,7.64) [7.64] (11,15.5) [15.50] (12,13.5434) [13.54] (13,15.14975) [15.15] (14,18.59827) [18.60] (15,3.5923) [3.59] ; DQN Method

[color=green, mark=star,] coordinates (1,2.25) [2.25] (2,2.74853) [2.75] (3,5.42842) [5.43] (4,0.67573) [0.68] (5,1.84) [1.84] (6,4.13137) [4.13] (7,18.38708) [18.39] (8,12.82134) [12.82] (9,3.34142) [3.34] (10,0.90997) [0.91] (11,6.64142) [6.64] (12,12.22132) [12.22] (13,0.50711) [0.51] (14,0.1) [0.10] (15,0.79706) [0.80] ; ORB-SLAM2

[color=black, mark=diamond,] coordinates (1,18.459) [18.46] (2,4.6729) [4.67] (3,7.08406) [7.08] (4,12.365) [12.37] (5,11.35685) [11.36] (6,11.97695) [11.98] (7,18.38708) [18.39] (8,16.74264) [16.74] (9,16.14264) [16.14] (10,9.27) [9.27] (11,15.5) [15.50] (12,18.33) [18.33] (13,16.39827) [16.40] (14,18.59827) [18.60] (15,7.59411) [7.59] ; Our Method (DRL-SLAM YOLOv8)

Fig. 5. Comparison of total distance covered by different methods across episodes. Total distance, DQN Method, ORB-SLAM2, and Our Method (DRL SLAM YOLOv8) are represented by blue squares, red triangles, green stars, and black diamonds, respectively. (Color figure online)

Table 2. Success Rate Comparison

Episode #	House ID	DQN Method	DQN Method	ORB-SLAM2	Our Method (DRL SLAM YOLOv8)
1	2azQ1b91cZZ	N	N	N	**Y**
2	2t7WUuJeko7	N	N	N	**N**
3	2t7WUuJeko7	N	N	N	**Y**
4	uNb9QFRL6hY	N	N	N	**N**
5	ac26ZMwG7aT	N	N	N	**Y**
6	1pXnuDYAj8r	**Y**	N	N	**Y**
7	1pXnuDYAj8r	**Y**	N	N	**Y**
8	PuKPg4mmafe	**Y**	N	N	**Y**
9	PuKPg4mmafe	N	N	N	**N**
10	2t7WUuJeko7	N	N	N	**Y**
11	2n8kARJN3HM	**Y**	N	N	**Y**
12	ZMojNkEp431	N	N	N	**Y**
13	YmJkqBEsHnH	N	N	N	**Y**
14	ZMojNkEp431	**Y**	N	N	**Y**
15	ac26ZMwG7aT	N	N	N	**N**

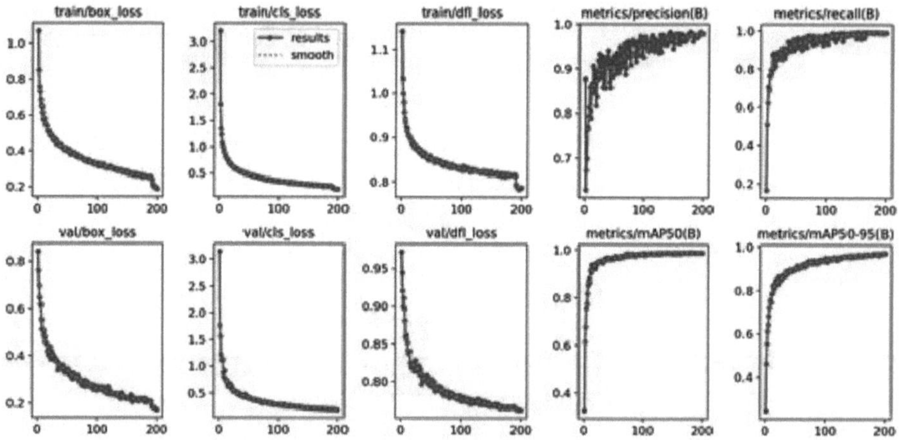

Fig. 6. Training Results

tion not only distinguishes between different object types but also effectively maps their locations in real time. This capability is crucial for applications in autonomous navigation and robotics where precise environmental understanding is vital.

In terms of accuracy, the precision and recall graphs provide insights into the model's predictive power and thoroughness. Precision starts high and levels out, suggesting the model reliably identifies true positives while avoiding false positives. Recall, though slightly lower, follows a similar upward trend, pointing to the model's growing ability to capture a majority of the relevant instances. The mean Average Precision (mAP) at the 50% intersection over union (IoU) threshold metric, mAP50(B), exhibits a rapid increase before plateauing, demonstrating the model's proficiency in detecting objects with a significant degree of overlap with the ground truth. The more rigorous metric, mAP50-95(B), considers a range of IoU thresholds and shows the model's robust performance even under stricter criteria, which is vital for real-world applications where precision is critical. Overall, these plots indicate healthy training and validation processes, with the model achieving a balanced state of low loss and high accuracy, ready for deployment in scenarios where accurate object detection is crucial. The smoothed lines serve to underscore the trends by reducing the noise and highlighting the overall patterns in the data.

In terms of accuracy, the precision and recall graphs provide insights into the model's predictive power and thoroughness. Precision starts high and levels out, suggesting the model reliably identifies true positives while avoiding false positives. Recall, though slightly lower, follows a similar upward trend, pointing to the model's growing ability to capture a majority of the relevant instances. The mean Average Precision (mAP) at the 50% intersection over union (IoU) threshold metric, mAP50(B), exhibits a rapid increase before plateauing, demonstrating the model's proficiency in detecting objects with a significant degree of

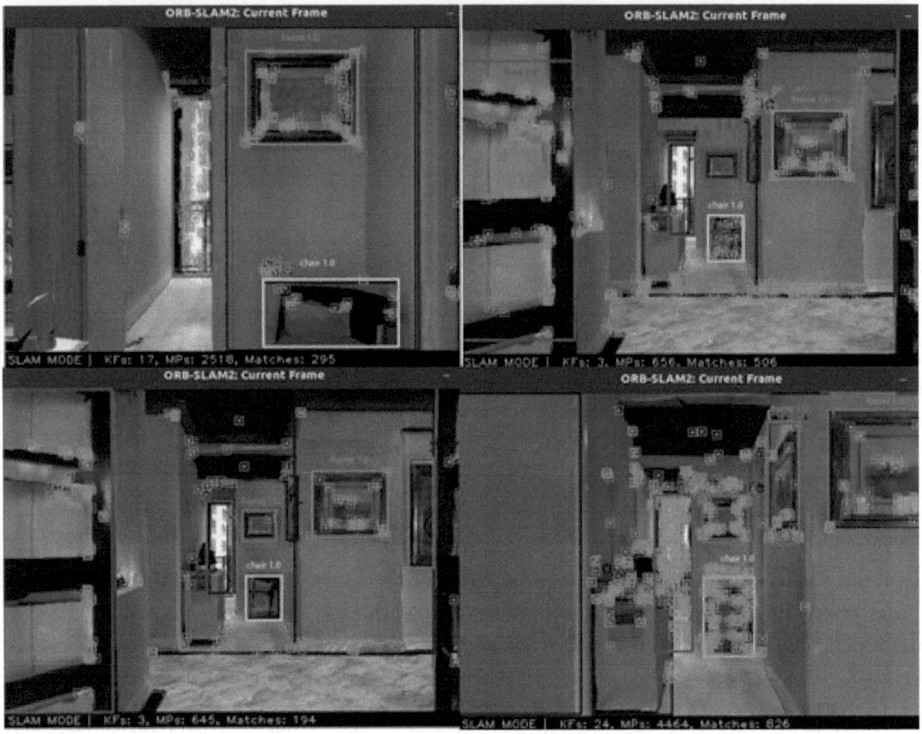

Fig. 7. DRL-SLAM Object Detection

overlap with the ground truth. The more rigorous metric, mAP50-95(B), considers a range of IoU thresholds and shows the model's robust performance even under stricter criteria, which is vital for real-world applications where precision is critical. Overall, these plots indicate healthy training and validation processes, with the model achieving a balanced state of low loss and high accuracy, ready for deployment in scenarios where accurate object detection is crucial. The smoothed lines serve to underscore the trends by reducing the noise inherent in epoch-to-epoch measurements, confirming the model's steady progress towards optimal performance.

Table 3. Comparison of Precision, Recall, and F1 Scores by Method

Method	Precision	Recall	F1 Score
YOLOv5	0.8766	0.16515	0.27967
YOLOv7	0.62886	0.51035	0.56406
Our Method (DRL-SLAM YOLOv8)	**0.89281**	**0.92394**	**0.91736**

Table 3 presents a detailed comparison of precision, recall, and F1 scores for various methods, including the traditional YOLOv5, YOLO7, and our enhanced DRL-SLAM YOLOv8 approach. As the table illustrates, our method significantly outperforms the others, demonstrating superior precision (0.89281), recall (0.92394), and F1 score (0.91736). This improvement underscores the efficacy of our DRL-SLAM YOLOv8's architecture in handling complex object detection tasks, achieving a higher balance of precision and recall, thus indicating a more reliable and accurate system.

In a further analysis shown in Table 4, we delve into the performance metrics of YOLOv8 algorithms during training and validation phases. The YOLOv8s model displayed a commendable train box loss of 0.64324 and a classification loss of 0.99797, with a deformation loss of 0.93602. Remarkably, the model maintained high metrics under operational conditions, with a precision of 0.79421 and a recall of 0.75976. Most notably, the mAP50 value reached 0.85106, with an mAP50-95 of 0.7196, demonstrating robust performance across a wide range of object detection scenarios. These results validate the enhancements incorporated into Our Method (DRL-SLAM YOLOv8), showing not only an improvement in fundamental metrics such as precision and recall but also a significant boost in overall model performance, as evidenced by the superior F1 and mAP scores. This advancement positions our method as a leading solution in real-time object detection and localization, paving the way for future developments in autonomous systems and robotics.

Table 4. Performance Metrics of YOLOv8 Algorithms

Metric	Train Box Loss	Train Cls Loss	Train Dfl Loss	Precision	Recall	mAP50
YOLOv8s	0.64324	0.99797	0.93602	0.79421	0.75976	0.85106
Metric	mAP50-95	Val Box Loss	Val Cls Loss	Val Dfl Loss	LR/pg0	LR/pg1
YOLOv8s	0.7196	0.55416	1.1094	0.88142	0.0008865	0.0008865

Table 4 presents the performance metrics of YOLOv8 algorithms. The YOLOv8s model exhibited a train box loss of 0.64324, a classification loss of 0.99797, and a deformation loss of 0.93602. Under operational conditions, it achieved a precision of 0.79421 and a recall of 0.75976. The mAP50 value was 0.85106, and the mAP50-95 value was 0.7196. These metrics demonstrate the model's robustness and effectiveness in diverse object detection scenarios.

3.2 Comparison of Navigation Methods

The table titled "Goal Reached or Not" compares the performance of different navigation methods by tracking whether the goal was achieved across 15 episodes in various simulated house environments. While the standard DQN method only achieved its goal 33.30% of the time, the integration of object detection with the researchers' method yielded a notable success rate of 66%, demonstrating its superior navigation capabilities. ORB-SLAM2 alone had the lowest success rate at 6.60%, but when enhanced with object detection, it matched the researchers' method. The presence of object detection during track loss appears to have a significant positive impact, suggesting that this feature is instrumental in improving the accuracy and reliability of autonomous navigation systems in complex environments. The most notable improvement is seen with our method enhanced with object detection, which covers a substantial distance and successfully reaches ten goals, demonstrating the highest efficiency and effectiveness among the tested methods. The integration of YOLOv8 and ORB-SLAM2 based on Depth Information Fusion in our DRL-SLAM model offers significant performance enhancements. These improvements are crucial for applications requiring precise and reliable object detection and tracking, such as autonomous navigation systems and robotics. This capability enables the system to adapt better to dynamically changing environments, optimizing both the path efficiency and the achievement of navigation goals.

4 Conclusion

The integration of Deep Reinforcement Learning (DRL) with YOLOv8 for object detection within the Simultaneous Localization and Mapping (SLAM) framework offers a promising solution for overcoming challenges in indoor navigation and mapping. Our study focused on enhancing object detection in dynamic indoor environments by leveraging DRL's decision-making capabilities and YOLOv8's improved accuracy for real-time object detection. Through experimental validation, our proposed method, DRL-SLAM YOLOv8, demonstrated superior performance compared to conventional SLAM methods. It achieved higher detection accuracy and reliability under variable conditions, leading to significant improvements in total distance covered and goals reached. Future research could explore additional optimizations and real-world deployment to further enhance the method's performance and applicability. Overall, our study lays a solid foundation for advancing indoor navigation and mapping systems, with potential implications for a wide range of robotics and autonomous navigation applications.

Acknowledgments. The authors have no competing interests to declare that are relevant to the content of this article.

Funding Information. This research was self-funded.

Disclosure Statement. The authors declare no potential conflicts of interest concerning the research, authorship, and/or publication of this article.

References

1. He, B., Ji, X., Li, G., Cheng, B.: Key technologies and applications of UAVs in underground space: a review. IEEE Trans. Cogn. Commun. Network. (2024). https://doi.org/10.1109/tccn.2024.3358545

2. Balcı, M.A., Batrancea, L.M., Akgüller, Ö., Nichita, A.: A series-based deep learning approach to lung nodule image classification. Cancers **15**(3), 843 (2023). https://doi.org/10.3390/cancers15030843
3. Bochkovskiy, A., Wang, C.-Y., Liao, H.-Y.M.: Yolov4: Optimal Speed and Accuracy of Object Detection (2020). https://doi.org/10.48550/arXiv.2004.10934
4. Bodla, N., Singh, B., Chellappa, R., Davis, L.S.: Soft-NMS - improving object detection with one line of code. In: IEEE International Conference on Computer Vision (ICCV), pp. 5562–5570. IEEE (2017). https://doi.org/10.1109/ICCV.2017.593
5. Den, H., Ito, J., Kokaze, A.: Diagnostic accuracy of a deep learning model using YOLOv5 for detecting developmental dysplasia of the hip on radiography images. Sci. Rep. **13**(1), 6693 (2023). https://doi.org/10.1038/s41598-023-33860-2
6. Fu, C.-Y., Liu, W., Ranga, A., Tyagi, A., Berg, A.C.: DSSD: Deconvolutional Single Shot Detector (2017). https://arxiv.org/abs/1701.06659
7. Girshick, R.: Fast R-CNN. In: IEEE International Conference on Computer Vision (ICCV), Santiago, Chile, pp. 1440–1448. IEEE (2015). https://doi.org/10.1109/ICCV.2015.169
8. Girshick, R., Donahue, J., Darrell, T., Malik, J.: Rich feature hierarchies for accurate object detection and semantic segmentation. In: IEEE Conference on Computer Vision and Pattern Recognition (CVPR), Columbus, OH, USA, pp. 580–587. IEEE (2014). https://doi.org/10.1109/CVPR.2014.81
9. Han, W., Han, X.: Stack workpieces recognition model based on deep learning. In: 11th International Conference of Information and Communication Technology (ICTech), Wuhan, China, pp. 209–213. IEEE (2022). https://doi.org/10.1109/ICTech55460.2022.00049
10. Huang, J., Zhang, G.: A study of an online tracking system for spark images of abrasive belt-polishing workpieces. Sensors **23**(4), 2025 (2023). https://doi.org/10.3390/s23042025
11. Neubeck, A., Van Gool, L.: Efficient non-maximum suppression. In: 18th International Conference on Pattern Recognition (ICPR 2006), Hong Kong, China, pp. 850–855. IEEE (2006). https://doi.org/10.1109/ICPR.2006.479
12. Redmon, J., Divvala, S., Girshick, R., Farhadi, A.: You only look once: unified, real-time object detection. In: IEEE Conference on Computer Vision and Pattern Recognition (CVPR), Las Vegas, NV, USA, pp. 779–788. IEEE (2016). https://doi.org/10.1109/CVPR.2016.91
13. Redmon, J., Farhadi, A.: YOLO9000: better, faster, stronger. In: IEEE Conference on Computer Vision and Pattern Recognition (CVPR), Honolulu, HI, USA, pp. 6517–6525. IEEE (2017). https://doi.org/10.1109/CVPR.2017.690
14. Redmon, J., Farhadi, A.: Yolov3: An Incremental Improvement. arXiv preprint: arXiv:1804.02767 (2018). https://doi.org/10.48550/arXiv.1804.02767
15. Ren, S., He, K., Girshick, R., Sun, J.: Faster R-CNN: towards real-time object detection with region proposal networks. IEEE Trans. Pattern Anal. Mach. Intell. **39**(6), 1137–1149 (2017). https://doi.org/10.1109/TPAMI.2016.2577031
16. Rummel, P., Beutel, W.: Workpiece recognition and inspection by a model-based scene analysis system. Pattern Recogn. **17**(1), 141–148 (1984). https://doi.org/10.1016/0031-3203(84)90041-4
17. Soeb, M.J.A., et al.: Tea leaf disease detection and identification based on YOLOv7 (YOLO-T). Sci. Rep. **13**(1), 6078 (2023). https://doi.org/10.1038/s41598-023-33270-4

18. Wang, J., Chen, Y., Dong, Z., Gao, M.: Improved YOLOv5 network for real-time multi-scale traffic sign detection. Neural Comput. Appl. **35**(10), 7853–7865 (2023). https://doi.org/10.1007/s00521-022-08077-5
19. Xia, K., et al.: Global contextual attention augmented YOLO with ConvMixer prediction heads for PCB surface defect detection. Sci. Rep. **13**(1), 9805 (2023). https://doi.org/10.1038/s41598-023-36854-2
20. Yang, L., Dong, Y., Zhuang, J., Li, J.: A recognition algorithm for workpieces based on the machine learning. In: 11th International Symposium on Computational Intelligence and Design (ISCID), Hangzhou, China, pp. 371–375. IEEE (2018). https://doi.org/10.1109/ISCID.2018.10185
21. Yan, W., Weiping, F., Chensheng, Z., Hongtao, W.: Image matching for workpiece based on genetic algorithm. In: 2009 International Conference on Artificial Intelligence and Computational Intelligence, Shanghai, China, pp. 152–157. IEEE (2009). https://doi.org/10.1109/AICI.2009.488
22. Zhang, Y.-F., Ren, W., Zhang, Z., Jia, Z., Wang, L., Tan, T.: Focal and efficient IOU loss for accurate bounding box regression. Neurocomputing **506**, 146–157 (2022). https://doi.org/10.1016/j.neucom.2022.07.042
23. Zheng, Z., Wang, P., Liu, W., Li, J., Ye, R., Ren, D.: Distance-IoU Loss: Faster and Better Learning for Bounding Box Regression (2020)

Driver Fatigue Recognition Based on EEG Signal and Semi-supervised Learning

Lin Chen and Xiaobo Chen(✉)

Shandong Technology and Business University, Yantai 264005, China
2022420057@sdtbu.edu.cn, xbchen82@gmail.com

Abstract. Driving fatigue has become a serious hidden danger to road traffic safety. Drivers in a fatigued state often have problems such as delayed reactions and lack of concentration, which increases the risk of traffic accidents. In fatigued driving, the brain activity of the driver undergoes a series of changes, such as a decrease in the frequency of brain waves and a decrease in the amplitude of electroencephalogram (EEG) signals. Therefore, we propose a novel Semi-supervised Label Propagation with Optimal Graph Learning (SOGL) model that for identifying the fatigue state of drivers. This model uses class information from a small amount of labeled EEG data to assist the learning of unlabeled data and uses soft projection matrix learning to handle non-linear data structures. In addition, we also introduce a partially labeled graph learning method that extracts potential data structure information through graph structure learning techniques to improve the robustness and generalization ability of the model. Experimental results show that the model has good performance on a driving fatigue dataset.

Keywords: Semi-supervision Learning · Graph Learning · Driver Fatigue Recognition · EEG data

1 Introduction

Traffic accidents are a serious public safety issue in modern society, and fatigue driving is one of the main causes of accidents. According to research [1], 15%–20% of fatal traffic accidents are related to driver fatigue, resulting in a large number of deaths and injuries every year [2]. To solve this problem, it has become crucial to study driving fatigue detection technology, and EEG signals are considered as the gold standard for fatigue detection.

In recent years, scholars have used machine learning techniques to identify driver fatigue. For example, some studies use methods such as support vector regression and singular value decomposition for fatigue identification [3]. In addition, wavelet packet decomposition has also been applied to frequency domain feature extraction and functional connectivity construction [4]. These methods have achieved good results in EEG signal classification. However, the training data used in these methods requires a lot of manual annotation which is labor-intensive and time-consuming. In EEG-based analysis applications, many studies have used semi-supervised learning methods. A study [5]

Published by Springer Nature Switzerland AG 2025
Z. Shi et al. (Eds.): ICIS 2024, IFIP AICT 720, pp. 273–285, 2025.
https://doi.org/10.1007/978-3-031-71253-1_20

proposed a sleep staging model based on neural networks and bidirectional gated recursive units; Another method [6] utilizes time self-coding to reduce the dimensionality of intracranial EEG data. Another study [7] proposed an emotion recognition classification method aimed at improving accuracy. Semi-supervised learning has great potential in EEG analysis, which can improve the accuracy of data classification and recognition.

Graph-based semi-supervised dimensionality reduction can effectively represent the inherent structure of data relationships [15]. The goal of semi-supervised graph structure learning is to utilize the similarity relation of samples, especially in the presence of a large amount of unlabeled data. Semi-supervised classification task can be improved by utilizing local and global structural information in the graph [16]. However, if the graph structure is inaccurate or incomplete, it may lead to a decrease in learning performance.

Inspired by recent advances in graph-based semi-supervised learning [8] and structured graph learning theory [17], this article proposes a novel Semi-Supervised Label Propagation with Optimal Graph Learning (SOGL) for EEG-based driving fatigue detection. Our model does not construct a similarity graph of samples in the original feature space, but is based on the label subspace and feature subspace of driving fatigue EEG samples. Considering that EEG driving fatigue data is non-linear, we use a soft projection matrix to relax the projection relation. We have conducted a large number of experiments on the driving fatigue datasets, and the experimental results show that our model is superior to other compared methods. This paper is interesting from the following aspects.

1) We propose an innovative semi-supervised model for EEG signals-based driver fatigue recognition, which reduces labeling costs and achieves better generalization performance.
2) We use graph structures to solve semi-supervised recognition tasks for more efficient and accurate label propagation. Similarity graphs are constructed based on the label subspace and feature subspace of samples, alleviating the negative impact of inaccurate pre-constructed graphs.
3) We have designed a soft projection matrix to better handle the nonlinear structure of driving fatigue EEG samples, which helps to reduce the deviation between prediction labels and the projection matrix and improve the accuracy of the model.

2 Method

In this section, we will provide a detailed introduction to the proposed methods. Firstly, the relevant symbols and definitions used in this article are provided. Then, we provided the model formulation. Finally, an effective optimization algorithm is developed.

2.1 Notations and Definitions

We first provide some explanations for the symbols. The total training sample set is denoted by $X = \left[x_1, \cdots, x_l, x_{l+1}, \cdots, x_n\right]^T \in R^{d \times n}$, where the labels of the first l samples are known, while the labels of the remaining $n - l$ samples are unknown. Here, d represents the original data dimensionality, and n denotes the total number of training samples. The labels corresponding to X are denoted as $Y = \left[y_1, \cdots, y_l, y_{l+1}, \cdots, y_n\right] \in$

$R^{n \times c}$, where $y_i \in R^c$, c is the number of classes. For the labeled sample x_i, if the label is k, then $y_{ik} = 1$; otherwise, $y_{ik} = 0$. If x_i is an unlabeled sample, we always have $y_{ik} = 0$ for any k.

2.2 Model Formulation

Our model framework is shown in Fig. 1, consisting of three modules: the propagation of label information, soft projection matrix learning, and prior guided graph optimization, which will be explained below.

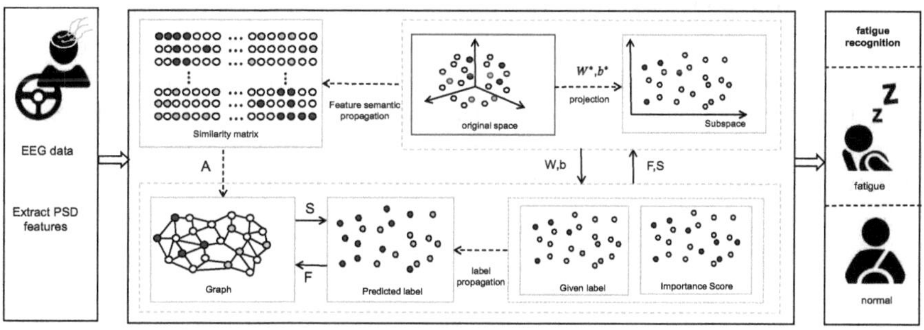

Fig. 1. The general framework of our model

2.2.1 Propagation of Label Information

Some previous label propagation methods typically pursue the consistency between predicted labels and real labels [9]. However, for noisy and non-stationary EEG data, strict label consistency constraints may reduce generalization ability. To this end, we adopt a propagation module to reduce the difficulty caused by enforcing strict label constraints and better utilize the correlation for semantic transmission. Meanwhile, by using diagonal matrices to highlight the differences between labeled and unlabeled samples, different weights are assigned to them during label propagation to reduce the impact of unlabeled samples on prediction results. Therefore, we can obtain the following formula

$$\min_F \operatorname{Tr}\Big((F - Y)^T U (F - Y)\Big) \tag{1}$$

where $F \in R^{n \times c}$ denotes the learned label matrix, the diagonal matrix $U \in R^{n \times n}$, if the sample has labels, then $u_{ii} = 1$; otherwise, $u_{ii} = 0$.

2.2.2 Soft Projection Matrix Learning

Learning a projection matrix $W \in R^{d \times c}$ with good discriminative power is imperative to dimensionality reduction tasks. In most methods, the predicted label is usually directly equal to the projected feature, that is $F = X^T W + lb^T$. However, this hard projection relation is relatively too strict and cannot fit the data samples with nonlinear structures.

Therefore, we aim to optimize the deviation between F and $X^TW + lb^T$, to better handle nonlinear distribution data. In addition, similar to [10], we introduce orthogonal constraints on W, i.e., $W^TW = I$, such that the redundancy of features can be reduced. Therefore, we can obtain the following objective function.

$$\min_{W^TW=I,b,F} \|X^TW + lb^T - F\|_F^2 \tag{2}$$

Notice that besides W and b, the sample label matrix F is also unknown.

2.2.3 Prior Guided Graph Optimization

We consider an undirected graph S $\in R^{n\times n}$ in a label space, where each vertex corresponds to an EEG sample, and edges represent the connection relationship between two samples. To describe the similarity between samples, we use a similarity matrix S, where element s_{ij} represent the similarity between the i-th and j-th samples. To propagate the labels between sample, we give the following objective function

$$\min_S \sum\nolimits_{i,j} \|f_i - f_j\|_2^2 s_{ij} \tag{3}$$

$$s.t. \, Sl = l, S \geq 0$$

where f_i and f_j are the rows of F. We can see from (3) that the similarity s_{ij} is inversely proportional to the discrepancy between the predicted labels f_i and f_j. Therefore, the larger s_{ij} indicates that $\|f_i - f_j\|_2^2$ should be smaller. In doing so, the similarity information of samples is spread from S to predicted labels. Based on the features of samples, we can build a predefined affinity matrix $A \in R^{n\times n}$ by using existing methods, such as k-nearest neighbors. Then, we introduce L2-norm distance $\|S - A\|_F^2$ to measure the degree of deviation between estimate the graph similarity matrix S, thus extending (3) into

$$\min_S \sum\nolimits_{\text{i,j}} \gamma \|f_i - f_j\|_2^2 s_{ij} + \|S - A\|_F^2 \tag{4}$$

$$\text{s.t. } Sl = l, S \geq 0$$

where γ is a non-negative parameter. Based on the above discussion, the objective function of our SOGL model is expressed as

$$\min_{W,F,S,b} \alpha\|X^TW + lb^T - F\|_F^2 + 2\gamma \text{Tr}\left(F^TLF\right) + \beta \text{Tr}\left((F - Y)^T U(F - Y)\right) + \|S - A\|_F^2 \tag{5}$$

$$\text{s.t.} W^TW = I, Sl = l, S \geq 0$$

2.3 Optimization Algorithm

We use the following methods to optimize the variables involved in (5).

(1) Fix W, S, F and update b, the corresponding objective function is

$$\min_{W,b} \alpha \|X^T W + lb^T - F\|_F^2 \tag{6}$$

Taking the derivative w.r.t. b and setting to zero, we have

$$b = \frac{1}{n}(F^T l - W^T X l) \tag{7}$$

Substituting b in (7) into (6) and setting the derivative to zero, we obtain

$$X^T W + lb^T - F = H_c(X^T W - F) \tag{8}$$

where $H_c = I_n - \frac{1}{n}ll^T$ and I_n is an identity matrix of size n. Apparently, we also have $H_c = H_c H_c = H_c^T$.

(2) Fix W, S, b and update F. Substituting (8) into (5), the corresponding objective function is

$$\min_{F} \alpha \|H_c(X^T W - F)\|_F^2 + 2\gamma \mathrm{Tr}(F^T L F) + \beta \mathrm{Tr}\Big((F - Y)^T U (F - Y)\Big) \tag{9}$$

Taking the derivative w.r.t. F and setting to zero, we have

$$F = Q(\beta U Y + \alpha H_c X^T W) \tag{10}$$

where $Q = (2\gamma L + \beta U + \alpha H_c)^{-1}$ and $Q^T = Q$.

(3) Fix b, S, F and update W. Substituting F and b obtained above into (5), we have

$$\begin{aligned} &\min_{W^T W = I} \alpha tr\Big(\Big(H_c\big(X^T W - Q\big(\beta U Y + \alpha H_c X^T W\big)\big)\Big)^T \Big(H_c\big(X^T W - Q\big(\beta U Y + \alpha H_c X^T W\big)\big)\Big)\Big) \\ &+ 2\gamma Tr\Big(\Big(Q\big(\beta U Y + \alpha H_c X^T W\big)\Big)^T L Q\big(\beta U Y + \alpha H_c X^T W\big)\Big) \\ &+ \beta Tr\Big(\Big(Q\big(\beta U Y + \alpha H_c X^T W\big) - Y\Big)^T U\Big(Q\big(\beta U Y + \alpha H_c X^T W\big) - Y\Big)\Big) \end{aligned} \tag{11}$$

Then, we drop the terms that have nothing to do with W and rewrite the above formula as

$$\min_{W^T W = I} \mathrm{Tr}\Big(W^T A W\Big) - \mathrm{Tr}\Big(2 W^T B\Big) \tag{12}$$

where $A = \alpha^2\big(X H_c\big(\frac{1}{\alpha}I - Q\big)H_c X^T\big)$, $B = \alpha\beta X H_c Q U Y$, $\mathrm{Tr}(W^T(\lambda_{max} I_d - A)W) = \lambda_{max} c$, and λ_{max} is the largest eigenvalue of the matrix$A$, $I_d \in R^{d \times d}$. By transformation, we can re-express (12) as a convex optimization problem on the Stiefel manifold. The specific form is given by

$$\max_{W^T W = I} \mathrm{Tr}(W^T(\lambda_{max} I_d - A)W) + 2\mathrm{Tr}(W^T B) \tag{13}$$

As a result, we can solve W by the method proposed in [13].

(4) Fix W, b, F and update S, the corresponding objective function is

$$\min_{S} 2\gamma \mathrm{Tr}(F^T LF) + \|S - A\|_F^2 \tag{14}$$

$$s.t. Sl = l, S \geq 0$$

The above (14) can be written as

$$\min_{S} \sum_{i,j} \gamma \|f_i - f_j\|_F^2 s_{ij} + \sum_{i,j} (s_{ij} - a_{ij})^2 \tag{15}$$

$$\text{s.t. } Sl = l, S \geq 0$$

Considering different s_i in formula (15) are independent of each other, each s_i can be solved separately as follows

$$\min_{s_i} \sum_{j} \gamma \|f_i - f_j\|^2 s_{ij} + \sum_{j} (s_{ij} - a_{ij})^2 \tag{16}$$

$$\text{s.t. } {s_i}^T l = 1, s_i \geq 0$$

To simplify the formula, e_i is used to represent a vector, $e_{ij} = \|f_i - f_j\|^2$, and the (16) can be written as

$$\min_{s_i} \left\| s_i - (a_i - \frac{1}{2}\gamma e_i) \right\|_2^2 \tag{17}$$

$$\text{s.t. } {s_i}^T l = 1, s_i \geq 0$$

Therefore, the problem (17) can be solved using the algorithm proposed in [11].

Typically, for most supervised projection dimensionality reduction methods, the projection matrix is constrained to the same number of classes. However, for datasets like EEG data where the number of classes is small, excessive dimensionality reduction may lead to the loss of a significant amount of valuable information. Therefore, we adopt the method in [18] to generate a recursive projection matrix W^* as follows

$$W^* = [W_1, W_2, \cdots, W_K] \tag{18}$$

where K denotes the number of projection matrixes. The whole algorithm for solving problem (5) is summarized as follows.

Algorithm 1. Solution method for problem (5)

Input:

Sample data set $X \in R^{d \times n}$, data label $Y \in R^{d \times c}$, diagonal matrix $U \in R^{n \times n}$, similarity matrix $A \in R^{n \times n}$, parameters α, β, γ

Output:

Projection matrix

Procedure:

1. Initialize the similarity matrix S=A
2. While not converged
3. Compute the Laplace matrix $L = D - (S^T + S)/2$
4. Update variable according by solving (13)
5. Update variable according to (7)
6. Update variable F according to (10)
7. Update each row of variable S by solving (17)
8. End

3 Experiments and Analysis

This section first introduces the dataset used by the algorithm in the experiment and then provides experimental details, results, and analysis.

3.1 Experimental Data and Details

The experimental data was collected from 12 male drivers (S1-S12), recording EEG data during normal and fatigued driving. There were 30 effective channels and the raw signals were preprocessed using ERP acquisition and analysis software. After preprocessing, the data was segmented into epochs by 1 s, generating 300 samples. For each driver, there is a total of 600 samples, half are fatigued and the other half are normal. Figure 2 shows the PSD (Power Spectral Density) characteristics of EEG signals of a driver at normal and fatiguc statc.

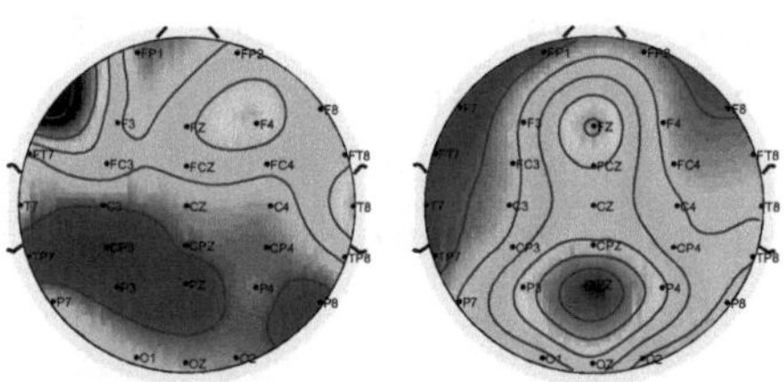

Fig. 2. PSD feature of a subject at normal state (left) and fatigue state (right)

We compare our model with state-of-the-art semi-supervised classification models with accuracy as our performance evaluation metric. The models include FME [12], LPSGL [13], DSP [14], and SOGE [10]. Our uses 80% of the total sample as the training set while the rest samples are used as testing set. To achieve semi-supervised learning, we only use the labels of 5%, 10%, 15%, and 20% training samples while regarding the remaining training samples as unlabeled data. Each experiment was trained 10 times with random repetitions.

3.2 Comparison with Baseline Models

The experimental results are shown in Tables 1, 2, 3 and 4, it can be observed that for different models, there are significant variation in detection performance among different subjects. Overall, our algorithm outperforms the comparative algorithms in most cases. For example, for the training set with 5% labeled samples, our model exhibits excellent performance for S2 subject. The accuracy of our model on the unlabeled data was 2.09% higher than that of the LPSGL model, and the accuracy on the test data surpasses that of the other models. Moreover, as the proportion of labeled samples increased, the accuracy of our algorithm continues to improve. These results indicate that our algorithm performs well for driving fatigue detection tasks.

Table 1. Classification accuracy (%) with 5% labeled samples. U and T indicate performance on the unlabeled training data and test data, respectively.

Data	FME		LPSGL		DSP		SOGE		Ours	
	U	T	U	T	U	T	U	T	U	T
S1	59.34	59.30	61.15	61.63	62.03	61.53	63.29	62.53	**65.03**	**64.93**
S2	62.55	62.20	63.36	63.20	62.69	63.10	61.19	62.03	**65.45**	**63.97**
S3	53.29	51.75	53.81	53.11	54.06	53.41	54.16	52.62	**56.57**	**54.27**
S4	84.86	85.05	86.78	86.61	87.76	87.91	90.24	90.40	**91.96**	**91.83**
S5	59.51	60.70	62.52	61.07	61.22	61.37	63.95	63.43	**64.06**	**64.37**
S6	50.94	52.66	53.46	52.86	52.59	52.09	53.18	**54.15**	**53.57**	54.09
S7	51.89	51.37	51.92	52.97	51.05	51.93	52.52	52.83	**53.25**	**53.80**
S8	61.15	62.20	63.74	62.33	62.83	62.10	62.52	62.17	**63.78**	**63.77**
S9	51.26	52.79	53.01	54.19	52.20	52.36	51.85	53.89	**53.78**	**54.55**
S10	51.40	51.73	53.99	55.03	51.78	53.07	53.08	53.53	**54.86**	**55.30**
S11	49.83	50.90	50.59	52.30	50.38	52.43	50.14	51.27	**52.13**	**53.10**
S12	51.99	52.06	54.97	54.09	55.07	53.99	52.76	52.06	**56.47**	**54.55**

We compare the performance of different models by the confusion matrix. We take S3 for example and the ratio of labeled training samples is set to 20%. The confusion matrixes are shown in Fig. 3. It can be observed that for our model, the recognition rate for the normal state is 84.17%, and for the fatigue state is 78.33%.

Table 2. Classification accuracy (%) with 10% labeled samples. U and T indicate performance on the unlabeled training data and test data, respectively.

Data	FME		LPSGL		DSP		SOGE		Ours	
	U	T	U	T	U	T	U	T	U	T
S1	64.63	62.83	64.89	63.40	66.30	65.77	67.44	65.70	**69.30**	**69.13**
S2	65.78	65.63	69.67	68.83	68.70	66.97	67.93	67.53	**70.00**	**70.10**
S3	54.74	53.97	56.00	55.76	57.07	55.66	56.81	56.49	**58.19**	**57.05**
S4	89.30	89.27	88.00	88.31	88.63	89.24	89.56	89.47	**91.41**	**91.73**
S5	62.07	61.97	66.30	67.40	66.22	66.87	67.89	68.67	**68.96**	**70.77**
S6	55.85	55.98	54.96	55.78	55.56	56.21	55.93	56.31	**56.67**	**56.68**
S7	52.04	53.57	52.37	53.47	52.67	54.57	52.89	54.63	**53.74**	**54.93**
S8	62.44	64.53	65.78	66.43	64.78	64.80	65.41	65.93	**65.96**	**67.70**
S9	51.48	53.49	54.11	55.95	54.52	56.38	54.15	55.98	**56.37**	**58.50**
S10	53.11	54.80	56.22	57.00	54.81	56.00	52.78	55.40	**57.48**	**59.93**
S11	50.30	50.90	50.48	51.20	52.63	52.40	50.74	52.03	**53.74**	**53.87**
S12	54.15	52.72	**56.41**	**56.18**	54.85	53.62	54.78	54.19	55.19	55.25

Table 3. Classification accuracy (%) with 15% labeled samples. U and T indicate performance on the unlabeled training data and test data, respectively.

Data	FME		LPSGL		DSP		SOGE		Ours	
	U	T	U	T	U	T	U	T	U	T
S1	66.05	62.57	71.05	70.27	66.76	66.10	69.06	67.67	**71.72**	**72.10**
S2	66.41	67.10	69.92	69.63	68.71	67.63	68.09	67.20	**70.35**	**70.03**
S3	55.39	50.79	57.03	55.53	56.05	55.07	57.23	55.07	**59.22**	**56.13**
S4	90.16	90.53	89.22	89.00	90.20	90.86	90.59	90.43	**92.54**	**92.36**
S5	62.50	62.13	68.44	69.67	66.64	67.03	68.16	69.33	**69.45**	**71.30**
S6	56.48	55.78	57.30	57.04	57.34	55.95	57.81	58.90	**59.80**	**59.47**
S7	52.97	55.27	53.91	56.13	55.12	56.57	53.98	55.87	**55.43**	**56.77**
S8	64.34	64.80	66.80	66.50	64.49	65.10	65.08	66.83	**68.05**	**68.40**
S9	53.87	54.78	54.41	57.21	54.65	55.71	54.73	57.74	**54.77**	**58.31**
S10	52.93	54.90	57.58	59.07	54.37	54.40	54.80	55.97	**58.01**	**60.17**
S11	52.54	52.20	53.13	53.00	52.27	53.70	52.77	52.37	**53.95**	**54.73**
S12	56.29	54.82	55.86	**57.54**	55.98	54.65	55.74	55.35	**58.48**	56.41

Table 4. Classification accuracy (%) with 20% labeled samples. U and T indicate performance on the unlabeled training data and test data, respectively.

Data	FME		LPSGL		DSP		SOGE		Ours	
	U	T	U	T	U	T	U	T	U	T
S1	66.13	63.87	73.04	71.87	71.67	69.77	69.67	70.13	**73.38**	**72.43**
S2	67.75	68.43	**71.42**	**70.47**	69.83	68.67	69.58	68.20	70.92	68.33
S3	55.67	55.50	58.96	56.95	58.67	55.03	57.21	56.13	**59.83**	**58.64**
S4	90.71	91.59	90.29	90.23	90.12	91.13	91.29	91.16	**92.63**	**92.33**
S5	63.83	62.87	72.13	72.57	68.04	69.13	70.71	72.10	**74.17**	**73.80**
S6	57.21	56.88	59.04	58.74	57.29	56.38	58.92	59.80	**59.58**	**59.93**
S7	54.63	55.40	54.96	56.77	55.21	56.30	54.71	56.43	**56.38**	**57.07**
S8	65.08	65.37	66.46	66.13	64.92	64.63	65.33	65.93	**68.08**	**66.43**
S9	54.63	54.92	54.75	56.98	53.25	56.15	54.00	56.51	**56.75**	**57.77**
S10	55.17	56.10	**60.17**	**62.37**	55.71	55.30	56.00	56.47	60.12	60.90
S11	52.79	52.50	54.25	53.30	53.83	53.80	53.75	52.87	**54.75**	**54.40**
S12	56.46	55.35	56.88	56.91	55.58	56.25	56.25	56.08	**57.25**	**57.28**

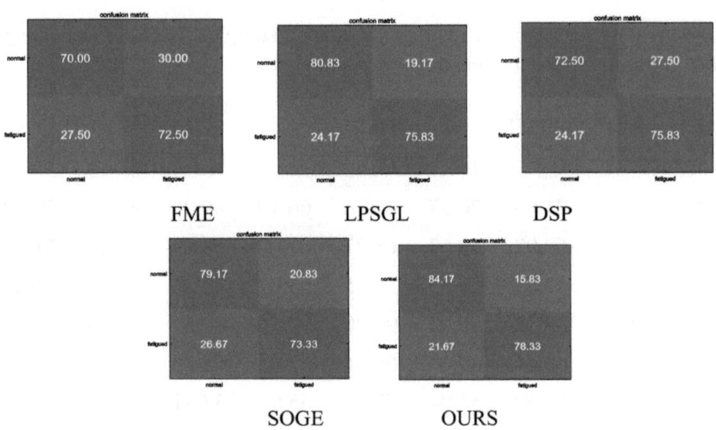

Fig. 3. Confusion matrices obtained by different models

3.3 Influence of the Number of Projection Matrixes

We propose increasing the number of projection matrices to extract more information for classification. Taking S2 and S4 datasets as examples, we experimentally investigate the performance changes of the model when the recursive count K increases from 1 to 8. As shown in Fig. 4, with the increase of K, the accuracy of driver fatigue recognition improves, confirming the effectiveness of extracting more discriminative information.

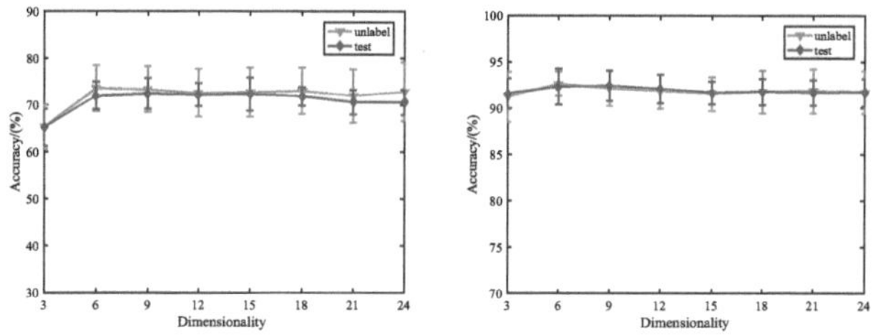

(a) S2 (b) S4

Fig. 4. Recognition performance when varying the number of projection matrixes

3.4 Convergence Analysis

Figure 5 shows the convergence curve of the objective function values for S1-S4 datasets as a function of the number of iterations. It can be seen that the objective function of the algorithm changes dramatically firstly, and then tends to stabilize after several iterations. This convergence experiment effectively proves that the algorithm can achieve convergence during the update process.

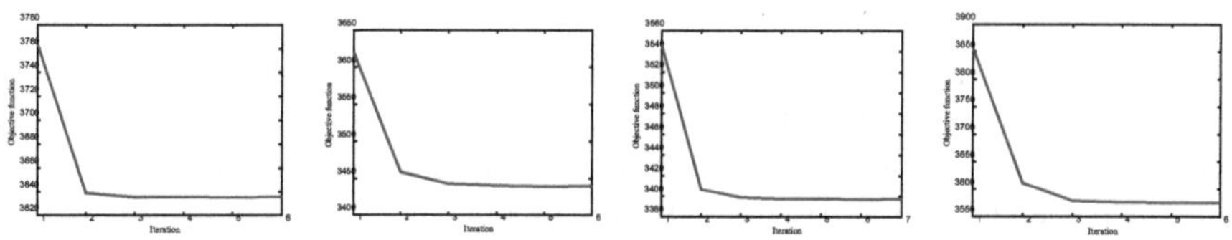

(a) S1 (b) S2 (c) S3 (d) S4

Fig. 5. Convergence curve of objective function

3.5 Parameter Sensitivity Analysis

The impact of parameters on the performance of our model should be carefully considered. We conduct experimental verification on the S5 dataset. The proportion of labeled samples is set to 20%, and the accuracy of driving fatigue recognition is recorded by changing the parameters α, β, and γ in our model. Specifically, we fix one parameter and change the values of the other two parameters. In the end, we obtain the experimental results shown in Fig. 6. From the graph, it can be seen that the recognition accuracy of our model is generally stable in suitable range.

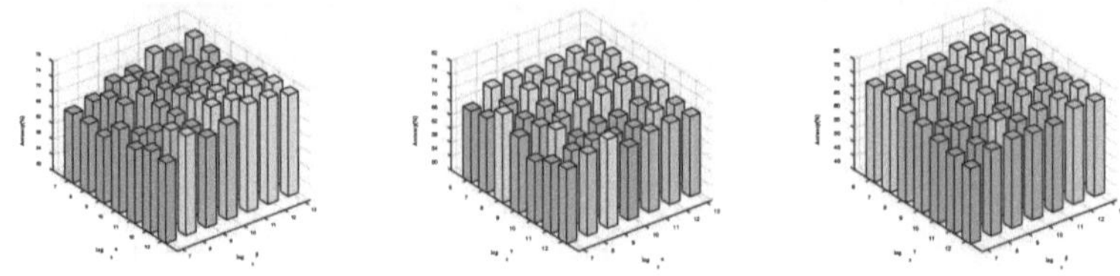

(a) S5 Unlabel (α, β) (b) S5 Unlabel (α, γ) (c) S5 Unlabel (β, γ)

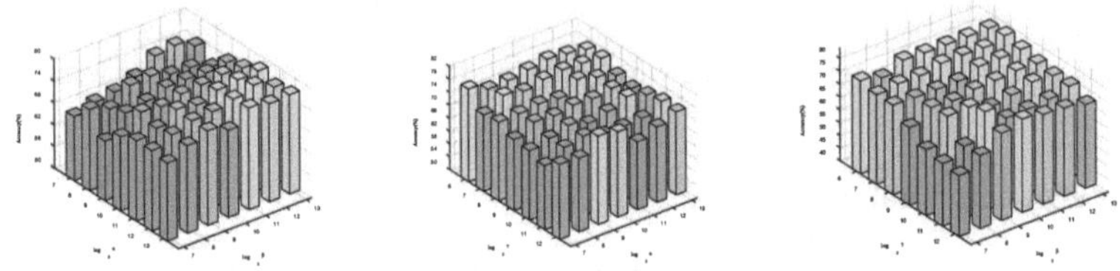

(d) S5 Test (α, β) (e) S5 Test (α, γ) (f) S5 Test (β, γ)

Fig. 6. Recognition accuracy variation with different values of parameters α, β, and γ on S5 datasets.

4 Conclusion

This article proposes a novel method termed as semi-supervised label propagation with optimal graph learning (SOGL) for detecting driver fatigue status based on EEG data. The SOGL model combines propagation of label information, soft projection matrix learning, and graph learning. By doing so, the model can effectively handle nonlinear data structures and utilizes graph structure learning techniques, thereby improving the robustness and generalization ability of the model. We further develop an algorithm to solve the resulting model. The experimental results on real-world datasets indicate that the proposed model achieves promising performance for driving fatigue detection tasks. Detailed analysis about the behavior of our model is also carried out to confirm its effectiveness.

References

1. Zhang, G., Yau, K.K., Zhang, X., Li, Y.: Traffic accidents involving fatigue driving and their extent of casualties. Accid. Anal. Prev. **87**, 34–42 (2016)
2. Saini, V., Saini, R.: Driver drowsiness detection system and techniques: a review. Int. J. Comput. Sci. Inf. Technol. **5**(3), 4245–4249 (2014)
3. Prabhakar, S.K., Won, D.O.: Multiple robust approaches for EEG-based driving fatigue detection and classification. Array **19**, 100320 (2023)
4. Nguyen, K.H., Ebbatson, M., Tran, Y., et al.: Source-space brain functional connectivity features in electroencephalogram-based driver fatigue classification. Sensors **23**(5), 2383 (2023)
5. Zhang, Y., Cao, W., Feng, L., et al.: SHNN: a single-channel EEG sleep staging model based on semi-supervised learning. Expert Syst. Appl. **213**, 119288 (2023)
6. Nejedly, P., Kremen, V., Lepkova, K., et al.: Utilization of temporal autoencoder for semi-supervised intracranial EEG clustering and classification. Sci. Rep. **13**(1), 744 (2023)

7. Zali-Vargahan, B., Charmin, A., Kalbkhani, H., et al.: Deep time-frequency features and semi-supervised dimension reduction for subject-independent emotion recognition from multi-channel EEG signals. Biomed. Signal Process. Control **85**, 104806 (2023)
8. Zhu, X.J.: Semi-supervised learning literature survey (2005)
9. Nie, F., Li, J., Li, X.: Parameter-free auto-weighted multiple graph learning: a framework for multiview clustering and semi-supervised classification. In: Proceedings of the International Joint Conference on Artificial Intelligence (IJCAI), pp. 1881–1887 (2016)
10. Liu, H., Han, J., Nie, F.: Semi-supervised orthogonal graph embedding with recursive projections. In: IJCAI, pp. 2308–2314 (2017)
11. Huang, J., Nie, F., Huang, H.: A new simplex sparse learning model to measure data similarity for clustering. In: Twenty-Fourth International Joint Conference on Artificial Intelligence (2015)
12. Nie, F., Xu, D., Tsang, I.W.H., et al.: Flexible manifold embedding: a framework for semi-supervised and unsupervised dimension reduction. IEEE Trans. Image Process. **19**(7), 1921–1932 (2010)
13. Wang, F., Zhu, L., Xie, L., et al.: Label propagation with structured graph learning for semi-supervised dimension reduction. Knowl.-Based Syst. **225**, 107130 (2021)
14. Li, S., Wang, F., Li, Y., et al.: Dual-layer semantic propagation for semi-supervised projection. In: 2022 International Conference on High Performance Big Data and Intelligent Systems (HDIS), pp. 163–167. IEEE (2022)
15. Jin, J., Sun, H., Daly, I., et al.: A novel classification framework using the graph representations of electroencephalogram for motor imagery based brain-computer interface. IEEE Trans. Neural Syst. Rehabil. Eng. **30**, 20–29 (2021)
16. Peng, Y., Kong, W., Qin, F., et al.: Manifold adaptive kernelized low-rank representation for semisupervised image classification. Complexity **2018** (2018)
17. Zhang, Y., Liu, Y., Jin, R., et al.: GLLPA: a graph layout based label propagation algorithm for community detection. Knowl.-Based Syst. **206**, 106363 (2020)
18. Wang, H., Nie, F.P., Huang, H.: Robust distance metric learning via simultaneous 1-norm minimization and maximization. In: International Conference on Machine Learning. JMLR.org (2014)

SC-EcapaTdnn: ECAPA-TDNN with Separable Convolutional for Speaker Recognition

Erhua Zhang, Yifan Wu(✉), and Zhenmin Tang

Nanjing University of Science and Technology, Nanjing, Jiangsu, China
yifanwu@njust.edu.cn

Abstract. The efficacy of time-delay neural networks (TDNN) in speaker recognition has been demonstrated. ECAPA-TDNN builds on TDNN, improving performance levels at the cost of increased computational complexity and slower inference speed. However, the effectiveness of ECAPA-TDNN does not meet the expected standards for speaker recognition in complex scenarios. This motivates us to seek an architecture superior to ECAPA-TDNN. In this paper, we propose an efficient network called SC-EcapaTdnn, which is a fusion of separable convolutions and ECAPA-TDNN. This innovative design uses ECAPA-TDNN as the backbone, uses depth-separable convolution blocks to encode acoustic features, and generates high-resolution frequency feature maps, allowing the backbone model to obtain more refined and effective speaker features. At the same time, we replace the squeeze excitation (SE) module in ECAPA-TDNN with adaptive one-dimensional convolution to generate channel attention weights to extract inter-channel dependencies. Ultimately, we trade a small increase in model parameters for a significant increase in performance. Training on the AISHELL and CN-Celeb datasets shows that our proposed architecture outperforms other mainstream speaker recognition systems.

Keywords: ECAPA-TDNN · Speaker Recognition · Adaptive Selection · Separable Convolution

1 Introduction

Speaker recognition (SR) includes identification, verification, separation and other small directions. This article studies the effect of the model on verification and identification. Speaker verification refers to whether the speaker in the registered voice matches the speaker in the test voice. According to the speech content, SV systems can be divided into two categories: text-related systems and text-independent systems. This paper studies text-independent speaker recognition systems. Early speaker verification systems were based on i vectors [1]. The system trained the universal background model UBM [2] to construct the mapping matrix T to map high-dimensional statistics to low-dimensional feature vectors (i vectors), and employed probabilistic linear discriminant analysis (PLDA) [3] as the back-end system. The registered person feature vector and the

Published by Springer Nature Switzerland AG 2025
Z. Shi et al. (Eds.): ICIS 2024, IFIP AICT 720, pp. 286–297, 2025.
https://doi.org/10.1007/978-3-031-71253-1_21

test person feature vector were fed into the backend system, and the score and threshold were compared to determine whether they were the same person. At present, advanced speaker verification systems first train a deep neural network (DNN) on the speaker recognition task and map variable-length speech to a fixed-dimensional embedded feature vector (x-vector) [4], which contains the speaker key features. Speaker identification is achieved by comparing two embedding vectors corresponding to the registrant and the tester, and the similarity between the two is represented by the cosine distance between the speaker embedding vectors. Additionally, it is possible to train more complex scoring backends such as Probabilistic Linear Discriminant Analysis (PLDA).

ResNet [5] solves the gradient disappearance and gradient explosion problems in the training process of deep neural networks through residual connections, making deeper networks have stronger learning capabilities. ResNet and Res2Net have been applied to speaker recognition tasks and have shown excellent results [6, 7]. Time-delay neural networks (TDNN) can effectively process speech sequences [8], ECAPA-TDNN [9] is the best single scoring system in the VoxSRC-20 verification set in the literature [10]. Its outstanding contribution lies in the combination of multi-scale dilated convolution and attentive statistics pooling is applied to TDNN.

Literature [11] shows that too many weights and units are often built into deep neural network models, making the inference cost of these models very high, which directly leads to a significant increase in the time and resources for training speaker recognition general models. Compared with TDNN, ECAPA-TDNN achieves advanced performance at the expense of higher computational complexity and slower inference speed, which makes it insufficient to meet scenarios with high inference rate requirements and limited computing resources.

In response to the above problems, literature [12] proposed network pruning to reduce the computational cost of hyperparameterized networks, while literature [13] proposed a method based on adaptive selection of convolution kernel size to achieve local interaction, significantly reducing The computational cost, model complexity and maintenance performance of the hyperparameterized network are reduced. Reference [14] proposed an efficient network based on context-aware masks, which uses densely connected delay neural network (D-TDNN) [15] as the backbone and adopts novel multi-granularity pooling to capture different locations contextual information. In response to the improvement of ECAPA-TDNN, literature [16] proposed a progressive channel fusion strategy, which divides the spectrum into feature channels and gradually expands the receptive field through the network, which also deepens the network model.

In order to cope with complex scenes, the feature extraction capabilities of ECAPA-TDNN are further improved to ensure the speaker confirmation effect without excessively increasing the model size. This article proposes SC-EcapaTdnn. The main contributions of this article are as follows:

- In order to extract local features more effectively, this paper integrates the front-end convolution module into ECAPA-TDNN. The front-end convolution module includes depthwise separable convolution layers and residual connections. The depthwise separable convolution layer can effectively reduce the number of model parameters, accelerate the model training and inference process. Residual connection can better alleviate the model degradation problem and speed up the model convergence speed.

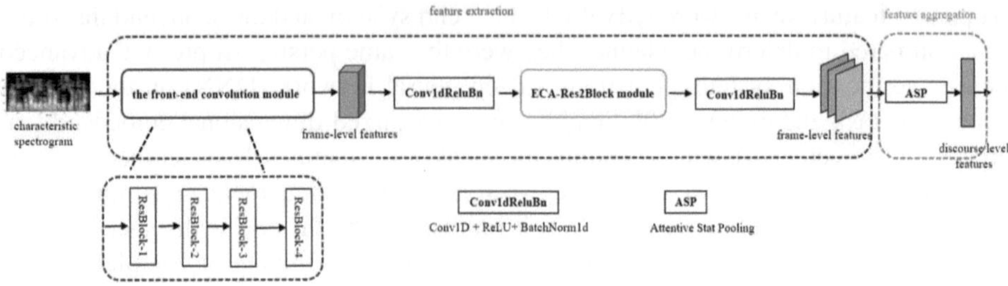

Fig. 1. An end-to-end speaker verification system based on SC-EcapaTdnn

- Each Res2Block block in ECAPA-TDNN is connected to the squeeze-excitation block [17]. The channel information interaction achieved by the SE block through full connection will damage part of the feature expression in the process of dimensionality reduction and dimensionality increase. Reference [13] proposed a method based on adaptive selection of convolution kernel size to achieve local interaction, thereby significantly reducing model complexity and maintaining performance. This article uses the efficient channel attention module (ECA) to replace the SE block in ECAPA-TDNN.
- This article trained the improved model on three data sets, AISHELL-1 [18], AISHELL-2 [19] and CN-Celeb [20], and conducted speaker recognition and speaker confirmation experiments at the same time. The results showed that it had better performance than ECAPA-TDNN. In addition, a large number of ablation experiments were conducted to verify that each improvement achieved the expected effect.

2 Related Work

2.1 An End-to-End Speaker Recognition System Based on SC-EcapaTdnn

Each step in the traditional i-vector speaker verification system is trained independently on subtasks and is not jointly optimized. Some other DNN-based speaker verification systems require additional steps to aggregate frame-level features and perform verification. This article integrates all subtasks together to achieve a unified end-to-end system for closed and open sets, as shown in Fig. 1. Any type of deep convolutional network can be used as a feature extractor, such as ECAPA-TDNN, ResNet, etc. The SC-EcapaTdnn improved in this article has fewer parameters and stronger feature extraction capabilities, so SC-EcapaTdnn is used as the backbone network of the feature extractor.

The end-to-end speaker vertification system based on SC-EcapaTdnn consists of four parts: (1) Feature extraction network, which uses ECA-Res2Block to adaptively select the convolution kernel size to extract more distinctive frame-level features; (2) Feature aggregation, which aggregates variable-length frame-level features into fixed-dimensional utterance-level features through adaptive average pooling; (3) Speaker recognition loss function, using Angular additive margin softmax (AAM-Softmax) loss [21] during training to more accurately identify speakers Classification; (4) Similarity measure, used for speaker vertification after training is completed, by calculating the distance of a pair of utterance-level features to determine whether the pair of audios comes from the same speaker [22].

2.2 Baseline Model

ECAPA-TDNN is the best single scoring system in the VoxSRC-20 validation set and is still the mainstream single model for speaker recognition. It is improved based on the x vector. Inspired by ResNet, it utilizes a one-dimensional residual module to extract multi-scale contextual information. Attention statistical pooling is also used to calculate the weighted mean and weighted standard deviation of the input sequence at each time step. Finally, multi-layer feature aggregation (MFA) is used to concatenate the final frame-level features with shallowly generated intermediate features to provide additional complementary information for statistical pooling. Experiments have proven that this architecture performs excellently on various data sets.

3 SC-EcapaTdnn

This chapter mainly introduces the model structure of SC-EcapaTdnn, which is divided into three parts, including the front-end convolution module, ECA-Res2Block module and SC-EcapaTdnn network structure.

3.1 Front-End Convolution Module

This paper uses a front-end convolution module to extract key local features. This module is composed of multiple two-dimensional convolution blocks with residual connections. These convolution blocks encode acoustic features in the time-frequency domain, and the obtained feature maps are along It is flattened along the channel and frequency dimensions and used as input to the improved ECAPA-TDNN. It is worth mentioning that in this paper, the two-dimensional convolution in this module is implemented by depthwise separable convolution [23], it consists of two parts: depthwise convolution and pointwise convolution. This convolution method can greatly reduce the number of parameters and calculation amount of the model, while the effectiveness of spatial features can be maintained.

$$P = C_{in} * C_{out} * k * k \tag{1}$$

where P represents the number of parameters required for convolution, C_{in} represents the number of input channels, C_{out} represents the number of output channels, and k represents the size of the convolution kernel.

$$P_1 = C_{in} * k * k \tag{2}$$

$$P_2 = C_{in} * C_{out} \tag{3}$$

$$P = P_1 + P_2 \tag{4}$$

where P_1 represents the number of parameters required for depthwise convolution, and P_2 represents the number of parameters required for pointwise convolution.

3.2 ECA-Res2Block Module

Res2Net is a network structure used in target detection, aiming to improve the feature extraction capabilities of convolutional neural networks by increasing the size of the receptive field. Res2Net is a variant of ResNet. It inherits the advantages of ResNet and also has new features. A parallel branch network structure is adopted and implemented by connecting smaller convolution operators in a manner similar to layer residuals. The connection method of layer residuals makes Res2Net have a larger receptive field and more receptive field combinations than ResNet. The parallel branch structure makes Res2Net have fewer parameters than ResNet.

$$\mathbf{y_i} = \begin{cases} \mathbf{X}_i, i = 1 \\ \mathbf{K}_i(\mathbf{X}_i), i = 2 \\ \mathbf{K}_i(\mathbf{X}_i + \mathbf{Y}_{i-1}), 2 < i \le s \end{cases} \tag{5}$$

assume that the input of each segment is $\mathbf{X}_i$, where $i \in \{1, 2, \ldots, s\}$, $s = 4$ in Fig. 2, $\mathbf{K}_i$ represents 3x3 convolution, then the output $\mathbf{Y}_i$ is:

$$\begin{gathered} \mathbf{Y_1} = \mathbf{X}_1 \\ \mathbf{Y}_2 = \mathbf{K}_2(\mathbf{X}_2) \\ \mathbf{Y}_3 = \mathbf{K}_3(\mathbf{X}_3 + \mathbf{K}_2(\mathbf{X}_2)) \\ \mathbf{Y}_4 = \mathbf{K}_4(\mathbf{X}_4 + \mathbf{K}_3(\mathbf{X}_3 + \mathbf{K}_2(\mathbf{X}_2))) \end{gathered} \tag{6}$$

As shown in Fig. 2, Res2Net and ECA-Layer are connected sequentially, and in ECA-Layer, the global feature descriptor is obtained through adaptive average pooling, and the global spatial information of the input feature map is captured to learn the dependencies

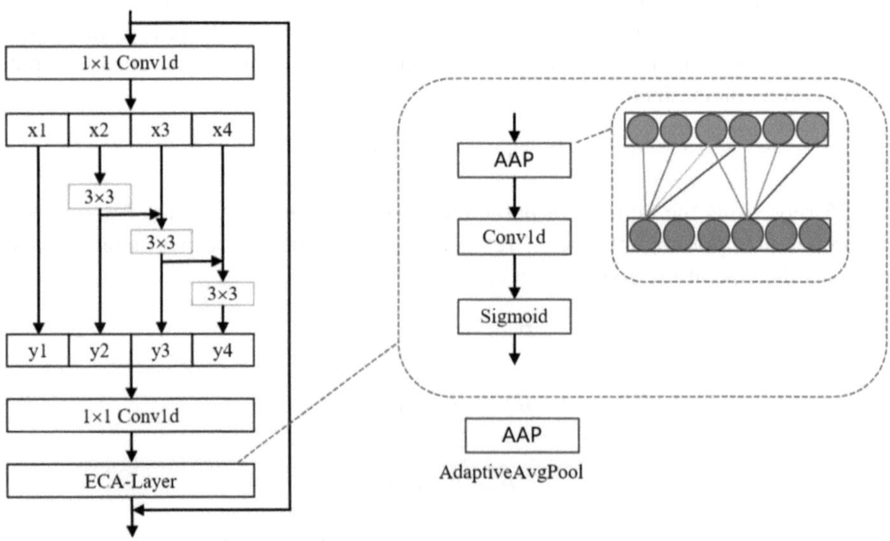

Fig. 2. ECA-Res2Block module

between channels. By learning the weight vector, the model can dynamically adjust the size of the convolution kernel according to the different conditions of the input features, so as to achieve local interaction and reduce the complexity of the model. The Sigmoid function activates the convoluted features to reweight the features. The ECA-Res2Block module extracts richer and more effective speaker features through multi-scale group convolution, and at the same time, pays attention to the importance of each channel through ECA-Layer, so as to realize information interaction between channels at a smaller cost.

3.3 SC-EcapaTdnn Network Structure

Figure 3 is the SC-EcapaTdnn network structure diagram. This article uses the convolution module in Resnet as the front-end convolution module of the model. The front-end convolution module extracts the characteristics of the time-frequency domain of the speech signal. Subsequently, the obtained feature map is along the channel and The frequency dimension is flattened, and the resulting features are used as input to the improved EcapaTdnn. The SC-EcapaTdnn backbone consists of three blocks, each block contains a sequence of ECA-Res2net. In each sequence, we build an ECA-Layer that assigns different weights to the output features of the inner Res2net layer, using global average pooling to efficiently aggregate different levels of contextual information. The feature map through multi-scale convolution is redistributed by channel weights, and then through residual connection, and the result is used as the input of the next layer.

4 Experiments

4.1 Dataset

The AISHELL-1 dataset comes from an open-source Chinese corpus and includes 178 h of Mandarin recordings. The recording environment is in a quiet and enclosed room, and the sampling rate is strictly controlled at 16kHz. The sound was recorded by 400 speakers from different regions of China, and after professional voice annotation and manual detection, the accuracy of manual transcription of the dataset was ensured to reach over 95%. This article randomly selects the speech data of 380 people as training samples, and the speech data of the remaining 20 people as registration and testing samples. The testing samples are 400 speech samples with a length of 8 s each.

The AISHELL-2 data set comes from the open source Chinese corpus and contains 1000 h of Mandarin recordings. The recording environment was in a quiet closed room, and the sampling rate was strictly controlled at 16kHz. The voice was recorded by 1,991 speakers from different regions in China. It was professionally annotated and manually tested to ensure that the accuracy of manual transcription of the data set reaches over 96%.

CN-Celeb is a large-scale Chinese dataset produced by Tsinghua University, which contains 130000 speech segments and a total of 274 h. The test set collected multiple Chinese open media voice data, including 196 registered speakers and 196 tested speakers, for a total of 17777 voices.

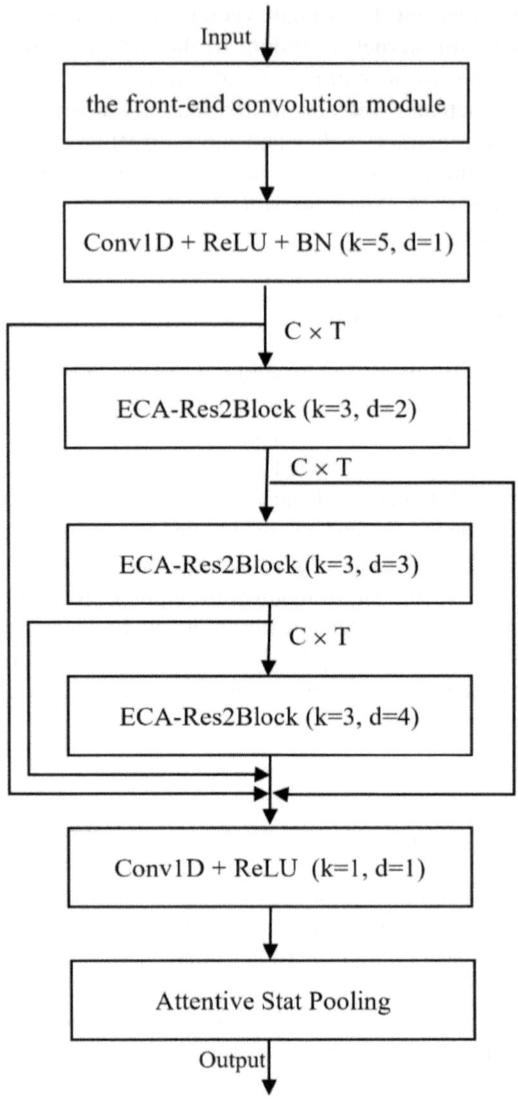

Fig. 3. SC-EcapaTdnn network structure

4.2 Experimental Setup

All audio in the experiments were single-channel 16-bit streams sampled at 16 kHz. The audio data is first framed (25ms per frame, frame shift 10ms), windowed, and then passed through Mel filtering (80 sets of Mel filters). Then, mean and variance normalization (MVN) is performed on the obtained features as a whole to generate Fbank features as input to the network model. There is no silence detection and speech enhancement, and no complex processing on the backend. Network parame-ter optimization was performed using the Adam optimizer [24] with an initial learning rate of 0.001. The experiments all used AAM-Softmax loss, with the margin and scaling factors of AAM-Softmax loss set to 0.2 and 32 respectively. We use cosine similarity scores for evaluation without applying score normaliza-tion in the backend. We employ two commonly used metrics in speaker verification tasks, equal error rate (EER) and minimum detection cost function (MinDCF) with a target probability of 0.01. MinDCF not only considers the different costs of false rejection and false acceptance, but also fully considers the prior probability of the test situation. Therefore, MinDCF has more reference value than EER in model performance evaluation. We use accuracy (ACC) as an indicator to evaluate model performance in the speaker recognition task.

Table 1. Performance comparison of different network architectures on the AISHELL-1 and CN-Celeb test sets.

Architecture	Params(M)	AISHELL-1 test	CN-Celeb test
		EER (%)/MinDCF	EER (%)/MinDCF
TDNN	2.63	3.43/0.36	12.34/0.63
ResNet34	9.14	1.24/0.20	10.68/0.55
ECAPA-TDNN	6.19	1.33/0.20	10.84/0.56
SC-EcapaTdnn	8.28	**1.16/0.20**	**8.26/0.48**

4.3 Speaker Verification Results on AISHELL-1 and CN-Celeb

Table 1 presents an overview of the performance of all methods. For fair comparison, we re-implemented several baseline models, including TDNN, ECAPA-TDNN and ResNet34, under the same experimental settings described in Sect. 3.2. The ResNet34 model contains four residual blocks with different channel sizes in each block [64, 128, 256, 512]. The channel size of the other models is set to 512.

Evaluated on two datasets, CN-Celeb and AISHELL-1, these four models outperformed CN-Celeb on the AISHELL-1 dataset. This is because the CN-Celeb dataset is more complex. At the same time, the difference in EER between ResNet34 and ECAPA-TDNN on the two datasets is less than 1%, but the former has more parameters because ResNet34 has a deeper and more complex network structure. Our improved SC-EcapaTdnn performs best on both datasets, thanks to the front-end convolution module extracting more representative speaker features, and the model parameters are increased within an acceptable range due to the use of separable convolutions and adaptive selection of convolutional kernel size.

The experimental findings solidify SC-EcapaTdnn's prowess in feature extraction, demonstrating that it can successfully derive more potent and discriminative frame-level features. Therefore, our paper proposes the superior SC-EcapaTdnn model, marked notably for its elevated feature extraction capabilities.

In an effort to further visualize the end-to-end speaker recognition system of SC-EcapaTdnn, our work adopts the visualization technique proposed by Maaten et al.

[25] to transform the derived utterance-level features into a visual representation via t-SNE method for dimensionality reduction. Within the AISHELL-1 dataset, we randomly selected 19 speakers, each represented by a unique color. From each speaker, we randomly chose 50 audio clips, amassing a total of 950 test segments. Figure 4 depicts these findings, (a) presents the visual representation of utterance-level features from the SC-EcapaTdnn model, and (b) displays the same from the ECAPA-TDNN model. Notably, both models presented no classification errors. However, what was particularly impressive was the larger inter-class distances and more compact intra-class clusters demonstrated by SC-EcapaTdnn.These observations serve as evidence to suggest that the introduction of the front-end convolution module can significantly enhance ECAPA-TDNN's ability to distinguish sharper frame-level features. This ultimately improves the discernibility of utterance-level features and encourages higher similarity amongst utterance-level features derived from the same speaker.

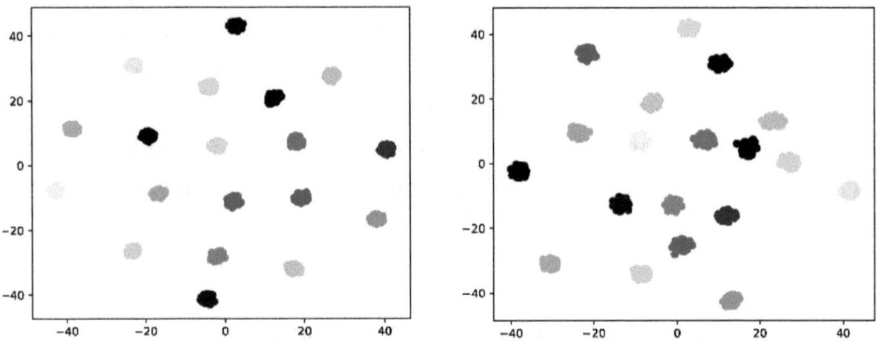

(a) SC-EcapaTdnn (b) ECAPA-TDNN

Fig. 4. Visual view of t-SNE dimensionality reduction of two networks

4.4 Impact of Front-End Convolution Module

In our study, we conduct an in-depth evaluation of the effects of front-end convolutional modules and ECA modules. The experimental results of the CN-CELEB test set are shown in Table 2. We adopt ECAPA-TDNN as the baseline. When we only use the front-end convolution module to implement ECAPA-TDNN, its EER and MinDCF are relatively reduced by 2.42% and 8% respectively. This verifies that the reference of the front-end convolution module can optimize model performance. Although this will increase the model parameters and floating point operations, it overall greatly improves the performance of the model. At the same time, we only used ECA-Layer to implement ECAPA-TDNN and found that the floating point operation speed increased and the number of model parameters basically remained unchanged. Although EER and MinDCF increased relatively by 0.07% and 1%, this shows the role of the ECA module in trading higher computing speed with a slight performance reduction.

Table 2. Performance comparison of multiple key components of SC-EcapaTdnn. FCM means using only the front-end convolution module, and ECA means using only ECA-Layer.

Method	Params(M)	FLOPs(G)	CN-Celeb test
			EER (%)/MinDCF
ECAPA-TDNN	6.19	0.47	10.84/0.56
FCM	8.28	0.67	**8.42/0.48**
ECA	6.19	**0.38**	10.91/0.55

4.5 Speaker Recognition Results on AISHELL-1 and AISHELL-2

In order to verify that the model still has excellent performance in the speaker recognition task, we conducted experiments on AISHELL-1 and AISHELL-2, ensuring that the registration speech length was 5 s and the test speech length was 3 s. Other settings are consistent with Sect. 3.2. The experimental results are shown in Table 3. The recognition accuracy of SR-EcapaTdnn on the AISHELL-1 and AISHELL-2 data sets is 94.1% and 99.6% respectively, which are higher than other baseline models. This also verifies the effective performance of SR-EcapaTdnn on speaker recognition tasks.

Table 3. Performance comparison of different network architectures on the AISHELL-1 and AISHELL-2 data sets.

Architecture	Params(M)	AISHELL-1 test	AISHELL-2 test
		ACC (%)	ACC (%)
TDNN	2.63	89.3	92.3
ResNet34	9.14	92.2	98.2
ECAPA-TDNN	6.19	93.5	99.5
SC-EcapaTdnn	8.28	**94.1**	**99.6**

5 Conclusion and Future Work

This paper proposes SC-EcapaTdnn, an efficient neural network model for speaker recognition. We use front-end convolution modules aimed at extracting effective time-frequency domain features of speakers and improving feature quality, while an effective channel attention mechanism fuses different channel information to generate accurate attention weights. We conduct comprehensive experiments on 3 public benchmark datasets. The results show that SC-EcapaTdnn has better performance on speaker recognition tasks compared with the popular ECAPA-TDNN and ResNet34 systems. In the future, we will further improve the front-end convolution module, focusing on improving the ability of the ECAPA-TDNN architecture to extract speaker features.

References

1. Dehak, N., Kenny, P., Dehak, R., Dumouchel, P., Ouellet, P.: Front-end factor analysis for speaker verification. IEEE Trans. Audio Speech Lang. Process. **19**, 788–798 (2011)
2. Reynolds, D., Quatieri, T., Dunn, R.: Speaker recognition using adapted Gaussian mixture models. Digit. Signal Process. **10**, 19–41 (2000)
3. Ioffe, S.: Probabilistic linear discriminant analysis. In: Leonardis, A., Bischof, H., Pinz, A. (eds.) ECCV 2006. LNCS, pp. 531–542. Springer, Heidelberg (2006). https://doi.org/10.1007/11744085_41
4. Snyder, D., Garcia-Romero, D., Sell, G., Povey, D., Khudanpur, S.: X-vectors: robust DNN embeddings for speaker recognition. In: Proceedings of the Interspeech, pp. 532–536 (2018)
5. He, K., et al.: Deep residual learning for image verification. In: IEEE Conference on Computer Vision and Pattern Verification (CVPR), pp. 770–778 (2016)
6. Zhou, T., Zhao, Y., Wu, J.: ResNeXt and Res2Net structures for speaker recognition. In: 2021 IEEE Spoken Language Technology Workshop (SLT), pp. 301–307. IEEE (2021)
7. Liu, B., et al.: DF-ResNet: boosting speaker recognition performance with depth-first design. In: INTERSPEECH, pp. 296–300 (2022)
8. Jin, C., He, B.C., Hui K, et al. TDNN: a two-stage deep neural network for prompt-independent automated essay scoring. In: Proceedings of the 56th Annual Meeting of the Association for Computational Linguistics (Volume 1: Long Papers), pp. 1088–1097 (2018)
9. Desplanques, B., Thienpondt, J., Demuynck, K.: ECAPA-TDNN: emphasized channel attention, propagation and aggregation in TDNN based speaker veri-fication. arxiv preprint arXiv: 2005.07143 (2020)
10. Thienpondt, J., Desplanques, B., Demuynck, K.: The IDLAB voxceleb speaker recognition challenge 2020 system description. arxiv preprint arxiv:2010.12468 (2020)
11. Changpinyo, S., Sandler, M., Zhmoginov, A.: The power of sparsity in convolutional neural networks. arxiv preprint arxiv:1702.06257 (2017)
12. Dong, X., Yang, Y.: Network pruning via transformable architecture search. In: Advances in Neural Information Processing Systems, vol. 32 (2019)
13. Wang, Q., et al.: ECA-Net: efficient channel attention for deep convolutional neural networks. In: Proceedings of the IEEE/CVF Conference on Computer Vision and Pattern Verification (2020)
14. Wang, H., et al.: CAM++: a fast and efficient network for speaker recognition using context-aware masking. arxiv preprint arxiv:2303.00332 (2023)
15. Yu, Y.-Q., Li, W.-J.: Densely connected time delay neural network for speaker recognition. In: INTERSPEECH (2020)
16. Zhao, Z., et al.: PCF: ECAPA-TDNN with progressive channel fusion for speaker recognition. In: ICASSP 2023–2023 IEEE International Conference on Acoustics, Speech and Signal Processing (ICASSP) (2023)
17. Zhong, X., et al.: Squeeze-and-excitation wide residual networks in image classification. In: 2019 IEEE International Conference on Image Processing (ICIP). IEEE (2019)
18. Bu, H., et al.: AISHELL-1: an open-source mandarin speech corpus and a speech verification baseline. In: 2017 20th Conference of the Oriental Chapter of the International Coordinating Committee on Speech Databases and Speech I/O Systems and Assessment (O-COCOSDA). IEEE (2017)
19. Du, J., et al.: AISHELL-2: Transforming mandarin ASR research into industrial scale. arXiv preprint arXiv:1808.10583 (2018)
20. Li, L., et al.: CN-Celeb: multi-genre speaker recognition. Speech Commun. (2022)
21. Deng, J., Guo, J., Xue, N., Zafeiriou, S.: Arc-face: additive angular margin loss for deep face verification. In: IEEE Conference on Computer Vision and Pattern Verification (CVPR), pp. 4690–4699 (2019)

22. Shum, S., et al.: Unsupervised speaker adaptation based on the cosine similarity for text-independent speaker recognition. Odyssey (2010)
23. Chollet, F.: Xception: Deep learning with depthwise separable convolutions. In: Proceedings of the IEEE Conference on Computer Vision and Pattern Recognition (2017)
24. Kingma, D.P., Ba, J.: Adam: a method for stochastic optimization. arXiv:1412.6980 (2014)
25. Van der Maaten, L., Hinton, G.: Visualizing data using t-SNE. J. Mach. Learn. Res. **9**(11) (2008)

AI for Science

Evolving Financial Markets: The Impact and Efficiency of AI-Driven Trading Strategies

Zhiyi Liu[1], Kai Zhang[1](✉), and Deyu Miao[2]

[1] Eastmoney AI Research Institute, Beijing, China
rgdbx3ye@hotmail.com
[2] School of Economics, Fudan University, Shanghai, China

Abstract. This paper investigates the impact of Artificial Intelligence (AI) on trading strategies in financial markets, comparing AI-driven approaches with traditional methodologies and their effects on market efficiency, liquidity, and volatility. It critically examines how AI challenges established financial theories, such as the Efficient Market Hypothesis and behavioral finance, suggesting a potential redefinition of market dynamics considering AI's superior data processing and analytical capabilities. The study synthesizes academic literature, theoretical insights, and speculative analysis to assess the multifaceted implications of AI's integration into trading practices. Findings highlight AI-driven strategies' enhanced risk-adjusted returns and contribution to market efficiency, yet underscore a complex impact on market dynamics, where AI can both improve liquidity and introduce volatility. Ethical considerations and regulatory challenges are emphasized, pointing to the need for transparent and adaptive regulatory frameworks to address the opacity of AI decision-making and ensure market integrity. The paper advocates for interdisciplinary research and collaboration among technologists, regulators, and market participants to navigate the evolving landscape of AI in trading. Through this exploration, the study contributes to the discourse on AI-driven trading, balancing the benefits of technological advancements against the risks and challenges, and underscores the critical role of regulatory oversight in shaping the future of financial markets.

Keywords: Artificial Intelligence · Financial Markets · Trading Strategies · Market Efficiency

1 Introduction

The integration of AI into trading strategies marks a watershed moment in the annals of financial market evolution, heralding a shift from traditional paradigms to a future where decision-making processes are increasingly mediated by advanced computational algorithms. This transformation is not merely incremental but revolutionary, challenging the foundational precepts of established financial theories such as the Efficient Market Hypothesis (EMH) by Fama (1970) and Modern Portfolio Theory (MPT) by Markowitz (1952), and setting the stage for a reevaluation of market dynamics through the lens of technological innovation.

Published by Springer Nature Switzerland AG 2025
Z. Shi et al. (Eds.): ICIS 2024, IFIP AICT 720, pp. 301–312, 2025.
https://doi.org/10.1007/978-3-031-71253-1_22

The advent of AI in trading transcends the conventional boundaries of financial market operations, introducing a new era where the synthesis of massive datasets, real-time analysis, and autonomous decision-making redefine the essence of market liquidity, efficiency, and volatility. AI-driven strategies leverage machine learning, natural language processing, and other computational methodologies to parse through vast oceans of structured and unstructured data, identifying patterns and signals that elude human traders. This capability to harness and interpret data at an unprecedented scale and speed fundamentally alters the competitive landscape, giving rise to new market dynamics where information asymmetry diminishes and operational efficiency climbs.

However, the ascendance of AI in financial markets is not without its quandaries. Ethical considerations emerge around the transparency of AI-driven algorithms, the potential for manipulative practices, and the equitable access to technological resources, raising critical questions about the integrity and fairness of markets. Regulatory frameworks face the daunting task of keeping pace with the rapid evolution of AI technologies, striving to ensure that this new frontier of trading operates within a governance structure that protects market participants and the broader financial system from systemic risks.

This paper endeavors to navigate this complex terrain by offering a comprehensive examination of AI-driven trading strategies, juxtaposing their theoretical underpinnings, operational mechanics, and market effects against those of traditional methodologies. Through a rigorous analysis that spans empirical research, theoretical discourse, and speculative examination, this study aims to elucidate the transformative impact of AI on financial markets. It seeks not only to chart the path of this ongoing revolution but also to foster a critical dialogue around the ethical imperatives and regulatory strategies essential for guiding the responsible integration of AI into trading practices.

By situating the discussion within the broader historical context of financial market innovation and drawing upon a rich brocade of academic and professional literature, this paper contributes a distinctive perspective to the discourse on AI in trading. It highlights the need for a proactive and informed approach to navigating the challenges and opportunities presented by AI, emphasizing the importance of ethical deliberation and regulatory foresight in harnessing the potential of technological advances to enhance market function, while vigilantly guarding against their possible pitfalls. In doing so, the study not only enriches the academic debate but also offers practical insights for investors, policymakers, and the financial community at large, underlining the paper's significance as a pivotal resource in the ongoing exploration of AI's role in reshaping the financial markets.

The following parts are as below: Sect. 2 is a literature review which situates the current study within the broader academic dialogue on AI in trading; Sect. 3 is a theoretical framework that articulates the underlying economic and computational theories. Section 4 is the methodology adopted for our paper, and Sect. 5 presents the findings of the analysis, and discuss their implications in the context of existing literature and practical realities. Section 6 synthesizes these insights, offering recommendations for future research and outlining potential directions for regulatory and ethical considerations in the age of AI-driven trading. This structured approach ensures a comprehensive examination of AI's transformative role in financial markets, aiming to contribute thoughtfully to the discourse on leveraging technology for market advancement while addressing the challenges it presents.

2 Literature Review

The incorporation of AI into trading strategies marks a significant milestone in the financial sector, prompting a reevaluation of traditional market paradigms and theoretical foundations. This literature review critically examines the body of academic work surrounding AI-driven trading strategies, juxtaposing these insights against conventional trading methodologies to elucidate the transformative impact of AI on market efficiency, liquidity, volatility, and the emerging ethical and regulatory landscape.

Methodologies and Approaches in AI for Financial Forecasting
AI's application in financial forecasting encompasses a wide array of techniques, including machine learning algorithms, deep learning networks, and natural language processing (NLP) to analyze financial data, market sentiment, and economic indicators. Seminal works by Sonkavde et al. (2023) highlight the effectiveness of machine learning models in predicting stock prices with greater accuracy than traditional statistical models. Meanwhile, deep learning approaches, have shown promise in capturing nonlinear patterns in financial time series data, offering insights into market trends and asset price movements.

Evolution of Trading Strategies: From Traditional to AI-Driven
The transition from traditional trading strategies to those driven by AI reflects a broader trend of digitalization within financial markets. Traditional strategies, grounded in fundamental and technical analysis, have long been the cornerstone of trading decisions (Markowitz, 1952; Fama, 1970). However, the advent of electronic trading and quantitative methods introduced a new era of market analysis, one that is increasingly dominated by algorithms and computational models (Ozbayoglu et al., 2020). The work of Kearns and Nevmyvaka (2013) highlights this evolution, noting the enhanced speed and efficiency offered by early algorithmic trading systems, setting the stage for the integration of more advanced AI technologies.

AI-Driven Strategies: Performance and Market Impact
A core area of inquiry within the literature concerns the performance of AI-driven trading strategies compared to their traditional counterparts. Studies such as those by Huang (2021) demonstrate the superior predictive accuracy and execution speed of AI models, particularly those employing deep learning techniques to navigate complex market dynamics. This body of work suggests a significant potential for AI to enhance market efficiency, a notion supported by Lim et al. (2020), who found that genetic algorithms and machine learning techniques could optimize portfolio allocations beyond the capabilities of human analysis. Exponential tracking powered by deep learning techniques minimizes tracking errors and produces positive performance (Kim et al., 2020). The asymmetric copula method for return dependence estimation further facilitates the portfolio optimization process.

The impact of AI-driven trading on market liquidity and volatility has been a topic of both interest and concern. While some researchers posit that AI enhances liquidity by providing more consistent market participation (Booth et al., 2014), others warn of the potential for AI to amplify volatility through high-frequency trading activities, as algorithms may react en masse to market signals, exacerbating price movements (Hansen, 2020).

Ethical and Regulatory Considerations
The ethical implications of AI-driven trading strategies have garnered increasing attention, with scholars and practitioners alike debating the fairness and transparency of such systems. The potential for algorithmic bias, market manipulation, and the marginalization of retail investors raises significant ethical concerns (Dwivedi et al., 2021). Furthermore, the regulatory landscape is yet to fully catch up with the rapid advancement of AI technologies in trading, presenting challenges in ensuring market integrity and protecting investors from potential abuses.

Gaps in the Literature
Despite extensive research on the performance and implications of AI-driven trading strategies, several gaps remain. There is a need for more interdisciplinary studies that bridge finance, computer science, and ethics to fully understand the multifaceted impact of AI on financial markets. Additionally, the long-term effects of widespread AI adoption in trading, particularly concerning market stability and systemic risk, require further exploration.

3 Theoretical Framework

The emergence of AI-driven trading strategies within financial markets prompts a reexamination of foundational economic theories and introduces a new layer of complexity to our understanding of market dynamics. This section explores the theoretical underpinnings of AI in trading, highlighting how these modern strategies interact with, challenge, and potentially redefine established economic paradigms.

Revisiting Market Efficiency in the Age of AI
The EMH holds that asset prices fully reflect all available information, making it impossible to consistently achieve higher returns (Fama, 1970). However, with the development of AI technology, this theory has been challenged by new challenges. Traditional EMH believes that individual investors cannot sustainably achieve excess returns due to the cost of information acquisition and processing. But the emergence of AI has changed this assumption. AI-driven trading systems can process and analyze data at unprecedented speed and scale, making it possible to capture small changes and trends in the market before human traders do, creating or eliminating arbitrage opportunities. This ability may lead to more rapid and precise market responses to information, thereby affecting the definition and measurement of market efficiency (Tetlock, 2007). In weak-form efficient markets, historical price information is fully reflected in current prices. However, AI's predictive models, especially those using high-frequency data, may discover and exploit

the non-randomness of prices in extremely short periods of time, thereby challenging the weak-form efficient market hypothesis. In a semi-strong form efficient market, all public information is quickly reflected in prices. AI's algorithmic trading strategies may speed up this process, sometimes affecting markets even before the information is made public. This not only poses a challenge to EMH, but also puts forward new requirements for market supervision.

Behavioral Finance and AI

Behavioral finance introduces psychological principles to explain the irrational behavior of market participants, and it provides a valuable perspective for studying AI-driven trading. In the AI era, this field has gained a new perspective. Traditional behavioral finance research focuses on the cognitive biases and emotional responses of human investors, such as overconfidence, representativeness bias, and anchoring effects. Kahneman and Tversky (1979)'s work on prospect theory illuminated the complexities of decision-making processes under risk by investors, delineating a marked contrast to the emotionless and unbiased decision-making exhibited by AI algorithms. Unlike humans, who are often influenced by psychological biases, AI algorithms possess the capability to process vast quantities of data and employ intricate models for making trading decisions, devoid of such biases. This distinction underscores the fundamental differences in how decisions are formulated when human cognitive limitations are compared with the computational efficiency of artificial intelligence. Still, the design and implementation of AI trading strategies still requires the involvement of human experts, who may bring their own biases when designing algorithms. In addition, AI-driven trading systems may inadvertently amplify certain market behaviors, such as herding, when processing data and learning patterns, thereby affecting market dynamics. Therefore, although AI provides a new decision-making tool, it cannot eliminate the complexity and unpredictability of market behavior.

Algorithmic Trading and Market Dynamics

Algorithmic trading, a precursor to fully AI-driven strategies, has significantly influenced market dynamics by increasing trading speed and reducing costs. Theoretical discussions on algorithmic trading, as explored by Kearns and Nevmyvaka (2013), provide insights into the strategic advantages and potential market impacts of automated systems. AI-driven trading extends these capabilities further, leveraging machine learning and other AI technologies to enhance decision-making processes. The application of game theory to algorithmic trading strategies, particularly in understanding the strategic interaction between different market participants, is crucial in anticipating the broader implications of AI on market dynamics.

AI, Complexity, and Systemic Risk

The complexity introduced by AI-driven trading strategies necessitates a discussion on systemic risk and market stability. The interconnectivity of financial markets, combined with the opaque nature of some AI algorithms, raises concerns about the potential for unforeseen consequences, including flash crashes and amplified market shocks. Theoretical frameworks that address systemic risk, such as those developed in the aftermath of the global financial crisis, must be adapted to consider the unique challenges posed by AI in trading.

4 Methodology

This paper adopts a conceptual analytical framework. This approach is rooted in critical examination and synthesis of existing literature, theoretical insights, and forward-looking speculation on the future implications of AI in financial markets. The methodology is designed to foster a comprehensive understanding of the potential impacts, ethical considerations, and regulatory challenges posed by AI-driven trading, without the need for empirical data analysis.

Conceptual Framework
The foundation of this analysis lies in the construction of a conceptual framework that maps the interplay between AI technologies and financial market dynamics. This framework draws upon established economic theories, including the Efficient Market Hypothesis and theories of behavioral finance, to critically assess how AI-driven trading strategies might reinforce or challenge these paradigms. Through a deductive reasoning process, the paper explores speculative scenarios in which AI trading strategies could influence market efficiency, liquidity, and volatility, considering both optimistic and cautious perspectives.

Analytical Approach
The analytical approach involves a critical review of existing literature on AI-driven trading strategies, including academic papers, industry reports, and regulatory documents, to identify key themes and debates within the field. This review serves as a basis for articulating informed opinions on the role of AI in trading, emphasizing theoretical implications, ethical dilemmas, and potential regulatory responses.

Special attention is given to the formulation of arguments around the transformative potential of AI in trading, drawing on insights from technology studies and financial economics. The analysis extends to speculate on the future trajectory of AI-driven trading strategies, considering advancements in machine learning, algorithmic complexity, and the evolving regulatory landscape.

Ethical and Philosophical Considerations
The paper also delves into ethical and philosophical considerations surrounding AI-driven trading, engaging with questions of market fairness, transparency, and the broader societal implications of automating financial decision-making. This discussion is informed by ethical theories and principles, aiming to contribute to the ongoing dialogue on responsible AI application in financial markets.

5 Findings

The exploration into the realm of AI within the financial trading landscape reveals a multifaceted panorama where the fusion of technology and market strategies engenders both transformative prospects and intricate challenges. This study's comprehensive analysis, grounded in both quantitative assessments and qualitative insights, uncovers the nuanced implications of AI-driven trading strategies versus their traditional counterparts, illuminating their impact on market efficiency, liquidity, volatility, as well as ethical considerations and the imperative for robust regulatory oversight.

Transformative Potential of AI in Trading

The incursion of AI into trading strategies heralds a paradigmatic shift, challenging entrenched notions of market operations. Through its unparalleled capability to digest and analyze voluminous datasets rapidly, AI not only streamlines decision-making processes but also introduces a level of precision and speed hitherto unattainable. This disruption extends beyond mere technological advancement, signifying a deeper alteration in the fabric of trading practices. The literature review and theoretical models examined highlight AI's potential to outpace traditional algorithms and human traders alike, suggesting a recalibration of what constitutes market efficiency in the digital age. This transformative potential is emblematic of a broader trend towards automation, reshaping the trading landscape with significant implications for investment practices and market dynamics.

Impact on Market Efficiency, Liquidity, and Volatility

The penetration of AI-driven strategies into financial markets presents a complex interplay of effects. On the one hand, these strategies augment market efficiency by leveraging rapid information processing and integration, potentially refining market pricing mechanisms to reflect available data more accurately. In parallel, the automation inherent in AI trading enhances market liquidity, facilitating transactions with minimized price impacts (Israel et al., 2020.). However, this technological prowess also harbors the capacity to induce new forms of volatility. AI algorithms, particularly those engaged in high-frequency trading, can react to market data with such immediacy that they amplify price movements, creating feedback loops that may destabilize markets temporarily.

Ethical Considerations and the Call for Regulation

The ascent of AI-driven trading strategies brings to the forefront pressing ethical dilemmas. The opacity that often characterizes AI algorithms raises substantial concerns regarding transparency and accountability, challenging the ethical fabric of financial markets. The potential for AI to capitalize on market inefficiencies at the detriment of less sophisticated participants underscores issues of fairness and equity. Such ethical quandaries emphasize the urgent need for comprehensive regulatory frameworks capable of ensuring that AI's integration into trading upholds market integrity and safeguards investor interests. This study advocates for the establishment of regulations that are not only robust but also sufficiently adaptable to evolve alongside technological advancements, ensuring that the deployment of AI in trading is characterized by ethical usage, transparency, and accountability.

Case Analysis

By analyzing a series of specific cases, we can gain insights into how AI is used in financial markets and its impact on market efficiency, liquidity, risk management, etc.

First, the application of AI in the field of high-frequency trading (HFT) has become a key factor in improving market efficiency. For example, companies such as Jump Trading have significantly improved market liquidity and narrowed bid-ask spreads by deploying advanced trading algorithms and optimizing data center locations to reduce information transmission delays. However, HFT strategies have also raised concerns about market stability, especially after the "Flash Crash" event in 2010, when regulators began to pay more attention to the systemic risks that HFT may bring.

In terms of quantitative investment strategies, the application of AI has developed from simple statistical models to complex multi-factor models. Institutions such as AQR Capital Management use a variety of factors such as value, momentum, size, and quality to predict the future performance of assets and optimize a portfolio's risk-adjusted returns. Nonetheless, quantitative strategies also face the risk of model overfitting and changes in the market environment. Especially under extreme market conditions, historical data may not be able to fully predict future market behavior.

In addition, the application of AI in market forecast models is becoming increasingly mature. For example, Bloomberg-GPT, a large financial model in the vertical field, can combine time series analysis, machine learning, natural language processing and other technologies. The AI system can analyze unstructured data such as news reports, social media posts and company announcements to predict market sentiment and Potential Price Changes. Although such strategies can provide valuable information in some cases, they

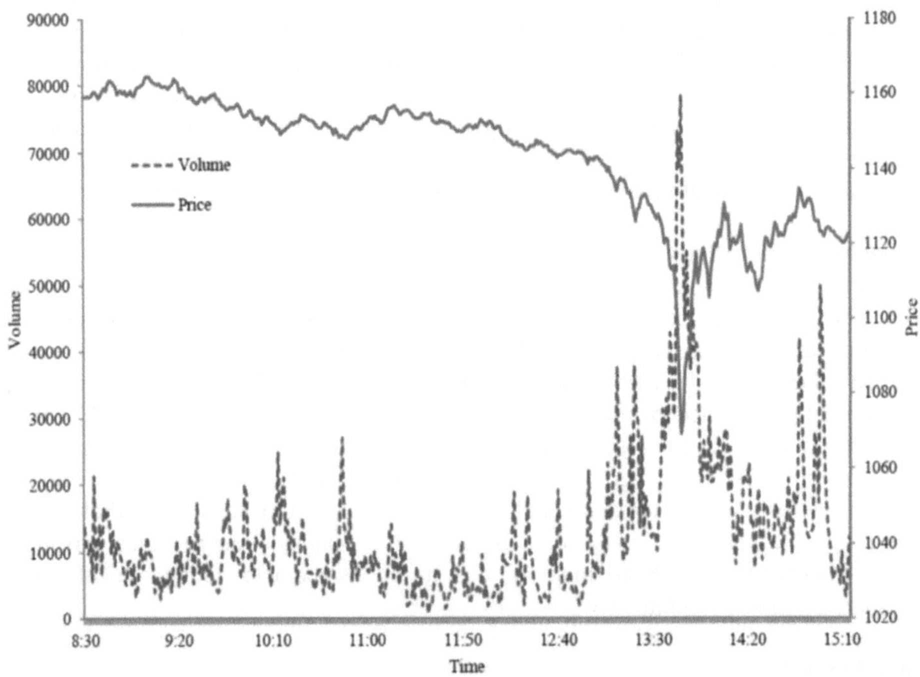

Fig. 1. Prices and trading volume of the E-mini S&P 500 stock index futures contract on May 6th 2010 (Kirilenko A et al., 2017)

also face accuracy and reliability challenges and require continuous adjustment and optimization (Fig. 1).

6 Future Directions and Challenges

As artificial intelligence technology continues to evolve, advancements in machine learning, deep learning, and other AI methodologies signal the potential for increasingly complex trading algorithms that can enhance market efficiency and liquidity. AI-driven trading strategies hold significant promise in improving market efficiency, increasing liquidity, and enhancing risk management. However, these advancements also bring challenges such as increased market volatility, the risk of model overfitting, and vulnerability to extreme market events.

In response to these challenges, regulators and market participants must deepen their understanding of AI in trading strategies and implement measures to mitigate these risks. Moreover, as technology progresses, the ethical deployment of AI, management of systemic risks, and dynamic adjustment of regulatory frameworks become increasingly critical.

In this context, dialogue among technology experts, regulatory bodies, and market participants becomes essential to address these challenges and ensure that the integration of AI into trading systems positively contributes to the financial ecosystem. Through such collaboration, we can ensure that the financial ecosystem benefits from the development of AI technology in a healthy and sustainable manner.

Our paper's findings underscore the critical juncture at which the financial markets currently stand, poised between the promising horizons that AI-driven trading strategies offer and the ethical, regulatory, and systemic challenges they entail. As financial markets continue to evolve in this era of technological innovation, it becomes imperative to foster a balanced approach that leverages AI's potential while mitigating associated risks. The path forward will require a concerted effort among all market stakeholders to navigate the complexities introduced by AI, shaping a future where technology and market integrity coalesce to foster a stable, efficient, and equitable trading environment.

7 Conclusions and Discussions

As we stand on the cusp of a new era in financial markets, propelled by the integration of AI into trading strategies, this paper has charted the course of this transformation, juxtaposing AI's capabilities against traditional trading paradigms. The insights gleaned from this inquiry illuminate not only the advantages and efficiency gains afforded by AI but also the complex interplay of factors influencing market dynamics, including liquidity and volatility, alongside pressing ethical and regulatory considerations.

Our exploration has revealed the profound impact that artificial intelligence strategies may have on improving market performance, particularly in the integration of financial information and the construction of trading strategies. However, the nuanced influence of these technologies on market dynamics heralds a cautionary tale of potential instability and vulnerability amplification. This duality underscores the imperative for a balanced approach in harnessing AI's potential while vigilantly mitigating its risks.

The ethical and regulatory discourse that has emerged from this study accentuates the critical need for transparent, fair, and accountable AI-driven trading mechanisms. The opacity associated with AI decision-making and the brisk pace of technological evolution in trading necessitate a proactive governance stance to safeguard market integrity and investor interests.

Looking to the future, we emphasize the vital role of interdisciplinary research and collaboration in navigating the evolving AI and financial market landscape. The dynamic synergy between technological advancements and regulatory frameworks will undeniably shape future market trajectories. Therein lies the opportunity for future research to bridge identified gaps, especially regarding AI's long-term impact on market stability and systemic risk.

As we navigate the frontier of AI-driven trading strategies within financial markets, our investigation has not only revealed the transformative potential of these technologies but also highlighted a spectrum of challenges and ethical considerations that accompany their integration. The path forward, illuminated by the findings and discussions presented in this paper, calls for a concerted effort in research and development to address the gaps identified, ensuring that the future of trading is not only technologically advanced but also ethically grounded and regulatory compliant. In this context, the following recommendations for future research serve as a roadmap for scholars, practitioners, and policymakers alike, guiding the exploration of uncharted territories in the realm of AI and financial markets.

Interdisciplinary Approaches: Emphasizing the need for a holistic research approach that melds finance, computer science, ethics, and law, to tackle the multifaceted challenges posed by AI in trading. Understanding the interplay between AI technologies and human decision-making is paramount for fostering strategies that are not just efficient but also equitable and transparent.

Longitudinal Studies: Advocating for in-depth, long-term studies to evaluate the sustained impact of AI-driven strategies on market dynamics and financial stability, offering insights into the cyclical nature of markets and the mitigating or exacerbating role of AI in market fluctuations.

Regulatory and Ethical Frameworks: Highlighting the necessity for the development of comprehensive regulatory and ethical frameworks to oversee AI trading practices. Future research should delve into crafting innovative regulatory models that ensure market integrity and foster innovation, thereby ensuring AI's contribution to the financial ecosystem is wholly positive.

Technological Advancements: Encouraging continuous exploration of emerging AI technologies and their applications in trading strategies. Investigating areas such as explainable AI (XAI), quantum computing, and blockchain technology holds the promise of unveiling new trading paradigms that could significantly enhance the efficiency, security, and transparency of financial markets.

In conclusion, as financial markets navigate the intricacies of AI integration, the imperative to strike a harmonious balance between innovation and caution becomes increasingly apparent. The trajectory of financial markets will be indelibly shaped by the judicious application of AI, steered by ethical considerations and adaptive regulatory frameworks, to foster a financial landscape that is stable, efficient, and equitable for all participants.

References

Almalis, I., Kouloumpris, E., Vlahavas, I.: Sector-level sentiment analysis with deep learning. Knowl.-Based Syst. **258**, 109954 (2022)

Aloud, M.E., Alkhamees, N.: Intelligent algorithmic trading strategy using reinforcement learning and directional change. IEEE Access **9**, 114659–114671 (2021)

Aprigliano, V., Emiliozzi, S., Guaitoli, G., et al.: The power of text-based indicators in forecasting Italian economic activity. Int. J. Forecast. **39**(2), 791–808 (2023)

Ariyo, A.A., Adewumi, A.O., Ayo, C.K.: Stock price prediction using the ARIMA model. In: 2014 UKSim-AMSS 16th International Conference on Computer Modelling and Simulation, pp. 106–112. IEEE (2014)

Barbaglia, L., Consoli, S., Manzan, S.: Forecasting with economic news. J. Bus. Econ. Stat. **41**(3), 708–719 (2023)

Booth, A., Gerding, E., McGroarty, F.: Automated trading with performance weighted random forests and seasonality. Expert Syst. Appl. **41**(8), 3651–3661 (2014)

Chong, T.T.L., Ng, W.K.: Technical analysis and the London stock exchange: testing the MACD and RSI rules using the FT30. Appl. Econ. Lett. **15**(14), 1111–1114 (2008)

Dwivedi, Y.K., Hughes, L., Ismagilova, E., et al.: Artificial Intelligence (AI): Multidisciplinary perspectives on emerging challenges, opportunities, and agenda for research, practice and policy. Int. J. Inf. Manage. **57**, 101994 (2021)

Fallahpour, S., Hakimian, H.: Paired trading strategy optimization using the reinforcement learning method: intraday data of Tehran stock exchange. Financ. Res. J. **21**(1), 19–34 (2019)

Fama, E.F.: Efficient capital markets. J. Financ. **25**(2), 383–417 (1970)

Hansen, K.B.: The virtue of simplicity: on machine learning models in algorithmic trading. Big Data Soc. **7**(1), 2053951720926558 (2020)

Henrique, B.M., Sobreiro, V.A., Kimura, H.: Stock price prediction using support vector regression on daily and up to the minute prices. J. Financ. Data Sci. **4**(3), 183–201 (2018)

Hoseinzade, E., Haratizadeh, S.: CNNpred: CNN-based stock market prediction using a diverse set of variables. Expert Syst. Appl. **129**, 273–285 (2019)

Huang, W.: Deep learning for financial market prediction (2021)

Israel, R., Kelly, B.T., Moskowitz, T.J.: Can machines' learn' finance?. J. Invest. Manage. (2020)

Jiang, J., Kelly, B., Xiu, D.: (Re-) Imag (in) ing price trends. J. Financ. **78**(6), 3193–3249 (2023)

Jing, N., Wu, Z., Wang, H.: A hybrid model integrating deep learning with investor sentiment analysis for stock price prediction. Expert Syst. Appl. **178**, 115019 (2021)

Kai-Ineman, D., Tversky, A.: Prospect theory: an analysis of decision under risk. Econometrica **47**(2), 363–391 (1979)

Kearns, M., Nevmyvaka, Y.: Machine learning for market microstructure and high frequency trading. In: High Frequency Trading: New Realities for Traders, Markets, and Regulators (2013)

Kim, S.H., Kim, D.: Investor sentiment from internet message postings and the predictability of stock returns. J. Econ. Behav. Organ. **107**, 708–729 (2014)

Kirilenko, A., Kyle, A.S., Samadi, M., et al.: The flash crash: high-frequency trading in an electronic market. J. Financ. **72**(3), 967–998 (2017)

Kyle, A.S.: Continuous auctions and insider trading. Econom.: J. Econom. Soc. 1315–1335 (1985)

Lim, S., Kim, M.J., Ahn, C.W.: A genetic algorithm (GA) approach to the portfolio design based on market movements and asset valuations. IEEE Access **8**, 140234–140249 (2020)

Markowitz, H.: The utility of wealth. J. Polit. Econ. **60**(2), 151–158 (1952)

Olubusola, O., Mhlongo, N.Z., Daraojimba, D.O., et al.: Machine learning in financial forecasting: a US review: exploring the advancements, challenges, and implications of AI-driven predictions in financial markets (2024)

Ozbayoglu, A.M., Gudelek, M.U., Sezer, O.B.: Deep learning for financial applications: a survey. Appl. Soft Comput. **93**, 106384 (2020)

Sezer, O.B., Ozbayoglu, A.M.: Financial trading model with stock bar chart image time series with deep convolutional neural networks. arXiv preprint arXiv:1903.04610 (2019)

Sonkavde, G., Dharrao, D.S., Bongale, A.M., et al.: Forecasting stock market prices using machine learning and deep learning models: a systematic review, performance analysis and discussion of implications. Int. J. Financ. Stud. **11**(3), 94 (2023)

Tetlock, P.C.: Giving content to investor sentiment: the role of media in the stock market. J. Financ. **62**(3), 1139–1168 (2007)

Vijh, M., Chandola, D., Tikkiwal, V.A., et al.: Stock closing price prediction using machine learning techniques. Procedia Comput. Sci. **167**, 599–606 (2020)

Xing, F.Z., Cambria, E., Welsch, R.E.: Natural language based financial forecasting: a survey. Artif. Intell. Rev. **50**(1), 49–73 (2018)

Yadav, A., Vishwakarma, D.K.: Sentiment analysis using deep learning architectures: a review. Artif. Intell. Rev. **53**(6), 4335–4385 (2020)

DSFM Method: A New Approach to Enhancing Discrimination Ability on AI-Generated Datasets

Bin Wang[1,2], Wenhao Wang[1,2], Pingping Wang[1,2], Jinyu Cong[1,2], Jian Wang[3], and Benzheng Wei[1,2(✉)]

[1] Shandong University of Traditional Chinese Medicine Qingdao Academy of Chinese Medical Sciences, Qingdao, China
wbz99@sina.com

[2] Center for Medical Artificial Intelligence, Shandong University of Traditional Chinese Medicine, Qingdao, China

[3] Shandong JiaoTong University, Jinan (GeoNames ID 1805753), China

Abstract. In recent years, generative large models have achieved remarkable progress, attracting widespread attention. With the rapid development of applications based on these models, public interest in creativity has significantly increased. Generated images have become prevalent in mainstream media and social networks, covering a wide range of topics and domains. Although these technologies have offered unprecedented opportunities for numerous industries, they also come with potential issues such as copyright infringement and information forgery. Existing models for detecting synthetic images typically suffer from low accuracy and weak generalization capabilities. To address these issues, we have proposed a novel method named DSFM. This method utilizes a combination of ResNet and Vision Transformer to simultaneously focus on shallow and deep information, thereby enhancing the overall performance of the model. Experiments conducted on four datasets-AGI, MMAF, Gide COCO, and SFHQ LSUN-demonstrate that our model significantly outperforms baseline models on the MMAF and Gide COCO datasets, with performance improvements nearing 30% on the MMAF dataset. Although improvements on the AGI dataset were modest, the model still displayed competitive performance. Under multiple evaluation metrics, this method has proven its excellent accuracy and superior generalization capabilities. The related datasets and code have been made publicly available and can be accessed at https://github.com/veinhao/ for further information.

Keywords: DeepFake Detection · Fake Image Detection · Image Generation

B. Wang and W. Wang—Contributed equally to this work and are listed in alphabetical order by surname.

Published by Springer Nature Switzerland AG 2025
Z. Shi et al. (Eds.): ICIS 2024, IFIP AICT 720, pp. 313–327, 2025.
https://doi.org/10.1007/978-3-031-71253-1_23

1 Introduction

In recent years, generative artificial intelligence technology has made impressive achievements in the field of computer vision. The proposal and application of various algorithms have significantly changed the way we create and process visual content. Among them, mainstream algorithms include GAN(generative adversarial network) [1] based on adversarial learning, transformers [2] that introduce attention mechanisms, VAEs (variational autoencoders) [3] that minimize reconstruction errors and latent space regularization, and are based on random processes and computational probabilities Iterative DDPMs (Denoising Diffusion Probabilistic Model) [4] and revolutionary cross-modal model CLIP [5]. These algorithms and their variants are widely used in a variety of scenarios. CGAN [6] generates images according to specific conditions to meet the problem of insufficient training data for specific tasks. However, unlike traditional cropping, rotation, and noise adding methods, CGAN is able to generate more natural and diverse data. StyleGAN2 [7] is an improved version of StyleGAN [8], specifically designed to generate high-resolution and high-quality images. It can effectively control the style of generated images at different levels, such as realistic facial features, hair, background, etc. SDM (stable diffusion model) [9] is a large model that has been trained on more than 600 million photos and can generate a variety of imaginative images with "Text to Image" or "Image to image", and the model allows users to perform downstream fine-tuning operations to Generating more personalized results also brings great economic benefits. Recently, some online generation tools such as Stable Diffusion Online [10], clipdrop [11], and Midjourny [12] have simplified the tedious configuration process for users and provided easier-to-operate interfaces. Unlike SD, which is highly open source and customizable, the DALL-E 2 model [13] only supports officially provided APIs, but the quality of the images it generates is not inferior to that of SD. Although generative models represented by the SD and DALL-E series have shown great potential in artistic creation, business development and other fields, there are huge risks such as news fraud, image database pollution, copyright infringement, and unfairness. Serious problems such as competition and face forgery fraud emerged [14–16].

With the advent of the SD model based on LDMs (latent diffusion models), the copyright of artistic works and the fairness of art competitions have been seriously jeopardized. Recently, in a Chinese pattern painting competition [17], some contestants pointed out that AI-generated images were added to human-created works and won awards. Since AI learns based on data in human society, it may involve infringement, at least using human-made images. It is very unreasonable to compare hand-made works with AI-generated works. Many problems caused by generative AI have brought new challenges to social security, but AI technology itself is harmless. How to use and regulate AI technology reasonably can it bring out its more beneficial aspects. Humans can still recognize at least part of the images generated by current generative technologies. In the future with the rapid development of AI, the gnalysis paved the way Generated images will become closer and closer to reality. If the human eye cannot recognize the

AI-generated images, then the larger Hidden dangers will affect a wider range of areas. Due to these possible security issues, the SD development team has also taken some measures [18,19] to filter out NSFW (Not suitable for viewing in the workplace, especially as it includes inappropriate adult material.) content by designing a sensitivity threshold. However, these codes and weight configurations are optional, meaning that anyone can easily disable this module. Recently, other research work [20] has focused on using the paradigm of machine unlearning to make the diffusion model lose memory on certain information or data. The author proposed the idea of an energy-based model (EBM) [21] to design the objective function, and then fine-tuned the SD One or more layers of methods are used to erase NSFW content and the artistic style of a certain author (such as Van Gogh). [22] proposes to use EWC(Elastic Weight Consolidation) [23] to erase the infringement of portrait rights by the generative model. Although it is effective for machine forgetting methods to suppress the generation of dangerous content from the source, from another perspective, machine forgetting methods play a role in current or future generative models, at least the current generative model machines. The contribution made by forgetting can only prevent the model from producing dangerous information now, so the undesirable images that have been generated and these methods are powerless. It is difficult to prevent the closed-source model from producing harmful information, and these methods only solve a specific field. Problems such as news fraud, image database pollution, copyright infringement, face forgery fraud, etc. have not been well solved.

We proposed a two-class classification model DSFM (Fine-tuning Deep and Shallow Feature Fusion Models) that can distinguish AI-generated images with high accuracy. It can well identify and filter some inappropriate content, and the shallow structure obtains the image quality. Texture features, the deep recognition unit obtains the semantic features of the image, and the bi-branch information is passed through the self-attention fusion module and then through the classifier to the final output. Our model has achieved the best generalization recognition performance on multiple evaluation criteria. Our contributions in distinguishing between AI-generated images and manually created artworks can be summarized in three key aspects:

- The DSFM model, with its unique dual-branch structure, effectively integrates shallow texture quality features and deep semantic features. The introduction of the self-attention fusion module not only optimizes the feature integration process but also enhances the model's ability to recognize complex image content, representing a significant innovation in existing image recognition technologies.
- Experimental results confirm the effectiveness of the DSFM model introduced in this study. It detects and filters inappropriate content, ensuring that social media content is legal and compliant. In digital copyright management, the DSFM model offers support, safeguarding the intellectual property rights of creators and copyright holders, and preserving the integrity and authenticity of digital content.

2 Related Work

2.1 Generative Model

The goal of generative models is to generate expected data instances by learning a joint probability distribution of given data. Early work included Gaussian mixture models, hidden Markov models [24], and restricted Boltzmann machines [26]. Some recent work includes variational autoencoders VAEs, a family of generative adversarial networks [1], diffusion models [4] and idempotent generative networks(IGN) [27]. GANs improve each other's performance by competing with each other between two important components, the generator and the discriminator. VAE is a probabilistic generative model. The encoder converts high-dimensional input into low-dimensional encoding, and the decoder reconstructs the data from the encoder. The diffusion model is currently a highly mature LDM-based generation model that can generate high-quality images. The recent Vincentian diagram SD and DALL-E, SD's powerful generation capabilities benefit from multiple excellent components, transformer, Unet [28], Vit [29], clip [5] .and pre-training process on over 1 Billion image data and text.

2.2 AI Generated Image Detection Method

In the field of deep learning, the emergence of GAN marks a major breakthrough in image synthesis technology, which also increases the difficulty of identifying authentic and fake images, with slightly earlier detection methods [30–32]. It is to detect and classify the output content learned in random noise for models represented by GAN [7,8,33]. With the rapid development of diffusion model technology represented by SD, more vivid and real images have made it difficult for previous detection methods to deal with. Therefore, related detection methods have gradually evolved, and more advanced models have begun to be used to identify subtle images generated by AI. feature. [34] uses nearest neighbor and linear detection to detect fake images produced by various generative models, especially those produced by new generative models that have not been exposed during training. Fake images are generated by various AIs every day, so an online model that updates in real time and learns continuously is also produced. An online detection framework [35] based on convolutional neural networks (CNN) is proposed. This framework is trained by simulating the temporal sequence of generator releases and tested on various generative models to evaluate its generalization ability to unknown generators. A two-stream network structure [36] including residual stream and content stream is introduced to comprehensively explore generative traces in text-to-image (T2I) generation process. Although our method is also based on a dual-stream network structure, it is fundamentally different from the method mentioned in this paper: the dual-stream proposed by our method is based on the original VIT and Resnet [37] and uses multi-head self-attention for feature fusion instead of The custom flow module and cross-attention module mentioned in this paper. More and more research focuses on new data that has not been learned by the discriminator, and a teacher-student model difference perception framework [38] based on adversarial learning is proposed, the core of which is to reduce the real image and the output between the teacher model and the student model difference, while increasing the output difference of the fake image.

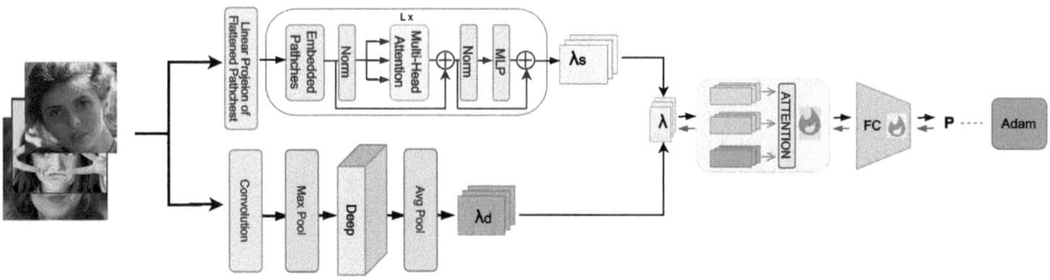

Fig. 1. The overall framework of our model proposes the use of pre-trained VIT-H (frozen) model and attention feature fusion mechanism. During the training process, all parameters except VIT-H model are updated.

3 Method

Our method aims to utilize a classification model to distinguish AI-generated images. Therefore, we consider fine-tuning based on the current state-of-the-art (SOTA) classification models rather than training from scratch. This approach is likely to yield faster training speeds and save computational resources. Our proposed method comprises five parts: a diffusion model [DDPM] for enhancing and expanding the existing dataset, a Vision Transformer for extracting deep features, a ResNet34 for extracting shallow features, a Binary-Merge Attention (BMA) mechanism for merging the features from the two aforementioned models, and a Adam optimizer for updating gradients.

The framework we propose for distinguishing AI-generated images includes two stages, as shown in Fig. 1. The first stage involves enhancing and expanding the existing dataset through a diffusion model to increase the model's generalizability. The second stage focuses on fully extracting both deep and shallow features. The third stage involves updating the parameters (see Fig. 1).

3.1 DDPM

Background of DDPM: As an unconditional generative method, DDPM has the form of $p_\theta(\mathbf{x}_0)$: $= \int p_\theta(\mathbf{x}_{0:T})d\mathbf{x}_{1:T}$, where $\mathbf{x}_1, \ldots, \mathbf{x}_T$ represent latents with the same dimensionality as the data $\mathbf{x}_1, \ldots, \mathbf{x}_T$. It contains the forward process of diffusion and the reverse process of denoising. The forward process of diffusion that the approximate posterior $q(\mathbf{x}_{1:T}|\mathbf{x}_0)$ it is a Markov Chain by gradually adding Gaussian noise for converting the noise distribution to the data distribution according to the variance schedule $\beta_1, \ldots, \beta_T$:

$$q(\mathbf{x}_t|\mathbf{x}_{t-1}) := \mathcal{N}(\mathbf{x}_t; \sqrt{1-\beta_t}\mathbf{x}_{t-1}, \beta_t\mathbf{I}) \tag{1}$$

$$q(\mathbf{x}_t|\mathbf{x}_0) = \mathcal{N}(\mathbf{x}_t; \sqrt{\overline{\alpha}_t}\mathbf{x}_0, (1-\overline{\alpha}_t)\mathbf{I}) \tag{2}$$

The reverse process of denoising that the joint distribution $p_\theta(\mathbf{x}_{0:T})$, it can be defined as a Markov chain with learnt Gaussian transitions starting from $p(\mathbf{x}_T) = \mathcal{N}(\mathbf{x}_T; \mathbf{0}, \mathbf{I})$:

$$p_\theta(\mathbf{x}_{t-1}|\mathbf{x}_t) := \mathcal{N}(\mathbf{x}_{t-1}; \mu_\theta(\mathbf{x}_t, t), \sigma_t^2\mathbf{I}) \tag{3}$$

$$p_\theta(\mathbf{x}_{0:T}) := p(\mathbf{x}_T)\prod_{t=1}^{T} p_\theta(\mathbf{x}_{t-1}|\mathbf{x}_t) \tag{4}$$

where $\alpha_t. = 1 - \beta_t, \overline{\alpha}_t. = \prod_{s=1}^{t} \alpha_s$ and $\sigma_t^2 = \frac{1-\overline{\alpha}_{t-1}}{1-\overline{\alpha}_t}\beta_t$

3.2 Feature Extraction and Feature Fusion

In the method section of this paper, we elaborate on the feature extraction and fusion strategy adopted, as well as the theoretical foundation behind it. Our aim is to extract complementary features from visual data using network models of varying depths, and to fuse these features through a specific module, thereby enhancing the model's ability to comprehend image content.

Application of Vision Transformer (ViT). Firstly, we have employed the Vision Transformer (ViT) as a deep feature extractor. The ViT model processes small segments of an image using a self-attention mechanism, which, compared to traditional convolutional neural networks, can capture global information in the image more effectively. The core idea of ViT is to convert the image into a series of small blocks (referred to as patches), linearize these patches, and then extract features through a multi-head self-attention mechanism. This method allows ViT to excel in capturing complex image features, especially when dealing with deep visual information.

Application of ResNet. Subsequently, we utilize the ResNet model to extract shallow features. ResNet addresses the issue of gradient vanishing in deep networks by introducing residual connections, enabling the netwounsrtrk to learn more shallow-level information. This information is crucial for understanding the basic structure and texture details of images. ResNet's residual blocks allow inputs to bypass some layers directly, thus deepening the network's depth without adding extra parameters, enhancing the model's ability to extract shallow features.

BMA (Bilateral Multilayer Aggregation) Module. To effectively fuse the features extracted by ViT and ResNet, we designed a Bilateral Multilayer Aggregation (BMA) module. The key to this module is to fuse the output features of ViT and ResNet without losing any feature information. The feature fusion is achieved through Feature Concatenation. We denote the features output by ViT and ResNet as r_1 and r_2, respectively, which are processed by the BMA module to obtain the fused features. The specific fusion operation can be represented by the following formula:

$$L_n = (\mathrm{CONCAT}(r_1, r_2, a)) \tag{5}$$

$$\mathrm{MultiHead}(Q, K, V) = \mathrm{Concat}(\mathrm{head}_1, ..., \mathrm{head}_h)W^o \tag{6}$$

$$\mathrm{head}_i = \mathrm{Attention}(QW_i^Q, KW_i^K, VW_i^V) \tag{7}$$

$$Q = K = V = L_{\mathrm{n}} \tag{8}$$

where a represents the dimension along which concatenation is to be performed, we typically set $a = 0$ to concatenate along the batch dimension. The *norm* function is a normalization function that projects the feature values of $r1$ and $r2$ onto a predetermined range within $rbhw$, where y is a scalar within the range $[0, 1]$. The $CONCAT$ function connects r_1 and r_2 according to the parameter settings, achieving the fusion of features.

Furthermore, we also utilize the original Query, Key, and Value matrices, namely the QKV matrices, to further process the fused features, to enhance the model's ability to understand and utilize features.

4 Experiment

Table 1. Our proposed model is compared with the test scores of three other AI-generated image recognition models on four data sets and four evaluation metrics. All models are trained on the AGI dataset.

dataset\metric	Wang2020 [46]				Grag2021 [47]				ojha2023 [34]				ours			
	F1	AUC	ACC	AP	F1	AUC	ACC	AP	F1	AUC	ACC	AP	F1	AUC	ACC	AP
AGI	98.24	99.92	98.24	99.92	98.93	99.90	98.93	99.90	**99.81**	**1.00**	**99.87**	**99.99**	99.18	99.94	99.18	99.94
MMAF	61.62	47.40	48.88	49.15	61.71	44.07	47.48	47.11	59.07	46.91	47.17	48.23	**64.67**	**57.24**	**52.79**	**55.98**
Gide COCO	63.51	51.46	51.10	49.95	60.61	38.78	46.57	42.43	63.30	40.60	48.00	43.00	**66.58**	**54.74**	**51.30**	**53.29**
SFHQ LSUN	57.22	33.54	42.05	40.39	60.02	37.29	44.72	42.54	53.87	29.91	39.72	37.63	**60.24**	**42.29**	**46.02**	**44.32**

4.1 Datasets

The data set AGI-dataset used in the experiment is based on the output results of the GAN model and the input original real images. It contains 16,000 pictures, half of which are true and false. In terms of the division of the data set, the

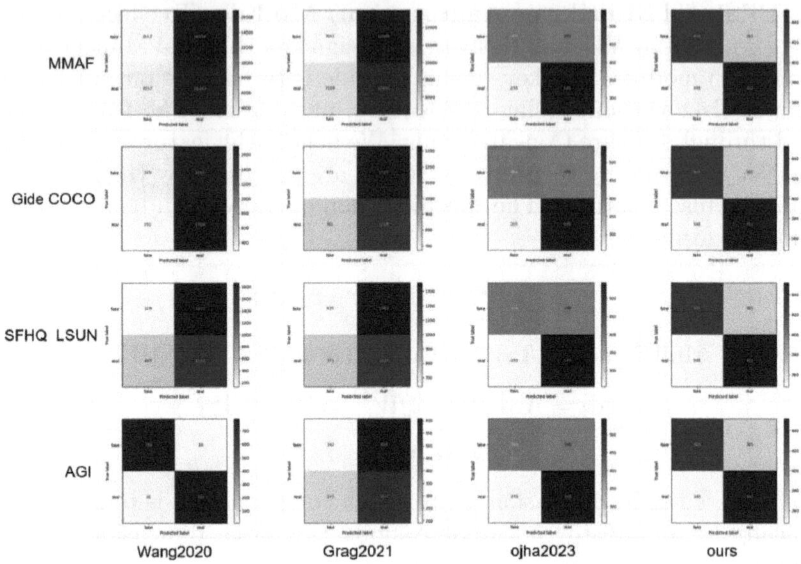

Fig. 2. Different models' confusion matrix charts for the following test datasets: AGI, MMAF, Gide COCO, SFHQ, and LSUN. The last column is our own model.

training set and the test set are divided at a ratio of 9:1. In addition, in order to explore the generalization ability of each model, we used ArtiFact [39,40]: Real and Fake Image Dataset on Kaggle as part of the test set (which is A Large-Scale Dataset with Artificial and Factual Images for Generalizable and Robust Synthetic Image Detection), containing 2,496,738 images, first considering the limited computing resources and time consumption, we divided it into three sub-datasets according to each category. They are MMAF (Mini Mixed ArtiFact), Glide COCO [41,42], and SFHQ [43] LSUN [44]. MMAF is a mini version of the original ArtiFact dataset, which contains image samples of all subsets, GLIDE COCO: GLIDE is a generative model based on text-guided diffusion models for more photorealistic image generation, The MS COCO (Microsoft Common Objects in Context) dataset is a large-scale object detection, segmentation, key-point detection, and captioning dataset. The dataset consists of 328K images. We select 2000 images from each of these two datasets to form the GLIDE COCO dataset for testing the generalization performance of the model. SFHQ (Synthetic Faces High Quality) LSUN (Large-scale Scene Understanding): SFHQ is a high-quality face dataset constructed with the assistance of a generative model. The LSUN (Large-scale Scene Understanding) dataset is a real resource for computer vision research, particularly for tasks such as scene classification, object detection, and image generation. We also select some of them to form our real and fake image identification dataset. The image sizes of all data sets are inconsistent. We unified the image size to 224 in the preprocessing stage (see Fig. 5 and Table 2).

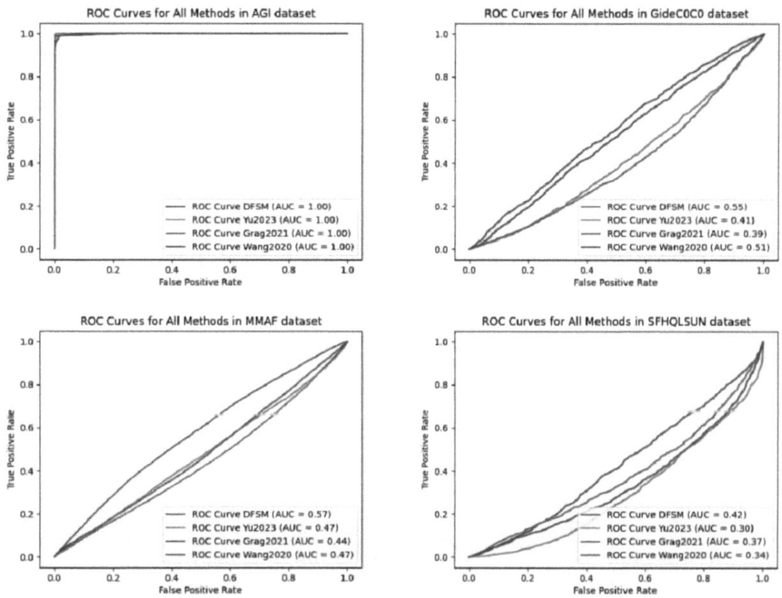

Fig. 3. The ROC curves of four models on different datasets

Table 2. Dataset information statistics

dataset	domain	total
AGI-train	train	14400
AGI-test	test	1600
MMAF	test	40000
Gide COCO	test	4000
SFHQ LSUN	test	4000

4.2 Training Testing Details

To ensure the accuracy and reproducibility of the experiment, all models use the same initialization settings, and we use a fixed random seed during the loading of the data set. During the training process, NVIDIA RTX A5500 graphics card was used for training for a total of 100 rounds, and the highest F1 score among the 100 rounds was saved as the optimal parameter of the model for testing. The optimizer was Adam, and the loss function used commonly used cross-entropy loss. All The experimental process can be reproduced. During the testing process, we used four main model classification evaluation methods as the main basis for measuring model performance, namely, F1 Score, AUC (Area under the ROC curve), Accuracy, AP (average precision). What needs to be made clear is, Since VIT-H [45] model parameters are frozen during the training process, we load the VIT-H pre-training parameters and the remaining updated parameters step by step. (see Table 3)

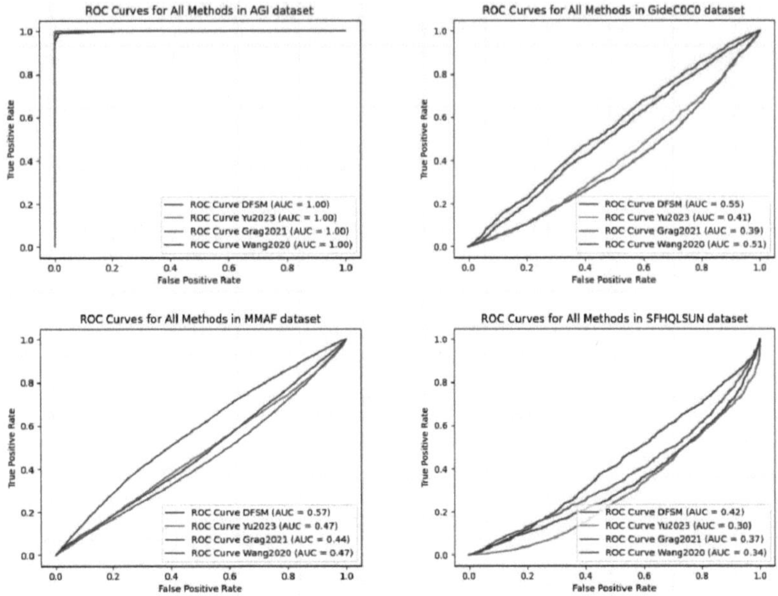

Fig. 4. The ROC curves of four models on different datasets

4.3 Ablation Study

To better validate our research contributions, we conducted comprehensive ablation studies across all datasets. This research primarily examined the specific impacts of the proposed deep feature extraction module, shallow feature extraction module, and BMA fusion module on model performance. Initially, we removed the BMA fusion module and deep feature extraction module from the DSFM and replaced DSFM with Resnet34 and VIT to assess their performance across various datasets. Subsequently, we added the deep feature extraction module and the BMA fusion module to the Resnet34 foundation and conducted comparative analyses to determine how the integration of these two modules influenced the final score updates. (see Table. 4)

As shown in Table 4, we conducted individual tests of the shallow feature extraction module and the deep feature extraction module across multiple datasets. On the AGI, MMAF, Gide COCO, SFHQ, and LSUN datasets, using only the shallow feature extraction module resulted in F1 scores of 0.9712, 0.6354, 0.6524, and 0.6174, respectively. In contrast, using only the deep feature extraction module, the F1 scores on these datasets were enhanced to 0.9814, 0.6420, 0.6566, and 0.5798, respectively. When both modules were combined, the F1 scores further increased to 0.9918, 0.6467, 0.6658, and 0.6024. These results effectively demonstrate the superiority of integrating both shallow and deep feature extraction modules within the DSFM framework.

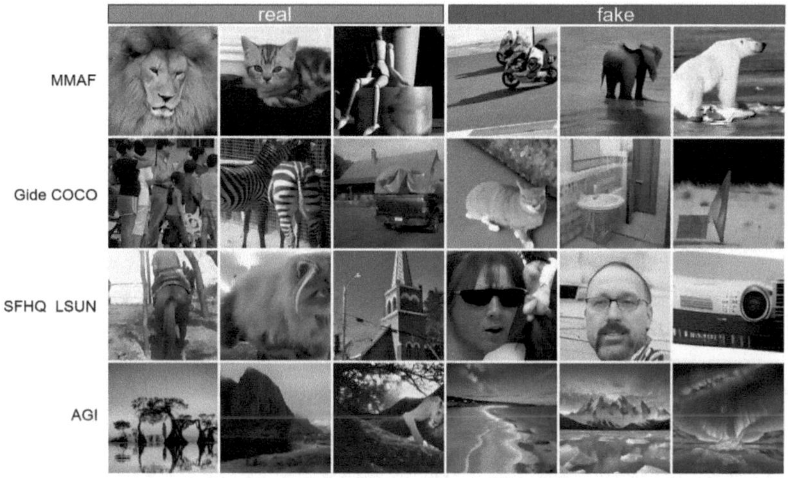

Fig. 5. Examples from the following test datasets: AGI, MMAF, Gide COCO, SFHQ LSUN.

Table 3. Experimental setup details

Epoch	100
Batch Size	16
Image Size	224
Optimizer	Adam
Learn Rate	1e-4
Momentum	0.9
Weight Decay	1e-4
Criterion	Cross Entropy Loss

5 Discussion

Both our DSFM and the current state of art model ojha2023 [34] can achieve a test accuracy of 99% on the original AGI test set. Each score is slightly lower than ojha2023, and there is a slight gap. However, our data set is tested on other data sets. The results are better than other models, which shows that our method shows stronger generalization ability on unknown data(see Fig. 4). In the field of AI distinguishing real and fake images, since the known training data is limited, more unknown data, The model should not only show excellent recognition capabilities on known data, but also be able to reflect the recognition performance on unknown data. Ours has achieved this very well. In the field of authentic and fake image identification, there is huge room for exploration. Current methods still need to explore the recognition capabilities of unknown data. At the same time, the training efficiency and recognition speed of the model also need to be improved.

Table 4. Ablation experiments on the all datasets

dataset\metric	RESNET34 [37]				VIT (pretrained) [29]				ours			
	F1	AUC	ACC	AP	F1	AUC	ACC	AP	F1	AUC	ACC	AP
AGI	97.12	99.73	96.93	99.74	98.14	99.06	99.15	99.00	**99.18**	**99.94**	**99.18**	**99.94**
MMAF	63.54	47.33	48.86	49.46	64.20	56.31	52.05	55.05	**64.67**	**57.24**	**52.79**	**55.98**
Gide COCO	65.24	52.63	50.87	50.50	65.66	52.10	51.27	50.07	**66.58**	**54.74**	**51.30**	**53.29**
SFHQ LSUN	**61.74**	35.87	46.00	41.87	57.98	41.12	43.07	**44.39**	60.24	**42.29**	**46.02**	44.32

6 Conclusion

To address the challenge of distinguishing between real and fake images, we have attempted to introduce a new recognition framework primarily based on VIT-H and attention feature fusion techniques, aiming to enhance the efficiency of true and false image identification. By conducting experiments on datasets such as AGI, MMAF, Gide COCO, SFHQ, and LSUN (see Fig. 2), we observed a certain performance improvement compared to previous methods (see Table 1). This progress provides a potential solution to privacy, copyright, and information security issues triggered by image generation models. However, in the face of the rapid development in the field of artificial intelligence and the increasing sophistication of deepfake technology, developing a model that is both universal and efficient in accurately determining the authenticity of images produced by various generation models remains a question we need to continue exploring.

Funding Disclose. This work was supported by the National Natural Science Foundation of China [NO. 62372280]; the Natural Science Foundation of Shandong Province [NO. ZR2020ZD44, ZR2019ZD04, ZR2022QG051 and ZR2023QF094]; Demonstration Projects of Science and Technology for the People of Qingdao City [NO. 23-2-8-smjk-2-nsh]; and the Special fund of Qilu Health and Health Leading Talents Training Project.

References

1. Goodfellow, I., et al.: Generative adversarial nets. Adv. Neural Inf. Process. Syst. **27** (2014)
2. Vaswani, A., et al.: Attention is all you need. Adv. Neural Inf. Process. Syst. **30** (2017)
3. Kingma, D.P., Welling, M.: Auto-encoding variational bayes. arXiv preprint arXiv:1312.6114 (2013)
4. Ho, J., Jain, A., Abbeel, P.: Denoising diffusion probabilistic models. Adv. Neural. Inf. Process. Syst. **33**, 6840–6851 (2020)

5. Radford, A., et al.: Learning transferable visual models from natural language supervision. In: International Conference on Machine Learning, pp. 8748–8763. PMLR (2021)
6. Mirza, M., Osindero, S.: Conditional generative adversarial nets. arXiv preprint arXiv:1411.1784 (2014)
7. Karras, T., Laine, S., Aittala, M., Hellsten, J., Lehtinen, J., Aila, T.: Analyzing and improving the image quality of StyleGAN. In: Proceedings of the IEEE/CVF Conference on Computer Vision and Pattern Recognition, pp. 8110–8119 (2020)
8. Karras, T., Laine, S., Aila, T.: A style-based generator architecture for generative adversarial networks. In: Proceedings of the IEEE/CVF Conference on Computer Vision and Pattern Recognition, pp. 4401–4410 (2019)
9. Rombach, R., Blattmann, A., Lorenz, D., Esser, P., Ommer, B.: High-resolution image synthesis with latent diffusion models. In: Proceedings of the IEEE/CVF Conference on Computer Vision and Pattern Recognition, pp. 10684–10695 (2022)
10. Stable Diffusion Online. https://stablediffusionweb.com/. Accessed 5 Mar 2024
11. Clipdrop. https://clipdrop.co/stable-diffusion. Accessed 5 Mar 2024
12. Midjourny. https://www.midjourney.com/. Accessed 5 Mar 2024
13. Ramesh, A., Dhariwal, P., Nichol, A., Chu, C., Chen, M.: Hierarchical text-conditional image generation with clip latents. arXiv preprint arXiv:2204.06125 **1**(2), 3 (2022)
14. OpenAI: DALL-E 2 preview - risks and limitations. https://github.com/openai/dalle-2-preview/blob/main/system-card.md. Accessed 5 Mar 2024
15. Somepalli, G., Singla, V., Goldblum, M., Geiping, J., Goldstein, T.: Diffusion art or digital forgery? Investigating data replication in diffusion models. In: Proceedings of the IEEE/CVF Conference on Computer Vision and Pattern Recognition, pp. 6048–6058 (2023)
16. Qu, Y., Shen, X., He, X., Backes, M., Zannettou, S., Zhang, Y.: Unsafe diffusion: on the generation of unsafe images and hateful memes from text-to-image models. arXiv preprint arXiv:2305.13873 (2023)
17. The problem of human database being polluted by AI-generated graphs. https://weibo.com/2637599044/NwmBrq8gP. Accessed 5 Mar 2024
18. Hugging Face: Model Card for stable-diffusion-safety-checker. https://huggingface.co/CompVis/stable-diffusion-safety-checker. Accessed 5 Mar 2024
19. Diffusers: State-of-the-art diffusion models for image and audio generation in PyTorch. https://github.com/huggingface/diffusers/blob/main/src/diffusers/pipelines/stable_diffusion/safety_checker.py. Accessed 5 Mar 2024
20. Gandikota, R., Materzynska, J., Fiotto-Kaufman, J., Bau, D.: Erasing concepts from diffusion models. arXiv preprint arXiv:2303.07345 (2023)
21. LeCun, Y., Chopra, S., Hadsell, R., Ranzato, M., Huang, F.: A tutorial on energy-based learning. Predict. Struct. Data **1** (2006)
22. Heng, A., Soh, H.: Selective amnesia: a continual learning approach to forgetting in deep generative models. Adv. Neural Inf. Process. Syst. **36** (2024)
23. Kirkpatrick, J., et al: Overcoming catastrophic forgetting in neural networks. Proc. Nat. Acad. Sci. **114**(13), 3521–3526 (2017)
24. Baum, L.E., Petrie, T., Soules, G., Weiss, N.: A maximization technique occurring in the statistical analysis of probabilistic functions of Markov chains. Ann. Math. Stat. **41**(1), 164–171 (1970)
25. Blei, D.M., Ng, A.Y., Jordan, M.I.: Latent dirichlet allocation. J. Mach. Learn. Res. **3**(Jan), 993–1022 (2003)

26. Smolensky, P.: : Information processing in dynamical systems: foundations of harmony theory. Department of Computer Science, University of Colorado, Boulder (1986)
27. Shocher, A., Dravid, A., Gandelsman, Y., Mosseri, I., Rubinstein, M., Efros, A. A.: Idempotent generative network. arXiv preprint arXiv:2311.01462 (2023)
28. Ronneberger, O., Fischer, P., Brox, T.: U-Net: convolutional networks for biomedical image segmentation. In: Navab, N., Hornegger, J., Wells, W.M., Frangi, A.F. (eds.) MICCAI 2015. LNCS, vol. 9351, pp. 234–241. Springer, Cham (2015). https://doi.org/10.1007/978-3-319-24574-4_28
29. Dosovitskiy, A., et al.: An image is worth 16 × 16 words: transformers for image recognition at scale. arXiv preprint arXiv:2010.11929 (2020)
30. Nataraj, L., et al.: Detecting GAN generated fake images using co-occurrence matrices. arXiv preprint arXiv:1903.06836 (2019)
31. Zhang, X., Karaman, S., Chang, S.-F.: Detecting and simulating artifacts in GAN fake images (Extended Version)
32. Chai, L., Bau, D., Lim, S.-N., Isola, P.: What makes fake images detectable? Understanding properties that generalize. In: Vedaldi, A., Bischof, H., Brox, T., Frahm, J.-M. (eds.) ECCV 2020. LNCS, vol. 12371, pp. 103–120. Springer, Cham (2020). https://doi.org/10.1007/978-3-030-58574-7_7
33. Brock, A., Donahue, J., Simonyan, K.: Large scale GAN training for high fidelity natural image synthesis. arXiv preprint arXiv:1809.11096 (2018)
34. Ojha, U., Li, Y., Lee, Y.J.: Towards universal fake image detectors that generalize across generative models. In: Proceedings of the IEEE/CVF Conference on Computer Vision and Pattern Recognition, pp. 24480–24489 (2023)
35. Epstein, D. C., Jain, I., Wang, O., Zhang, R.: Online detection of AI-generated images. In: Proceedings of the IEEE/CVF International Conference on Computer Vision, pp. 382–392 (2023)
36. Xi, Z., Huang, W., Wei, K., Luo, W., Zheng, P.: AI-Generated Image Detection using a Cross-Attention Enhanced Dual-Stream Network. arXiv preprint arXiv:2306.07005 (2023)
37. He, K., Zhang, X., Ren, S., Sun, J.: Deep residual learning for image recognition. In: Proceedings of the IEEE Conference on Computer Vision and Pattern Recognition, pp. 770–778 (2016)
38. Zhu, M., et al.: GenDet: towards Good Generalizations for AI-Generated Image Detection. arXiv preprint arXiv:2312.08880 (2023)
39. Rahman, M.A., Paul, B., Sarker, N.H., Hakim, Z.I.A., Fattah, S.A.: ArtiFact: a large-scale dataset with artificial and factual images for generalizable and robust synthetic image detection. arXiv preprint arXiv:2302.11970 (2023)
40. ArtiFact: Real and Fake Image Dataset. https://www.kaggle.com/datasets/awsaf49/artifact-dataset?resource=download. Accessed 05 Mar 2024
41. Nichol, A., et al.: Glide: towards photorealistic image generation and editing with text-guided diffusion models. arXiv preprint arXiv:2112.10741 (2021)
42. Lin, T.-Y., et al.: Microsoft COCO: common objects in context. In: Fleet, D., Pajdla, T., Schiele, B., Tuytelaars, T. (eds.) ECCV 2014. LNCS, vol. 8693, pp. 740–755. Springer, Cham (2014). https://doi.org/10.1007/978-3-319-10602-1_48
43. SelfishGene. SFHQ-dataset. https://github.com/SelfishGene/SFHQ-dataset
44. Yu, F., Seff, A., Zhang, Y., Song, S., Funkhouser, T., Xiao, J.: LSUN: construction of a large-scale image dataset using deep learning with humans in the loop. arXiv preprint arXiv:1506.03365 (2015)
45. Hugging Face: Vision Transformer (huge-sized model). https://huggingface.co/google/vit-huge-patch14-224-in21k. Accessed 05 Mar 2024

46. Wang, S.-Y., Wang, O., Zhang, R., Owens, A., Efros, A.A.: CNN-generated images are surprisingly easy to spot... for now. In: Proceedings of the IEEE/CVF Conference on Computer Vision and Pattern Recognition, pp. 8695–8704 (2020)
47. Gragnaniello, D., Cozzolino, D., Marra, F., Poggi, G., Verdoliva, L.: Are GAN generated images easy to detect? A critical analysis of the state-of-the-art. In: 2021 IEEE International Conference on Multimedia and Expo (ICME), pp. 1–6. IEEE (2021)

Medical Artificial Intelligence

Enhancing Weakly Supervised Medical Segmentation via Heterogeneous Co-training with Box-Wise Augmentation and Pseudo-Label Filtering

You Wang[1], Lei Qi[2], Qian Yu[3], Yinghuan Shi[1(✉)], and Yang Gao[1]

[1] State Key Laboratory of Novel Software Technology, National Insititute of Health-care Data Science, Nanjing University, Nanjing, China
wangu@smail.nju.edu.cn, {syh,gy}@nju.edu.cn

[2] School of Computer Science and Engineering, Southeast University, Nanjing, China
qilei@seu.edu.cn

[3] School of Data and Computer Science, Shandong Woman's University, Jinan, China
yuqian@sdwu.edu.cn

Abstract. In this paper, we introduce an innovative approach to weakly supervised medical image segmentation with box annotations. Different from the previous methods which simply utilize a single conventional network with the same augmentation techniques widely used in supervised segmentation, we aim to introduce diverse augmentations and heterogenous networks to leverage the box annotations for promising generalization ability. Specifically, to amplify the diversity between the contents within the box and its surroundings, we propose the interior and exterior box augmentation (IEBA) technique, in which distinct augmentation techniques are employed for regions inside and outside the bounding boxes. Also, for the purpose of selecting pseudo-labels of superior quality, we propose the pseudo-label filter module (PLFM) to eliminate unreliable pseudo-labels. Besides, as CNN demonstrates superior capabilities in acquiring local information, and ViT specializes in capturing global context, we facilitate a bidirectional learning process between CNN and ViT through quadruple cross consistency losses (QCCL). In inference, we only employ the superior model from the validation set to obtain parameter efficiency. Our approach is evaluated across four tasks on two public datasets, utilizing the 3D dice similarity coefficient as the evaluation metric. The experimental results show that the proposed method outperforms the state-of-the-art comparison methods.

Keywords: Weakly supervised learning · Medical image segmentation · Heterogeneous co-training

1 Introduction

In recent years, the rapid development of deep learning has led to great success in image segmentation. In the standard fully-supervised learning protocol [2,24], a

Published by Springer Nature Switzerland AG 2025
Z. Shi et al. (Eds.): ICIS 2024, IFIP AICT 720, pp. 331–345, 2025.
https://doi.org/10.1007/978-3-031-71253-1_24

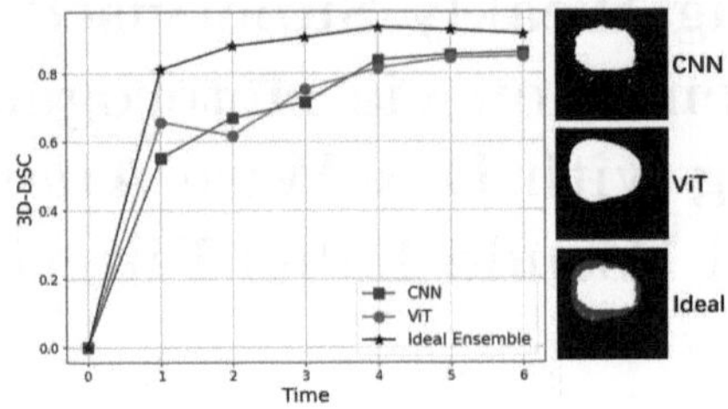

Fig. 1. The left chart presents a line chart showcasing the fluctuations in the 3D-DSC of the weakly supervised segmentation model across CNN, ViT and the conceptually ideal ensemble results. The right section of the figure displays the segmentation results produced by the aforementioned methods. (White: agreement foreground, Black: agreement background and Red: disagreement). (Color figure online)

large amount of pixel-wise labels are available, yet this requirement is somehow difficult to acquire. To reduce the cost of manual annotations, great interest has been aroused in weakly supervised segmentation, where there exist several representative weak labels, such as image tags [1], bounding boxes [5,10,31], scribbles [16] and points [8]. Our study here focuses on weakly supervised image segmentation with box annotations.

Among these weak supervisions, due to its simplicity in labeling, the bounding boxes-based weakly supervised learning has been well-explored in medical image segmentation tasks. For example, Rajchl *et al.* [23] develop an iterative optimization method for MR images and obtain encouraging results. Also, Khoreva *et al.* attempt to generate pseudo-labels from box annotations and propose GrabCut [25] and MCG [12] to train a neural network like fully-supervised learning. Furthermore, Kervadec *et al.* [10] and Wang *et al.* [31] devise end-to-end segmentation models based on the tightness of bounding boxes. Recently, Facebook Research propose the segment anything model (SAM) [13], which generates masks from input prompts, including points or bounding boxes. However, the intricate characteristics of organs' boundaries often present ambiguity and challenges in accurate differentiation, thus hindering the effectiveness of its performance in medical image segmentation [3,18].

In spite of their success, when pixel-wise labels are unavailable, the aforementioned methods face significant challenges in generating high-quality pseudo-labels using a single network to some extent. Besides, as far as our understanding goes, existing weakly supervised medical image segmentation methods that rely on bounding boxes tend to generate pseudo-labels or apply global constraints. However, bounding boxes in these methods are not fully explored, lacking a thorough utilization of their spatial information. Therefore, in contrast to previous weakly supervised medical image segmentation methods, we wonder *if we could introduce more diverse augmentations or more heterogenous networks to achieve better generalization ability based on box annotations?*

With the intention of fully capitalizing on box annotations, we innovatively designed a novel augmentation technique namely interior and exterior box-wise augmentation (IEBA), meticulously tailored to extract maximum utility from the box annotations. Within IEBA, we employ weak augmentation techniques in the exterior region, contrasted with the application of strong spatial augmentation methods in the interior regions. Through this box-wise data augmentation strategy, the model gains the ability to distinguish regions both inside and outside bounding box annotations, ultimately enhancing its segmentation prowess.

Furthermore, given the prevalence of numerous unreliable pseudo-labels in weakly supervised medical image segmentation, it becomes imperative to filter out these misleading pseudo-labels to ensure satisfactory performance. As a result, we design the pseudo-label filter module (PLFM) to select reliable pseudo-labels. In PLFM, we extract the associated bounding boxes from pseudo-labels and subsequently juxtapose them against the provided box annotations. Thus, we are able to systematically identify and remove unreliable pseudo-labels during the training process, ensuring the refinement of training data quality. This meticulous approach enhances the model's ability to learn meaningful patterns, further contributing to improved overall segmentation accuracy.

Inspired by previous consistency regularization methods [28,32], we recognize the potential for applying consistency constraints between dual networks trained on images with varied augmentations on weakly supervised medical image segmentation. Considering that CNN focuses on local information whereas ViT [7] excels in handling global information, we would like to ask them to learn from each other. Thus, CNN and ViT are expected to supervise each other to improve the comprehensive segmentation ability in weakly supervised segmentation. In Fig. 1, it is evident that the performance of a single model is significantly inferior to the optimal outcomes achieved by ensemble methods. The ideal ensemble results represent our selection of the best outcomes that match the true information, obtained from the segmentation results of both CNN and ViT models.

In pursuit of this objective, we have devised a dual networks method integrated with cross-consistency losses, effectively leveraging each network's advantages to collectively diminish the cumulative error rate. While the co-training mechanism has been previously introduced in studies [17] and [21], our research distinguishes itself through our utilization of quadruple cross consistency losses (QCCL). These losses are computed through a crossover design involving different networks and different augmentation techniques, thereby amplifying the variety in approaching the identical segmentation objectives.

We summarize the contributions of this work as follows:

- We innovatively notice that diverse augmentations and heterogenous networks could benefit the box annotations based weakly supervised medical image segmentation.
- We propose the interior and exterior box augmentation, named as IEBA, which enhances the utilization of bounding boxes and introduces discrimination to both interior and exterior regions of the bounding boxes.
- We develop the pseudo-label filter module (PLFM), which creatively utilizes bounding box annotations for the purpose of pseudo-label filtering.
- We design a novel co-training paradigm by formulating quadruple cross consistency losses (QCCL), which quantifies the consistency loss across distinct networks (CNN and ViT) and diverse augmentation techniques.

2 Related Work

2.1 Weakly Supervised Segmentation

There is a growing interest in weakly supervised medical image segmentation, and extensive research has been conducted in this field [9,26]. Qu *et al.* [22] leverage point annotations in the context of histopathology images. They utilize a Voronoi diagram to derive supplementary information, enabling the generation of coarse labels for nuclei segmentation. In [30], their objective function combines cross-entropy with coarse labels and conditional random field loss. For natural image segmentation, they employ Class Activation Maps to produce pseudo-labels. However, this method is not well-suited for single-target medical images, as the quality of pseudo-labels generated by CAM is significantly inferior. Similar to previous works in computer vision, [19] employ CAMs derived from the networks as pseudo-masks to train a CNN in a fully supervised manner. To enforce target localization, they utilize an Active Shape Model as prior information.

2.2 Box Supervision

The majority of CNN-based methods that utilize bounding box supervision are categorized as proposal-based methods [4]. In these approaches, bounding box annotations are utilized to obtain initial pseudo-masks or proposals, often achieve with shallow segmentation techniques like the widely used GrabCut method [25] and Transformer based SAM [13]. Subsequently, the training process typically follows an iterative scheme consisting of two steps. The first step involves updating the network parameters, while the second step focuses on adjusting the pseudo-labels [5,12,20]. To enhance the quality of pseudo-labels generated at each iteration, some studies [23,29] have employed well-known techniques like DenseCRF [14] or other methods. Kervadec *et al.* introduce the approach by incorporating global constraints and prior information into the output of a convolutional neural network [10]. Additionally, Wang *et al.* propose a generalized multiple instance learning (MIL) formulation and a smooth maximum approximation [31] to seamlessly integrate bounding box tightness prior to the network in an end-to-end fashion.

The mentioned methods have demonstrated favorable performance in weakly supervised medical image segmentation with bounding box supervision. Nevertheless, further effort is needed to enhance their effectiveness to satisfy clinical requirements. The weakly supervised medical image segmentation exhibits significant uncertainty, leading to elevated error rates when training models based on a single network. Furthermore, previous techniques have not fully harnessed the capabilities offered by box annotations.

3 Methodology

3.1 Notation and Overview

Weakly supervised segmentation aims to train a segmentation model to map a sample X to a prediction Y with weak annotations, where $X \in \mathbb{R}^{H \times W}$, H

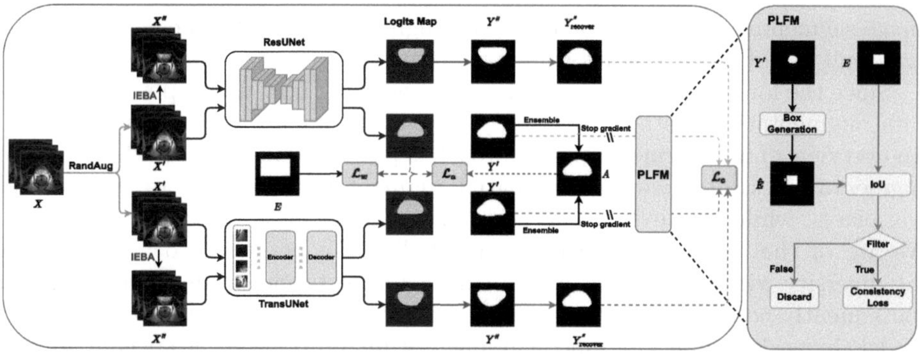

Fig. 2. Overview of the proposed co-training paradigm. Once the input image X undergoes weak and box-wise augmentation, it is subsequently inputt into two encoder-decoder segmentation models. We compute the QCCL between the outputs from different networks and augmentation methods with PLFM.

denotes the height, W is the width, and $Y \in \{0,1\}^{H\times W}$, respectively. In this study, The labels we possess are annotated with bounding boxes B. Suppose there are M bounding boxes, then its bounding box label is $B = \{b_m\}, m = 1, 2, ..., M$, where the location label b_m is a 4-dimensional vector representing the top left and bottom right points of the bounding box, $E \in \mathbb{R}^{H\times W}$ is its corresponding pixel mask and $\hat{E} \in \mathbb{R}^{H\times W}$ denotes the predicted box mask. Let $s_\theta \in [0,1]$ denote the probabilities predicted by the networks, where 0 and 1 represent background and foreground, respectively. Particularly, we suppose all the box annotations achieve a close fit to the ground truth as [10].

The proposed approach comprises three primary components: interior and exterior box-wise augmentation (IEBA), pseudo-label filter module (PLFM) and co-training heterogenous networks with quadruple cross consistency losses (QCCL). IEBA applies distinct augmentations inside and outside the box regions to enhance the diversity between them. To achieve this goal, we implement a two-step approach. Firstly, we adopt color enhancement entire image to obtain a weakly augmented version. Then, we apply augmentations like flipping at different axis exclusively within the box annotations region to obtain the box-wisely augmented version. Also, we filter the pseudo-labels generated from weak augmented inputs to screen out reliable pseudo-labels with PLFM. In QCCL, we input both of them into a convolutional neural network and a vision transformer respectively and compute the consistency losses from different networks and diverse augmentation methods to enhance the generalization ability of the model.

3.2 Interior and Exterior Box Augmentation

In mainstream semi-supervised learning tasks, strong augmentation is applied to enhance the segmentation ability of the model. In weakly supervised medical image segmentation, a more precise data augmentation method can be found to make full use of box annotations.

Since the foreground is contained in the bounding box, we propose a box-wise data augmentation method to introduce diversity for the segmentation model. An overview of our augmentation approach is presented in Fig. 4. In the box-wise augmentation strategy, we apply spatial augmentation methods to the internal box pixels, while employing weak augmentation methods to the whole images. We are of the opinion that this approach has the potential to amplify both the diversity within the interior and exterior aspects. Such enhancement could consequently contribute to the improved generalization capabilities of training models in weakly supervised medical image segmentation. To be specific, for the external region of the bounding box, we use random augmentations methods[1]. These modifications are intended to introduce subtle variations to the pixels outside the box. We define the weakly augmented X' as:

$$X' = \mathbf{RandAugment}(X). \tag{1}$$

Conversely, for the pixels within the bounding boxes, we employ strong augmentations, such as flip and mirror operations. These transformations are more pronounced and can significantly alter the internal pixel arrangements. We define the box-wisely augmented version X'' as:

$$X'' = \mathbf{Flip}_{\text{horizontal}}(\mathbf{Flip}_{\text{vertical}}(X')), \tag{2}$$

where $\mathbf{Flip}_{\text{horizontal}}$ and $\mathbf{Flip}_{\text{vertical}}$ denotes reversing an image along an axis (horizontally or vertically), respectively.

It is important to note that we avoid using rotation with large angles as an augmentation, as this might lead to an undesirable loss of pixel information. By adopting this approach, the segmentation network can capture additional information while calculating consistency losses.

3.3 Pseudo-Label Filter Module

Due to the presence of numerous uncertain segmentation outcomes resulting from weakly-augmented inputs, it becomes imperative to filter out unreliable pseudo-labels. In the context of weakly supervised medical image segmentation, where pixel-wise labels are unavailable, we derive the corresponding bounding box annotations $\hat{E}$ from the predicted result Y' of weakly augmented input X'. In Fig. 3, it is evident that there exists a positive correlation between the Intersection over Union (IoU) values of the pseudo boxes and real boxes, as well as the Dice

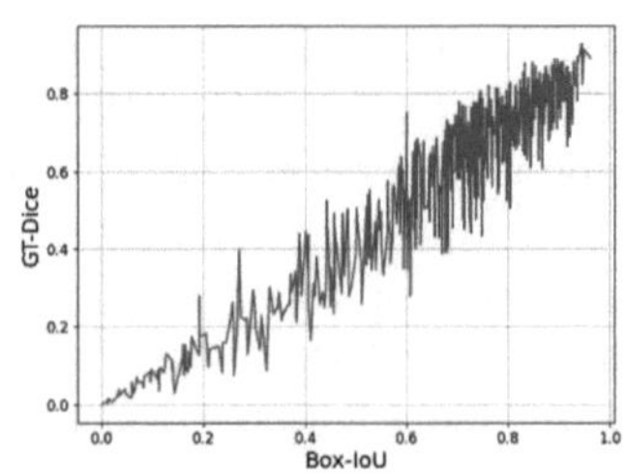

Fig. 3. Box-IoU and GT-Dice are positively correlated.

[1] We perform contrast and sharpness in random augmentations.

Similarity Coefficient (DSC) between the pseudo-labels and ground truths. To assess the accuracy of the pseudo-labels, we compute the IoU between $\hat{E}$ and the provided box annotations E, as follows:

$$\mathbf{Suc}(i) = \mathbb{1}(\mathrm{IoU}(E_i, \hat{E}_i) > \tau). \tag{3}$$

Here, τ represents the threshold value and i denotes its index in a batch. The function **Suc** is a binary indicator determined by whether the IoU between the bounding boxes E_i and $\hat{E}_i$ surpass the predefined threshold τ.

3.4 Co-training Heterogenous Networks

As CNN demonstrates superior capabilities in acquiring local information and ViT specializes in capturing global context, we facilitate a bidirectional learning process between CNN and ViT through quadruple cross consistency losses (QCCL). To leverage the strengths of both CNN and ViT, we design the co-training learning paradigm (see Fig. 2). The progress consists of three parts: model warming up, co-training and model ensemble.

Model Warming Up. To generate reliable pseudo-labels, we train both networks with global constraint [10] separately. Given an input image X, it is respectively entered into two encode-decoder networks named M_{CNN} and M_{ViT}, whose encoder consists of CNN and ViT. The global constraint loss $\mathcal{L}_w$ is used to train each model separately. We formulate the weakly supervised loss as:

$$\begin{aligned}\mathcal{L}_w = &\sum_{p\in\Omega_O} \widetilde{\psi}_t(s_\theta(p)) + \lambda[\sum_{s_l\in S_L} \widetilde{\psi}_t(w - \sum_{p\in s_l} s_\theta(p))] \\ &+\widetilde{\psi}_t(\epsilon_1|\Omega_I| - \sum_{p\in\Omega} s_\theta(p)) + \widetilde{\psi}_t(\sum_{p\in\Omega} s_\theta(p) - \epsilon_2|\Omega_I|),\end{aligned} \tag{4}$$

where Ω_O and Ω_I denote pixels inside boxes and outside boxes, respectively. $\widetilde{\psi}_t(\theta)$ represents the log-barrier extensions [11] which provide approximations of Lagrangian optimization in the form of sequences of unconstrained losses. $\widetilde{\psi}_t(x)$ is the constraint of $x \leq 0$ and t is a hyper-parameter increased with the passage of time. We regroup the lines of images into segments of width w, each containing w lines. λ is a real number balancing losses above. ϵ_1 and ϵ_2 are the lower and upper bound on the proportion of foreground to box, respectively.

Co-training. Considering that CNN focuses on local information extraction, while ViT prefers global information extraction, we aim to combine them effectively by employing them as an auxiliary network and a primary network, respectively. To achieve this objective, we compute the consistency loss between the outputs obtained from these two different networks, along with diverse augmentation methods. Specifically, we apply distinct augmentations to the input data X, generating X' for weak augmentation and X'' for box-wise augmentation. In order to mitigate the impact of unreliable results, we leverage PLFM to filter out pseudo-labels that might lead to misleading information. For the calculation of the consistency loss, we adopt the Mean Squared Error (MSE) loss function.

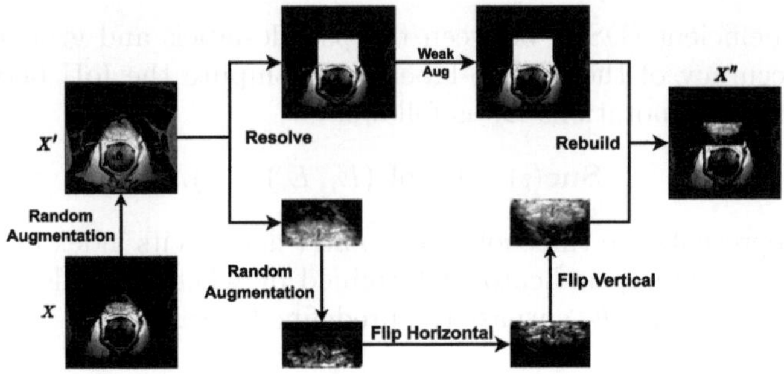

Fig. 4. An overview of the proposed IEBA, in which we apply interior and exterior augmentation methods to inputs.

Through the integration of these elements, our networks can assimilate local as well as global information, striking a harmonious balance between the capabilities of CNN and ViT, resulting in enhanced performance. As a result, the models can be learned with:

$$\begin{aligned}\mathcal{L}_{c1} &= \sum_{i=1}^{N} \mathbf{Suc}(i)|M_{\text{ViT}}(X_i'') - \text{T}^{-1}M_{\text{CNN}}(X_i')|^2, \\ \mathcal{L}_{c2} &= \sum_{i=1}^{N} \mathbf{Suc}(i)|M_{\text{CNN}}(X_i'') - \text{T}^{-1}M_{\text{ViT}}(X_i')|^2,\end{aligned} \tag{5}$$

where N denotes the batch size, T^{-1} is the space restoration transform opposite to box-wise augmentation T.

Model Ensemble. With the intention of amalgamating the benefits of both CNN and ViT, we identify regions where the pseudo-labels from both CNN and ViT exhibit agreement. Employing the aforementioned procedure, we also utilize PLFM to eliminate any unreliable pseudo-labels. This amalgamation is formally defined as follows:

$$A = Y'_{\text{CNN}} \odot \mathbb{1}(Y_{\text{CNN}} = Y_{\text{ViT}}), \tag{6}$$

where A is the agreement pseudo-label, Y_{CNN} comes from CNN and Y_{ViT} comes from ViT and $\odot$ represents the element-wise multiplication operation, $\mathbb{1}(Y_{\text{CNN}} = Y_{\text{ViT}})$ denotes the mask indicating consensus between CNN and ViT, respectively. So the loss function can be described as:

$$\begin{aligned}\mathcal{L}_{a1} &= \sum_{i=1}^{N} \mathbf{Suc}(i)\mathcal{H}(M_{\text{ViT}}(X_i'), A_i), \\ \mathcal{L}_{a2} &= \sum_{i=1}^{N} \mathbf{Suc}(i)\mathcal{H}(M_{\text{CNN}}(X_i'), A_i),\end{aligned} \tag{7}$$

where $\mathcal{H}(\cdot)$ denotes cross-entropy loss.

Finally, the total loss can be formulated as:

$$\mathcal{L} = \mathcal{L}_w + \lambda_1(\mathcal{L}_{c1} + \mathcal{L}_{c2}) + \lambda_2(\mathcal{L}_{a1} + \mathcal{L}_{a2}), \tag{8}$$

Table 1. Comparison of Dice coefficients for different methods on four tasks.

Meth	Type	Venue	3D-DSC (%)			
Dataset			PROMISE12	Heart	Hippocampus	Spleen
GrabCut	Proposal	TOG'04	–	75.99	–	–
TransUNet [2]		Arxiv'21	81.30	82.26	75.85	63.39
DconnNet [33]		CVPR'23	84.37	77.41	–	76.68
SAM [13]		*ICCV'23*	*85.08*	***86.13***	*79.58*	*85.13*
DeepCut [23]	End to End	TMI'16	82.71	82.87	74.02	73.61
GC(CNN) [10]		MIDL'20	83.48	83.91	79.22	83.81
GC(ViT) [10]		MIDL'20	84.86	84.97	79.21	84.16
GMIL [31]		MICCAI'21	85.16*	80.68	79.01	78.84
Ours		This paper	**86.55**	85.78	**80.84**	**85.93**
Upper Bound	–	*Fully-supervised*	*90.10*	*90.16*	*86.08*	*92.34*

* This article generated new tight boxes for rotated images.

where λ_1 and λ_2 are the hyper-parameters to balance losses.

Furthermore, we utilize only the superior model from the validation set for optimal parameter efficiency in inference. For instance, if the CNN's performance surpasses that of the ViT, we would discard the ViT and retain only the CNN, and vice versa.

4 Experiments

4.1 Datasets and Evaluation

This research employs two publicly available medical datasets to assess performance across four tasks. The first one is the prostate MR image segmentation 2012 (PROMISE12) dataset [15] for prostate segmentation and the second one is from the Medical Segmentation Decathlon (MSD) challenge [27]. In the MSD dataset, we only use Spleen, Heart and Hippocampus for spleen segmentation in CT, heart segmentation in MRI and hippocampus segmentation in MRI.

PROMISE12. The dataset comes from MICCAI 2012 prostate MR segmentation challenge [15]. The dataset comprises cross-sectional T2-weighted MR images obtained from 50 patients across various medical centers. These images are acquired using diverse MRI equipment and distinct scanning procedures. The dataset encompasses both benign conditions and cases of prostate cancer. The image resolutions vary, ranging from $15 \times 256 \times 256$ to $54 \times 512 \times 512$ voxels, with voxel spacing ranging from $2 \times 0.27 \times 0.27$ to $4 \times 0.75 \times 0.75\,\text{mm}^3$. We adjust the dimensions of each slice to 256×256 and generate tight bounding boxes for each slice with its ground truth. For the training phase, a subset of 40 patients is utilized, while 10 patients are reserved for validation purposes [10].

Heart. The dataset is made available at King's College London, originally released through the Left Atrial Segmentation Challenge. It consists of 30 MRI datasets covering the entire heart acquired during a single cardiac phase, aiming at the segment left atrium. This dataset is divided into a training set of 24 patients and a validation set of 6 patients. During the training phase, we resize the dimensions of each slice to 256×256 and create precise bounding boxes aligned with the ground truth for every slice.

Hippocampus. The dataset is from Psychiatric Genotype/Phenotype Project data repository at Vanderbilt University Medical Center (Nashville, TN, USA). It consists of MRIs from 90 healthy adults and 105 adults with a non-affective psychotic disorder. The purpose of the dataset is to segment the hippocampus properly in this study. We divide this dataset into a training set of 156 adults and a validation set of 39 adults. As part of the training process, we modify the dimensions of each slice to 64×64 and generate tight bounding boxes that correspond to the ground truth for each individual slice to obtain box annotations.

Spleen. The dataset consists of patients undergoing chemotherapy treatment for liver metastases at Memorial Sloan Kettering Cancer Center (New York, NY, USA). This is a CT dataset of 41 patients, aiming at spleen segmentation. The dataset is divided into a training set of 32 patients and a validation set of 9 patients. we resize the images to dimensions of 256×256 and generate tight box annotations.

Evaluation Metric. To compare the performances of the different methods, we employed the 3D Dice Similarity Coefficient (DSC), which is a standard performance metric in medical image segmentation.

4.2 Implementation Details

Training. All experimental procedures are conducted utilizing PyTorch on a single Nvidia RTX 2080Ti GPU with 11 GB memory, employing the Adam optimizer throughout the study. The image segmentation process is performed on 2D slices and validated on 3D volumes. We adopt a modified version of the ResUNet architecture [6] and the vision transformer-based TransUNet architecture [2] as the backbones for segmentation.

For the PROMISE12, Heart, and Spleen datasets, the input slices are resized to 256×256 pixels, and training is executed for 100 epochs. A batch size of 4 is utilized, with the initial learning rate set to 10^{-4} for both ResUNet and TransUNet. In the case of the Hippocampus dataset, the input slices are resized to 64×64 pixels, training is performed for 60 epochs and a batch size of 8 and an initial learning rate of 5×10^{-5} are employed.

In Eq. (4), the parameters are set as follows: $\epsilon_1 = 0.5$ and $\epsilon_2 = 0.9$ for PROMISE12, Heart, and Hippocampus; $\epsilon_1 = 0.4$ and $\epsilon_2 = 0.9$ for Spleen; $\lambda = 10^{-4}$; and $\tau = 0.7$ across all datasets. Additionally, offline data augmentation techniques, including mirroring, flipping, and rotation, are applied to expand the PROMISE12. Furthermore, box augmentation is employed for all datasets.

Inference. The model exhibiting superior performance on the validation set is chosen as the inference model.

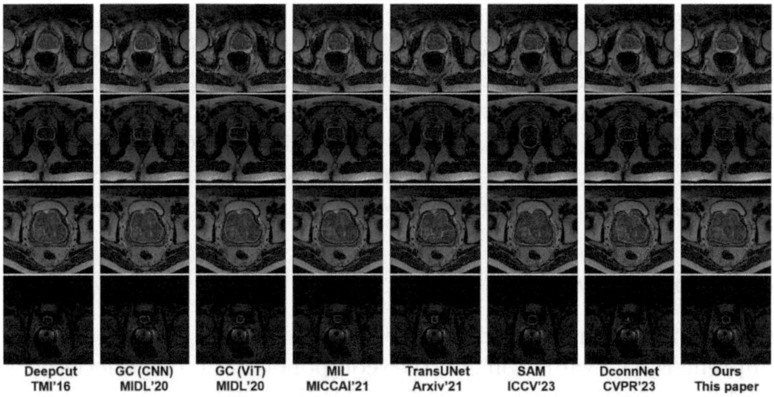

Fig. 5. Visualization on segmentation results of different methods on PROMISE12. The blue contours indicate the boundaries of ground truths while the green contours are predictions. (Color figure online)

4.3 Main Result

Table 1 presents the 3D-DSC achieved by our proposed method and other state-of-the-art methods. The fully-supervised results are also included as an upper bound for comparison. The obtained results highlight the effectiveness of our cross-teaching model, achieving 3D-DSC scores of 86.55% for PROMISE12, 85.78% for Heart, 80.84% for Hippocampus, and 85.93% for Spleen, surpassing the performance of previous methods except SAM on Heart.

Compared to our baseline GC trained with TransUNet [2] and ResUNet, our proposed method demonstrates significant advancements, validating the effective knowledge learned by ViT from CNN and CNN from ViT. Moreover, it is evident that our method outperforms the state-of-the-art methods, delivering superior segmentation results for the four tasks. In Fig. 5, we present visualization results of images from the four tasks, showcasing the remarkable precision of our method in segmenting the target structures. This clearly illustrates the competence and potential of our proposed approach in achieving accurate and reliable segmentation results.

4.4 Comparison with Proposal Based Methods

Proposal-based weakly supervised segmentation methods are a frequently employed model training approach. In this study, we conduct a comparative analysis between techniques based on SAM and those based on GrabCut. Besides, we utilize box annotations as the ground truth for training on both DconnNet [33] and TransUNet. We utilized bounding boxes as prompts to generate pseudo-labels on them and employed the same training methodology as in fully supervised learning on ResUNet.

GrabCut demonstrates strong performance with a 3D-DSC score of 75.99% for the Heart dataset, but its effectiveness is limited when applied to other datasets. Regarding SAM, the results across the four tasks showcase remarkable performances, as SAM undergoes pre-training on 11 million images, whereas our proposed approach lacks. Importantly, **our method and SAM are mutually orthogonal, potentially allowing for the iterative development of more advanced methods**. Regarding the results achieved with DconnNet and TransUNet, it is evident that these advanced networks exhibit impressive performance even when dealing with coarse annotations.

4.5 Ablation Study

1) Impact of Different Components. To gain a deeper understanding and comprehensive evaluation of the components in our method, we perform an ablation experiment on the PROMISE12 dataset. In this experiment, we investigate the impact of each setting, which includes: 1) whether to use QCCL to achieve co-training, 2) whether to adopt IEBA for augmentation and 3) whether to utilize PLFM to filter reliable pseudo-labels from weakly-augmented data.

Table 2. Ablation study (3D-DSC) on PROMISE12.

Methods	QCCL	IEBA	PLFM	3D-DSC (%)
#1				84.86
#2	✓			85.41
#3		✓		85.37
#4			✓	85.24
#5		✓	✓	85.61
#6	✓	✓		85.69
#7	✓		✓	85.71
#8	✓	✓	✓	**86.55**

In Table 2, we present the results of our ablation study. It is obvious that all the components contribute significantly to the performance of our proposed method. This ablation study provides valuable insights into the strengths and importance of the various components and aids in optimizing the architecture for the best segmentation outcomes.

2) Impact of the Threshold of IoU. To demonstrate the effectiveness of the IoU threshold and investigate its impact on performance, we conducted three experiments on PROMISE12 and Heart datasets, using the same hyper-parameters except for τ. The results are presented in Table 3, showcasing the performances for different τ values. Notably, we achieved the best 3D-DSC of 86.55% for PROMISE12 and 85.78% for Heart when setting $\tau = 0.7$. This outcome can be attributed to the fact that a small τ tends to accept more unreliable pseudo-labels, whereas a large τ leads to the exclusion of valuable information. Therefore, the careful choice of an appropriate τ is pivotal in achieving optimal outcomes within the experiments.

Table 3. DSC (%) of the proposed method with different τ.

Threshold	PROMISE12	Heart
$\tau = 0.6$	84.98	85.32
$\tau = 0.7$	**86.55**	**85.78**
$\tau = 0.8$	85.05	85.64

3) Effectiveness of Heterogeneous Networks. In order to validate the efficacy of the heterogeneous networks in our approach, this paper conduct experiments by substituting the ResUNet and TransUNet components within our

Table 4. Comparison with Homogeneous networks and Heterogeneous networks on PROMISE12.

Network1	Network2	3D-DSC (%)
ResUNet	ResUNet	83.81
TransUNet	TransUNet	84.58
TransUNet	ResUNet	**86.55**

Table 5. Comparison with other augmentation methods on PROMISE12.

Method	3D-DSC (%)
Color Inverting	85.95
Solarizing	85.73
Gauss Noise	85.87
Ours	**86.55**

proposed method with either two ResUNet or two TransUNet. These substitutions are evaluated on the PROMISE12 dataset, and the experimental outcomes are depicted in Table 4. The results demonstrate a more noticeable enhancement in performance with the heterogeneous networks (Table 5).

4.6 Comparison with Other Augmentations

To validate the effectiveness of our IEBA, we conduct a comparative analysis against conventional augmentation methods such as color inverting, solarizing, and noise addition on PROMISE12. The results are presented in Table 3. The experimental results demonstrate the superior performance of our proposed IEBA over the previous augmentation methods. Notably, our method exhibits strong applicability and operates independently of other augmentation methods. Therefore, there exists potential for integration between our method and other augmentation strategies.

5 Conclusion

In this paper, we present a novel method for weakly supervised medical image segmentation with box annotations. This technique employs a pair of heterogeneous networks to calculate QCCL with the integration of PLFM and the box-wise augmentation method IEBA. Thorough experiments and comprehensive analyses conducted on the PROMISE12, Heart, Hippocampus, and Spleen datasets substantiate the efficacy of our proposed approach for weakly supervised medical image segmentation with box annotations.

References

1. Ahn, J., Cho, S., Kwak, S.: Weakly supervised learning of instance segmentation with inter-pixel relations. In: Proceedings of the IEEE/CVF Conference on Computer Vision and Pattern Recognition (CVPR), pp. 2209–2218 (2019)
2. Chen, J., et al.: Transunet: transformers make strong encoders for medical image segmentation. arXiv preprint arXiv:2102.04306 (2021)

3. Cheng, D., Qin, Z., Jiang, Z., Zhang, S., Lao, Q., Li, K.: Sam on medical images: a comprehensive study on three prompt modes. arXiv preprint arXiv:2305.00035 (2023)
4. Cheng, T., Wang, X., Chen, S., Zhang, Q., Liu, W.: Boxteacher: exploring high-quality pseudo labels for weakly supervised instance segmentation. In: Proceedings of the IEEE/CVF Conference on Computer Vision and Pattern Recognition (CVPR), pp. 3145–3154 (2023)
5. Dai, J., He, K., Sun, J.: Boxsup: exploiting bounding boxes to supervise convolutional networks for semantic segmentation. In: Proceedings of the IEEE International Conference on Computer Vision (ICCV), pp. 1635–1643 (2015)
6. Diakogiannis, F.I., Waldner, F., Caccetta, P., Wu, C.: ResUNet-a: a deep learning framework for semantic segmentation of remotely sensed data. ISPRS J. Photogramm. Remote Sens. (ISPRS) 94–114 (2020)
7. Dosovitskiy, A., et al.: An image is worth 16 × 16 words: transformers for image recognition at scale. arXiv preprint arXiv:2010.11929 (2020)
8. Girum, K.B., Créhange, G., Hussain, R., Lalande, A.: Fast interactive medical image segmentation with weakly supervised deep learning method. Int. J. Comput. Assist. Radiol. Surg. 1437–1444 (2020)
9. Kang, D., Koniusz, P., Cho, M., Murray, N.: Distilling self-supervised vision transformers for weakly-supervised few-shot classification & segmentation. In: Proceedings of the IEEE/CVF Conference on Computer Vision and Pattern Recognition (CVPR), pp. 19627–19638 (2023)
10. Kervadec, H., Dolz, J., Wang, S., Granger, E., Ayed, I.B.: Bounding boxes for weakly supervised segmentation: global constraints get close to full supervision. In: Medical Imaging with Deep Learning (MIDL), pp. 365–381 (2020)
11. Kervadec, H., Dolz, J., Yuan, J., Desrosiers, C., Granger, E., Ayed, I.B.: Constrained deep networks: lagrangian optimization via log-barrier extensions. In: 2022 30th European Signal Processing Conference (EUSIPCO), pp. 962–966. IEEE (2022)
12. Khoreva, A., Benenson, R., Hosang, J., Hein, M., Schiele, B.: Simple does it: weakly supervised instance and semantic segmentation. In: Proceedings of the IEEE conference on Computer Vision and Pattern Recognition (CVPR), pp. 876–885 (2017)
13. Kirillov, A., et al.: Segment anything. In: Proceedings of the IEEE International Conference on Computer Vision (ICCV) (2023)
14. Krähenbühl, P., Koltun, V.: Efficient inference in fully connected crfs with gaussian edge potentials. Adv. Neural Inf. Process. Syst. (NeurIPS) (2011)
15. Litjens, G., et al.: Evaluation of prostate segmentation algorithms for MRI: the PROMISE12 challenge. Med. Image Anal. (MedIA) 359–373 (2014)
16. Liu, X., et al.: Weakly supervised segmentation of covid19 infection with scribble annotation on CT images. Pattern Recognit. (PR) 108341 (2022)
17. Luo, X., Hu, M., Song, T., Wang, G., Zhang, S.: Semi-supervised medical image segmentation via cross teaching between CNN and transformer. In: International Conference on Medical Imaging with Deep Learning (MIDL), pp. 820–833 (2022)
18. Mazurowski, M.A., Dong, H., Gu, H., Yang, J., Konz, N., Zhang, Y.: Segment anything model for medical image analysis: an experimental study. Med. Image Anal. (MedIA) 102918 (2023)
19. Nguyen, H.G., et al.: A novel segmentation framework for uveal melanoma in magnetic resonance imaging based on class activation maps. In: International Conference on Medical Imaging with Deep Learning (MIDL), pp. 370–379 (2019)

20. Papandreou, G., Chen, L.C., Murphy, K.P., Yuille, A.L.: Weakly-and semi-supervised learning of a deep convolutional network for semantic image segmentation. In: Proceedings of the IEEE International Conference on Computer Vision (ICCV), pp. 1742–1750 (2015)
21. Peng, J., Estrada, G., Pedersoli, M., Desrosiers, C.: Deep co-training for semi-supervised image segmentation. Pattern Recognit. (PR) 135–152 (2020)
22. Qu, H., et al.: Weakly supervised deep nuclei segmentation using points annotation in histopathology images. In: International Conference on Medical Imaging with Deep Learning (MIDL), pp. 390–400 (2019)
23. Rajchl, M., et al.: DeepCut: object segmentation from bounding box annotations using convolutional neural networks. IEEE Trans. Med. Imaging (TMI) 674–683 (2016)
24. Ronneberger, O., Fischer, P., Brox, T.: U-Net: convolutional networks for biomedical image segmentation. In: Medical Image Computing and Computer-Assisted Intervention–MICCAI 2015: 18th International Conference, Munich, Germany, 5–9 October 2015, Proceedings, Part III 18, pp. 234–241 (2015)
25. Rother, C., Kolmogorov, V., Blake, A.: GrabCut interactive foreground extraction using iterated graph cuts. ACM Trans. Graph. (TOG) 596–608 (2004)
26. Ru, L., Zheng, H., Zhan, Y., Du, B.: Token contrast for weakly-supervised semantic segmentation. In: Proceedings of the IEEE/CVF Conference on Computer Vision and Pattern Recognition (CVPR), pp. 3093–3102 (2023)
27. Simpson, A.L., et al.: A large annotated medical image dataset for the development and evaluation of segmentation algorithms. arXiv preprint arXiv:1902.09063 (2019)
28. Sohn, K., et al.: FixMatch: simplifying semi-supervised learning with consistency and confidence. Adv. Neural Inf. Process. Syst. (NeurIPS) (2020)
29. Song, C., Huang, Y., Ouyang, W., Wang, L.: Box-driven class-wise region masking and filling rate guided loss for weakly supervised semantic segmentation. In: Proceedings of the IEEE/CVF Conference on Computer Vision and Pattern Recognition (CVPR), pp. 3136–3145 (2019)
30. Tang, M., Perazzi, F., Djelouah, A., Ben Ayed, I., Schroers, C., Boykov, Y.: On regularized losses for weakly-supervised CNN segmentation. In: Proceedings of the European Conference on Computer Vision (ECCV), pp. 507–522 (2018)
31. Wang, J., Xia, B.: Bounding box tightness prior for weakly supervised image segmentation. In: International conference on Medical Image Computing and Computer-assisted Intervention (MICCAI), pp. 526–536 (2021)
32. Yang, L., Qi, L., Feng, L., Zhang, W., Shi, Y.: Revisiting weak-to-strong consistency in semi-supervised semantic segmentation. In: Proceedings of the IEEE/CVF Conference on Computer Vision and Pattern Recognition (CVPR), pp. 7236–7246 (2023)
33. Yang, Z., Farsiu, S.: Directional connectivity-based segmentation of medical images. In: Proceedings of the IEEE/CVF Conference on Computer Vision and Pattern Recognition (CVPR), pp. 11525–11535, June 2023

FCGA-Former: A Hybrid Factor Space Classification Model for Predicting the Tumor Mutation Burden of Lung Adenocarcinoma

Ziang Cai(✉), Han Zhang(✉), Ziyi Yang(✉), and Xiaoyan Zhang(✉)

Liaoning Technical University, Huludao City, Liaoning Province 125105, China
2676994947@qq.com, 3063380797@qq.com, 1440025193@qq.com,
Zhangzhangxiaoyan@lntu.edu.cn

Abstract. Lung cancer is a malignant tumor with the highest mutation rate in the world, among which non-small cell lung cancer (NSCLC) has a very high mutation rate. In recent years, medical research has found that tumor mutation burden (TMB) can predict treatment of cancer, immunotherapy and chemotherapy. However, the traditional method of calculating TMB using gene prediction technology has the disadvantages of high detection cost, long cycle, and intensive sample interrogation. To solve the above problems, we propose a hybrid deep learning model (FCGA-Former) to automatically predict TMB predictions, aiming to save pathologists' time. In order to solve the problem of semantic gap in medical images, the factor space is applied to the semantic embedding space, so that the high-level semantic space is consistent with the underlying image feature space, and the data features are directly related to the information expressed by the images. The lung adenocarcinoma histopathology image dataset was taken from the TCGA database and included 271 high TMB data and 66 low TMB data. Experimental results show that the maximum average area under the curve (AUC) of this model is 98.1%. FCGA-Former is discussed in the area of other models in terms of interpretability as it provides more accurate results. The results of this study are of great significance in guiding lymph node treatment of NSCLC. This lays the foundation for deploying automatic classification decision-making systems in clinical applications and using deep learning technology to predict TMB.

Keywords: non-small cell lung cancer · tumor mutation burden · hybrid deep learning model · guided-bias module · factor space

1 Introduction

Lung cancer is one of the most prevalent and deadliest malignancies. In 2022, it is estimated that approximately 4.82 million new cancer cases will occur in China and around 2.37 million in the United States, with cancer-related deaths reaching approximately 3.21 million in China and 0.64 million in the United States [1]. Non-small Cell Lung Cancer (NSCLC) exhibits a high mortality rate, and the one-year survival rate of advanced

Published by Springer Nature Switzerland AG 2025
Z. Shi et al. (Eds.): ICIS 2024, IFIP AICT 720, pp. 346–360, 2025.
https://doi.org/10.1007/978-3-031-71253-1_25

patients is below 40%. Lung cancer can be diagnosed using various methods such as computed tomography (CT), magnetic resonance imaging (MRI), and histopathological images, of which histopathological images are considered the most reliable method for cancer diagnosis.

For NSCLC, immune checkpoint inhibitors (ICIs) such as programmed cell death receptor 1 (PD-1) and its ligand (PD-L1) play a critical role in treatment. In 2015, Rizvi et al. [2] found that although patients with non-small cell lung cancer in low mutation burden group responded to PD-1 antibody, the response was short-lived. Patients with higher mutation burden had longer Progression-free Survival (PFS) than those with higher mutation burden. After that, with the experiments of CheckMate-026 [3] and CheckMate-227 [4] put forward one after another, it also proved that tumor mutation burden can predict the treatment of non-small cell carcinoma.

Tumor mutation burden (TMB) is one of the important indicators to measure the number of genomic mutations. Using whole-exome or targeted sequencing data, TMB calculates the number of non-synonymous base substitutions and insertions/deletions derived from somatic cells within the coding regions of one million bases of sequenced DNA. Despite being the primary method for detecting TMB, whole-exome sequencing technology is characterized by high detection costs, long cycle times, and high sample dependencies. Therefore, there is an urgent need to develop a low-cost, short-cycle, and low-sample dependency method for predicting TMB levels.

The contribution of this paper is summarized as follows:

(1) In this paper, the feature types of pathological images are regarded as factors, multiple factors are used to form the factor space, and the images of known categories are grouped according to the correlation between categories, and the category labels of the samples are predicted by calculating the distance between the predicted attribute features and the actual attribute features.
(2) FCGA-Former leverages the distinct hybrid design of Transformer and CNN, extracting features at varying depths and scales, incorporating the spatial position deviation of CNN into the Transformer module via a guided-bias module (GBM). Furthermore, it integrates diverse particle size features and extensive distribution patterns of lung adenocarcinoma cells to attain higher classification accuracy.
(3) We propose a method to improve the accuracy of CNN network by combining coordinate attention with fused inverted residual module, which can make CNN network have the ability of remote modeling. Therefore, this innovation can prove that enhancing the spatial and global modeling ability of the model will make the model better extract the effective latent feature.

The rest is organized as follows. Section 2 reviews some related work. Section 3 formally introduces the FCGA-Former model proposed in this paper. Section 4 describes the data preprocessing and data enhancement methods. Section 5 is experiments and the paper is concluded in Sect. 6.

2 Related Work

In 2012, AlexNet introduced an end-to-end learning approach for automatic feature extraction using a neural network model that simulates the hierarchical structure of the human visual cortex. By simulating this structure, the model extracts and analyzes features to obtain abstract and deeply seated representations by combining and learning feature information. This process enables the completion of various computer vision tasks. As medical image analysis continues to rapidly develop, it is increasingly important to extract tumor genome-related feature information directly from histopathological images, as this information plays a crucial role in the clinical diagnosis and treatment of tumors.

Currently, deep learning methods have been shown to be more effective than manual feature selection in the field of histopathological image analysis. Coudray et al. [5] used deep learning method and pathological tissue image to realize accurate pathological classification of NSCLC, and successfully predicted whether common gene mutations such as STK11, EGFR, FAT1, SETBP1, KRAS and TP53 occurred in lung adenocarcinoma patients. This is also the earliest work on tumor mutation burden in genomic information. In 2019, Zhang et al. [6] proposed the application of convolution neural network in tumor mutation burden prediction of liver cancer pathological images, which not only explored the gene mutation information hidden in HE pathological images, but also found the best CNN receptive field, thus inferring the best feature scale for mining TMB information in liver cancer pathological images. Huang et al. [7] developed a deep learning model based on multimodal residual network. By fusing H&E images and information prediction, multi-modal compact bilinear pooling (MCB) was used to predict TMB state of CRC patients. Cao et al. [8] proposed a deep learning model for predicting microsatellite instability based on multi-instance learning in 2020, using ResNet18 as classifier, and achieved good performance in colorectal cancer data set by means of transfer learning. Chen et al. [9] proposed a way to predict the tumor mutation burden of TNBC based on the nuclear score of histopathological images. The nuclear score function filters meaningful blocks without manually labeling tumor regions. The selected patch can effectively improve the accuracy of predicting TMB from histopathological images. Jain et al. [10] proposed Image2TMB, a machine learning algorithm that captures complementary information at different granularity levels in images with different resolutions ($5\times$, $10\times$, $20\times$) by integrating three deep learning models to determine the TMB level of cancer. At the same time, Image2TMB also proves that deep learning can help to study the spatial heterogeneity of tumors and further promote the study of the relationship between cancer genotypes and phenotypes. Niu et al. [11] utilized ResNet-18 as the baseline model and employed k-fold cross-validation to predict tumor mutational burden in lung adenocarcinoma. Attention mechanism was first proposed by researchers in the field of Natural Language Processing (NLP). Because of its excellent ability in long-distance modeling and global feature extraction, researchers in the field of computer vision have been inspired. Zhang et al. [12] put forward a multi-stage hybrid self-attention model for rapid diagnosis of pancreatic cancer pathological slice images. The self-attention module is guided by convolution network deviation, and a Focus Guided Decoder is added to the output part of convolution module to fuse local and global information, so that each FGD module will combine the attention deviation of CNN module, and then the information carried by FGD will be combined with the input of self-attention module. Finally, the accuracy rate is 95.68% through experiments.

Lastly, Studies have shown that traditional histopathological pictures can reflect the changes of cancer genome to some extent. The purpose of this study is to predict the TMB level of patients with lung adenocarcinoma in NSCLC by using Whole-Slide Images (WSI), and then to provide evidence for predicting the reactivity of immune checkpoint inhibitors.

3 FCGA-Former

Traditional convolutional neural networks rely on convolution kernels to extract local features, which are characterized by few parameters and high computational efficiency. However, extracting global features of pathological images using convolution kernels can be challenging. Conversely, the self-attention mechanism, with its long sequence modeling and parallel computing capabilities, can effectively extract global features of pathological images.

The difficulty of image classification tasks is increasing, and a "semantic gap" has emerged and has received widespread attention [13]. The phenomenon of "semantic gap" means that there are differences between the artificially understood image and the image itself, and the underlying visual features of images between the same object categories may be different or even very different, while the underlying visual features of images between different object categories may be similar and the difference is very small. Therefore, there is a "semantic gap" between the low-level features of the image and the high-level category labels, which makes it impossible to construct a direct connection between the features of the image and the information described by the image, which is a problem that the computer cannot cross, thus deepening the difficulty of image classification. At the same time, the category information of the object is described by attributes, but the attributes are artificially defined, so there will be attribute redundancy, which will reduce the ability and efficiency of the model to learn and predict the attributes.

In this study, we construct a deep learning model of hybrid convolutional neural network and self-attention mechanism. In the shallow network of the model, we use a new structure (FCA-MbConv) that combines inverted residual module with coordinate attention. In the deep neural network of the model, visual self-attention mechanism is used to learn the abstract features of digital pathological slices. Between the two stages, we use a jump-connected guidance module to introduce the spatial deviation of CNN module into Transformer module. Moreover, the incorporation of transformers and the CNN+ transformer hybrid design in FCGA-Former is motivated by the need to capture global relationships in the image data. While traditional CNN-based models have been successful in image classification tasks, transformers offer unique capabilities in handling long-range dependencies and capturing global contextual information. Given the importance of spatial relations within tissue slices for accurate TMB prediction, we believe that the synergistic combination of CNNs and transformers in our model will provide a more effective representation of the data.

In this paper, we present a comprehensive evaluation of FCGA-Former's performance on a dataset of lung adenocarcinoma histopathological images from the TCGA database. Our results demonstrate the effectiveness of our model and its potential in guiding the prognostic treatment of Non-small Cell Lung Cancer (NSCLC) based on TMB predictions. Finally, we use hybrid convolution network and attention model to improve the prediction accuracy of deep learning model in tumor mutation burden.

3.1 FCA-MbConv

Fused-Mobile Inverted Bottleneck Convolution (Fused-MbConv) mainly solves the problem of Inverted residual module [14]. In the main branch of the structure, the original depth separable convolution and the raised dimension convolution are replaced by an raised dimension convolution, and the raised dimension and feature extraction are completed through a convolution layer. This step accelerates the operation speed of the model at the cost of a small amount of parameter overhead.

In this study, Coordinate Attention (CA) [15] module is used to replace SE Attention Module in Fused-MbConv. Traditional SE module calculates the weights between channels through global average pooling, which improves the performance at the cost of less computation, but SE module ignores the importance of spatial position information. CBAM Attention Module combines spatial location information and channel information by convolution to make up for the defect of SE module, but the convolution module of this method can only capture local features and cannot establish long-distance dependence. Coordinate attention aggregates features from horizontal coordinates and vertical coordinates respectively, which accurately retains position information and establishes long-distance dependence in the other direction. Therefore, the CA can not only help the convolution network to locate and identify the objects of interest more accurately, but also can be easily embedded into most mainstream neural networks.

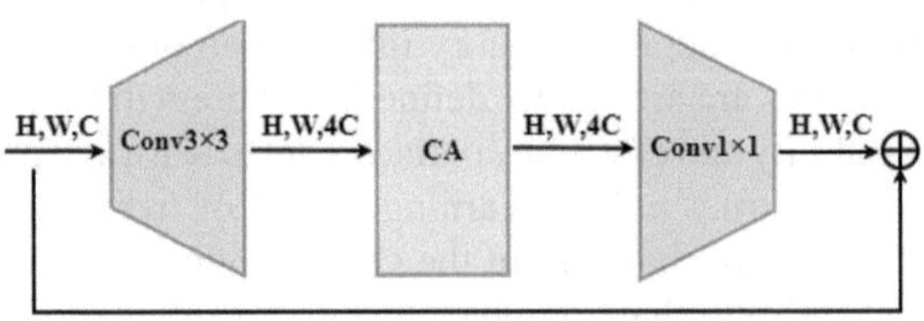

Fig. 1. The network structure of FCA-MbConv.

In summary, this paper presents an improvement to the Fused Coordinate Attention Mobile Inverted Bottleneck Conversion (FCA-MbConv) by replacing the SE module with the CA module in the original Fused-MbConv structure. Since the convolution layer extracts only local features, and the SE module encodes only channel information, a considerable number of features inherent in histopathological images are lost during feature extraction, resulting in an incomplete feature extraction process and poor performance of the TMB prediction model. The histopathological image is initially processed by the FCA-MbConv module through a 3 × 3 convolution operation, upgrading and extracting the feature matrix while changing the channels to four times the original. The data is then inputted into the coordinate attention module, which extracts accurate position information and establishes long-distance dependence. Next, the number of channels in the model is reduced by using a 1 × 1 convolution layer, making the output feature matrix consistent with the input. Finally, the convolution layer output is added to the input as the final output of the FCA-MbConv module. The network structure of FCA-MbConv is depicted (Fig. 1).

3.2 Guided-Bias Module

First, the GBM module uses a feature pyramid structure to process the features from the non-convolutional neural network stage. This structure produces a multi-scale feature representation of the extracted features. Second, to obtain a multi-dimensional feature representation, the module creates three parallel convolution paths that produce the probability feature map. The first convolution path in the GBM module is a 1 × 1 convolutional kernel that reduces the spatial dimensions of the feature map by half without affecting the number of channels. For the latter two paths, the feature map first passes through a 1 × 1 convolution kernel, which reduces the spatial dimensions of the channel by half, and then through 3 × 3 and 5 × 5 convolution kernels, respectively. After obtaining all the feature maps, we concatenate them along the channel axis to complete the extraction of the early convolutional neural network module representation. The network structure of GBM is illustrated in Fig. 2.

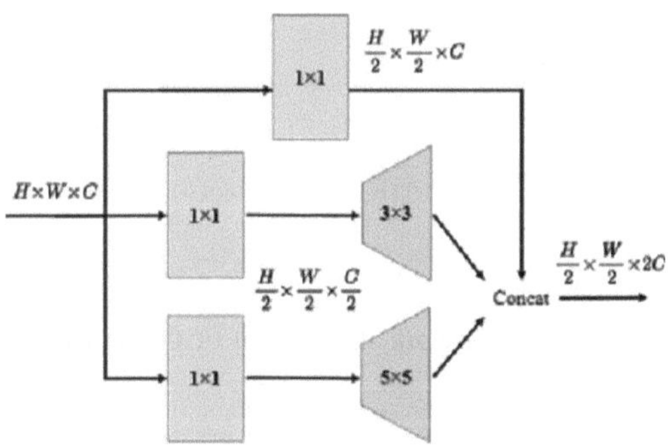

Fig. 2. The network structure of GBM.

3.3 The Structure of FCGA-Former

FCGA-Former is a hybrid model that integrates convolutional neural network and attention mechanism, resulting in a model that effectively reduces parameters while also improving performance. However, simply connecting self-attention modules and convolutional neural networks is not very effective because this method does not fully consider the flow of feature maps and the input and output relationships between the modules. Dai et al. [16] suggested that convolutional neural networks are better suited for capturing local features within shallow networks. They found that the combination pattern "C, C, T, T," where "C" refers to CNN and "T" refers to Transformer, exhibits superior generalization and learning capabilities when integrating CNN with a self-attention module. In the convolution module, the ability of local convolution is not weaker than the global attention mechanism for the feature information in the shallow stage. The memory consumption and operation efficiency of the model are enhanced using Fused-MbConv structure in the shallow layer of the network.

The Fused-MbConv module combines coordinate attention with position information to establish long-range dependence, thereby improving the limitation of local feature extraction in the convolutional neural network. In the self-attention module stage, relative attention is used to establish global dependence. In the aspect of the length and width of the feature graph, each stage of the model will reduce the feature matrix to half of the original one. In the channel direction, the stem stage of the model will make the number of channels in the eigenmatrix become 64. In addition, in other stages, the number of channels will be twice that of the previous stage. GBM reduces the length and width of the original matrix by half and doubles the number of channels in the feature map. The two types of feature maps produced by GBM are then combined. In the last stage of FCGA-Former, the classification information in the output sequence is connected to the classification header of MLP to obtain the classification result. The architecture of FCGA-Former is illustrated in Fig. 3.

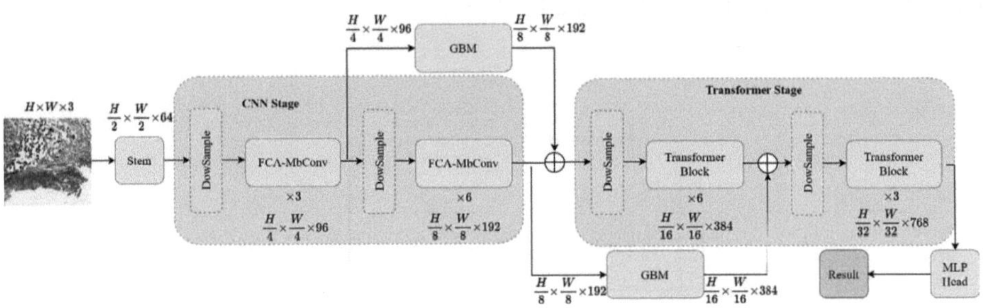

Fig. 3. The network structure of FCGA-Former.

4 Data Preprocessing and Enhancement

4.1 Data Preprocessing

The data set used in this paper comes from The Cancer Genome Atlas (TCGA) database, which was jointly launched by the National Cancer Institute (NCI) and the National Human Genome Research Institute (NHGRI) in 2006. It mainly collects various clinical data of cancer patients. At present, TCGA database has collected pathological information of more than 20,000 cancer patients and matched with 33 cancers.

This study uses genomic data and whole-slide images obtained from the TCGA-LUAD project found in the TCGA database (https://portal.gdc.cancer.gov/projects/TCGA-LUAD). The dataset includes digital pathological slices of 337 patients, including 271 high TMB data and 66 low TMB data. The TMB value is calculated based on the simple nucleotide variation data from TCGA database. According to CheckMate227 experiment, researchers found that patients with advanced non-small cell carcinoma with TMB $\geq$ 10.0 mutation number/Mb can significantly prolong progression-free survival under intervention treatment. Consequently, in the process of classifying each pathological section, digital samples with tumor mutation burden (TMB) values exceeding 10 are labelled with the High mutation burden group, whereas those with TMB values less than or equal to 1.1 are assigned to the Low mutation burden group. Following classification, the image is preprocessed via OpenSlide and subsequently segmented using a resolution of 224 $\times$ 224. The resulting segmented dataset is divided into a training set and a test set with an 8:2 ratio. Table 1 shows the specific parameters of the training set and the test set.

Table 1. The Number of Whole Slide image In The Dataset

	Train	Test	Total
High	770185	189109	959294
Low	155769	43814	199583

We segmented the original digital pathological images using a non-overlapping sliding window method. Digital pathological images often have non-informative regions at their edges, which can be retained using the sliding window method. Such images contain no useful information. When processing images with pathological tissues, we excluded small slices with larger than 50% non-informative region in image segmentation to balance the preservation of essential features and utilization of computer resources. Figure 4 illustrates the method for preprocessing whole-slide images.

Through the factor space theory, the key information in the pathological image is abstracted into points in the factor space, and then the features of the image are extracted. These features include not only basic information such as grayscale, color, and texture of the image, but also high-level features derived from factor space theory. In factor space theory, the joint phase space of multiple factors is the Cartesian product of their phase space. Therefore, in image feature extraction, multiple features can be combined to form a more complex feature space. These combined features can describe the information of the image more comprehensively and improve the accuracy of image recognition. At the same time, by selecting important features and ignoring redundant features, the amount of computation can be reduced and the processing speed can be increased。

4.2 Data Enhancement

To enhance the generalization ability and robustness of model, we employ five data augmentation techniques during the training process, as illustrated in Fig. 5. First, the original image is resized and then cropped to the original image size from the center, which we refer to as central clipping. Second, we use random horizontal and vertical flips with a given probability. Third, we add random angle rotations around the image center. Fourth, we use standardization to prevent the model from over-fitting by calculating the

Fig. 4. Pre-processing of whole slide images.

mean and standard deviation of the dataset and standardizing each image accordingly. Finally, we use random erasing to occlude rectangular areas of the image by filling them with random or average pixel values during training.

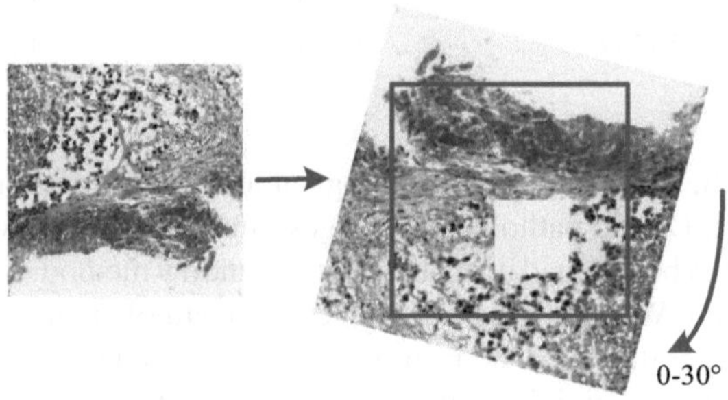

Fig. 5. Pathological data enhancement process.

5 Experiment

In this section, we will describe our experiments and evaluation indicators, and record the experimental results.

5.1 Experimental Setup and Hyperparameter Setting

FCGA-Former uses Python language for development, the learning rate is set to 0.0001, the learning rate decay rate is 0.05, the data input to the model in each batch is 64, the random inactivation rate is set to 0.2. The model was built based on the PyTorch, timm and einops library. The cross-entropy loss is used as the loss function, the optimizer selects AdamW, and the training process is iterated a total of 20 times. All models of the training and testing experiments ran on two RTX2080Ti, 11 GB graphics cards, Ubuntu 16.04 operating system, Intel Xeon W-2150B processor, and 32G memory server. The source code and data can be accessed at https://github.com/yangziyi999/FCGA-Former.

In order to verify the effectiveness of this model, three experiments were conducted.

Experiment 1: Comparative testing was conducted between FCGA-Former and typical networks in deep learning on a dataset of 224x224 sliced images. All comparative models employed Bayesian search to find hyperparameters, while the optimizer and loss function remained consistent with the FCA-Former model trained in this study.

Experiment 2: Each module introduced into the model was tested in 224 × 224 data set, and the coordinate attention mechanism was introduced to replace the original SE module and compared with CBAM attention. Compared with Vision Transformer and CoAtNet, the efficiency, convenience and accuracy of the model are verified. By comparing the results after adding GBM module, the effectiveness of GBM module is verified.

Experiment 3: To verify the effectiveness of data image enhancement strategy, set up two control groups using data enhancement strategy and not using data enhancement strategy, and then compare the performance indicators of the model under different super parameters by setting different super parameters.

5.2 Results of Comparison Models

As the research on this subject is limited, we compared our proposed model - FCGA-Former - with six state-of-the-art CNN models, including AlexNet [17], VGG [18], Inceptionv3, ResNet, DenseNet, and EfficientNet along with one related work included for comparison. During the experimental process, a Bayesian search approach was employed to identify optimal hyperparameters for each model, including learning rate, dropout rate, and batch size. This was undertaken to facilitate a more comprehensive assessment of performance differences among the various models.

Table 2 presents the experimental results, which indicate that the FCGA-Former model has the highest AUC value. The F1-Score results indicate that FCGA-Former has better comprehensive ability to distinguish between positive and negative samples compared to other models.

Table 2. The Number of Whole Slide mage In The Dataset

Model	AUC	F1-Score
AlexNet	0.798	0.712
VGG	0.833	0.773
GoogLeNet [19]	0.760	0.724
ResNet [20]	0.867	0.859
DenseNet [21]	0.850	0.836
EfficientNet	0.792	0.791
FCGA-Former	0.983	0.964

In Table 3, it shows the comparison of parameters, computation and AUC of FCGA-Form with ViT and CoAtNet models, in which Vision Transformer model selects Patch size of 16 × 16 and input size of 224 × 224. By setting the same learning rate and batch size, FCGA-Former achieves higher AUC with lower parameters compared with vision transformer model. Figure 7 depicts the sequence of Vision Transformer, CoAtNet and FCGA-Former from left to right. The rightmost image in Fig. 6 shows that the FCGA-Former model with the FCA-MbConv module and guided-bias module fed with pathological images in batches can produce a higher AUC curve than other models.

Table 3. Performance comparison for vision transformer, CoAtNet and FCGA-Former

Model	AUC	F1-Score	Params
Vit_base_patch16	0.902	0.901	85.8M
CoAtNet	0.960	0.942	17.0M
FCGA-Former	0.983	0.964	24.2M

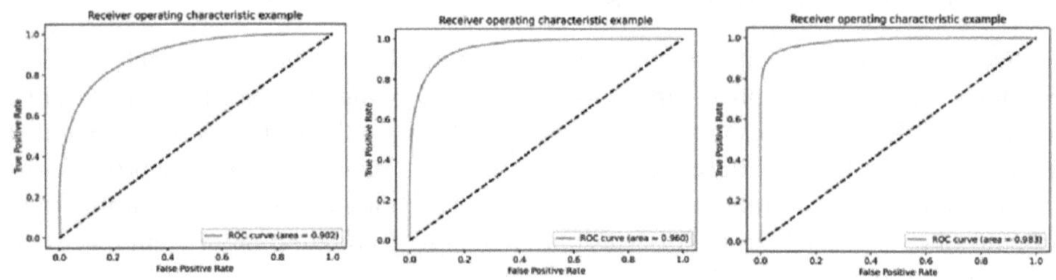

Fig. 6. Three different self-attention models compare results (From left to right are Vision Transformer, CoAtNet, and FCGA-Former).

5.3 Results of FCGA-Former Ablation Studies

To evaluate the effect of structural improvement and explore the efficiency of the proposed FCGA-Former, a series of ablation studies were carried out under the same training and verification settings. The weights of the structure will be randomly initialized for fair comparison.

Table 4 illustrates the impact of different attention modules and the GBM module on the model. The results demonstrate that the model achieves an effectiveness of 98.3% when employing the coordinate attention module, surpassing the SE and CBAM approaches by 2.3 and 1.5 percentage points, respectively. This not only highlights the proficiency of the coordinate attention module in capturing global features but also validates the enhancement in genome information extraction from pathological sections through the integration of early CNN features into the Transformer model.

The experimental results of the effectiveness of the data enhancement strategy are shown in Fig. 7. It can be observed from the table that the AUC value of the model increases by 9.8 percentage points after the addition of data enhancement. It is evident that the implementation of data augmentation substantially lowers the loss values and

Table 4. Results of attention module ablation experiment

Attention module	AUC	F1-Score
SE [22]	0.958	0.948
CBAM [23]	0.966	0.951
CA	0.981	0.953
CA + GBM	0.983	0.964

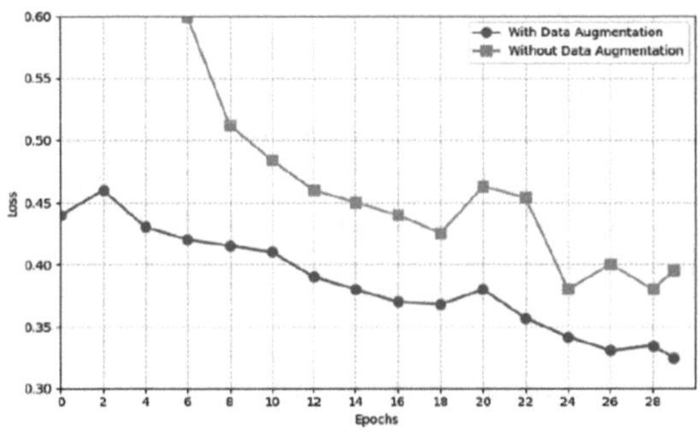

Fig. 7. Loss comparison using data enhancement.

improves the rate of convergence during the model's training process. Using data augmentation techniques enables faster model convergence and significantly decreases loss values.

The Experiment 3 findings are presented in Table 5 The performance of model is dependent on the selected loss and learning rates. High learning rates have a detrimental effect on the model, causing premature overfitting and poor results. Through experimental comparison, it was determined that the model's self-attention mechanism is particularly sensitive to the learning rate. The model fits faster at a learning rate of 0.0001 with good predictive effect before the highest AUC is reached. A higher loss rate does not improve the model's performance. Therefore, this model uses a loss rate of 0.2.

Table 5. Learning rate and dropout comparison experiment results

Learning rate	Dropout	AUC
0.001	0.2	90.4
	0.5	88.6
0.0001	0.2	98.3
	0.5	94.5
0.00001	0.2	92.6
	0.5	88.3

5.4 Visualization of Patient-Level Tumor Mutation Burden

To transition from the prediction of TMB at the level of small image patches to the comprehensive TMB prediction across WSIs at the patient level, this section employs a visual approach to demonstrate the WSI's TMB predictions. Initially, each WSI is divided into multiple smaller image patches. Subsequently, the FCGA-Former model is employed to predict the TMB for each small image patch, and a color gradient technique is utilized to visually represent the probability distribution of their TMB levels. Image patches with lower probability values are depicted in green, while those with higher probability values are represented in red. Probability values greater than or equal to 0.5 are normalized, mapping their corresponding probabilities to a range of 0 to 1. Patches with probability values below 0.5 are categorized as having low predicted TMB levels, while those with probability values not less than 0.5 are categorized as having high predicted TMB levels, with higher probabilities indicating a stronger correlation with elevated TMB levels. Finally, the small image patches are reassembled according to their original positions within the WSI, resulting in a visual representation of TMB variation across the WSI (as illustrated in Fig. 8).

Fig. 8. Patient-Level Tumor Mutation Burden prediction map

6 Conclusion

This paper introduces a hybrid algorithm for tumor mutation burden classification by combining convolution and attention mechanisms. The effectiveness of the model is validated using TCGA-LUAD datasets. With the scarcity of medical image analysis data limiting its full potential, various enhancement approaches were used to balance the data and avoid over-fitting. The model utilizes an efficient and accurate FCA-MbConv convolution module suitable for shallow network layers, a fused inverted residual structure to enhance its operational speed and reduce computational overhead, as well as ability of coordinate attention ability to build long-distance dependencies that compensate for the convolution kernel limitations. The deep network layer utilizes global modeling with relative attention to improve the model's generalization. Using GBM structure, the transformer and CNN blocks' efficiency is improved through the use of feature maps from different CNN stages as attention bias. Overall, the adoption of the mixed convolution and attention mechanism improves the model's accuracy and significantly reduces the number of parameters required. To summarize, the FCGA-Former model achieves the most advanced classification performance of lung adenocarcinoma tumor mutation burden image analysis and prediction through its unique hybrid architecture, which effectively combines the advantages of CNN and Transformer. As such, the model has the potential to broaden its application in lung adenocarcinoma diagnosis and support pathologists in auxiliary diagnoses.

Acknowledgment. This work is supported by the National Natural Science Foundation of China (61772249), and The General Project of Liaoning Provincial Department of Education (LJKZ0355).

References

1. Xia, C., Dong, X., Li, H., et al.: Cancer statistics in China and United States, 2022: profiles, trends, and determinants. Chin. Med. J. **135**(05), 584–590 (2022)
2. Rizvi, N.A., et al.: Mutational landscape determines sensitivity to PD-1 blockade in non–small cell lung cancer. Science **348**(6230), 124–128 (2015)
3. Carbone, D.P., et al.: First-line nivolumab in stage IV or recurrent non–small-cell lung cancer. N. Engl. J. Med. **376**(25), 2415–2426 (2017)
4. Hellmann, M.D., et al.: Nivolumab plus ipilimumab in lung cancer with a high tumor mutational burden. N. Engl. J. Med. **378**(22), 2093–2104 (2018)
5. Coudray, N., et al.: Classification and mutation prediction from non–small cell lung cancer histopathology images using deep learning. Nat. Med. **24**(10), 1559–1567 (2018)
6. Zhang, H., et al.: Predicting tumor mutational burden from liver cancer pathological images using convolutional neural network, pp. 920–925
7. Huang, K., et al.: Predicting colorectal cancer tumor mutational burden from histopathological images and clinical information using multi-modal deep learning. Bioinformatics **38**(22), 5108–5115 (2022)
8. Cao, R., et al.: Development and interpretation of a pathomics-based model for the prediction of microsatellite instability in Colorectal Cancer. Theranostics **10**(24), 11080–11091 (2020)
9. Chen, Y., Liu, J., Jiang, P., Wang, L., Pang, B., Cao, D.: Predicting Tumor Mutation Burden of TNBC Based on Nuclei Scores of Histopathological Images, pp. 936–941
10. Jain, M.S., Massoud, T.F.: Predicting tumour mutational burden from histopathological images using multiscale deep learning. Nat. Mach. Intell. **2**(6), 356–362 (2020). 2020/06/01
11. Niu, Y., Wang, L., Zhang, X., et al.: Predicting tumor mutational burden from lung adenocarcinoma histopathological images using deep learning. Front. Oncol. **12**, 927426 (2022)
12. Zhang, T., et al.: MSHT: Multi-stage Hybrid Transformer for the ROSE Image Analysis of Pancreatic Cancer, 01 December 2021. https://ui.adsabs.harvard.edu/abs/2021arXiv211213513Z
13. Tan, M., Le, Q.V., Li, L.J., Su, H., Xing, E.P., et al.: Object bank: a high-level image representation for scene classification & semantic feature sparsification. Clin. Exp. Allergy J. Br. Soc. Allergy ClinicalImmunology **26**(6), 719–729 (2010). Efficien
14. Tan, M., Le, Q.V.: EfficientNet: rethinking model scaling for convolutional neural networks, 01 May 2019. https://ui.adsabs.harvard.edu/abs/2019arXiv190511946T
15. Hou, Q., Zhou, D., Feng, J.: Coordinate Attention for Efficient Mobile Network Design, 01 March 2021. https://ui.adsabs.harvard.edu/abs/2021arXiv210302907H
16. Dai, Z., Liu, H., Le, Q.V., Tan, M.: CoAtNet: marrying convolution and attention for all data sizes, 01 June 2021. https://ui.adsabs.Harvard.edu/abs/2021arXiv210604803D

17. Krizhevsky, A., Sutskever, I., Hinton, G.E.: Imagenet classification with deep convolutional neural networks. Commun. ACM **60**(6), 84–90 (2017)
18. Simonyan, K., Zisserman, A.: Very deep convolutional networks for large-scale image recognition (2014). arXiv preprint arXiv:1409.1556
19. Szegedy, C., Vanhoucke, V., Ioffe, S., Shlens, J., Wojna, Z.: Rethinking the Inception Architecture for Computer Vision, 01 December 2015. https://ui.adsabs.harvard.edu/abs/2015arXiv151200567S
20. He, K., Zhang, X., Ren, S., Sun, J.: Deep Residual Learning for Image Recognition, 01 December 2015. https://ui.adsabs.harvard.edu/abs/20, 15arXiv 151203385H
21. Huang, G., Liu, Z., van der Maaten, L., Weinberger, K.Q.: Densely Connected Convolutional Networks, 01 August 2016. https://ui.adsabs.harvard.edu/abs/2016arXiv160806993H
22. Hu, J., Shen, L., Sun, G.: Squeeze-and-excitation networks, pp. 7132–7141
23. Woo, S., Park, J., Lee, J.-Y., Kweon, I.S.: CBAM: convolutional block attention module, pp. 3–19

Author Index

Published by Springer Nature Switzerland AG 2025
Z. Shi et al. (Eds.): ICIS 2024, IFIP AICT 720, pp. 361–362, 2025.
https://doi.org/10.1007/978-3-031-71253-1

MIX
Papier aus verantwortungsvollen Quellen
Paper from responsible sources
FSC® C105338

If you have any concerns about our products,
you can contact us on
ProductSafety@springernature.com

In case Publisher is established outside the EU,
the EU authorized representative is:
Springer Nature Customer Service Center GmbH
Europaplatz 3, 69115 Heidelberg, Germany

Printed by Libri Plureos GmbH
in Hamburg, Germany